Business in Real-Time Using Azure IoT and Cortana Intelligence Suite

Driving Your Digital Transformation

Bob Familiar

Jeff Barnes

Apress®

Business in Real-Time Using Azure IoT and Cortana Intelligence Suite: Driving Your Digital Transformation

Bob Familiar
Sudbury, Massachusetts, USA

Jeff Barnes
Miami, Florida, USA

ISBN-13 (pbk): 978-1-4842-2649-0
DOI 10.1007/978-1-4842-2650-6

ISBN-13 (electronic): 978-1-4842-2650-6

Library of Congress Control Number: 2017943349

Cover image designed by Freepik

Managing Director: Welmoed Spahr
Editorial Director: Todd Green
Acquisitions Editor: Natalie Pao
Development Editor: James Markham
Technical Reviewers: Alina Stanciu and Jim O'Neil
Copy Editor: Kezia Endsley
Coordinating Editor: Jessica Vakili

Distributed to the book trade worldwide by Springer Science+Business Media New York, 233 Spring Street, 6th Floor, New York, NY 10013. Phone 1-800-SPRINGER, fax (201) 348-4505, e-mail orders-ny@springer-sbm.com, or visit www.springeronline.com. Apress Media, LLC is a California LLC and the sole member (owner) is Springer Science + Business Media Finance Inc (SSBM Finance Inc). SSBM Finance Inc is a **Delaware** corporation.

For information on translations, please e-mail rights@apress.com, or visit http://www.apress.com/rights-permissions.

Apress titles may be purchased in bulk for academic, corporate, or promotional use. eBook versions and licenses are also available for most titles. For more information, reference our Print and eBook Bulk Sales web page at http://www.apress.com/bulk-sales.

Any source code or other supplementary material referenced by the author in this book is available to readers on GitHub via the book's product page, located at www.apress.com/978-1-4842-2649-0. For more detailed information, please visit http://www.apress.com/source-code.

Printed on acid-free paper

This book is dedicated to all those who seek to "live life in the fast lane"
by exploiting technology to help drive digital disruption and positively transform
their businesses so they may truly operate at Internet speed.

To my incredible wife, Mandy, who is a continuous stream
of inspiration, and to my children, Ariana and Bobby, who never cease to
amaze me with their talent, insight, and intelligence.

—Bob Familiar

This book is the culmination of many long, sacrificed nights and weekends.
To that end, I would like to thank my wife Susan, and my children, Ryan,
Brooke, and Nicholas, for their constant love, support, and encouragement.

—Jeff Barnes

Contents at a Glance

Contents

About the Authors

Bob Familiar is the National Practice Director for Application Services at BlueMetal, an Insight company. As National Director, Bob leads a team of seasoned principal architects who are responsible for industry research and development, rapid prototyping and outreach to the technology community, and providing strategy and guidance to BlueMetal clients on their most important and challenging projects. Bob is an accomplished software professional, evangelist, and author. Bob has been working in the software industry for over 30 years and holds a patent in object relational architecture and technology and is the author of *Microservices, IoT, and Azure,* available from Apress.

Jeff Barnes is a Cloud Solution Architect on the Microsoft Partner Enterprise Architect Team (PEAT), where he helps global Microsoft partners with pre-sales Azure architecture technical support. Jeff has been in the IT industry for over 30 years and has been with Microsoft for the last (18+) years. During that time, he has held several key software architect roles at Microsoft, including consulting, evangelism, and partner divisions. Prior to Microsoft, Jeff worked for several Fortune 500 financial, manufacturing, and retail companies. Jeff holds a Bachelor's degree in Management Information Systems from Florida State University and is the author of *Microsoft Azure Essentials: Azure Machine Learning by Microsoft Press*.

About the Technical Reviewers

Alina Stanciu is a senior program manager of the Microsoft Azure IoT team, where she drives deep engagements with Microsoft partners worldwide to accelerate their migration path to Azure IoT services. Alina works directly with customers and top-tier partners to get product feedback for continuous innovation of the Azure IoT platform. Her support of the Azure IoT community ranges from training, to workshops and hackathons, to deep architectural reviews. She not only leads training sessions for internal events, such as Microsoft MVP Summit, Microsoft TechReady, and Microsoft C+E University, but she also participates in external events, such as the Microsoft Worldwide Partner Conference or IoT Solutions World Congress. Before joining the Azure IoT team, Alina worked for the Microsoft Cloud Infrastructure Operations, where she delivered hyper-scale operations management platform for Microsoft Data Centers.

Jim O'Neil has over 25 years of experience in the software industry, spanning the disciplines of software prototyping, military and commercial software development, technical support, and developer evangelism. Jim's current passion is the intersection of devices (mobile and IoT) with cloud infrastructure, focusing on agility, scalability, and reliability. Jim joined BlueMetal, an Insight Company, in January 2014 after six years in the Microsoft Developer Evangelism organization where he hosted workshops, hackathons, and conferences to bring new technologies to a wide developer audience. In his spare time, Jim is the cofounder of New England GiveCamp, an annual hackathon supporting non-profits in the New England region; a perennial facilitator at National Junior Classical League Conventions; and the de facto family genealogist.

Acknowledgments

We would like to thank Kevin Miller, Alina Stanciu, and Nayana Singh, for their guidance and support and the Azure IoT engineering team, for their in-depth technical reviews and highly constructive feedback.

A warm and heartfelt thank you to Jim O'Neil for his thorough review covering both the technical content as well as educating us on the proper use of the Oxford comma.

The following people, all members of the BlueMetal team, have been instrumental in making this book possible through their support and technical expertise—Michael Griffin, Raheel Retiwalla, Ron Bokleman, Mike Shir, Scott Jamison, Matt Jackson, Priya Gore, and Rich Woodbury.

A big thank you to the team at Apress for their awesome support and guidance on this journey.

Introduction

It is often said that change is the only constant in the modern business world. In fact, this idea has been with us for centuries. In 1531, writing in his *Discourses on Livy*, Niccolò Machiavelli observed that, "Whosoever desires constant success must change his conduct with the times."

It is, in my view, too early for us to determine if the Internet of Things (IoT) will come to be seen as the harbinger of another great evolution of human productivity, rivaling those spurred by the industrial revolution in the 18th and 19th centuries, or by the move to computer automation and information technology (IT) in the 20th. However, it is already clear that IoT is a disruptive technology, and with any disruption comes both challenge and opportunity.

Like many advances in technology, IoT is a new name for a collection of ideas that have been developing for many years. The central enabling technologies of IoT solutions—sensors, telemetry streams, data storage and analysis, and system-level command and control—have existed for decades. Certainly, the systems of the NASA space program in the mid-20th century were IoT systems without that name. What has changed is that maturing technologies have been matched by dramatic economic changes, and together these have increased capabilities while simultaneously driving down costs. Today IoT solutions can be built which would have been economically infeasible only a short time ago.

At this point, the potential impact of IoT solutions includes most areas of human endeavor—industrial systems; logistics and manufacturing; smart homes, buildings, and cities; autonomous vehicles; efficient and personalized healthcare; tailored retail experiences; and many others, including systems that enrich fans' experiences in following their favorite sports figures. Bob and Jeff have been early practitioners of IoT solutions in many of these areas, and what they have learned along the way informs and enriches this book.

IoT solutions typically connect devices, provide analysis of the data from those devices (usually paired with data from other data repositories), and then operationalize the insights derived from that analysis to act. That action could be sending command and control messages back to the connected devices, or initiating workflows in existing business systems. Very often IoT solutions connect systems that have not previously been connected, and machine learning on this newly visible data can create not only new efficiencies in existing environments, but also transformed understanding of what is possible.

Many business leaders have adopted a "disrupt or be disrupted" approach to IoT, leveraging the deeper understanding IoT solutions provide to lead a digital transformation of their organizations and position them for future success.

At Microsoft, our ongoing goal for Azure IoT is to simplify the creation of solutions that provide compelling customer value. This book explains how businesses can leverage our platform to realize their own digital transformations.

In this book, Bob and Jeff illustrate how solutions come together across the landscape of devices, sensors, device management, real-time analytics, and predictive analytics. They also provide a needed focus on how to create actionable intelligence from the system, exposed in this case via mobile dashboards and real-time text and e-mail alerts. They have created a cookbook for creating a complete solution based on a wide variety of Azure platform services, and they share with the reader all the individual recipes that make up the solution along the way. I'm delighted that they have chosen to share their expertise in this way.

April 2017

Kevin Miller
Principal Program Manager, Azure IoT
Microsoft Corporation

Chapter Overview

Chapter 1: Business in Real-Time

This chapter provides a business context for the technical topics covered in the book. What business conditions are driving the need for real-time data? What is the impact on the organization if these new mission-critical applications, big data stores and advanced analytics are deployed to the cloud? How will they be managed and maintained? Is there a logical approach and a technology roadmap that will point the way to a successful transformation to a real-time business? A principled approach and reference architecture are introduced that provide the roadmap on how to design and implement a highly scalable, secure IoT and advanced analytics SaaS solution on Azure.

Chapter 2: DevOps Using PowerShell, ARM, and VSTS

DevOps is best summed up as the union of people, process, and tools. It's an alignment of the development and operations teams, the automation of development, test, and release processes, and the selection of a consistent set of tools used to facilitate automation of the build, test, and release cycles. The goal of adopting a DevOps approach is to create a streamlined product development lifecycle that removes, to the greatest degree possible, errors that are introduced through manual steps. This chapter details how you can use Azure PowerShell, Azure Resource Manager (ARM) templates, and Visual Studio Team Services to automate the provision, build, and deploy steps of Azure hosted services.

Chapter 3: Device Management Using IoT Hub

Connecting people, places, and things to the cloud, while not trivial, may be one of the easier aspects of IoT as the techniques and protocols are very well defined. The real work begins when you have thousands of devices connected to the cloud and you need to manage the day-to-day operations of this extremely distributed system. In addition to monitoring and managing the cloud services that are providing analytics, storage, dashboards, alerts, and notifications, you also need to monitor and manage your beacons, devices, and edge gateways. This chapter examines the Device Management features of Azure IoT Hub that support command and control, device twin, and direct methods.

Chapter 4: Sensors, Devices, and Gateways

This chapter provides a glimpse into the world of sensors and devices. It touches on some of the more common sensor and device scenarios that you will encounter and how they relate and work together to create a consistent, reliable network of connected things. Patterns for the implementation of device firmware are covered.

Chapter 5: Real-Time Processing Using Azure Stream Analytics

In this chapter, we examine the use of Microsoft Azure Streaming Analytics to create jobs to process our incoming data streams from our various sensors, perform data transformations and enrichment, and finally, provide output results in various data formats.

Chapter 6: Batch Processing with Data Factory and Data Lake Store

In this chapter, we examine the use of Azure Data Factory and Azure Data Lake and where, why, and how these technologies fit within the capabilities of a modern business running at Internet speed. We first cover the basic technical aspects and capabilities of Azure Data Factory and Azure Data Lake. Following that, we detail three major pieces of functionality for our reference implementation—how to leverage reference data in our Stream analytics jobs, how to retrain an Azure machine learning model, and how to move to data from Azure blob storage to Azure Data Lake.

Chapter 7: Advanced Analytics with Azure Data Lake Analytics

The Data Lake analytics tools and capabilities help make it easier and more efficient to solve today's modern business analysis and reporting problems. It is more efficient because it offers virtually unlimited storage, with immediate access to that storage for running analytical operations on top of it. Data Lake offers the ability to persist the raw data in its native form and then run transformational and analytical jobs to create new analysis, summarizations, and predictions across structured and unstructured data. This analysis is always based on the original data. All this adds up to a "faster-time-to-value" for a modern business seeking to maximize its true potential. In this chapter, we examine the use of Azure Data Lake Analytics (ADLA), which is Microsoft's new "big data" toolset that runs on top of Azure Data Lake.

Chapter 8: Advanced Analytics Using Machine Learning and R

We are truly living in exciting times as three major trends are converging in the IT industry today—big data and the Internet of Things (IoT), cloud computing and cheap cloud-based storage, and business intelligence capabilities. Some would say that the combination of these forces is helping to usher in the fourth Industrial Revolution. It has been predicted that artificial intelligence (AI) and machine learning (ML) capabilities will be incorporated into an ever-increasing number of platforms, applications, and software services as we approach the next year. These new AI and ML capabilities will enable a new generation of business and it professionals to take advantage of artificial intelligence and machine learning capabilities without having to understand exactly how they work. In this chapter, we explore the exciting new world of machine learning and predictive analytics using Azure Machine Learning and the R programming language.

Chapter 9: Data Visualizations, Alerts, and Notifications with Power BI

In this chapter, we explore the use of data visualizations, alerts, and notifications to help today's modern business provide useful communications to their employees and customers to successfully manage their operations in real time. We start the chapter with a brief look at today's modern reporting landscape, then take a look at how Microsoft technologies like Power BI and Azure Functions can help provide quick and easy solutions. We then demonstrate enabling these technologies as part of our reference implementation scenario. We conclude the chapter by demonstrating the use of a C# .NET "SIMULATOR" application to automatically generate thousands of sample test data transactions through our Azure Cloud applications. The simulated data will be processed in real time using Azure Streaming Analytics. We also implement a Power BI dashboard that provides outputs for our new Lambda cloud architecture. Lambda architectures are designed to handle massive quantities of data by taking advantage of both batch and stream-processing methods. Our new Power BI dashboard will display outputs for all three "temperatures" of the Lambda architecture processing model and provide visualizations for our cold, warm, and hot data paths.

Chapter 10: Security and Identity

Cybercrime and IoT security have been front and center in the news this past year. Deploying an IoT solution using public cloud platforms requires an understanding of the surface areas of vulnerability and the attack vectors that cyber criminals might leverage to define your security strategy. Security is a not a solution; it is an ongoing process that requires discipline and constant analysis, review, and action. Identity is all about who can access your applications, APIs, and the underlying data that's at the heart of your IoT solution. You will want the ability to provide users some level of self-service for registration, password management, and profile updates while maintaining restrictive protocols for application capabilities and access to data. This chapter outlines a framework for analyzing potential threat vectors and the tools and protocols that Azure provides to mitigate these threats. We also examine how to implement a multi-tenant application using Azure Active Directory B2C.

Chapter 11: Epilogue

In this chapter, we reflect on each of the topics covered in the book and provide some advice on how you can get started down the path to your digital transformation.

CHAPTER 1

■ ■ ■

Business in Real-Time

Every business today is going through a digital transformation due to disruptive forces in the market, from born-in-the-cloud competitors to the increasing demands of customers, partners, and employees to engage through modern digital experiences. They are evolving from relying only on historical data to learning to use both historical and real-time data to drive innovation, evolve business strategy, and automate critical business processes.

As businesses evolve and transform to take advantage of real-time data, they will drive impact through operational efficiencies as well as create new revenue opportunities. For example, a product manufacturer can gather information about how their products in remote locations are performing and automate the scheduling of field service engineers only as needed. Retail outlets can provide real-time inventory to drive an Omni-channel shopping experience for their customers. Companies that have a need to increase worker safety can track environmental conditions such as temperature, humidity, and wind speed along with employee biometrics such as heart rate, body temperature, and breathing rate to be able to determine if an employee's physical condition would create a worker safety issue.

In each of these scenarios, companies are finding that to stay competitive, improve operational efficiencies, and engage their customers more deeply, they must learn to leverage modern software development patterns and practices. They are transforming to become Software-as-a-Service (SaaS) providers skilled in the dark arts of data science and the Internet of Things (IoT). They are learning to create applications that connect people, places, and things. They are providing real-time data visualization, alerts, and notifications. They are integrating these connected products with existing line-of-business systems and providing seamless authentication for customers, partners and employees through immersive, beautiful experiences that work on any device and are available 24/7. They are transforming to become a *Real-Time Business*.

A Platform Approach

To maximize the investment in transforming to a Real-Time Business, it is necessary to increase reuse of common business and technology capabilities. This is most effectively achieved by leveraging a platform approach. A platform approach seeks to create a common underlying set of capabilities that are accessed through managed APIs so that many verticalized applications can be built on this common substrate, as depicted in Figure 1-1.

© Bob Familiar and Jeff Barnes 2017
B. Familiar and J. Barnes, *Business in Real-Time Using Azure IoT and Cortana Intelligence Suite*,
DOI 10.1007/978-1-4842-2650-6_1

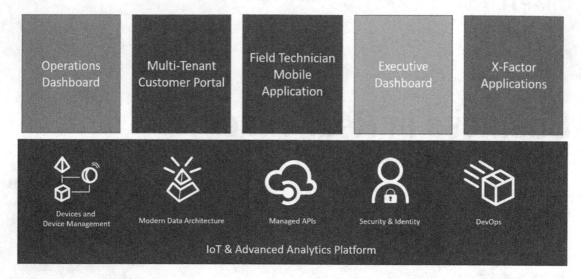

Figure 1-1. *IoT and the Advanced Analytics Platform model*

Regardless of vertical industry, there are a set of common, reusable components that you need to operationalize an IoT solution. Once those capabilities are in place, a business can build many applications that target different types of users and different vertical markets. One of the huge benefits of this approach is that all the data from all those vertical markets ends up in a common advanced analytics sub-system where cross-business insights can be drawn. These insights result in what we call *X-Factor applications,* those new revenue opportunities that were undiscoverable due to the siloed nature of the previous business model.

Real-Time Business Platform

Transforming to a Real-Time Business requires an investment in people, process, and tools. To meet the expectations of your customers and provide the business with a platform for driving impact at velocity, a new approach is required in the design, development, and deployment of your software products. Real-Time Business solutions are SaaS applications that support frequent release cycles, work on any device, and provide a multi-tenant authentication scheme and secure access to the underlying information for customers, partners, and employees.

A Real-Time Business implies that you are adopting the latest sensor, beacon, and smart device technologies for connecting products, physical environments, and people to generate real-time data. It implies that you are leveraging advanced analytics techniques such as stream processing, map reduce, and machine learning to perform real-time analytics on the constant stream of data flowing into the system. Through that analysis, you will be able to provide visual and system level alerts and notifications and high-value data visualization for consumers of the information. In addition, you will be able to integrate with existing lines of business systems to automate critical business processes.

As depicted in Figure 1-2, to be successful on this journey, organizations must apply a set of unwavering principles that provide the guideposts and rules that are used to influence each product decision along the way.

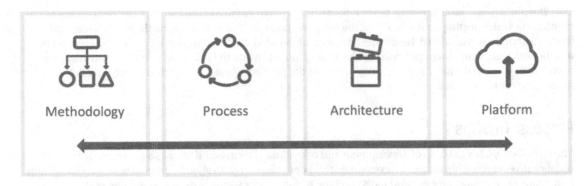

Figure 1-2. *Methodology, Process, Architecture, Platform*

These principles include a well-defined software development methodology, a standard software development process that includes not only development but also operations, the adoption of software architecture patterns that provide scalability, elasticity, and agility, and a software platform that provides the foundational services for modern software.

Methodology: Lean Engineering

Lean engineering has its root in manufacturing where the primary concept is to maximize customer value while minimizing waste, i.e., creating more value for customers with fewer resources. Applied to the software development lifecycle, the product team engages customers early in the development process by operationalizing a minimal-viable-product (MVP) and asking for feedback. Using this approach, the software product team can more easily adjust or even course-correct and thus increase product quality.

The lean engineering lifecycle, as depicted in Figure 1-3, is called Build-Measure-Learn and promotes continuous delivery, continuous analytics, and continuous feedback.

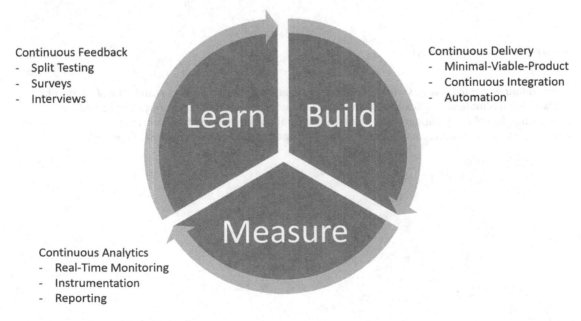

Figure 1-3. *Lean engineering cycle*

The Build phase represents the development and deployment activities; the Measure phase focuses on monitoring and reporting on the health of the software; Learn is all about engaging the customer to gather feedback that then is used to drive the next iteration of the product development lifecycle. The creation of dashboards, either custom or provided by third-party tools, provide the real-time and historical analytics from which you can derive insights quickly and steer the product development effort in the direction that meets your customer's needs.

Process: DevOps

The term *DevOps* is a mashup of development and operations. The mashup implies a deeper, more collaborative relationship between development and operations organizations. The goal of that collaboration is to define how people, process, and tools combine to automate a software development lifecycle.

DevOps, as depicted in Figure 1-4, implies the creation of cross-functional teams, combining developers, testers, and architects along with operations who together own the entire deployment pipeline from build through test to staging through to production.

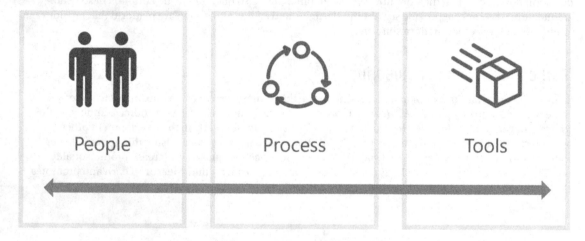

Figure 1-4. *DevOps framework*

It requires that these teams work collaboratively to adopt common processes and tools. This simple explanation has massive implications to an organization. It does not happen overnight and should be approached in a phased manner using small teams that adopt the new methods and best practices and then transition to become subject matter experts, transferring their knowledge to the rest of the staff.

Architecture: Microservices

The key attributes of microservices are:

- *Autonomous and Isolated*: Microservices are self-contained units of functionally with loosely coupled dependencies on other services and are designed, developed, tested, and released independently.

- *Reusable, Fault Tolerant, and Responsive*: Microservices must be able to scale appropriately depending on the usage scenario. They must be fault-tolerant and provide a reasonable timeframe for recovery if something does go awry. Finally, they need to be responsive, providing reasonable performance given the execution scenario.

- *Programmable*: Microservices rely on APIs and data contracts to define how interaction with the service is achieved. The API defines a set of network-visible endpoints, and the data contract defines the structure of the message that is either sent or returned.

- *Configurable*: Microservices are configurable. To be both reusable and able to address the needs of each system that chooses to employ its capabilities, a microservice must provide a means by which it can be appropriately molded to the usage scenario.

- *Automated*: The lifecycle of a microservice should be fully automated, from design all the way through deployment.

Microservice architecture has become a popular pattern in the development of highly scalable, fault-tolerant SaaS applications as it provides a more robust application architecture, supports a high velocity release cycle, and places an emphasis on managed APIs as the means to access the underlying data, analytics, and business operations. One of the benefits of this approach is that the APIs have the potential to become a new revenue channel for the business.

Platform: Cloud

Modern applications require an infrastructure and software platform that can provide high availability, fault tolerance, elastic scale, on-demand storage and compute, APIs, and tools to fully automate every interaction with the platform. The cloud platforms must also provide the foundational building block services that span IoT, big data, and predictive analytics.

Internet of Things (IoT) and Big Data

IoT is not new. The ability to connect devices to networks, gather telemetry, and display that information to garner insight and act has been around for some time. NASA pioneered the concept of data being collected by sensors and sent across space and time to be analyzed in near-real-time so that status could be visualized, insights gleaned, and action taken in an emergency (see Figure 1-5).

Figure 1-5. *Neil Armstrong (image credit NASA)*

NASA's Mission Control, seen in Figure 1-6, consisted of hundreds of people, each with his own collection of monitors providing data visualization of key metrics coming from the command module or an astronaut's suit. That data was an immediate measure of mission status and safety. Truly amazing when you think about what that organization accomplished given the state of technology at the time.

Figure 1-6. *NASA's Mission Control (image credit NASA)*

The Tipping Point

The one thing that NASA had that made them unique was a budget. Billions of dollars enabled NASA to put humans on the moon and, in the process, define IoT for the rest of us.

It is not likely that you have a NASA-sized budget, but you are in luck. It is no longer necessary to break the bank to IoT-enable your products and connect them to the cloud to gather telemetry, transform and store the data, gather insight, and act. Sensors and miniature microprocessor boards are inexpensive and getting cheaper and more powerful all the time. The ability to develop the code to gather sensor readings, connect to a secure cloud endpoint, and send messages has never been easier.

What is driving this thirst for IoT is data. This data will reveal the quality of the product and how it is used by customers, as well as give you the ability to calculate mean time to failure for its components and provide immediate business value through the automation of scheduled preventive maintenance. Using predictive and prescriptive analytics, you can provide an enhanced customer experience, increase product quality, and create a competitive advantage.

Big Data

What you learn very quickly with IoT is that once you have sensor-enabled people, places, and things, then it becomes all about the data. There are approximately 2 billion PCs on the planet in 2017 and about 10 billion mobile devices. By 2020, it is projected there will be over 50 billion connected devices driving Exabytes of data into the cloud.

How are we going to be able to ingest, transform, store, and analyze this data, and even more importantly, how are going to query and visualize the data so that we can quickly draw insights and act? We need to learn new skills and leverage new cloud capabilities to deal with this influx of massive amounts data.

Advanced Analytics

If data is the ore, then knowledge is the gold. One of the goals of collecting all this data is to be able to mine insight from real-time data visualizations that improve business value and automate critical business processes. A typical IoT data processing pattern is to set up cold, warm, and hot path routes for the data where the cold path provides long-term storage, the warm path provides storage for real-time dashboards, fast batch and slow batch processing, and the hot path delivers the messages via a queue to a microservice that provides real-time notification services for alerts and alarms.

Predictive analytics is a popular choice for real-time solutions because it is a data-mining process focused on predicting a future state. Data models are created from historical or sample data. These models are used along with statistical algorithms to examine real-time data streams and make a prediction. Manufacturing companies can use predictive analytics to determine when component parts of their products are about to fail and use that to automate the process of scheduling a field service engineer to visit and perform maintenance. A medical clinic may use predictive analytics to examine genomic data to see if a population is predestined for a medical condition. A retail outlet may use this approach applied to real-time inventory levels to predict when it will run out of a popular product.

Real-Time Business Reference Architecture

To realize the benefits a Real-Time Business solution requires a set of business and technical capabilities that define the process by which you ingest device events, perform advanced analytics, gather insight, and act.

The business will need to develop a model that demonstrates how processes will be improved to reduce cost and what new revenue channels will be identified and leveraged to increase profit. For example, a manufacturer can reduce costs by only sending field technicians to perform maintenance when needed. That same manufacturer may find that they can offer more flexible service contracts and thus increase sales and monthly service contract revenue.

A product development team who is responsible for supporting this new business model will need a reference architecture that provides a roadmap for how they can construct a real-time system from connected devices and cloud services.

Figure 1-7 depicts a reference architecture for Real-Time Business. Each component of the architecture represents the combination of foundational cloud services for implementing a real-time data pipeline, advanced analytics, big data storage, APIs, and the supporting automation scripts and security protocols. Together these components provide the technical capabilities of a Real-Time Business platform.

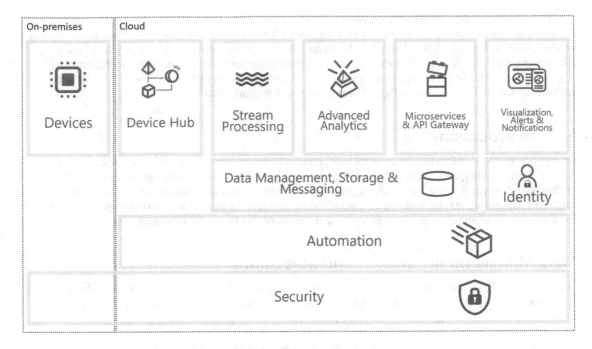

Figure 1-7. *Real-Time Business reference architecture*

Devices

Each IoT scenario requires analysis and strategy on how best to sensor-enable the product, the environment, or the people to efficiently and securely gather the data needed to drive the business case. This may involve RFID tags for location and product identification; environmental sensors for temperature, humidity, or wind speed; mechanical sensors for tracking gear revolutions or hydraulic pump iterations; or in the case of people, biometric sensors for heart rate, skin temperature, or blood glucose.

In addition to the sensors, you will need devices with an embedded operating system such as Linux or Windows 10 IoT, to host the code that manages the connectivity to sensors and the physical environments in which the device is deployed, secure connectivity via wired, wireless and/or cellular network, secure authentication to the cloud, device-to-cloud messaging such as heartbeat and telemetry, and cloud-to-device messaging for command and control and device management. Advanced scenarios may add analytics, filtering, business rules and alerts, and notification at the edge. The device will also participate in the device-management protocols for managing device state, firmware upgrades, and other remote control operations.

Device Hub

A *device hub* is a cloud-hosted service that provides secure device connectivity, telemetry ingestion, and remote command and control. This service should provide these capabilities at scale so that, as the number of connected devices grows, the service never fails. This service may provide a transient store for all incoming messages. This transient store allows real-time analytics of the message events, analysis of messages over short periods of time, as well as the ability to go back in time to reassess the events.

Device management is typically incorporated into the device hub service. Device management provides the ability to register devices using their unique identifier such as serial number. Once registered, the device will be able to connect securely to the device hub for communication purposes. Device management may leverage the concept of a *device twin,* which is a digital representation of the state of the device kept synchronized with physical devices. The device twin provides the ability to synchronize property values of the device in the cloud with the devices in the field, essentially performing desired state configuration (DSC) at scale.

Stream Processing

Stream processing is a cloud-hosted service that provides real-time analytics on incoming telemetry. The service allows you to query across the incoming messages in real time, select messages of a certain type or that contain certain values, apply aggregation and calculations over time (windowing), transform the messages, identify alarm conditions, and then act on the result of the analytics. In most cases, this service routes the resulting message to a storage location, API, or message queue for further processing.

Data Management, Storage, and Messaging

To get the most out of the real-time data now coursing through the cloud, you will want to provide various types of storage and data management, each optimized for the next step in the data processing pipeline.

- *Blob Storage*: Blob storage is typically used for event archival.

- *Store and Forward Messaging*: To provide integration with event-driven microservices or on-premises line-of-business systems, queues and pub/sub mechanisms provide loosely coupled messaging.

- NoSQL and Relational Databases: For time-based query capabilities and integration with traditional applications and modern dashboards, you can leverage relational or NoSQL storage services.

- *Data Lake*: A Hadoop Distributed File System (HDFS) that provides big data storage and cross-language query access and can be used with advanced analytics engines.

- *Extract, Transform, and Load*: You may look to use an ETL service to perform data integration and transformation operations.

Advanced Analytics

Advanced analytics is a catch phrase for all the possible big data analytics you may look to perform on your real-time data. This may involve combining the real-time data with historical and reference data and leveraging the distributed query capabilities of a Hadoop engine, using ETL tools to integrate into a data warehouse or train a predictive model to automate preventive maintenance. It is also possible to use the latest advances in Azure Cognitive APIs and artificial intelligence bots along with this real-time data to create new immersive, conversational experiences for your customers.

Microservices and API Gateways

A microservice provides a business or platform capability through a well-defined API, data contract, configuration, and an underlying data storage necessary to function. It provides this function and only this function. It does one thing and it does it well. Microservices represent business capabilities defined using domain-driven design, implemented using object-oriented best practices, tested at each step in the deployment pipeline, and deployed through automation as autonomous, isolated, highly scalable, resilient services in a distributed cloud infrastructure. An IoT solution may have three types of microservices:

- *Transactional*: Transactional microservices are responsible for writing messages to an appropriate store.

- *Event Driven*: Event-driven microservices listen on message queues and act on the event of a message arriving on the queue. These microservices are typically used to drive alert and notification business processes or integrate with other lines of business systems that require special message handling.

- *API Contracts*: These microservices leverage ReST endpoints and JSON data models and provide the cross-cutting concerns and business capabilities that you want exposed to any consuming application.

API gateways provide secure API proxies that wrap your ReST APIs, organize APIs into products, provide restricted access to API products via the definition of developer groups, provide a subscription capability, provide policy injection, throttling, quotas, etc., and provide analytics at the product, API, and operation levels. API gateways provide the ability to segregate your APIs into private, semi-private (partner access), or public access and then monetize the APIs to create a new revenue channel.

Visualization, Alerts, and Notifications

Now that you can ingest, analyze, and store your real-time data, you will want to create customer-, partner-, and employee-facing applications that provide impactful data visualizations, visual and device-centric alerts and notifications using your APIs and event-driven microservices. You may leverage third-party services such as Twilio and Send Grid to provide text, voice, and e-mail notifications. In addition, you may look to use cloud-hosted mobile notification services for real-time updates on mobile devices.

Identity

You will want to provide access to the applications you create to your customers, partners, and employees. The identify service provides a single sign-on or a multi-tenant authentication and authorization mechanism such that the person logging into your application can only see the data and application functionality that their role provides. The identity service can provide these features in both a Business-to-Consumer (B2C) and Business-to-Business (B2B) model, including integration with your company's directory services.

Automation

Designing, developing, deploying, and operationalizing an IoT solution requires the adoption of an automated approach to the software product lifecycle. The popular term for this today is DevOps. DevOps implies that you are organized into a software product team model that places an emphasis on product quality as the code moves through an automated deployment pipeline. The team has a well-defined process and uses a set of tools to automate its work, reducing errors and improving quality. The team leverages the cloud platform to automate the provisioning of cloud infrastructure, performing build, test, and release management, and the monitoring and gathering of runtime health metrics.

Security

IoT solutions have four security zones; local, device, cloud gateway, and cloud service. The local zone is the physical environment that the device is deployed into. The device zone represents the IoT device, how it is configured with the local zone and its internal workings, the operating system and applications. The cloud gateway zone represents the public facing endpoints that devices connect and communicate with. Finally, the cloud service zone provides access to the incoming messages to internal cloud-hosted services that provide data ingestion, stream processing, storage, advanced analytics, and application integration.

Here are a few things to keep in mind with respect to securing an IoT and advanced analytics solution:

- Secure the wired/wireless network that your devices are running on.

- Make sure the embedded operating systems that are running your devices are up to date and remotely patchable through an automated firmware upgrade process.

- Use TLS to secure the connection from the smart device and/or edge gateway to the cloud.

- Encrypt messages at rest and in fight.

- Make sure your public cloud endpoints are secured using SSL and you are using some form of authentication and authorization such as Basic, OAuth, managed certificates, or Shared Access Policies.

- Leverage an identify service for access to your applications.

- Leverage a key management service to provide governance and limited secure access to your certificates.

Microsoft Azure IoT and Cortana Intelligence Suite

Microsoft provides a feature-rich and complete set of IoT and advanced analytics resources on which you can build your Real-Time Business platform. For each of the capabilities in the reference architecture, there are one or more Azure services that provide that function through a scalable, configurable finished service. The key is knowing how to bring them all together using a combination of code, configuration, and best practices (see Figure 1-8).

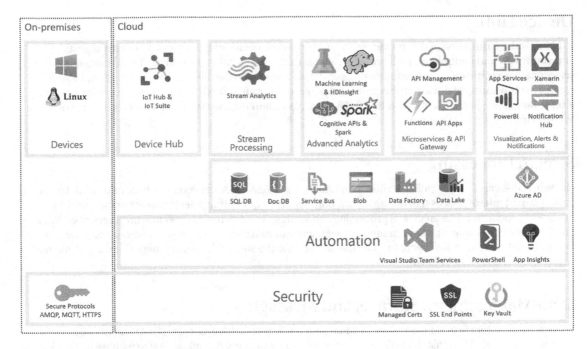

Figure 1-8. *Reference architecture and Azure mapping*

Automation

Azure provides complete support for a continuous integration and continuous delivery process using PowerShell, Azure Resource Manager (ARM) Templates, and Visual Studio Team Services (VSTS). Open source and third-party tools are also supported providing a rich and diverse ecosystem of automation tools and utilities regardless of your choice of operating system or programming language. See Chapter 2 for more detail on automation using PowerShell, ARM Templates, and VSTS.

Security and Identity

Security is a key concern with any distributed system and with the introduction of devices, sensors, beacons, edge gateways, and new networking protocols, we must be diligent in defining the security threats to the system and design the solution from the start with security in mind. Azure provides foundational services for self-service managing of end user's identity that, combined with a model for subscription management and customer and organization identification, you can provide create a seamless experience for your customers, partners, and employees. See Chapter 10 for details on security and identity using Azure AD B2C.

Devices

Microsoft provides the IoT Gateway SDK, an open source, cross-platform library that provides the infrastructure and plug-and-play modules to create IoT gateway solutions. Using the SDK, you can develop applications that enable devices to communicate with Azure IoT Hub. The SDK provides a collection of modules that can perform operations such as message aggregation and transformation, mathematical analytics, local storage, local alerts and notification, and so on. The modules communicate in a pipeline fashion and pass messages along via a message broker. You can extend the SDK by developing your own modules. See Chapter 4 for details on devices.

Device Hub

IoT Hub is the Azure service that provides device registration, device management, telemetry ingestion, and command and control. IoT Hub provides reliable device-to-cloud and cloud-to-device messaging at scale, enables secure communications using per-device security credentials and authentication, includes extensive monitoring of device connectivity and properties through the device twin, and provides access via a set of language-specific SDKs including C, C#, Java, Node, and Python. See Chapter 3 for coverage of Azure IoT Hub and device management.

Stream Processing

On Azure, this capability is called Azure Stream Analytics or ASA. ASA lets you rapidly develop and deploy small grained microservices that define inputs, outputs, and a query that selects subsets of messages for analytical processing. The analytical processing can leverage windowing, aggregating messages over time, application of rules against values in the messages, and external calls to Azure Functions or Machine Learning APIs to determine where to route the message for the step in the data analytics pipeline. Chapter 5 covers Stream Analytics in detail.

Data Management, Storage, and Messaging

There are many storage options on Azure including but not limited to blob storage, SQL Database, Cosmos DB, and Data Lake, a Hadoop Distributed File System as a service capability that allows you to manage large volumes of data and file sizes in the petabyte range. Azure provides Data Factory for performing ETL operations on data that is stored in Azure or moving in and out of on-premises storage locations. And finally, Azure provides Service Bus for store and forward messaging, pub/sub scenarios, and high-volume data ingestions using Event Hubs. See Chapters 6 and 7 for details on Data Factory and Data Lake.

Advanced Analytics

Azure provides a rich set of fully managed analytics capabilities including HDInsight, Microsoft's Hadoop as a Service, machine learning for predictive analytics, and Data Lake analytics for large-scale distributed analytics that leverage Yarn and U-SQL. Microsoft also provides a set of cognitive APIs that provide advanced machine learning intelligence for language understanding, facial recognition, sentiment analytics, and more. See Chapter 8 for coverage of Azure Machine Learning and the R programming language.

Microservices and API Gateway

As you build out your solution on Azure and its foundational services, you will want to leverage a microservice architecture to optimize your use of the on-demand features of Azure and to be able to support a continuous delivery development pipeline and high-velocity release cycle. You have several choices in how you package and deploy your microservices on Azure including App Services, Service Fabric, Azure Container Services (ACS), and Docker.

For those microservices that expose ReST APIs, Azure provides API Management to publish your APIs using the subscription model for both internal as well as external developers. They can apply policies, gather statistics, and provide security to protect them from abuse. Chapter 2 provides details on Azure API Management.

Visualization, Alerts, and Notifications

A key feature of Real-Time Business solutions is the real-time data visualization provided through self-updating dashboards, alerts, and notifications that are provided through dashboards and mobile devices as well as through system integration, which could include cloud-hosted applications such as Dynamics CRM and on-premises line-of-business applications such as SAP.

There are a myriad of technologies that allow you to create these types of user experiences, from responsive web using Node.JS, Angular.JS, D3, and other popular JavaScript libraries to native or cross-platform mobile frameworks such as Xamarin and off-the-shelf data visualization products like PowerBI. Chapter 9 demonstrates how to implement alerts and notifications using Azure functions and data visualization using PowerBI.

Worker Health and Safety: A Reference Implementation

As you navigate through the chapters of this book, we will cover each of components in the reference architecture. We have provided a reference implementation to demonstrate the patterns and practices leveraging Azure IoT and Cortana Intelligence Suite. The solution is called *Worker Health and Safety*. The repository has been designed to support a linear progression through the book as each chapter builds on the previous chapters.

To follow along with the exercises in this book, you need an Azure account. Be aware that, by following the exercises, you will incur a cost for the Azure services that you provision and run.

■ **Note**   You can sign up for an Azure account by visiting `http://azure.net`.

Backstory

The solution scenario is that you provide a SaaS solution that allows your customers to connect their employees who work in dangerous conditions using sensor-enabled clothing and wearables. The sensors provide a rich set of biometric data that is collected in real time and is used to feed a predictive analytics engine that will raise alerts before an employee reaches a level of exhaustion or stress.

Three fictitious companies have been defined that present your customers. Each company has 15 employees who are being monitored.

- *WigiTech*: A technology firm that wants to monitor factory floor employees who work in dangerous conditions

- *Tall Towers*: A utilities service company whose employees perform maintenance on communications towers that sit atop skyscrapers

- *The Complicated Badger*: A trucking company that specializes in moving heavy equipment in and out of mining and logging sites wants to monitor their employees to make sure they are fit to handle to the difficult driving conditions

Solution Architecture

The solution architecture is best depicted as three cooperating sub-systems (see Figures 1-9, 1-10, and 1-11):

- *IoT Sub-System*: The services necessary to provide device connectivity, two-way communication, and device management

- *Analytics Sub-System*: The services necessary to perform real-time analytics and event routing, big data storage and data management, and predictive analytics

- *Application Services Sub-System*: The services necessary to provide secure access to applications, APIs, and the underlying data as well as the tools that provide automation for provision, build, test, deployment, and monitoring

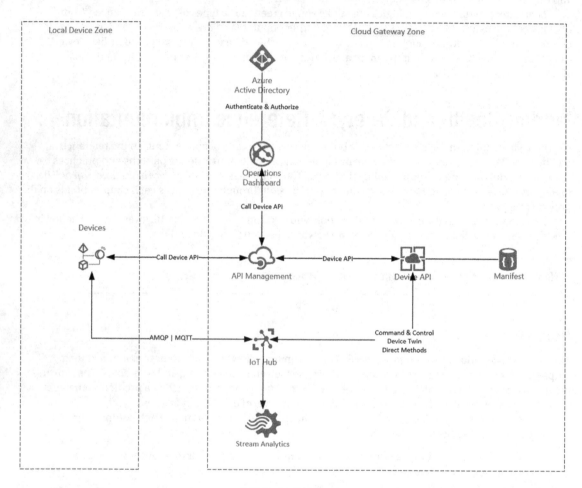

IoT Sub-System

Figure 1-9. *IoT sub-system*

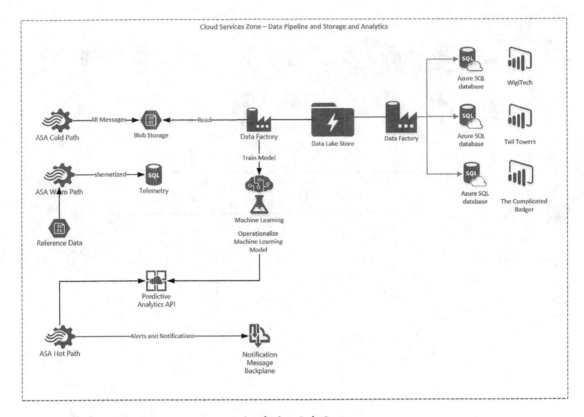

Analytics Sub-System

Figure 1-10. *Analytics sub-system*

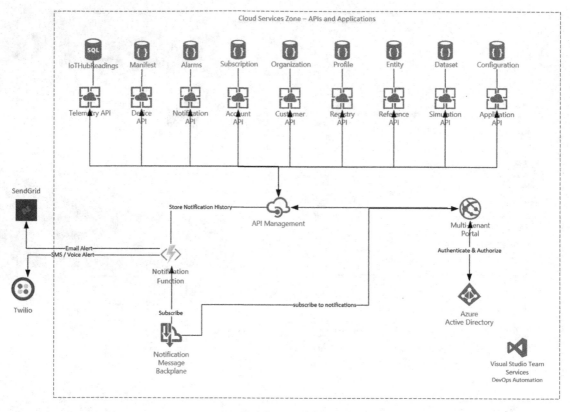

Application Sub-System

Figure 1-11. *Application services sub-system*

Downloading the Repository

If you would like to leverage the hands-on exercises in each of the chapters, we have provided a reference implementation code repository as a starting point. The repository is located here:

`https://github.com/brtbook/brt`

Clone the repository to your local environment. The exercises in Chapter 2 will detail the setup and configuration of your development environment. Note that an Azure subscription is required and that you will incur costs for the services that you provision in your Azure environment.

Summary

In this chapter, we introduced the concept of a Real-Time Business, the challenges as well as the benefits. We provided an overview of the core tenants of modern software development, lean engineering, DevOps, microservices, and the cloud.

We introduced the Real-Time Business reference architecture, which provides a roadmap for how you can design a highly scalable SaaS IoT and advanced analytics solution. Finally, we mapped the reference architecture to the foundational resources on Azure that we will need to bring our solution to market at velocity.

Each subsequent chapter will cover an area of the reference architecture along with the relevant Azure services that map to that area. We will use the reference implementation for Worker Health and Safety to demonstrate the patterns and practices.

CHAPTER 2

DevOps Using PowerShell, ARM, and VSTS

DevOps is best summed up as the union of people, processes, and tools (see Figure 2-1), an alignment of the development and operations teams, the automation of development, test and release processes and the selection of a consistent set of tools to facilitate automating the provision, build, test and release cycles. The goal of adopting a DevOps approach is to create a streamlined product development lifecycle that removes, to the greatest degree possible, errors that are introduced through manual steps, i.e., errors introduced through human error.

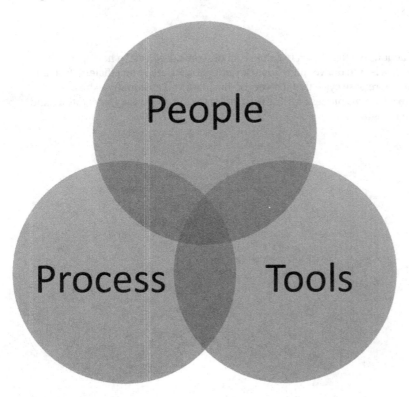

Figure 2-1. *DevOps framework*

© Bob Familiar and Jeff Barnes 2017
B. Familiar and J. Barnes, *Business in Real-Time Using Azure IoT and Cortana Intelligence Suite*,
DOI 10.1007/978-1-4842-2650-6_2

Through a combination of empirical studies and firsthand experience, software professionals have come to realize that small, cross-functional teams are optimal for the creation of modern software applications. Lean Engineering, Agile, Scrum, et al. have grown in popularity to fill the methodology and process void, and the tools have evolved to promote automation to a first-class citizen in the engineering domain.

Every organization must find its own path to DevOps. How a company measures success will differ based on where they are experiencing the most pain. The metrics used to measure success therefore will be different for each organization. Some common metrics include more frequent deployments, faster recovery from failures, lower failure rates and time to market. Determining the metrics that are most important to your organization will require some self-reflection and collaboration between all the teams that would be affected by the inherent change.

People

When introducing DevOps into your organization, the people aspect can be the most challenging. Introducing impactful change into an organization is difficult without the support from leadership and buy-in from the engineering staff. To facilitate this change, your company may need to introduce new organizational structures and new teaming models, breaking down the walls between development and operations. The engineering staff may need to learn new skills, change their daily habits, and learn to work more collaboratively. You may need to hire new skills, retrain staff, and, my favorite, hire professional services firms to assist in these transitions.

Process

Process is defined as a series of actions or steps taken to achieve an outcome. The goal in having a well-defined product development lifecycle is to deliver high quality, valuable software in an efficient, fast, and reliable manner, enabling a frequent release cycle that delivers on business and customer desires.

There are three key stages to a DevOps process—Infrastructure as Code, Continuous Integration, and Continuous Delivery—as shown in Figure 2-2.

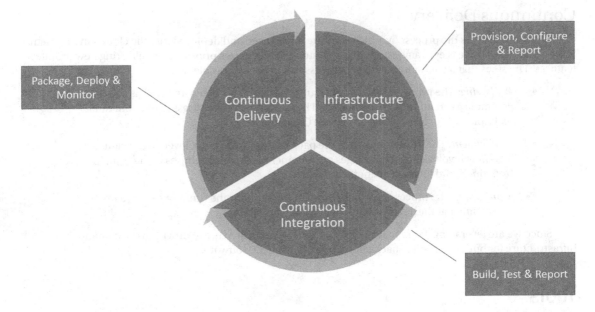

Figure 2-2. *DevOps process*

Infrastructure as Code

Infrastructure as Code is the process of defining Infrastructure-as-a-Service (IaaS) and Platform-as-a-Service (PaaS) configurations consisting of networks, virtual machines, and software services using templates and then orchestrating their creation via automation scripts and utilities. Using this approach, it is possible to instantiate and configure all the compute, storage, and software services needed for sophisticated, on-demand distributed systems.

Continuous Integration

Continuous integration is the process by which code is developed and checked in to the source code repository triggering an automatic run of unit and functional tests. If tests fail, developers are informed through the automation of work items that are added to their individual backlog.

Continuous integration provides fast feedback to developers on the quality of their code. Code is only accepted into the master branch if it passes through these quality checks. If the build fails, fixing the build becomes the highest priority. This process should be running "continuously," hence the name, as this process lays the foundation for continuous delivery, making sure that the current software build is stable and deployable throughout its lifecycle.

Continuous Delivery

Continuous delivery is the process by which software is packaged and deployed into the cloud environment. It is critical that if there is ever any issue with these steps, fixing it takes priority over delivering new product features. The steps that a continuous delivery process would be responsible for are:

- *Packaging*: The process by which software is packaged for deployment. This can be as simple as creating a ZIP file that used by the deployment process to use container technologies such as Docker and Azure Container Services.

- *Deployment*: The process by which the packaged software is deployed to the cloud. This may involve copying packages or container images on-premises to the cloud or from one cloud location to another.

- *Monitoring*: The process by which the team can monitor the running software to determine that the deployment is healthy and functional.

Since we are leveraging Azure to host this solution, we can use Azure to provision on-demand infrastructure for building, testing, packaging, and deploying the software.

Tools

An entire industry has grown up around continuous integration and continuous delivery. There is a myriad of products and tools both from independent software vendors as well as the open source community. These tools provide capabilities across the entire software product development lifecycle including source code management, building automation, testing frameworks and testing automation, project management tools, bug tracking, Integrated Development Environments (IDEs), packaging and deployment process automation, desired state configuration, and the list goes on.

Your choice of tools will depend on your development frameworks, cloud platform, language skills and likely existing investments in tooling by your company. To increase the quality of your continuous integration and continuous delivery processes, tool integration will be a major factor. The recommendation is to focus on how each of the frameworks, languages, automation tools and platforms you use allows you to eliminate manual steps and provide reporting and visibility into the health of your build and runtime environments.

DevOps and Azure

Azure provides a rich set of SDKs, APIs, tools, frameworks, and command-line utilities for managing Azure resources and defining and managing your continuous integration and continuous delivery processes. Azure has evolved to provide not only support for Microsoft's traditional development tools and languages, i.e. Visual Studio, .NET Framework, and C#, but also provides full support for teams that want to leverage *nix, Java, node.js, Docker, Jenkins, Octopus, Chef, Puppet, Jira, CA Rally or just about any other open source or ISV Continuous Integration/Continuous Deliver (CICD) product. Whether you develop in .NET, Java, Ruby, Python, PHP or Node, the same level of capability is available for creating an automated continuous delivery process.

It would be impossible to cover all the possible combinations, so for our purposes, we will focus on using PowerShell and Visual Studio Team Services along with Azure Resource Manager Templates to implement a fully automated CICD process that provides the provisioning, build, and deploy steps for our solution.

PowerShell

Windows PowerShell is an object-oriented task automation and configuration management framework from Microsoft consisting of a command-line shell and associated scripting language built on the .NET Framework. PowerShell has been migrated to .NET Core and has been open sourced as of August 2016, making it a viable automation tool on Mac and Linux.

The PowerShell Console (see Figure 2-3) is the command-line utility that you can use to execute PowerShell scripts. When using PowerShell to administer Azure from a desktop, it is recommended that you run this utility as an administrator.

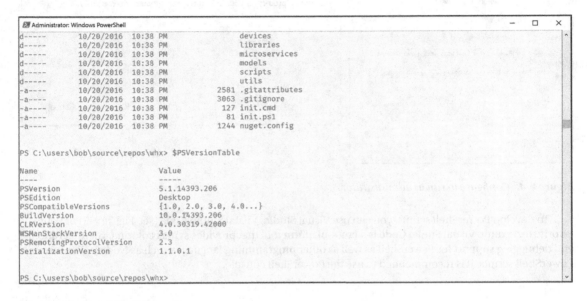

Figure 2-3. PowerShell Console

■ **Tip**   Pin this utility to your taskbar, bring up the Property dialog box for the application, and click on the Advanced Properties button. On the Advanced Properties dialog box, check Run as Administrator (see Figure 2-4).

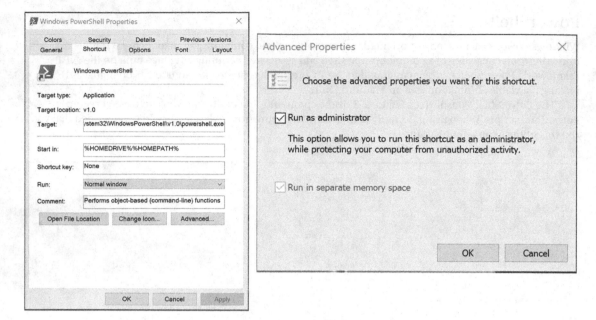

Figure 2-4. *Configure to run as administrator*

To develop PowerShell scripts, you can use Visual Studio, Visual Studio Code (see Figure 2-5) or your favorite text editor. Visual Studio Code is a cross-platform tool that provides syntax coloring, Git integration, and debugging support for PowerShell as well as other programming languages such as Node.js. For running PowerShell scripts, it is recommended to use the PowerShell console.

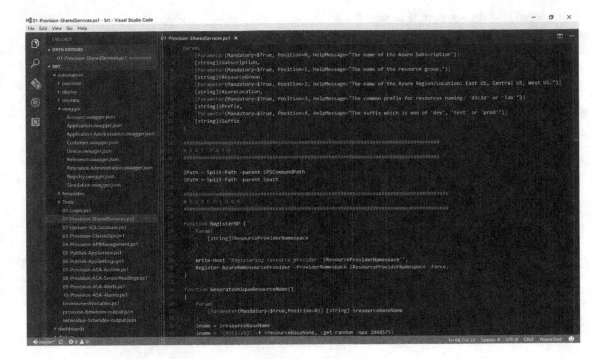

Figure 2-5. *Visual Studio Code*

Script Constructs

The PowerShell scripts provided in the accompanying Git repo uses a few standard PowerShell techniques. The first technique is that most scripts will take a standard set of input parameters so that they are reusable. At the top of each script, there is a param section that defines five standard parameters:

```
param(
    [string]$Subscription,  # Azure subscription
    [string]$ResourceGroup, # resource group
    [string]$AzureLocation, # region, i.e. East US, Japan
    [string]$Prefix,        # the prefix for naming services
    [string]$Suffix         # the suffix for naming services
)
```

Here is an example of passing these parameters to a script from the command line:

```
PS C:\> .\somescript.ps1
    -subscription bobs-azure
    -resourcegroup dev001
    -azurelocation "East US"
    -prefix bob
    -suffix dev
```

The PowerShell scripts reside in the code repository. At times the scripts will need to reference files located in the repository. To reference files throughout the repository, the the current path location is captured and then used to construct paths to other files.

```
$Path = Split-Path -parent $PSCommandPath
$Path = Split-Path -parent $Path
```

A PowerShell variable is a name that starts with $. To declare a variable, you use this syntax:

```
$storageAccountName = $Prefix + "blobstorage" + $Suffix
$storageAccountType = "Standard_LRS"
```

Note the use of the $Prefix and $Suffix common parameters. These parameters are used to make sure unique names are created for each of the Azure resources. At the start of each script, the error cache is cleared and the start time is recorded so the runtime of the script can be calculated and reported at the end of the script.

```
$Error.Clear()

# Mark the start time.
$StartTime = Get-Date

$ErrorActionPreference = "Stop"

#--------------------
# body of script here
#--------------------

# Mark the finish time.
$FinishTime = Get-Date

#Console output
$TotalTime = ($FinishTime - $StartTime).TotalSeconds
Write-Verbose -Message "Elapse Time (Seconds): $TotalTime" -Verbose
```

Azure PowerShell

Azure PowerShell is a scripting environment that you can use to control and automate the creation, configuration, and management of Azure resources as well as your custom code and configuration in Azure. Azure PowerShell provides *cmdlets* (PowerShell commands) that encapsulate Azure's ReST APIs. To configure the Azure PowerShell environment, download and run the Azure SDK installation.

■ **Tip**   To install PowerShell and the Azure PowerShell extensions, visit https://azure.microsoft.com/en-us/downloads.

After installation is complete, run the PowerShell console as administrator and execute the following commands.

```
PS C:\> Set-ExecutionPolicy Unrestricted
```

Install the Azure Resource Manager Modules:

```
PS C:\> Install-Module AzureRM
PS C:\> Import-Module AzureRM
```

Install the Azure Classic Modules:

```
PS C:\> Install-Module Azure
PS C:\> Import-Module Azure
```

Invoking Azure Cmdlets

Azure PowerShell cmdlets wrap the Azure ReST APIs and make it straightforward to apply Azure Resource Manager (ARM) templates and invoke commands to configure and manage existing services. Azure Resource Templates are covered in more detail later in this chapter. For example, to select an Azure subscription, you would use the Set-AzureRmContext cmdlet:

```
Set-AzureRmContext -SubscriptionName $Subscription;
```

This next bit of code will check to see if a resource group exists, and if it does not exist, it will create it:

```
$rg = Get-AzureRmResourceGroup
    -Name $ResourceGroup
    -ErrorAction SilentlyContinue

if(!$rg)
{
    New-AzureRmResourceGroup
        -Name $ResourceGroup
        -Location $AzureLocation
}
Else
{
    Write-Verbose"Using existing resource group"
}
```

Azure Resource Manager

The reference implementation comprises many cooperating software services and components. Azure Resource Manager (ARM) is the construct in Azure to organize and relate the resources for your solution and provide the ability to create, configure, update, and delete them as a single unit. Let's define the terminology:

- *Resource*: A manageable item that is available through Azure. Some common resources are a virtual machine, storage account, web app, database, a virtual network, etc.

- *Resource Group*: A named collection of related resources for an Azure solution. The resource group can include all the resources for the solution, or only those resources that you want to manage as a group. You decide how you want to allocate resources to resource groups based on what makes the most sense for your organization. It is not uncommon to designate resource groups for development, test, staging, and production through a naming convention.

- *Resource Provider*: A service that supplies the resources you can deploy and manage through a resource manager. Each resource provider offers operations for working with the resources that are deployed. Some common resource providers are `Microsoft.Compute`, which supplies the virtual machine resource, `Microsoft.Storage`, which supplies the storage account resource, and `Microsoft.Web`, which supplies resources related to web apps.

- *Resource Manager Template*: A resource manager template, also referred to as an ARM template, is a JavaScript Object Notation (JSON) file that defines one or more resources to deploy to a resource group. It also defines the dependencies between the deployed resources. The template can be used to deploy the resources consistently and repeatedly.

There are many benefits to defining your Azure environments using JSON templates rather than implementing it all in script.

- The templates can be versioned, added to your code repository, and kept in sync with the code that implements the solution.

- You can leverage these templates repeatedly and consistently throughout the lifecycle of your continuous delivery process.

- You can apply role-based access control on the deployed resources to define who can access which capabilities in the environment.

- You can apply tags to individual Azure resources. Querying your Azure environment for tagged resources provides you views that span across resource groups. This can be helpful if you want to create a billing view for all the resources that are associated with `test` or with `accounting` as an example.

ARM Templates

ARM templates are JSON files that define the resources to be provisioned and configured in a resource group. The ARM template file has six sections.

Part 1. $schema

Location of the JSON schema file that describes the version of the template language.

```
"$schema": https://schema.management.azure.com/schemas/2015-01-01/deploymentTemplate.json#
```

Part 2. Content Version

The version of the template (such as 1.0.0.0).

```
"contentVersion": "1.0.0.0"
```

Part 3. Parameters

Defines the input parameters to the template. Good use of input parameters makes your script reusable and dynamic. Here we are defining input parameters for Azure location, storage account name, and so on. These input parameters make the script dynamic and reusable. The values can be accessed in other areas of the template using this notation: [parameters('param-name')].

```
"parameters": {
        "azureLocation": {"type": "string"},
        "storageAccountName": {"type": "string"},
        "servicebusNamespace": {"type": "string"},
        "docDbAccount": {"type": "string"},
    ...
```

Part 4. Variables

Reusable JSON script fragments that provide common settings or simplification of complex code constructs. These named variables can be accessed in other areas of the template using the notation: [variables('variable-name')].

```
"variables": {
  "iotHubResourceId":
    "[resourceId(
      'Microsoft.Devices/Iothubs',parameters('iotHubName'))]",
  "iotHubKeyName": "iothubowner",
    ...
```

Part 5. Resources

This part of the template lists the resources that you want provisioned in Azure, such as an instance of DocumentDB, a service bus namespace, or a web site. To identify the type of resource, use the resource provider syntax, for example:

```
'Microsoft.Storage/storageAccounts'
```

or

```
'Microsoft.DocumentDb/databaseAccounts'.
```

Here is a snippet of a resources section in an ARM template:

```
"resources": [
 {
  "type": "Microsoft.Storage/storageAccounts",
  "name": "[parameters('storageAccountName')]",
  "apiVersion": "2015-06-15",
  "location": "[parameters('azureLocation')]",
  "properties": {"accountType":
      "[parameters('storageAccountType')]"}
 },
 ...
```

Part 6. Outputs

The outputs section allows you to request settings that result from the creation of Azure resources so that you can reuse them with other scripts and templates. These values are typically items such as connection strings and are shared access policy keys.

```
"outputs": {
  "iotHubHostName": {
    "type": "string",
    "value": "[reference(
        variables('iotHubResourceId')).hostName]"
  },
  "iotHubKey": {
    "type": "string",
    "value": "[listkeys(
        variables('iotHubKeyResource'),
        variables('iotHubVersion')).primaryKey]"
  },
  ...
```

To execute a template, you need to first create a matching parameters JSON file that contains the input parameters as defined by the template. The following PowerShell code will generate a JSON file that contains the input parameters for an ARM template and then passes that file along with the template to the **New-AzureRMResourceGroupDeployment** cmdlet. When the command completes, the output parameters are written to a file with the name **provision-[ResourceGroupName]-output.json**.

```
Try
{
    $JSON = @"
{
    "$schema": "https://schema.management.azure.com/schemas/2015-01-01/deploymentTemplate.
     json#",

    "contentVersion": "1.0.0.0",

    "parameters": {
        "azureLocation": {"value": "$AzureLocation"},
        "storageAccountName": {"value": "$storageAccountName"},
        "storageAccountType": {"value": "$storageAccountType"},
        "servicebusNamespace": {"value":
            "$servicebusNamespace"},
        "docDbAccount": {"value": "$databaseAccount"},
        "iotHubName": {"value": "$iotHubName"},
        "prefix":{"value":"$Prefix"},
        "suffix":{"value":"$Suffix"},
    }
}
"@
    $ParamsPath = $Path
        + "\Automation\Templates\whx-arm-template-params.json"
```

```powershell
    # write the parameters file to disk
    $JSON | Set-Content -Path $ParamsPath

    $TemplatePath = $Path
        + "\Automation\Templates\whx-arm-template.json"
    $OutputPath = $Path
        + "\Automation\provision-$ResourceGroup-output.json"

    # validate the template files
    Test-AzureRmResourceGroupDeployment
        -ResourceGroupName $ResourceGroup
        -TemplateFile $TemplatePath
        -TemplateParameterFile $ParamsPath

    # perform the deployment
    New-AzureRmResourceGroupDeployment
        -ResourceGroupName $ResourceGroup
        -TemplateFile $TemplatePath
        -TemplateParameterFile $ParamsPath
        | ConvertTo-Json
        | Out-File  "$OutputPath"
}
Catch
{
    Write-Verbose -Message $Error[0].Exception.Message
    Write-Verbose
     -Message "Exiting due to exception: ARM Template Failed."
}
```

The output file will contain both the input parameters to the template as well as each of the requested output settings as requested by the template. By saving the output as a JSON file, any other script in the provisioning, build, and deployment processes can parse the file and access the stored values.

To provide this parsing capability for the other PowerShell scripts in our solution, you can create a PowerShell script that loads the output JSON file and initializes a PowerShell object to make it easy to access the settings.

```powershell
$provisionOutputPath = $Path
    + "\automation\provision-$ResourceGroup-output.json"
$provisionInfo = ConvertFrom-Json
    -InputObject (Gc $provisionOutputPath -Raw)
```

To include this script in another file, you can use this PowerShell command:

```powershell
$includePath = $Path + "\Automation\EnvironmentVariables.ps1"
."$includePath"
```

To access one of the input parameters or output values from the execution of the ARM template, you use the $provisionInfo object as follows:

```
$iotHubHostName = $provisionInfo.Outputs.iotHubHostName.Value
$iotHubKey = $provisionInfo.Outputs.iotHubKey.Value
$iotHubConnectionString =
    $provisionInfo.Outputs.iotHubConnectionString.Value
$iotHubname = $provisionInfo.Parameters.iotHubname.Value
```

■ **Tip**   Useful Azure ARM Template Resources

Azure Resource Manager Template Best Practices

https://docs.microsoft.com/en-us/azure/azure-resource-manager/resource-manager-template-best-practices

Using Azure PowerShell with Azure Resource Manager

https://github.com/Azure/azure-content/blob/master/articles/powershell-azure-resource-manager.md

Azure Quick Start ARM Templates

https://github.com/Azure/azure-quickstart-templates

Now that you have a handle on how Azure PowerShell cmdlets and ARM templates are used, the next part of this chapter will take you through a series of exercises that will use the Git repo together with Visual Studio Team Services to orchestrate a provisioning, build, and deployment CICD process.

Visual Studio Team Services

Visual Studio Team Services (VSTS) is a source code control, project management, continuous integration, and continuous delivery Software-as-a-Services (SaaS) offering in Azure.

To get started with VSTS, you simply instantiate an instance in your Azure subscription, providing a unique name for the instance.

CREATE AN INSTANCE OF VISUAL STUDIO TEAM SERVICES

In the Azure Portal, select New ➤ Developer Tools ➤ Team Project and fill out the form with your instance name, version control, and process template (see Figure 2-6).

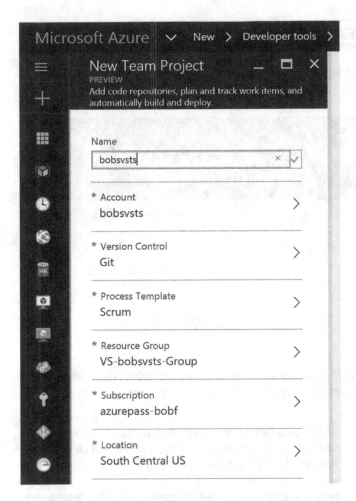

Figure 2-6. *New Visual Studio Team Services instance*

Once this process completes, you can navigate to your VSTS instance at the URL http://[your-vsts-hostname].visualstudio.com and start to configure your team development environment.

ADDING TEAM MEMBERS TO VSTS

Once your instance is provisioned, you can provide access to VSTS for your teammates by selecting the Users option from the VSTS account home page (see Figure 2-7).

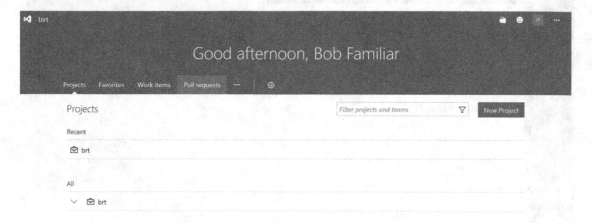

Figure 2-7. *VSTS account home page*

By clicking the ellipsis (…) in the menu, you can access the Users page. You can register users with this instance of VSTS on this page. Once users are registered with the service, they can be added to individual projects.

VSTS provides five free Basic user accounts and an unlimited number of MSDN developer accounts. You can also add an unlimited number of stakeholder accounts; stakeholders are users who do not perform development tasks but access the reporting features of the service (see Figure 2-8).

Figure 2-8. *Managing VSTS users*

If you require additional Basic users, you can purchase licenses for a monthly fee.

CREATING VSTS PROJECTS

Once you log in, you are presented with the Welcome screen and can begin creating project repositories, clone those repositories to your local development environment, add source files, and commit those changes back to the repository. When you are creating projects, you also have the option of using a Team Foundation Server (TFS) repository format and choosing what type of process template you prefer—Agile, Scrum, or CMMI (see Figure 2-9).

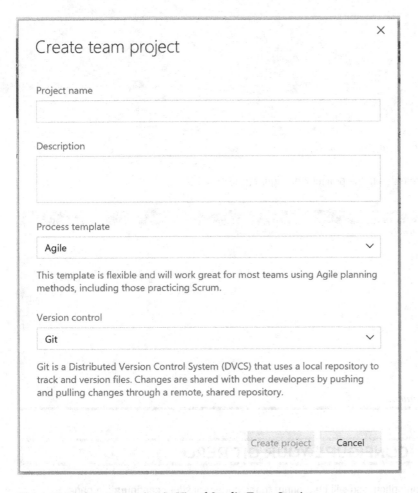

Figure 2-9. *Create a project in Visual Studio Team Services*

After you create a project, you need to add users to the project team. From the project home page, click on the gear icon in the toolbar to get to the project configuration page (see Figure 2-10).

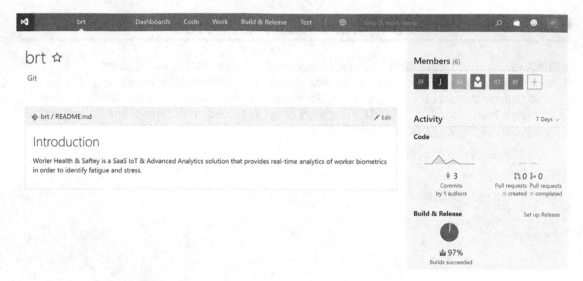

Figure 2-10. *VSTS project home page*

From here you can add teammates to the project (see Figure 2-11).

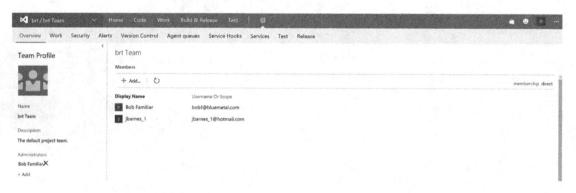

Figure 2-11. *Add project team members*

CONFIGURE YOUR GIT REPO

If you click on the Code menu option, you will be brought to the code repository configuration page. You can access the endpoint for the repository for cloning, download Git for Windows, import an existing repository, and download plugins for your IDE (see Figure 2-12). Once you have configured your repo, you can use Git commands or other Git tools to clone the repo to your local environment and begin coding.

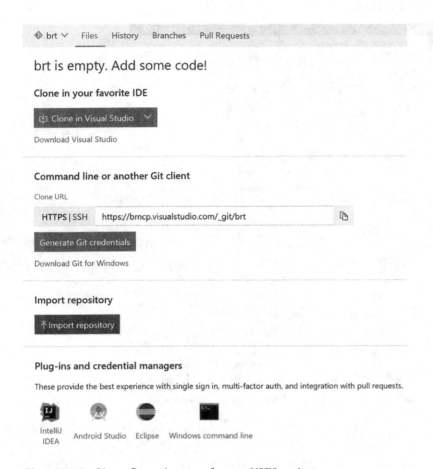

Figure 2-12. *Git configuration page for new VSTS project*

There are plugins for many popular IDEs including Eclipse, IntelliJ, Android Studio, Visual Studio, Visual Studio Code, and others (see Figure 2-13).

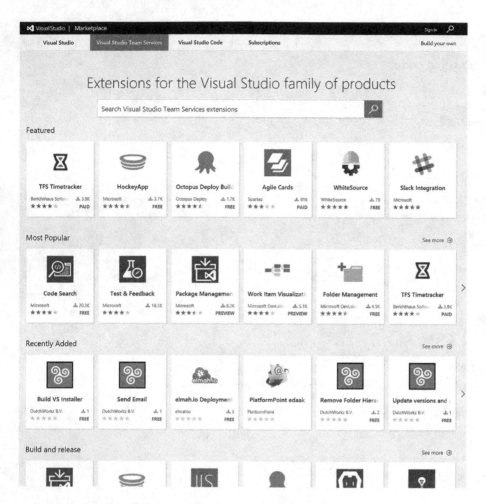

Figure 2-13. *Visual Studio Marketplace*

There is a marketplace of extensions that provide integration with Octopus, Git Hub, Slack, Trello, and many more. You can also build your own extensions.

CONFIGURE A PACKAGE FEED

VSTS has a package management extension that allows you to set up an Azure-hosted repository feed that can be used to enable continuous delivery workflows. The service can host components and packages and make them available to your builds and releases. At the time of this writing, the Package Management extension supports NuGet, and there are plans to support additional package types such as Docker, Maven, and others in the future (see Figure 2-14).

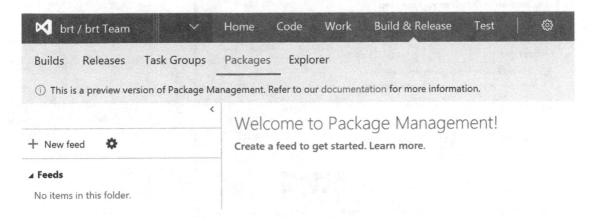

Figure 2-14. *Visual Studio Team Services package feed*

■ **Tip**   To install the Package Management extension, visit `https://marketplace.visualstudio.com/items?itemName=ms.feed`.

After the Package Management extension has been installed, visit the Packages page and click New Feed to create your NuGet feed. Set the name, add a description, and specify who can contribute packages (see Figure 2-15).

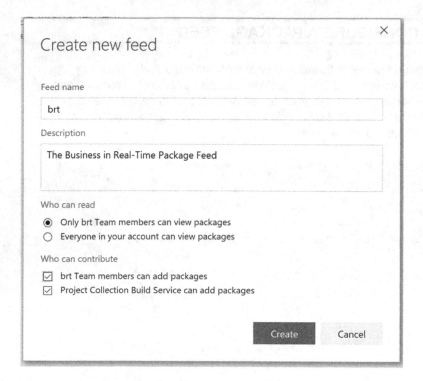

Figure 2-15. *Create a new package feed*

■ **Note**   Make sure to check "Project Collection Build Service Can Add Packages" so that build tasks can publish packages to the feed.

Once you create the feed, you will be able to access the connection details. Click the Connect to Feed button to display the Connect to Feed dialog box. Here you will see the package source URL as well as download the VSTS credential provider (see Figure 2-16).

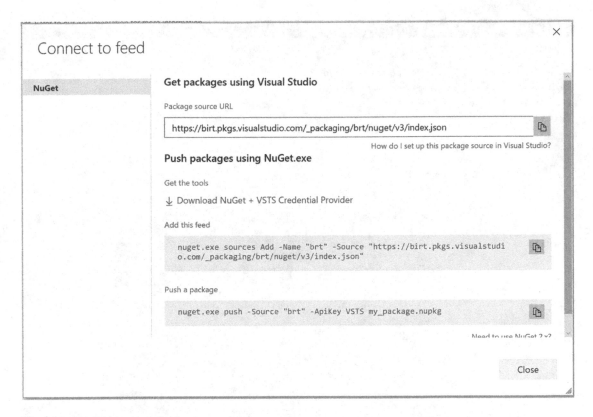

Figure 2-16. *Connect to a feed*

This is required to enable the local development environment to authenticate to the feed. Each member of the development team will need to do this in his or her own environment.

CONFIGURE THE NUGET PACKAGE FEED

To authenticate to the package feed, you will need to create a personal access token and set up a NuGet.config for the solution. From the VSTS Account home page, click on your account in the toolbar and select Security. Select Personal Access Tokens and then click Add. Give your token a name and click Create Token (see Figure 2-17).

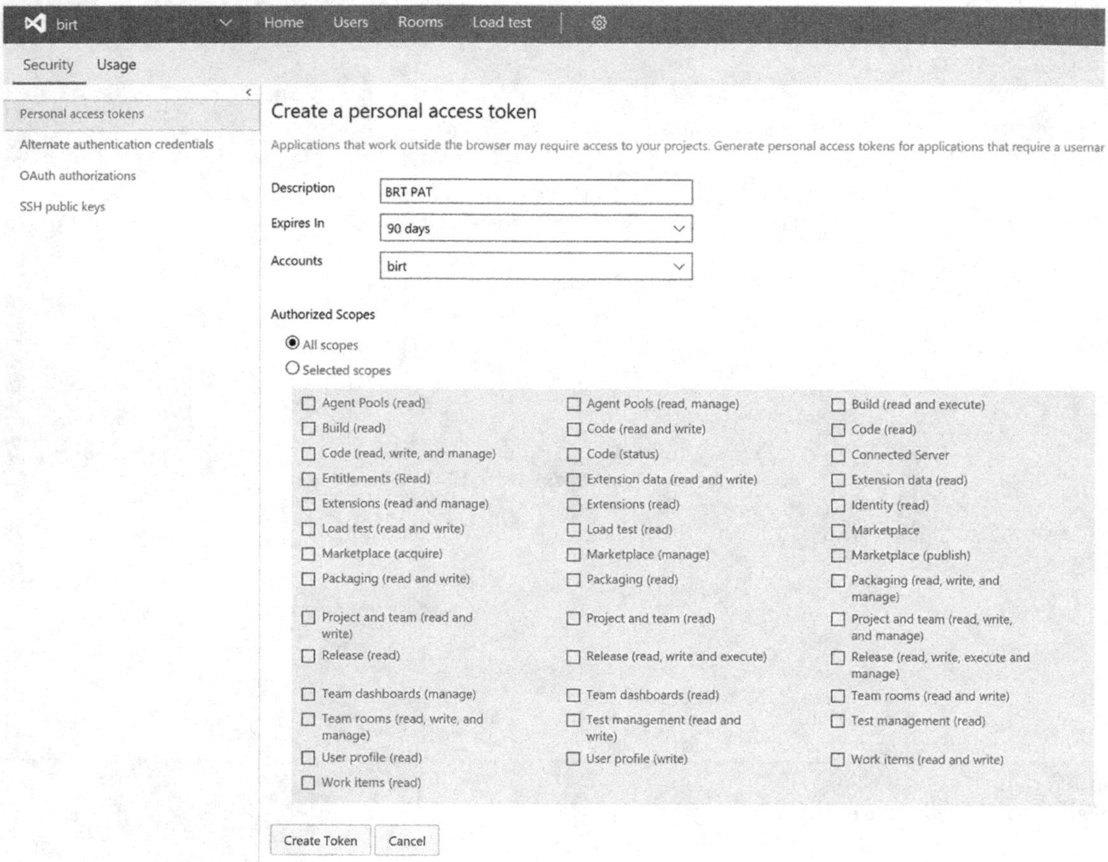

Figure 2-17. *Create a personal access token*

Copy the generated token and set it aside as you will use it in a subsequent step. Using the PowerShell console, navigate to the top-level folder of your repo and execute this command:

```
PS C\:> Invoke-WebRequest https://dist.nuget.org/win-x86-commandline/latest/nuget.exe
-OutFile nuget.exe
```

This command will download a copy of NuGet.exe. Add a NuGet.config file to the root of your repo. Here is a basic NuGet.config file you can use. Save this to the root of your repo.

```
<?xml version="1.0" encoding="utf-8"?>
<configuration>
  <packageSources>
    <clear />
    <add key="vss-package-management"
        value="https://www.myget.org/F/vss-package-
          management/api/v2" />
```

```
    <add key="nuget.org"
        value="https://api.nuget.org/v3/index.json" />
  </packageSources>
  <activePackageSource>
    <add key="All" value="(Aggregate source)" />
  </activePackageSource>
</configuration>
```

Next, execute the following command to add your feed to the `NuGet.config` file and to store your feed authentication credentials:

```
PS C:\> .\nuget.exe sources add -name {your feed name}
-source {your feed URL}
```

You will be promoted for a username. This can be anything. Next you are promoted for a password. Copy and paste your personal access token and press Enter. Your feed will be added to the `NuGet.config` file and your development environment will be automatically authenticated to the feed for downloading and publishing packages. Finally, remove the copy of `NuGet.exe` from your current directory.

```
PS C:\> rm nuget.exe
```

To add this feed to Visual Studio, from the menu click Tools ➤ NuGet Package Manager ➤ Package Manager Settings. Click the + sign to add a package source and paste the package source URL into the Source field. Give it a friendly name (see Figure 2-18).

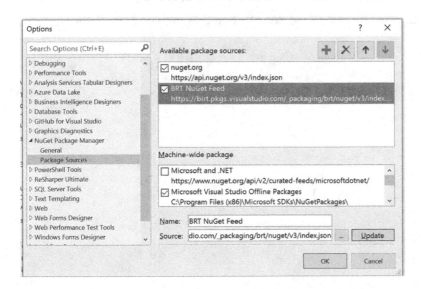

Figure 2-18. *Package Manager settings*

Package feeds provide a single source of versioned NuGet packages for your team, thus promoting reuse and collaboration. In the next exercise, you will build the NuGet packages and publish them to this newly configured feed.

CREATING A BUILD DEFINITION

Now that your development environment is configured, you can get down to the work of creating the automation definitions that will define the continuous integration and continuous delivery processes.

The reference implementation Git repository can be cloned using this URL:

https://github.com/bobfamiliar/brt.git

The repo has the following folders:

- *Automation*: PowerShell scripts and ARM templates
- *Dashboards*: Customer and employee dashboard and operations dashboard
- *Devices*: Device simulators
- *Libraries*: Common libraries for ReST and DocumentDB
- *Microservices*: Solution and cross-cutting services
- *Models*: Data models used by devices and microservices
- *Utilities*: Utility applications

The first task will be to create the automation definitions that build the Library and Model NuGet packages. The build definition will execute against the source code that has been committed to the repo and will leverage auto-provisioned compute resources in Azure to run the build steps.

Click Build & Release in the top menu bar of VSTS and then click New Definition (see Figure 2-19).

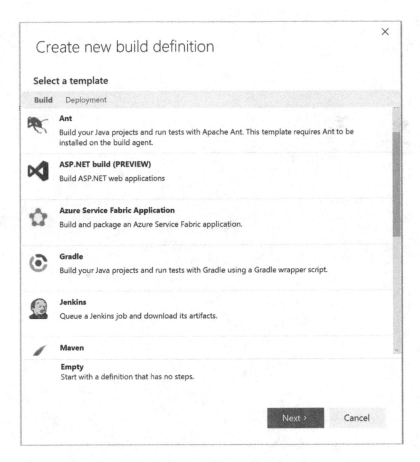

Figure 2-19. Create new build definition template list

VSTS has several built-in templates. For this scenario, select the empty template and click the Next button.

On the next page of the wizard, take the default settings but check the box to turn on continuous integration (see Figure 2-20).

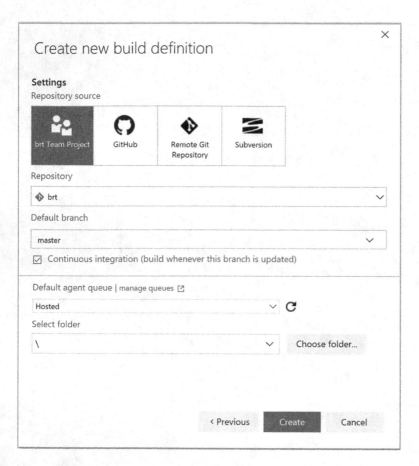

Figure 2-20. *Create new build definition settings*

Click Add Build step. The resulting task catalog contains build, utility, test, packaging and deployment tasks that you can use in combination to define a build (see Figure 2-21).

Figure 2-21. Task catalog

This build definition requires four tasks. You can select each of the four tasks while on this dialog box and add them to the build definition.

- Select the Package category and add the NuGet Installer Task

- Select the Build category and add the MSBuild Task

- Select the Package category and add the NuGet Packager Task

- Add the NuGet Publisher Task

- Click the Close button

When you return, your build definition should look as depicted in Figure 2-22.

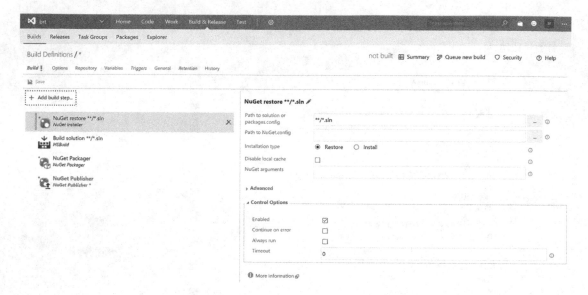

Figure 2-22. *Build definition under development*

Each task has a collection of settings. Fill out the settings for each task as shown in Table 2-1 to define a build for the wire library. The build definition will produce a NuGet package that is published to the package feed you created earlier. Note that some settings are hidden and you need to click on the Advanced button to expose additional settings.

Table 2-1. *Build Wire NuGet Package Build Definition*

NuGet Installer Settings	
Path to Solution	`libraries/Wire/Wire.sln`
Path to NuGet.Config	`nuget.config`
NuGet Arguments	`-outputdirectory packages`
MSBuild Settings	
Path to Solution	`libraries/Wire/Wire.sln`
Configuration	`debug`
NuGet Packager	
Path to CSProj	`libraries/Wire/Wire.csproj`
Package Folder	`nugets`
Include Referenced Projects	Yes (checked)
Configuration to Package	`debug`
NuGet Publisher	
Path to NuPkg	`nugets/wire*.nupkg`
Feed Type	Internal
Internal Feed URL	[URL to your package feed]

Click Save and provide a name such as `Build Wire NuGet Package`. To test the build definition, click the Queue New Build link in the upper-left side of the screen. The build request will be queued and will execute when a build agent becomes available. A build agent is an Azure-hosted virtual machine that is provisioned on demand to execute your build definition.

The build definition will queue up and start the build process once a build agent becomes available. If there are build errors, you can use the console output to debug any issues with the task settings (see Figure 2-23). The supplied build log files are also provided.

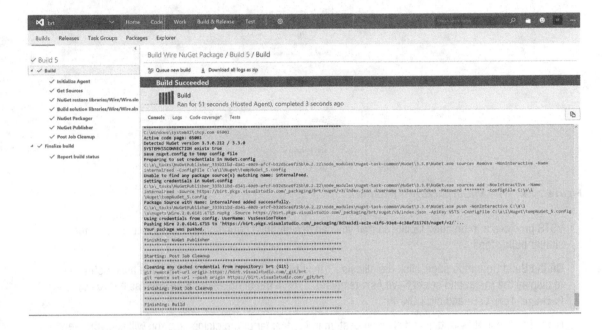

Figure 2-23. *Build success*

Your package feed now contains the Wire NuGet package, as shown in Figure 2-24.

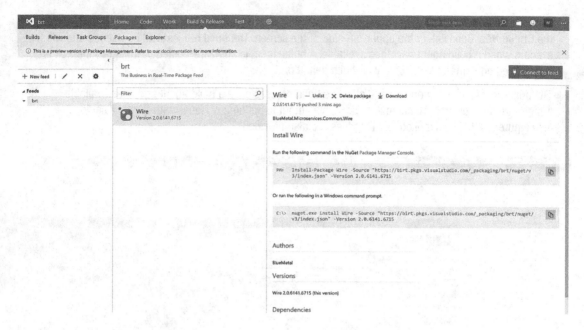

Figure 2-24. *Wire NuGet package is published*

VSTS provides a templating facility so that you can design build definitions once and reuse them for similar build steps.

On the Build Definition page, click the ellipsis … next to the Build Wire NuGet Package build definition to display the menu and select Save As a template…. Give the template a name such as `Build NuGet Package Template` and click OK.

Next click the + New button and click on Custom in the toolbar of the dialog box. You will see your newly created template. Select the template and click Next and then click Create (see Figure 2-25).

Figure 2-25. *Create new build definition from a custom template*

Update the settings to point to the Store library in the libraries/store folder. Save the definition and queue the build to publish the Store NuGet Package. Add a build definition for the Reference model, which is in the models/reference folder. This will create the NuGet package that represents the data model for the Reference microservice.

Once you complete this exercise, you should have three NuGet packages in your feed—Wire, Store, and Reference.

CREATE A PROVISIONING BUILD DEFINITION

The provisioning build definitions use PowerShell scripts and ARM templates to create and configure the foundational Azure resources that our solution requires.

For this exercise, we create a build definition that executes the script creating our resource group and provisions these shared services:

- Service bus namespace

- Storage account

- DocumentDB

- SQL database

- IoT Hub

Before creating this build definition, you will need to configure a service endpoint from your VSTS environment to your Azure subscription so that the build definitions can connect to that subscription and execute PowerShell and ARM templates.

Hover over the gear icon in the toolbar and select Services from the drop-down menu. Click + Add New Service endpoint and select Azure Resource Manager from the list (see Figure 2-26).

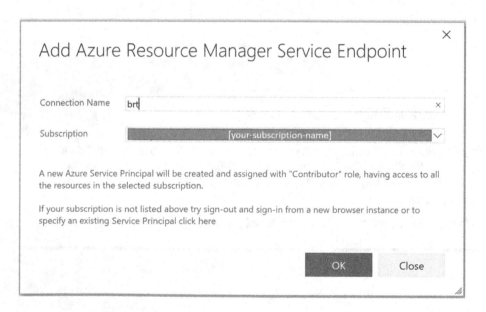

Figure 2-26. *Add Azure Resource Manager Service Endpoint*

Select your subscription from the drop-down and provide a friendly name. Click OK.

This build definition will generate an output file that contains the connection strings and keys to the shared services. Check this file into the repo so that it can be used by subsequent build definition scripts. To do that, give the Build Agent permission to contribute to the repository.

Click on Version Control in the menu bar and then the name of your Git repo. Select the Project Collection Build Service and allow the following permissions, then save your changes (see Figure 2-27).

- Branch creation: Allow

- Contribute: Allow

- Read: Inherited allow

- Tag Creation: Inherited allow

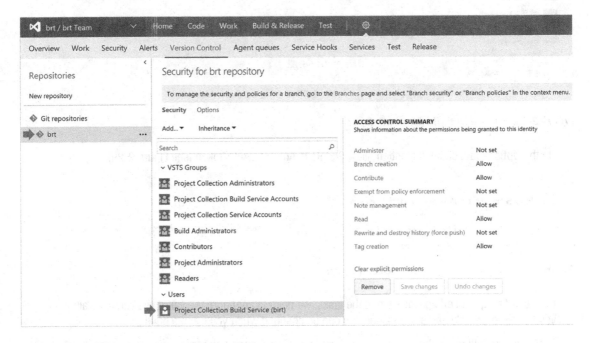

Figure 2-27. *Configure security on the repository*

Create an Empty build definition template. Click the + Add build step… button and add four tasks to the definition (see Figure 2-28).

- Select the Deploy category and add two tasks of type Azure PowerShell

- Select the Utility category and add three tasks of the type command line

- Move the command-line tasks between the two Azure PowerShell tasks, as depicted in Figure 2-28

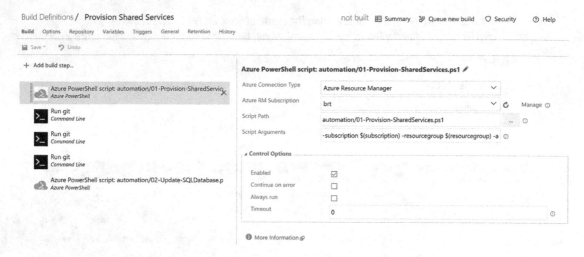

Figure 2-28. *Provision Build definition tasks*

On the Options tab, check the option Allow Scripts to Access OAuth Token (see Figure 2-29).

☑ **Allow Scripts to Access OAuth Token**

Enables scripts and other processes launched during the build to access the OAuth Token via the System.AccessToken variable

Figure 2-29. *Allow Scripts to Access OAuth Token*

Before defining the settings for each of the tasks, we need to configure the variables. Variables allow you to create friendly names for values that can be changed when you run the build.

Each build definition can have its own set of variables. The PowerShell scripts, as you may recall, take a set of command-line parameters. You will use the variables to provide these parameter values at runtime. Click on Variables in the menu and add the variable definitions listed in Table 2-2 and depicted in Figure 2-30.

Table 2-2. *Variable Definitions for Provision Build Definition*

Name	Value	Allow at Q Time
subscription	[your-subscription-name]	Yes
resourcegroup	[resource-group-name]	Yes
azurelocation	[azure-region]	Yes
prefix	[prefix]	Yes
suffix	[suffix]	Yes
System.prefergit	True	No

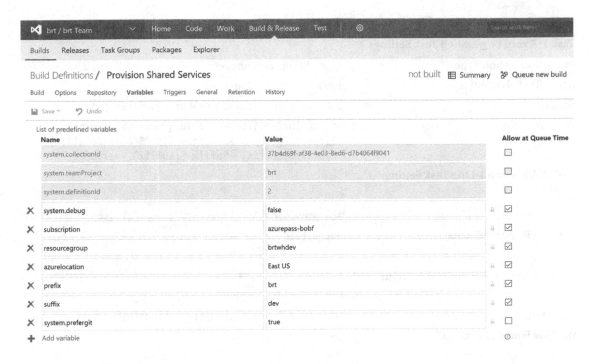

Figure 2-30. *Build definition variables*

Click on Build in the menu and fill out the settings for the Azure PowerShell and command-line tasks.

The first PowerShell script will apply the ARM templates that were reviewed early in this chapter. The script and template provision the shared services and then generate an output file that contains the connection strings and keys for the shared services.

The command-line tasks execute Git commands to add the generated file to the repository and commit it.

Finally, we will run a PowerShell script that generates the relational tables in the SQL database. We will use the variables to pass dynamic parameters to the scripts.

Fill out the settings for each of the build tasks outlined in Table 2-3.

Table 2-3. *Provision Shared Services Build Definition*

Task 1: Azure PowerShell Task Settings	
Azure Connection Type	Azure Resource Manager
Azure RM Subscription	`[your-subscription-name]`
Script Path	`automation/01-Provision-SharedServices.ps1`

Script Arguments	`-subscription $(subscription) -resourcegroup`
	`$(resourcegroup) -azurelocation '$(azurelocation)'`
	`-Prefix $(prefix) -Suffix $(suffix) -verbose`

Task 2: Command-Line Task Settings	
Tool	Git
Arguments	`add provision-$(resourcegroup)-output.json`
Working Folder (Advanced)	`automation`
Fail on Standard Error	Yes
Task 3: Command-Line Task Settings	
Tool	Git
Arguments	`commit -m "commit provision output"`
Working Folder (Advanced)	`automation`
Fail on Standard Error	Yes
Task 4: Command-Line Task Settings	
Tool	Git
Arguments	`push origin HEAD:master`
Working Folder (Advanced)	`automation`
Fail on Standard Error	No
Continue Error	Yes
Task 5: Azure PowerShell Task Settings	
Azure Connection Type	Azure Resource Manager
Azure RM Subscription	`[your-subscription-name]`
Script Path	`automation/02-Update-SQLDatabase.ps1`

Script Arguments	`-subscription $(subscription) -resourcegroup`
	`$(resourcegroup) -azurelocation '$(azurelocation)'`
	`-Prefix $(prefix) -Suffix $(suffix) -verbose`

Save the definition by providing a name such as `Provision Shared Services` and queue the build.

When this script completes you will have created a resource group in your subscription that contains the shared services; generated an output file that contains the connection strings and keys for other build definitions; and checked that new file into the Git repo (see Figure 2-31).

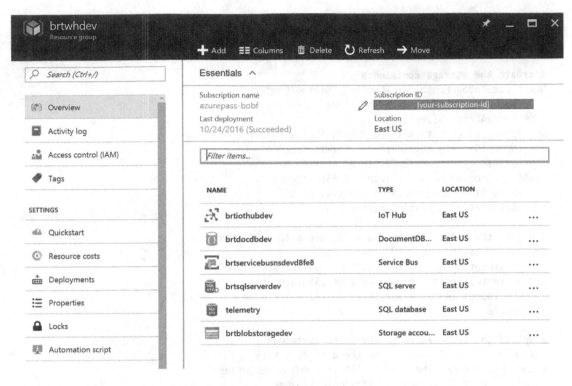

Figure 2-31. *Resource group with provisioned shared services*

PROVISION USING AZURE CLASSIC COMMANDS

There are a few operations that require the PowerShell script to execute in what is called Azure Classic mode (meaning that they do not work within the ARM context). These commands relate to creating blob storage containers and accessing and saving the service bus connection string. The commands reside in a file called 03-Provision-ClassicOps.ps1 in the automation folder. Let's review the code.

```
# get the path
$Path = Split-Path -parent $PSCommandPath
$Path = Split-Path -parent $Path
```

```
# pull in the environment variables
$includePath = $Path +
    "\Automation\EnvironmentVariables.ps1"
."$includePath"
```

```
# get the storage key and context
$storageKey = (Get-AzureRmStorageAccountKey -AccountName
    $storageAccountName -ResourceGroupName
    $ResourceGroup)[0]
```

```powershell
$StorageContext = New-AzureStorageContext
    -StorageAccountName $storageAccountName
    -StorageAccountKey $storageKey.Value

# create the storage containers
New-AzureStorageContainer -Context $StorageContext
    -Name $ArchiveContainerName -Permission Off
    -ErrorAction SilentlyContinue
New-AzureStorageContainer -Context $StorageContext
    -Name $RefDataContainerName -Permission Off
    -ErrorAction SilentlyContinue
New-AzureStorageContainer -Context $StorageContext
    -Name $ImageContainerName -Permission Off
    -ErrorAction SilentlyContinue

# Upload the rules file to the reference data container
$refdata = $path +
    "\automation\deploy\rules\$TempSensorRulesFilename"
Set-AzureStorageBlobContent -Context $StorageContext
    -Container $RefDataContainerName -File $refdata
    -Force

# Upload the image files to the image container
# $_.mode -match "-a---" scans the data directory
# and only fetches the files, filtering out directories
$imagedir = $path + "\automation\deploy\images"
$files = Get-ChildItem $imagedir -force| Where-Object {$_.mode -match "-a---"}

# iterate through all the files and start uploading data
foreach ($file in $files)
{
    #fq name represents fully qualified name
    $fqName = $imagedir + "\" + $file.Name

    #upload the current file to the blob
    Set-AzureStorageBlobContent -Blob $file.Name
        -Context $StorageContext
        -Container $ImageContainerName
        -File $fqName -Force
}

# save the service bus connection string
$sbr = Get-AzureSBAuthorizationRule -Namespace $serviceBusNamespace

$JSON =@"
{
    "ServiceBusConnectionString":
        "$sbr.ConnectionString",
}
"@
```

```
$ServiceBusInfo = $Path + "\automation\servicebus-$resourcegroup-output.json"
$JSON | Set-Content -Path $ServiceBusInfo
```

Before you can create a build definition to run this provisioning script, you need to create a connection between the build environment and the Azure subscription for executing Azure Classic commands.

Navigate to the Services Configuration page, add an endpoint of type Azure Classic, and fill out the form (see Figure 2-32).

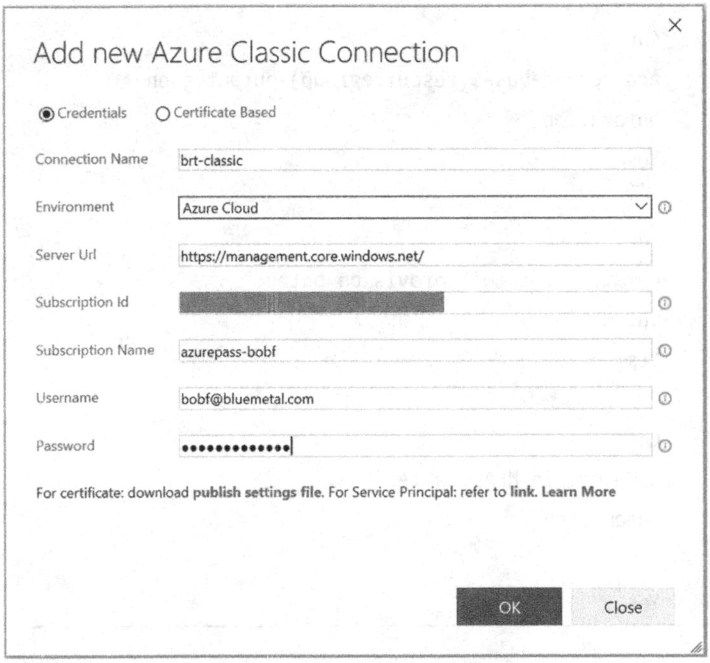

Figure 2-32. *Configure Azure Classic connection*

Create an empty build definition and add a Deploy task of type Azure PowerShell Script and then three utility tasks of type command line. Configure the settings shown in Table 2-4.

Table 2-4. *Provision Classic Resources Build Definition*

Task 1: Azure PowerShell Task Settings	
Azure Connection Type	Azure Classic
Azure Classic Subscription	`[your-classic-subscription-connection-name]`
Script Path	`automation/03-Provision-ClassicOps.ps1`
Script Arguments	`-subscription $(subscription) -resourcegroup` `$(resourcegroup) -verbose`
Task 2: Command-Line Task Settings	
Command	`Git`
Arguments	`add servicebus-$(resourcegroup)-output.json`
Working Folder	`automation`
File on Standard Error	Yes
Task 3: Command-Line Task Settings	
Command	`Git`
Arguments	`commit -m "commit provision output"`
Working Folder	`automation`
File on Standard Error	Yes
Task 4: Command-Line Task Settings	
Command	`Git`
Arguments	`push origin HEAD:master`
Working Folder	`automation`
File on Standard Error	No
Continue on Error	Yes

Define the variables for this build definition as shown in Table 2-5.

Table 2-5. *Variable Definitions for Provision Classic Resources Build Definition*

Name	Value	Set a Q Time
subscription	`[your-subscription-name]`	Yes
resourcegroup	`[resource-group-name]`	Yes

To validate the script, navigate to your storage account and examine the blob storage containers. You should see that several image files have been uploaded to the images container. These are the employee headshots (see Figure 2-33).

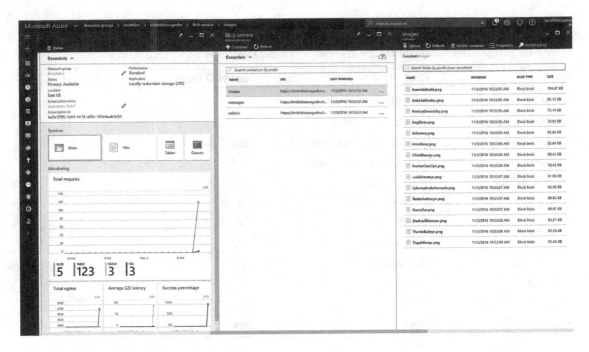

Figure 2-33. *Image container created and files uploaded*

There is also now a new file in the automation folder called `servicebus-[resource-group-name]-output.json` that contains the service bus connection string. This file has also been checked into the repository.

CREATE A DEPLOYMENT BUILD DEFINITION

In this exercise, you will create a deployment build definition for the microservice Reference API that will execute the following steps:

- Build and package the Reference microservice

- Create the Reference database and Entity collection in Document DB

- Upload a sample set of reference data to DocumentDB

- Provision an App Service Plan and App Service in the resource group

- Deploy the Reference API package to the App Service

- Configure the App Service settings with the connection info for DocumentDB

Since you have created a new NuGet feed with new versions of the NuGet packages that the microservice project requires, you will need to open the Reference API solution, which is in the `microservices/reference` folder, and build the solution. Performing a local build will update the NuGet references. Once complete, check in the updates to the repository.

Create a new build definition using an empty template and define the variables as shown in Table 2-6.

Table 2-6. *Variable Definitions for Deploy Reference API Build Definition*

Name	Value	Set at Q Time
BuildPlatform	Any CPU	Yes
BuildConfiguration	[debug | release]	Yes
Subscription	[your-subscription-name]	Yes
Resourcegroup	[resource-group-name]	Yes
Azurelocation	[azure-region]	Yes
Prefix	[project-code]	Yes
Suffix	[dev | tst | prd]	Yes
ServiceName	ReferenceAPI	No
ServicePlan	AppServicePlan	No
Database	Reference	No
Collection	Entity	No
DeployData	false	Yes

Add the tasks to the build definition as shown in Table 2-7.

Table 2-7. *Tasks for the Deploy Reference API Build Definition*

Category	Task
Package	NuGet Installer
Build	Visual Studio Build
Deploy	Azure PowerShell
Deploy	Azure App Service Deployment ARM
Deploy	Azure PowerShell

Configure each build step as shown in Table 2-8.

Table 2-8. Deploy Reference API Build Definition

Task 1: NuGet Installer Task Settings	
Path to solution	`microservices/Reference/ReferenceAPI.sln`
Path to nuget.config	`nuget.config`
NuGet Arguments	`-outputdirectory packages`
Task 2: Visual Studio Build Task Settings	
Solution	`microservices/Reference/ReferenceAPI.sln`
MSBuild Arguments	`/p:DeployOnBuild=true;DefaultPackageFilename=ReferenceAPI.` `zip /p:PublishUrl=$(Build.StagingDirectory)/ReferenceAPI`
Platform	`$(BuildPlatform)`
Configuration	`$(BuildConfiguration)`
Task 3: Azure PowerShell Task Settings	
Azure Connection Type	Azure Resource Manager
Azure RM Subscription	`[your-subscription-connection-name]`
Script Path	`automation/05-Publish-AppService.ps1`
Script Arguments	`-Subscription $(Subscription) -ResourceGroup` `$(ResourceGroup) -AzureLocation '$(AzureLocation)' -Prefix` `$(Prefix) -Suffix $(Suffix) -ServiceName $(ServiceName)` `-ServicePlan $(ServicePlan) -Database $(Database)` `-Collection $(Collection) -DeployData:$$(DeployData)`
Task 4: Azure App Service Deployment ARM Task Settings	
Azure RM Subscription	`[your-subscription-connection-name]`
App Service Name	`$(Prefix)ReferenceApi($Suffix)`
Package Folder Name	`microservices/reference/ReferenceAPI/obj/Debug/Package/` `ReferenceAPI.zip`
Publish Using Web Deploy	Yes
Remove Additional Files	Yes
Task 5: Azure PowerShell Task Settings	
Azure Connection Type	Azure Resource Manager
Azure RM Subscription	`[your-subscription-connection-name]`
Script Path	`automation/06-Publish-AppSettings.ps1`
Script Arguments	`-Subscription $(Subscription) -ResourceGroup` `$(ResourceGroup) -AzureLocation '$(AzureLocation)' -Prefix` `$(Prefix) -Suffix $(Suffix) -ServiceName $(ServiceName)` `-Database $(Database) -Collection $(Collection)`

Save the build definition providing a name such as `Deploy Reference Microservice` and queue the build.

Set the Deploy Data variable to true. This will trigger the creation of the Reference Database and Entity Collection as well as upload sample reference data into the DocumentDB collection.

Once the build completes, you will see both an App Service Plan and the Reference API App Service listed in your resource group. The App Service Plan defines the scale up and scale out settings for any App Services that are associated with the plan (see Figure 2-34).

Figure 2-34. *Reference microservice deployment*

If you click on application settings, you will see that the runtime settings this service requires have been configured by the deployment definition (see Figure 2-35). The values for these settings are pulled from the file that was generated by the provisioning build definition and injected dynamically when this service is built and deployed.

App settings

collection	Entity	☐ Slot setting	...
database	Reference	☐ Slot setting	...
docdburi	https://brtdocdbdev.docum...	☐ Slot setting	...
apiss	810ecd57-e305-43ec-89ad-...	☐ Slot setting	...
docdbkey	N8ZLwHk5SE8zogBRcF6lvZ...	☐ Slot setting	...
Key	*Value*	☐ Slot setting	...

Figure 2-35. *Dynamic application settings*

You can test the Reference microservice by clicking on the URL on the Overview screen. The service will spin up and take you to the default home page of the API application (see Figure 2-36).

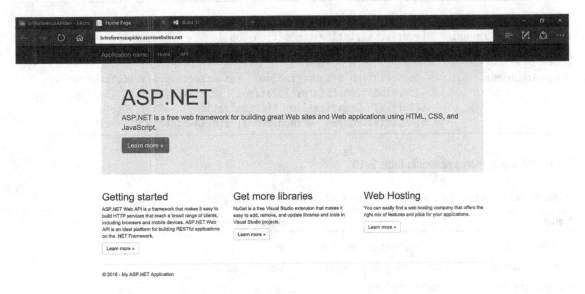

Figure 2-36. *Reference Microservice default home page*

In the next exercise, you'll provision API management and configure the API proxy. Once that is complete, we can smoke test the API and validate that the database and collection in DocumentDB has been properly initialized.

CREATE THE PROVISION APIM BUILD DEFINITION

API management is an Azure service for publishing APIs to developers. You use API management to define a proxy endpoint for which you can track analytics, define security access, engage a subscription model, inject policies such as throttling or custom headers, and more.

Once API management is provisioned, you will have both an Administrator Portal and a Developer Portal. The Administrator Portal is used to manage APIs, developer groups, and API products and policies, as well as review the analytics reports. The Developer Portal provides developers the ability to register and subscribe to APIs that they have been given access to. Once subscribed, the developer receives a subscription key that must be used on every call to an API. The portal also supplies a console page for each API where the developer can access documentation and test the API to see how it functions.

To create a build definition for provisioning API management, start with an empty build definition and add a single build task from the Deploy category, adding an Azure PowerShell build task with the settings shown in Table 2-9.

Table 2-9. *Provision APIM Build Definition*

Task 1: Azure PowerShell Task Settings	
Azure Connection Type	Azure Resource Manager
Azure RM Subscription	`[your-subscription-connection-name]`
Script Path	`automation/04-Provision-APIManagement.ps1`
Script Arguments	`-subscription $(subscription) -resourcegroup $(resourcegroup)` `-azurelocation '$(azurelocation)' -Prefix $(prefix) -Suffix` `$(suffix) -Organization '$(organization)' -APIServiceName` `$(apiservicename) -APIAdminEmail $(APIAdminEmail)  -verbose`

Define the variables shown in Table 2-10.

Table 2-10. *Variable Definitions for Provision APIM Build Definition*

Name	Value	Set at Q Time
Subscription	`[your-subscription-name]`	Yes
ResourceGroup	`[resource-group-name]`	Yes
AzureLocation	`[azure-region]`	Yes
Prefix	`[project-code]`	Yes
Suffix	`[dev	tst	prd]`	Yes
Organization	`[your company name]`	Yes
APIServiceName	`[project-code]`	Yes
APIAdminEmail	`[your-email]`	Yes

■ **Note**   The default build time for the free VSTS Build Agent is 30 minutes. It may take more than 30 minutes to provision API management. This will result in the build reporting a failure. Even though the build reports failure, the provisioning process is still running and will most likely complete successfully.

If you do encounter an issue, you can also run the provisioning script from your laptop using the PowerShell console. Execute these commands from the `automation` folder.

```
PS C:\> .\00-Login.ps1
PS C:\> .\04-Provision-APIManagement.ps1
```

After the provisioning process has completed, you should see an instance of API management in your resource group, as shown in Figure 2-37.

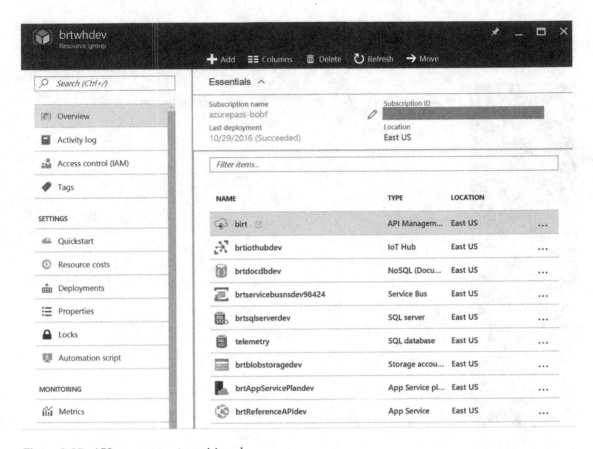

Figure 2-37. *API management provisioned*

Click on the service name in the resource group to navigate to the API Management blade. From there you can launch the Publisher Portal or the Developer Portal. Launch the Publisher Portal (see Figure 2-38).

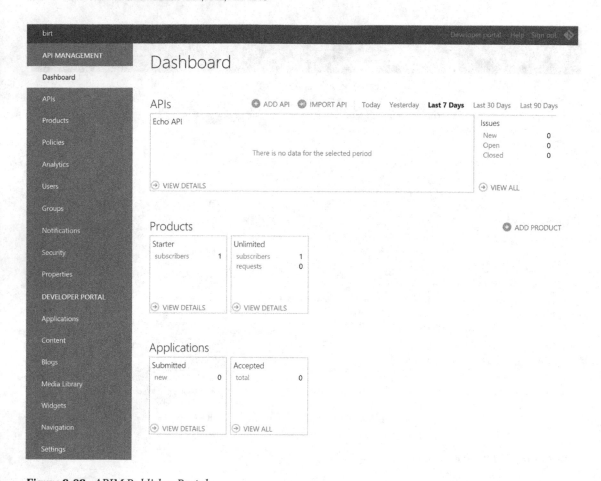

Figure 2-38. APIM Publisher Portal

The Publisher Portal provides access to all the API management settings and functions. Let's examine the publisher features:

- *Dashboard*: The Dashboard provides a summary overview of products, groups, and API activity.

- *Products*: Products are an organizational construct for APIs. By organizing APIs into products, you can control who can access the APIs.

- *Groups*: Groups provide an organizational construct for memberships. For example, you can create developer groups that represent different teams, internal and external developers, operations, etc. The groups are then assigned to products, which limits access to only the APIs that are published as part of those products.

- *Users*: Users provide the administrator visibility to developer subscriptions. You can add developers and invite developers to the service.

- *APIs*: An API defines a API proxy, including documentation, operations, and security settings.

- *Policies*: Policies provide a mechanism by which you can inject operations on both inbound requests and outbound responses such as injecting a header, setting quotas, configuring CORS, and so on.

- *Analytics*: Analytics provides usage and health reports for each of the API's operations, bandwidth usage and visibility into which users are calling which APIs.

- *Notifications*: Administrator alerts are reported here.

- *Security*: Security allows you to configure the security settings for the API Management service including Active Directory integration and access to the Management API.

- *Properties*: Property values are strings that may contain secrets and can be referenced from policies. Use properties to re-use values across policies and avoid specifying secrets within policies.

- *Developer Portal*: The Developer Portal section of the Administrator Portal gives you the ability to customize the Developer Portal.

In these next exercises, you will configure the APIM environment and define the proxy for the Reference API.

ADD APIM GROUPS

Click Groups in the Publisher Portal navigation menu and click Add Group. Provide the name and description `BRT Developers` and click Save. Create a second group called `BRT Operators` (see Figure 2-39).

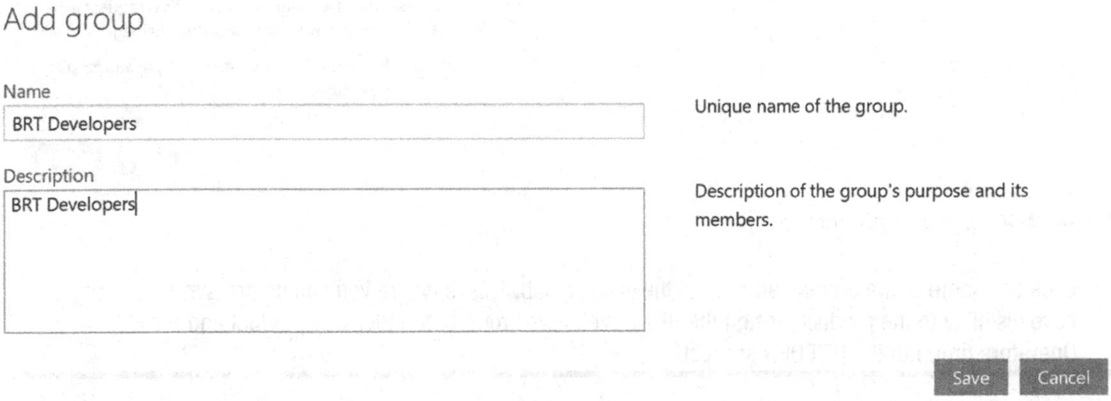

Add group

Name

| BRT Developers |

Unique name of the group.

Description

| BRT Developers |

Description of the group's purpose and its members.

Save   Cancel

Figure 2-39. Create an APIM group

ADD APIM PRODUCTS

Click on Products and then Add Product. Provide the title and a description `BRT.DEV` and `BRT Developer APIs`, respectively.

Since you are provisioning the developer environment, we recommend using a naming convention that makes it clear that these APIs are part of that environment. By default, the APIs require a subscription.

You have the option of requiring administrator approval for access to the APIs in this product. Click Save and then create a second product called `BRT.OPS` with the description BRT Operations APIs (see Figure 2-40).

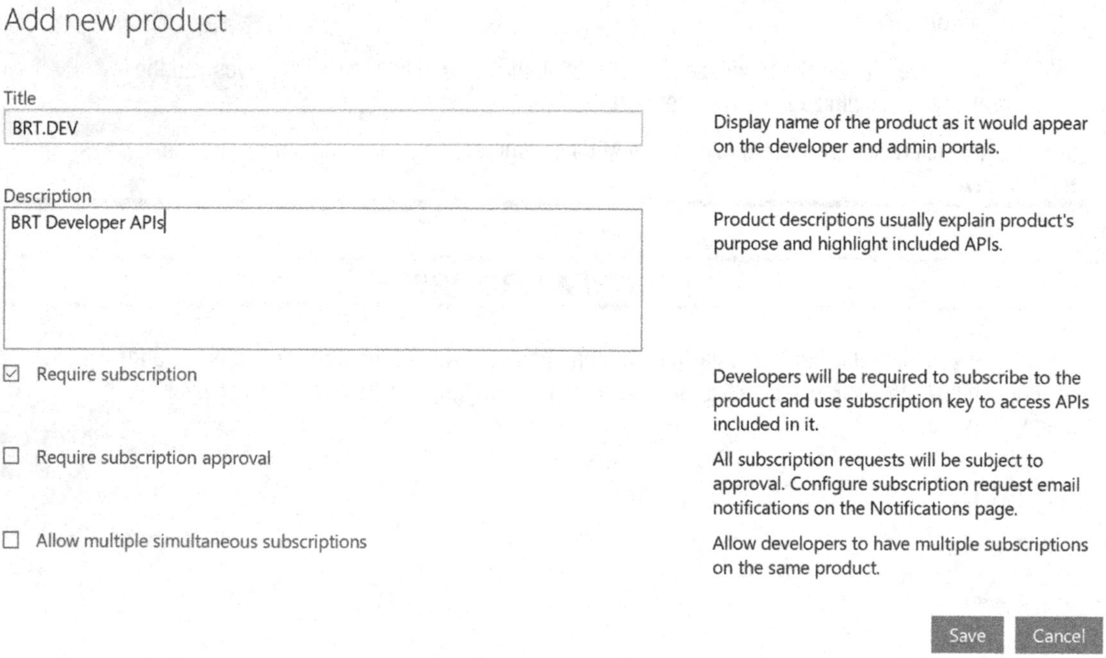

Add new product

Title

| BRT.DEV |

Display name of the product as it would appear on the developer and admin portals.

Description

| BRT Developer APIs |

Product descriptions usually explain product's purpose and highlight included APIs.

☑ Require subscription

Developers will be required to subscribe to the product and use subscription key to access APIs included in it.

☐ Require subscription approval

All subscription requests will be subject to approval. Configure subscription request email notifications on the Notifications page.

☐ Allow multiple simultaneous subscriptions

Allow developers to have multiple subscriptions on the same product.

[Save] [Cancel]

Figure 2-40. *Create a product*

Click the name of the product and select the Visibility tab. This is where you can control which groups have visibility to the product. Assign the BRT Developers group to the BRT.DEV product and the BRT Operators group to the BRT.OPS product.

DEFINE AN API PROXY

To streamline the process of defining the API proxies, we will import Swagger definitions. Swagger is standard JSON format for defining ReST APIs. Here is Swagger fragment for the reference API:

```
{
  "swagger": "2.0",
  "info": {
    "title": "Reference.Dev",
    "version": "1.0"
  },
  "host": "[prefix]referenceapi[suffix].azurewebsites.net",
  "basePath": "/reference",
  "schemes": [
    "https"
  ],
  "paths": {
    "/entities/domain/{domain}": {
      "get": {
        "operationId": "Get Entities by Domain",
        "parameters": [
          {
            "name": "domain",
            "in": "path",
            "description": "",
            "required": true,
            "type": "string"
          },
          {
            "name": "Ocp-Apim-Subscription-Key",
            "in": "header",
            "description": "subscription key in header",
            "type": "string"
          }
        ],
        "responses": {}
      }
    },
...
```

Swagger definitions have been provided for each of the microservices. You can find them in the automation/swagger folder. You will need to update these files to point to your deployed services in Azure.

Update the Reference.Swagger.json and Reference.Adminstration.Swagger.json files by replacing the [prefix] and [suffix] placeholders with the values you used during deployment.

Click APIs and then Import API.

Select From File and Swagger format, navigate to the automation/swagger directory, and select the Reference.Swagger.json.

Select New API and enter the URI suffix `dev/v1/reference`. This creates a new endpoint for the API that provides additional environment and versioning. Finally, add the API to the BRT.DEV group and click Save (see Figure 2-41).

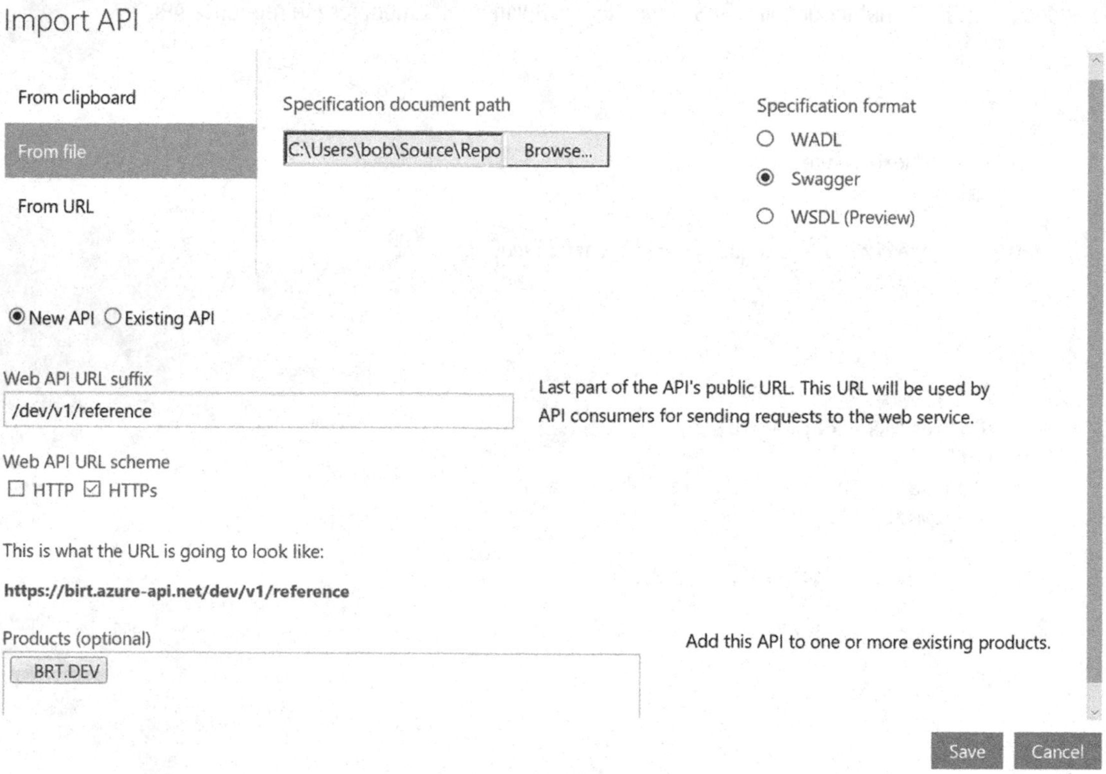

Import API

From clipboard	Specification document path	Specification format

		○ WADL
From file	`C:\Users\bob\Source\Repo` [Browse...]	● Swagger
		○ WSDL (Preview)
From URL		

● New API ○ Existing API

Web API URL suffix

`/dev/v1/reference`

Last part of the API's public URL. This URL will be used by API consumers for sending requests to the web service.

Web API URL scheme
☐ HTTP ☑ HTTPs

This is what the URL is going to look like:

https://birt.azure-api.net/dev/v1/reference

Products (optional)

Add this API to one or more existing products.

[BRT.DEV]

[Save] [Cancel]

***Figure 2-41.** Import reference API*

Repeat these steps using the swagger file `Reference.Adminstration.Swagger.json`.

This API endpoint is provided by the same running service, Reference API, but administration operations are only available to the operations team. Enter the URI suffix `dev/v1/reference/admin`, add the API to the BRT.OPS group, and click Save (see Figure 2-42).

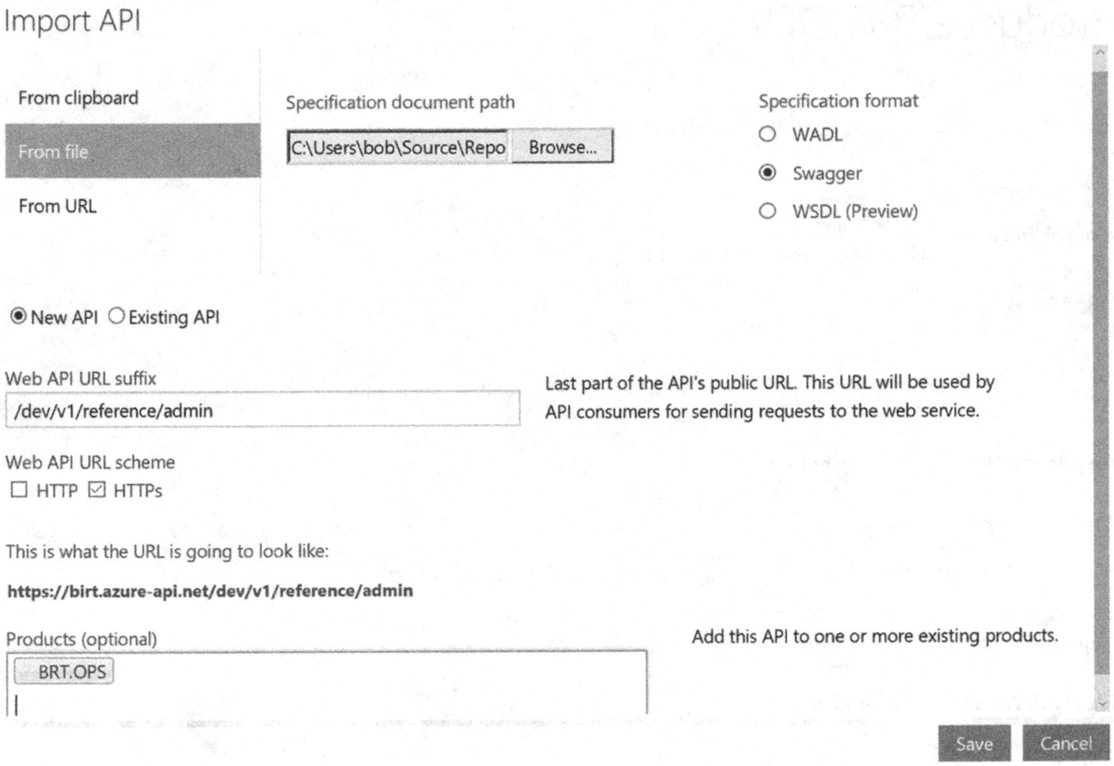

Import API

From clipboard	Specification document path	Specification format
From file	C:\Users\bob\Source\Repo Browse...	○ WADL
		● Swagger
From URL		○ WSDL (Preview)

● New API ○ Existing API

Web API URL suffix

/dev/v1/reference/admin

Last part of the API's public URL. This URL will be used by API consumers for sending requests to the web service.

Web API URL scheme
☐ HTTP ☑ HTTPs

This is what the URL is going to look like:

https://birt.azure-api.net/dev/v1/reference/admin

Products (optional)

Add this API to one or more existing products.

BRT.OPS

Save   Cancel

Figure 2-42. *Import reference administration API*

For registered developers and operators to have visibility to the APIs, the API products need to be published.

Click Products and then click the product name and then the Publish button. Do this for the BRT.DEV and BRT.OPS products (see Figure 2-43).

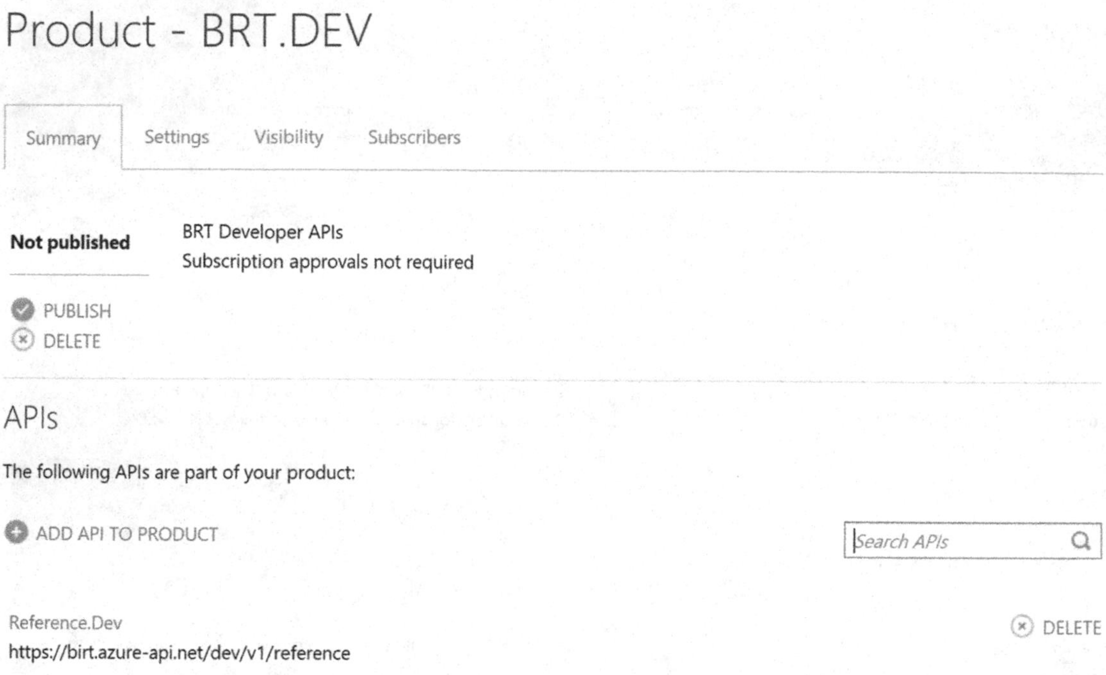

Product - BRT.DEV

Summary | Settings | Visibility | Subscribers

Not published

BRT Developer APIs
Subscription approvals not required

✅ PUBLISH
✖ DELETE

APIs

The following APIs are part of your product:

➕ ADD API TO PRODUCT

Search APIs 🔍

Reference.Dev
https://birt.azure-api.net/dev/v1/reference

✖ DELETE

Figure 2-43. *Publish a product*

CREATE APIM PROPERTIES

There are several ways to secure ReST APIs including OAuth, managed certs, and other techniques. This application will use a combination of the subscription key provided by API management and a shared secret that is known only to the API service and API management. To set up a shared secret mechanism, you will use a combination of API management properties and policies.

As you can see in Figure 2-44, if an application tries to call the API Proxy without the subscription key, access is denied. If an application tries to go around API management and call the API directly without the shared secret, access is denied. In either case, if the call is not made using SSL, the invocation will fail (see Figure 2-44).

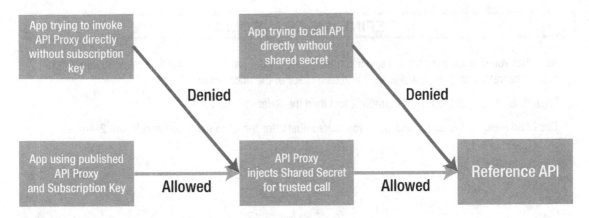

Figure 2-44. *Securing APIs with subscription keys and shared secrets*

Properties are used to define the secrets in the policy definitions. The API configuration for this application requires SSL and that a shared secret be passed into the service in a header called `apiss`. If the header is not present or the value in the header does not match the shared secret value known to the API, access will be denied.

A default shared secret value is provided in the file `EnvironmentVariables.ps1` in the `automation` folder. You should update the value in this file using the `GenSharedSecret` console utility that can be found in the `utility` folder.

Once you have your new shared secret value, click Properties in the Publisher Portal and then Add Property. Create a property with the name `SSHeaderName` and set the value to `apiss`. Check the This Is a Secret check box. Repeat these steps and create a property with the name `SSHeaderValue`. Set the value to your generated shared secret (see Figure 2-45).

Add property		Add property	
Name	Alphanumeric string used for referencing the property in the policies.	Name	Alphanumeric string used for referencing the property in the policies.
SSHeaderName		SSHeaderValue	
Value	A string or an expression representing property value.	Value	A string or an expression representing property value.
apiss		{your=shared-secret-value}	
☑ This is a secret	When checked, it means that the property value contains a secret.	☑ This is a secret	When checked, it means that the property value contains a secret.
Tags	Tags, when provided, can be used to filter the property list.	Tags	Tags, when provided, can be used to filter the property list.
	Save Close		Save Close

Figure 2-45. *Create a property*

■ **Note**   If you update the shared secret, remember to redeploy your APIs so that the application settings are updated with the new shared secret value.

DEFINE AN APIM POLICY

Now that you defined the properties, you can use a Set Header policy on inbound requests to inject the shared secret making API management a trusted caller of the microservices.

Click Policies, select the BRT.DEV product, and then the Reference.DEV API.

Click Add Policy in the editor and place your cursor just after the `<inbound>` tag (see Figure 2-46).

Figure 2-46. *Policy Editor*

Scroll down the list of policies and inject the Set Header policy into the policy document. Modify the header using the property syntax.

To reference the shared secret header name, use `{{SSHeaderName}}`, and to reference the value use `{{SSHeaderValue}}`. Set `exists-action` to `override`. Click Save (see Figure 2-47).

```
<set-header name="{{SSHeaderName}}" exists-action="override">
  <value>{{SSHeaderValue}}</value>
</set-header>
```

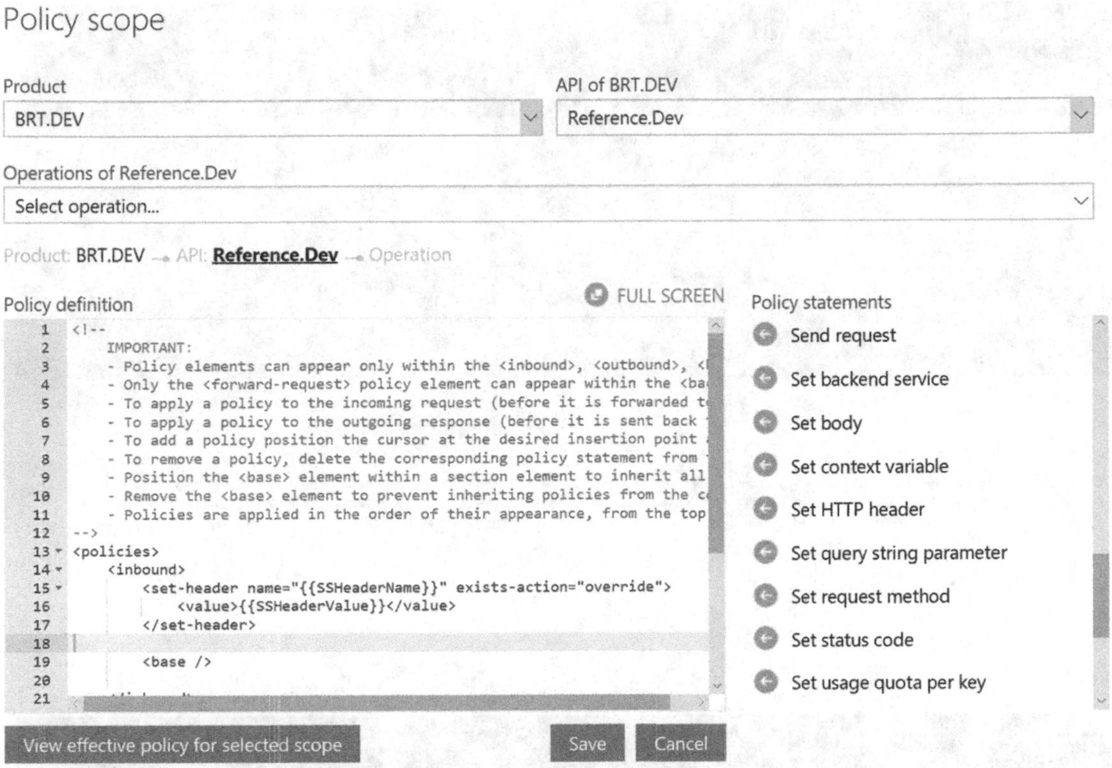

Policy scope

Product
BRT.DEV

API of BRT.DEV
Reference.Dev

Operations of Reference.Dev
Select operation...

Product: BRT.DEV → API: **Reference.Dev** → Operation

Policy definition   ☁ FULL SCREEN

```
1   <!--
2       IMPORTANT:
3       - Policy elements can appear only within the <inbound>, <outbound>, <
4       - Only the <forward-request> policy element can appear within the <ba
5       - To apply a policy to the incoming request (before it is forwarded t
6       - To apply a policy to the outgoing response (before it is sent back
7       - To add a policy position the cursor at the desired insertion point
8       - To remove a policy, delete the corresponding policy statement from
9       - Position the <base> element within a section element to inherit all
10      - Remove the <base> element to prevent inheriting policies from the c
11      - Policies are applied in the order of their appearance, from the top
12   -->
13   <policies>
14       <inbound>
15           <set-header name="{{SSHeaderName}}" exists-action="override">
16               <value>{{SSHeaderValue}}</value>
17           </set-header>
18
19           <base />
20
21
```

Policy statements

◉ Send request
◉ Set backend service
◉ Set body
◉ Set context variable
◉ Set HTTP header
◉ Set query string parameter
◉ Set request method
◉ Set status code
◉ Set usage quota per key

View effective policy for selected scope   Save   Cancel

Figure 2-47. *Set the header policy using property reference syntax*

Repeat these steps for the Reference.Administration.Dev API.

TEST THE REFERENCE APIS

From the Administrator Portal, navigate to the API Management Developer Portal (see Figure 2-48). This portal is auto-generated and provides a self-service portal for developers to access your APIs. When developers visit this portal the first time, they will be asked to register. The administrator will receive an e-mail notification and will also see a notification in the Notifications area of the Publisher Portal. Once membership has been approved, the developer will be able to see the published products. Since you are the API management administrator, you already have direct access.

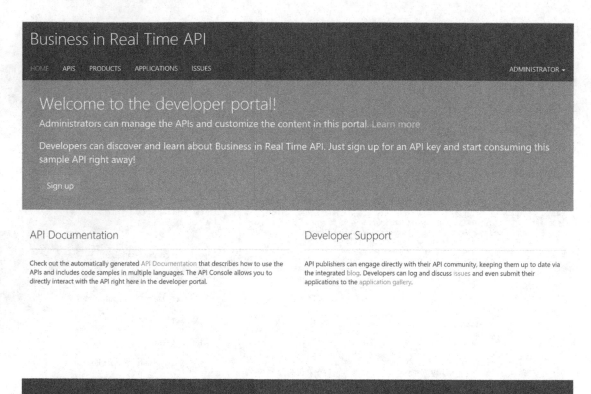

Figure 2-48. *The Developer Portal*

Click on APIs to see the list of published APIs. Select the Reference.DEV API. You will see the list of operations. The operation pages provide the request URL and code samples as well as the ability to invoke the API to learn how it works. Select the Get Reference Entities by Domain operation and then click Try It (see Figure 2-49).

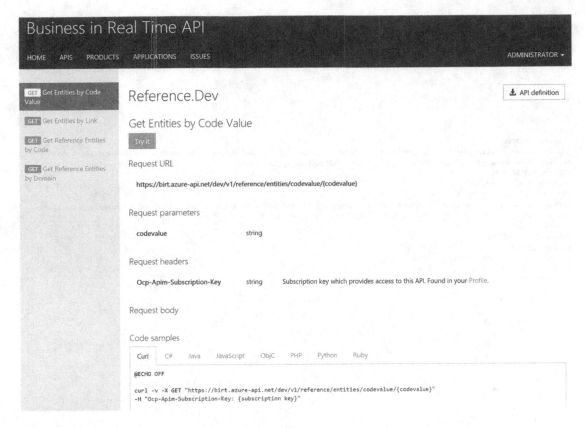

Figure 2-49. *Reference API operations*

Reference data is information that is common to many applications like lists of states, country codes, ZIP codes, language codes, and so on. You do not want to allow just any application to modify this data and corrupt the lookup lists; therefore, the Reference operations have been partitioned into a read-only public API (Reference API) and an API with update capabilities (Reference Administration API). Earlier, we configured the Reference API to be visible to developers and the Reference Administration API to be visible only to operators.

The "Get Reference Entities by Domain" operation takes an entity domain, States for example, and returns all the entities that are part of that domain. Enter States in the domain field and then click the Send button (see Figure 2-50).

| Response | Trace |

Response status

200 OK

Response latency

731 ms

Response content

```
Pragma: no-cache
Ocp-Apim-Trace-Location: https://apimgmtst3ghpmngpm4njv0f.blob.core.windows.net/apiinspectorcontainer/yqTdEFksNypllExsrzuGgA2-3?
sv=2015-07-08&sr=b&sig=5Zios1qZYijFnZdGpkDw11ZM%2BuaWzoTLBwqO%2BR6defg%3D&se=2016-11-01T00%3A57%3A58Z&sp=r&traceId=bf79f08e79154
9529899e083150df88b
Cache-Control: no-cache
Date: Mon, 31 Oct 2016 00:57:59 GMT
Set-Cookie: ARRAffinity=e1c9f2959b97bd8a16b9f8bae2c6c2e9ae828b3cb08cee1ae6e04c5116edda9a;Path=/;Domain=brtreferenceapidev.azurew
ebsites.net
X-AspNet-Version: 4.0.30319
X-Powered-By: ASP.NET
Content-Length: 14009
Content-Type: application/json; charset=utf-8
Expires: -1

{
  "list": [
    {
      "domain": "States",
      "code": "AL",
      "codevalue": "Alabama",
      "link": "US",
      "sequence": 0,
      "attributes": [
        {
          "key": "Capitol",
          "val": "Montgomery"
        },
        {
          "key": "Population",
          "val": "4779736"
        },
        {
          "key": "Square Miles",
          "val": "52419"
        }
      ],
```

Figure 2-50. *Response from the reference API*

RETRIEVE THE PRODUCT SUBSCRIPTION KEYS

To retrieve the subscription keys for the published products, navigate to the Profile page on the Developer Portal (see Figure 2-51). You will see that there are two sets of keys for the BRT.DEV Product and BRT.OPS products. Each product provides two keys, a primary and secondary. Whenever you are presented with keys in Azure, you are always provided two so that you can keep the primary private and hand out the secondary. If security issues arise, you can always use the primary key to access the service and regenerate the secondary to prevent additional access by users of the previous key.

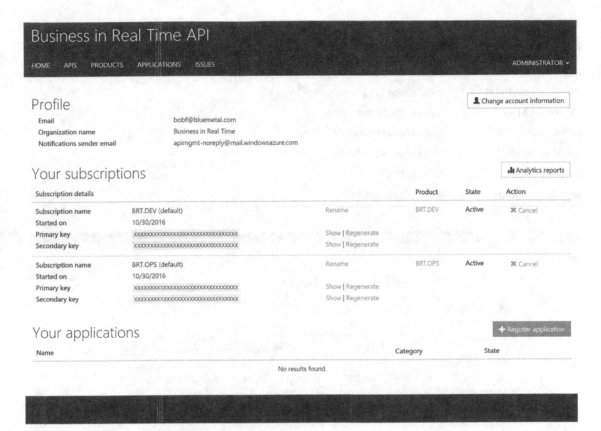

Figure 2-51. *Developer Portal profile page*

Make a note of the secondary keys for both products, as you will use them to access the APIs in subsequent steps.

COMPLETE THE DEPLOYMENT

To complete the deployment, you need to create build definitions for the remaining models and microservices.

Recall that you can save existing build definitions as templates so you do not have to start from scratch when creating new definitions. Use this feature to create a template for microservice deployments based on the Deploy Reference Microservice build definition.

Create and queue build definitions for the NuGet packages listed in Table 2-11. The complete NuGet feed is depicted in Figure 2-52.

Table 2-11. *Business in Real-Time NuGets*

Project Name	Location
Account Model	models/account
Application Model	models/application
Customer Model	models/customer
Device ModelNet4	models/device/net4/
Message ModelNet4	models/message/net4
Registry Model	models/registry
Simulation Model	models/simulation

Figure 2-52. *Complete package feed*

To associate the microservice solutions with your NuGet feed, you will need to open each one in Visual Studio and perform a local build and check in the updated solutions.

Next, create the following deployment build definitions:

- Deploy Account Microservice
- Deploy Application Microservice
- Deploy Customer Microservices
- Deploy Device Microservice
- Deploy Registry Microservice
- Deploy Simulation Microservice

When you run these builds the first time, set the DeployData input parameter to true so that the DocumentDB database and collection are created.

The database and collection names for each of the microservices are shown in Table 2-12.

Table 2-12. *Databases and Collections*

Account	Database	**Account**
	Collection	**Subscription**
Application	Database	**Application**
	Collection	**Configuration**
Customer	Database	**Customer**
	Collection	**Organization**
Device	Database	**Device**
	Collection	**Manifest**
Registry	Database	**Registry**
	Collection	**Profile**
Simulation	Database	**Simulation**
	Collection	**DataSet**

Update and import the Swagger definitions and configure the shared secret policy for the following APIs:

- Account API
- Application API
- Application Administration API
- Customer API
- Device API
- Registry API
- Simulation API

As shown in Figure 2-53, the microservice deployment and configuration is now complete. In the next exercise, you will bootstrap the deployment with sample data and provision a set of IoT simulated devices.

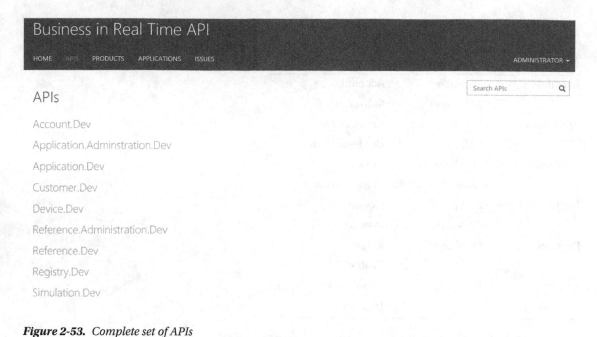

Figure 2-53. *Complete set of APIs*

BOOTSTRAP THE DEPLOYMENT

Once you have completed the provisioning and deployment process and configured your managed APIs, you can use the Bootstrap utility to initialize the environment with sample data and provision a set of simulated devices.

The Bootstrap utility can be found in the `utilities\bootstrap` folder. The utility will perform the following operations.

1. *Create Registry Profiles:* Create three faux company profiles and 16 employee profiles per company. The faux companies are:

   a. *WigiTech:* Manufacturer of high-tech components and products

   b. *Tall Towers:* Utility services firm that specializes in servicing radio towers on skyscrapers

   c. *The Complicated Badger:* A trucking firm that specializes in moving heavy equipment

2. *Create Customer Organizations:* Define a set of three teams per company where each team is made up of five employees. The 16th employee per company represents management.

3. *Create Account Subscriptions:* Define three customer accounts for the three companies and define their subscription levels.

4. *Create Application Configurations*: Since each company is using the same multi-tenant solution, this information represents the customization of the solution for that company. Some simple examples of this are logo, colors, etc., but can expand to more sophisticated customizations that may require access to advanced modules.

5. *Create Device Manifests*: Create a device registration and associated manifest for each employee. Each device is associated with an employee and represents the set of sensors that collect the biometric data.

These operations need to be run in order, as each step of the sample data generation process builds on the previous step.

To use the Bootstrap utility, you need to update the application so that it can use your managed APIs.

Load the solution in Visual Studio and open the `app.config` file. Update the App Settings adding your subscription keys from API management and the API management hostname for each of the APIs.

```
<add key="DevSubKey"
    value="subscription-key=[your-dev-key]" />
<add key="OpsSubKey"
    value="subscription-key=[your-dev-key]" />
<add key="ProfileAPI"
    value="https://[your-apim-host].azure-api.net/dev/v1/registry"/>
<add key="AccountAPI"
    value="https://[your-apim-host].azure-api.net/dev/v1/account"/>
<add key="ApplicationAPI"
     value="https://[your-apim-host].azure-api.net/dev/v1/application"/>
<add key="CustomerAPI"
    value="https://[your-apim-host].azure-api.net/dev/v1/customer"/>
<add key="DeviceAPI"
    value="https://[your-apim-host].azure-api.net/dev/v1/device"/>
```

■ **Note** The Bootstrap utility uses the Microsoft Access Database Engine to read the profile sample data from Excel.

If your development environment does not have this runtime installed, the utility will throw an exception. Install the Access Database Engine from this location:

```
https://www.microsoft.com/en-us/download/details.aspx?id=13255
```

Build and run the utility (see Figure 2-54). You will be presented with the menu. Select option 1 and press Enter.

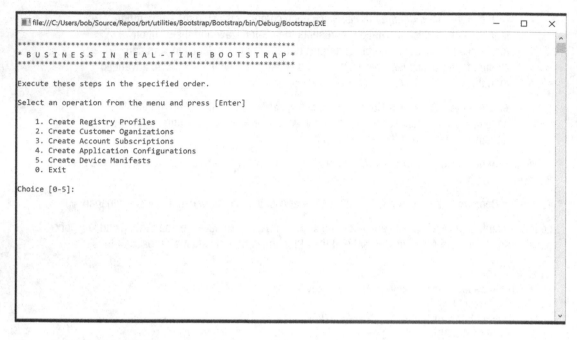

Figure 2-54. *Bootstrap utility*

You will return to the main menu after the completion of each step. Continue through menu options 2 through 5 to complete the sample data generation process. If you run into any issues, it is likely related to API configuration settings. Review your managed API settings and test within the Developer Portal to make sure your APIs are functioning properly.

LOAD SIMULATION DATA

To load the simulation data, you will use the DocumentDB Data Migration Tool (DT). This is a free utility from Microsoft that provides both a command-line and GUI application version. The command-line version of DT is used by the deployment PowerShell scripts to create the DocumentDB databases and collections as well as upload the sample reference data. Since the simulation data is significantly larger in size than the reference data, we will perform this operation from our development environment.

The simulation data is provided as a collection gzip'ed JSON documents in the `automation\simdata\gzip` folder. There are ~64KB documents of simulation data where each document represents a collection of biometrics readings from 1 of 15 teammates.

The DT desktop utility is in the `automation\Tools\dt\dt-1.7` folder and is called `DTUI.EXE`. Run the utility and configure the source to be the gzip folder. Check the Decompress Data box (see Figure 2-55).

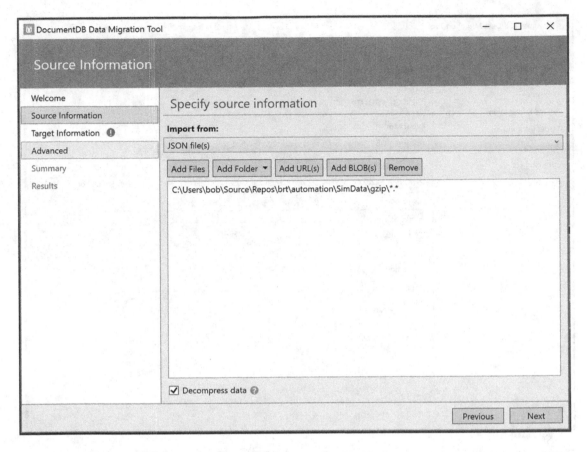

Figure 2-55. *DocumentDB data migration utility*

Click Next and add the connection string to your instance of DocumentDB. Append the name of the database, Simulation, to the end of the connection using the syntax Database=Simulation;. Set the collection name to be DataSet (see Figure 2-56).

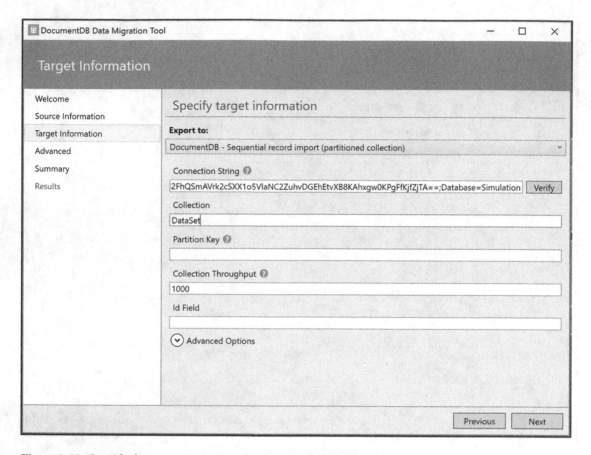

Figure 2-56. *Provide the connection string, database, and collection names*

Click Next until you get to the last screen and run the `import` operation. The utility will decompress the data files and upload them to DocumentDB.

Once the process completes, you can validate the process by testing the simulation API using API management. Navigate to the Developer Portal and select the Get Simulation Dataset by Name endpoint, click Try It, and then provide the name `teammate1` as the parameter. Click Send. If the data import succeeded, you will receive a `200` response code and the JSON will be displayed in the output window (see Figure 2-57).

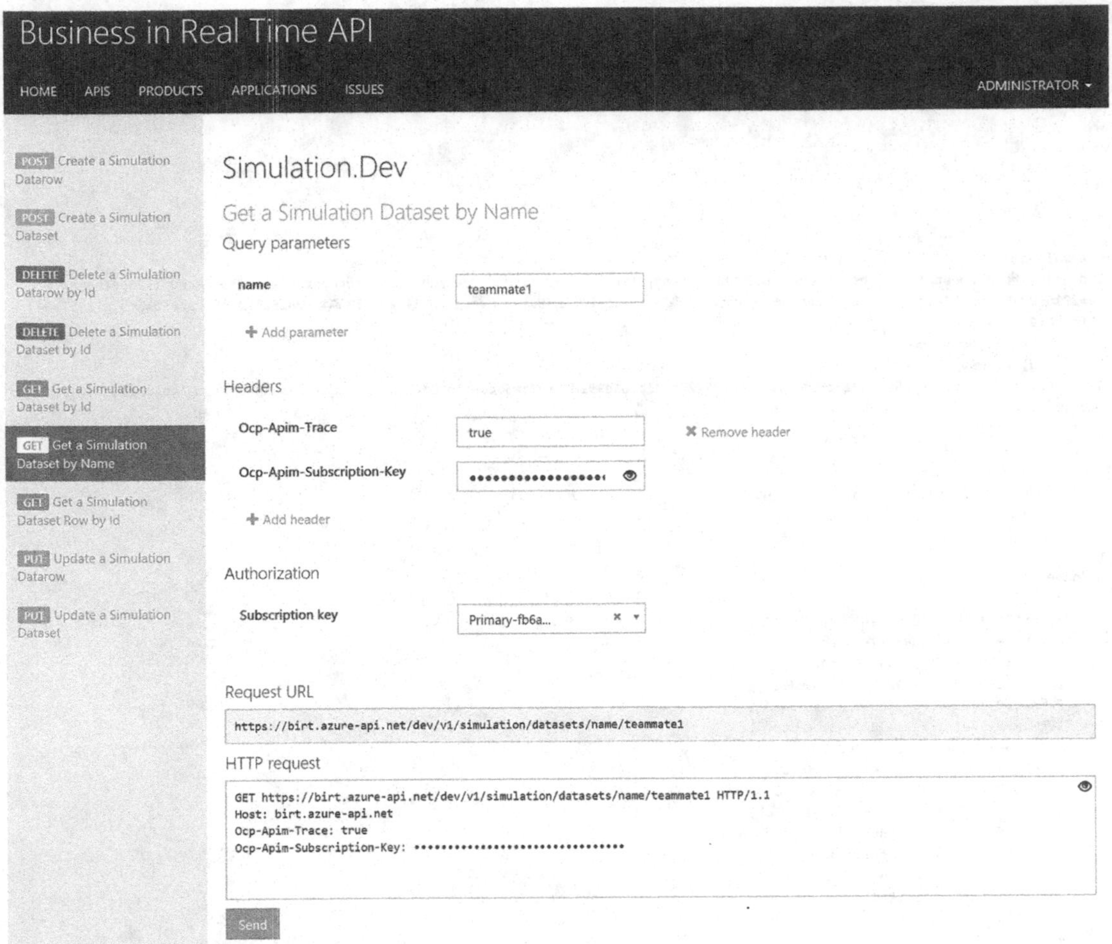

Figure 2-57. *Test the simulation API*

Response	Trace

Response status

200 OK

Response latency

46739 ms

Response content

```
Pragma: no-cache
Ocp-Apim-Trace-Location: https://apimgmtst3ghpmngpm4njv0f.blob.core.windows.net/apiinspectorcontainer/yqTdEFksNypllExsrzuGgA2-4?
sv=2015-07-08&sr=b&sig=glet8uQLo22uyd9OFgIjnfnJDbDy%2Bh8wa1QaLA%2Bf8g4%3D&se=2016-11-03T23%3A49%3A23Z&sp=r&traceId=8f57a73457aa4
72fb3a2b9bff2a50cf7
Cache-Control: no-cache
Date: Wed, 02 Nov 2016 23:50:09 GMT
Set-Cookie: ARRAffinity=56646929c62d005e2f4e8ce9726ccc1bfe6e992d29e06ca36cede1ba3e46d768;Path=/;Domain=brtsimulationapidev.azure
websites.net
X-AspNet-Version: 4.0.30319
X-Powered-By: ASP.NET
Content-Length: 163886
Content-Type: application/json; charset=utf-8
Expires: -1

{
  "name": "teammate1",
  "rows": [
    "664da22f-12cd-406e-a03a-8332a597dbb2",
    "48ae820e-8cdc-4d58-8297-331cb60c0920",
    "3985e739-95a7-417b-84aa-351c418d81e4",
    "866efe1c-67dd-4d78-9917-fcd4f85092bc",
    "28bd1c58-1b95-4446-9765-f22925e13af0",
    "29c61a38-c7e1-467a-ab08-7e4afbce6a0f",
    "1476fb96-29f4-4c83-b961-e837b85710be",
    "0eeb747e-f0f0-4f3d-aff4-b685b1f9ad56",
    "9f8dc477-0440-44c8-841a-5a1507cadc06",
    "cc5e302f-1e42-44a8-91ee-57f1ae37cb7b",
    "d792976d-4937-4364-966f-cc5fa7dedf6f",
    "4752d00d-2869-4bf4-b0f4-c169c9b0f5ff",
    "d12382cc-6106-40bc-aea1-f9bddc7772fb",
    "24e18d53-6d06-4dd6-88fb-d72f4cb1b7a6",
    "cf3ff920-fc49-4026-9f4b-b418eeda704c",
    "404d4e5b-b521-4cb3-b0ef-aec6e0282d34",
    "458a4511-6843-4f1f-9735-cd2256e681de",
    "acc50856-08c2-4cd0-b829-1487232b4a50",
    "8b63e603-1687-4452-b815-cbd7a5b01463",
    "ace33cc1-2b96-47c9-9aca-63c252f0c3c7",
    "bb0ff865-495f-4786-8790-5e1a475c0c5c",
    "35af05b1-8809-425e-bd7b-0eec2b7a9000",
    "a6d6d5ac-5d7b-4287-8306-6be559e81b88",
    "c616eb17-8958-4258-8dfb-d74fb54df11e",
```

Figure 2-57. (*continued*)

Summary

DevOps is all about people, processes, and tools. It implies the creation of cross-functional teams, combining developers, testers, and architects along with operations personnel who together own the entire deployment pipeline, from build through test to staging and production. It requires that these teams work collaboratively to adopt common processes and tools. Your ability to deliver modern software that leverages microservice architecture and cloud platforms is rooted in your ability to organize teams, define continuous processes, and use the right set of tools and technologies to automate your software product lifecycle.

In this chapter, we examined how one could use PowerShell, Azure resource management templates, and Visual Studio Team Services to create automation definitions that handle provisioning Azure services, building software packages and services and deploying software builds to Azure. Every step of the continuous integration and continuous delivery process was executed in Azure, providing a seamless experience for the DevOps team. In addition, the scripts were designed so that these operations can be performed against a development, test, or production environment simply by modifying the input parameters.

If you have successfully completed the exercises in this chapter, you are well positioned to maximize your learning from subsequent chapters as we continue to build on this newly provisioned IoT and advanced analytics solution.

CHAPTER 3

■ ■ ■

Device Management Using IoT Hub

Connecting people, places, and things to the cloud, while not trivial, may be one of the easier aspects of IoT as the techniques and protocols are very well defined. The real work begins when you have thousands, possibly millions, of devices connected to the cloud and you need to manage the day-to-day operations of this extremely distributed system. In addition to monitoring and managing the cloud services that are providing analytics, storage, dashboards, alerts, and notifications, you also need to monitor and manage your beacons, devices, and edge gateways.

What is my device inventory? Are the devices powered on and connected? Are they taking sensor readings? Are they sending telemetry messages? Are any devices reporting errors? Do they need to be rebooted or reconfigured? What version of firmware are they running, and do we need to upgrade any devices to the new firmware revision?

These device conditions need to be diagnosed and managed remotely and securely by the operations team using a set of software services accessed through an intelligent Device Management dashboard.

The Device Management Lifecycle

The operations team will require a set of software tools that support a well-defined process for managing a device throughout its entire life, from provisioning and configuration through to retirement (see Figure 3-1).

© Bob Familiar and Jeff Barnes 2017
B. Familiar and J. Barnes, *Business in Real-Time Using Azure IoT and Cortana Intelligence Suite*,
DOI 10.1007/978-1-4842-2650-6_3

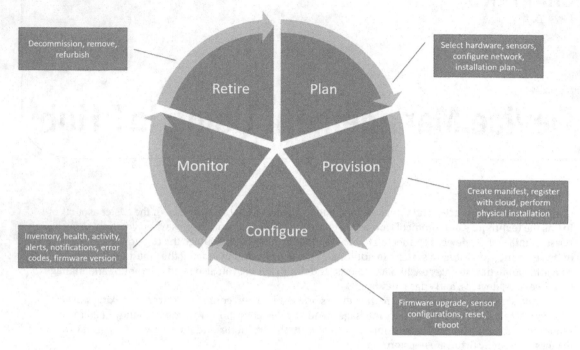

Figure 3-1. *Device management lifecycle*

This chapter will take you through each of the device management lifecycle phases. At the close of the chapter is a collection of exercises that demonstrate common device management patterns including reboot, firmware upgrade, and sensor configuration.

The Real-Time Business sample provides an operations dashboard, a managed device API, and device simulators that work in conjunction with Azure IoT Hub to demonstrate device management software services (see Figure 3-2).

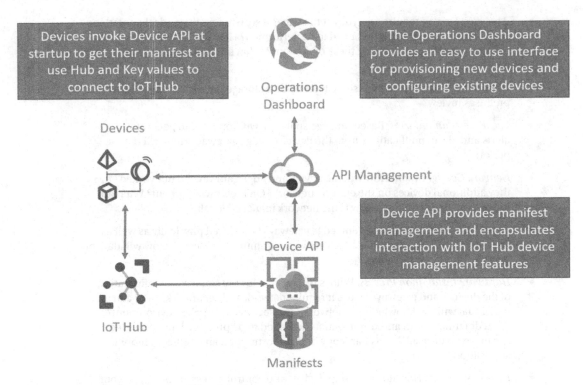

Figure 3-2. *Device management lifecycle software services*

Planning

When planning an IoT device strategy, there are several areas of research, design, and process that need to be considered. Each IoT solution has its own unique challenges given the environments where the devices are deployed. As is true with any project, the planning phase is critical to success. The goal is to eliminate assumptions and reduce risk.

Here are a few examples of questions that, when answered, will help eliminate assumptions and reduce risk leading to a well-defined device management strategy:

- *Hardware and Software Platform*: Will you use an off-the-shelf IoT device and edge gateway or do you require a custom-built enclosure? How will it be powered? What are the environmental conditions where the device and edge gateways will be deployed? Temperature? Humidity? Dust? What is the expected lifetime of the hardware? What operating system will be installed?

- *Communications*: What communication mechanism do you require? Cellular, wireless, wired, or some combination?

- *Sensors*: What sensors will be used? What are the power requirements? How will these be connected to the hardware platform? Direct connect, sensor gateway, Modbus, BACnet, CAN bus, or other? What are the ranges of readings that define normal, warning, and alerts conditions for each sensor? How often are messages sent for each type of reading, and what data do those messages contain?

- *Analytics*: Do you require analytics at the edge? If so, what mathematical operations or Machine Learning analyses need to be performed? How many readings need to be aggregated before applying these operations? What filtering, if any, needs to be applied?

- *Local Storage*: Do you require some level of local storage for edge analysis or on-premises review?

- *Local Alerts and Alarms*: Based on edge analytics, will you need to generate alerts and alarm notifications from the device or edge gateway? How will that be performed?

- *Network Configuration*: How will the device and edge gateways be networked? Are they additional devices on the existing network? On their own segment? What are the firewall requirements? How is the network managed locally?

- *Security*: How will the devices and edge gateways be secured physically as well as digitally? How do devices and edge gateways communicate locally? How will data be encrypted in flight and at rest?

- *Hardware Installation Process*: Who is responsible for the setup and configuration of the devices and gateways? Does it require network and security skills, or can an individual with no knowledge of networks and security set up the environment? What documentation and training materials need to be produced and provided? Are these made available as hardcopy or digitally through an intelligent mobile application?

- *Device Grouping:* How do you group devices and control access according to your organization's needs?

Developing a comprehensive device management strategy is foundational to a successful IoT solution. It requires collaboration among operations and software and hardware engineers to design a secure and manageable approach to the provisioning, deployment, and operating processes that will scale to tens of thousands, possibly millions, of devices.

Provisioning

Provisioning is the process by which the operating system and firmware is installed, unique device IDs are generated, devices are registered with the cloud, and a digital document (a manifest) is created to store and track device details throughout its life.

The task of generating unique identifiers may involve integrating with line-of-business systems or Enterprise Resource Planning (ERP) systems such as SAP. ERP systems are often used to supply master data for product codes, track inventory, and provide asset reporting services. CRM systems can provide customer information such as the physical address of the company, what product and services have been purchased by the customer, and the location where the devices and gateways will be installed. In addition, information such as geolocation coordinates and details such as building, floor, and room numbers may be provided.

Device metadata will provides the software services the necessary details to orchestrate a comprehensive device management process. Let's examine how this information is used by the Device API and Azure IoT Hub software services.

Azure IoT Hub

Azure IoT Hub is a fully managed service that provides secure communication and management services for your devices. These include:

- Device-to-cloud and cloud-to-device communication for secure two-way communication as well as file transfer using asynchronous command and control messages and synchronous request and reply methods

- A highly scalable event hub based transient store providing storage of messages from one to seven days and a cursor based access to the event stream providing state management and synchronization

- Secure communication using WebSockets on port 443, AMQP, MQTT, or HTTPS protocols

- Monitoring device connectivity, the event stream, and identity management events

- SDKs for many popular languages and operating systems

- Device management capabilities

- Built-in declarative message routing to other Azure services

---

■ **Note**   This chapter focuses on the device management features of IoT Hub. If you need additional detail on IoT Hub, refer to the IoT Hub documentation and download the IoT Reference Architecture PDF.

https://docs.microsoft.com/en-us/azure/iot-hub/

http://download.microsoft.com/download/A/4/D/A4DAD253-BC21-41D3-B9D9-87D2AE6F0719/Microsoft_Azure_IoT_Reference_Architecture.pdf

---

Azure IoT Hub provides a rich set of device management capabilities including Device Registration, Device Twin, Direct Methods, Jobs, and Queries. Before we dive into Azure IoT Hub, let's examine the device microservice, a managed ReST API that encapsulates the calls to IoT Hub as well as manages a document repository that tracks each device's metadata throughout its lifetime.

The Device API and the Device Manifest

The Business in Real Time reference implementation provides a managed API called *Device* that is used to create and manage the metadata about each device as well as encapsulate operations that use the IoT Hub device management features.

■ **Note**   The source code for the Device API can be found in the `microservices/device` folder of the code repository.

If you performed the exercises in Chapter 2, you will have a fully deployed managed instance of the Device API, as shown in Figure 3-3.

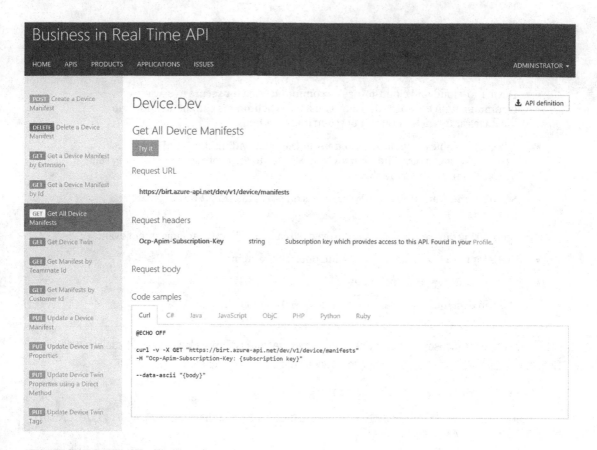

Figure 3-3. *Managed device API*

The Device API provides operations to create, update, and query a JSON document called the *Manifest*. The manifest is created at the start of the provisioning process and initialized with the information an organization requires to track the device throughout its lifecycle. Each time the device is configured, updated, or de-provisioned, the manifest is updated, thus providing an historical record (see Figure 3-4).

```
4896d607-d582-43ce-a2f9-1c09c68c7597                                    —  ☐  ✕
Document
💾 Save    🔁 Discard    🗑 Delete    🔃 Refresh    ☰ Properties

1  {
2      "Created": "2016-11-25T05:10:29.5924996Z",
3      "Modified": "2016-11-25T05:10:29.5924996Z",
4      "Type": 1,
5      "Key": {
6          "PrimaryKey": "██████████████████████████",
7          "SecondaryKey": "██████████████████████████",
8      },
9      "Extensions": [
10         {
11             "Key": "heartbeat",
12             "Val": "30000"
13         },
14         {
15             "Key": "telemetry",
16             "Val": "10000"
17         },
18         {
19             "Key": "customerId",
20             "Val": "██████████████████"
21         },
22         {
23             "Key": "teammateId",
24             "Val": "██████████████████"
25         }
26     ],
27     "Longitude": -71.216035,
28     "Latitude": 42.221322,
29     "Hub": "████████.azure-devices.net",
30     "DeviceDescription": "WigiTech Worker Health Simulator",
31     "FirmwareVersion": "1.0.0.0",
32     "HardwareVersion": "1.0.0.0",
33     "Manufacturer": "WigiTech",
34     "ModelNumber": "WT-SIM-001",
35     "SerialNumber": "██████████████████████",
36     "Timezone": "EST",
37     "Utcoffset": "UTC-5:00",
38     "id": "██████████████████",
39     "cachettl": 10
40 }
```

Figure 3-4. *Device manifest JSON document*

The device manifest provides a collection of useful properties such as:

- *Created*: The date/time the manifest document was created.

- *Modified*: The date/time the manifest document was last updated.

- *Type*: The type of device; simulator, smart device, edge gateway, mobile phone, etc.

- *Serial Number*: The unique ID for the device. This value is used to register with Azure IoT Hub and to uniquely identify messages.

- *Longitude/Latitude*: The geolocation of the device. This value can be set at provisioning time and then dynamically updated if the device has GPS capabilities. This is especially useful for devices that are on the move or scenarios where you want to map the location of devices.

- *Manufacturer/Model Number*: The manufacturer and model number of the physical device.

- *Firmware Version/Hardware Version*: Details of the version of firmware installed on the device and the version of the hardware.

- *Extensions*: A key/value pair list that can be used to extend the data model. Our implementation uses the extensions collection to hold the heartbeat and telemetry cadence, the customer profile ID, and the teammate profile ID associated with the device.

- *Hub and Key*: The IoT Hub hostname and security key.

The Device API provides a *Create Manifest* operation that will register the device with IoT Hub and store the manifest in DocumentDB.

Here is a C# code sample that creates a manifest for a simulated device and calls the Device API to perform the registration. The manifest is passed as the payload to the ReST call.

```
// initialize a new device manifest
var manifest = new Manifest
{
    Latitude = [latitude-value],
    Longitude = [longitude-value],
    SerialNumber = [unique-device-id],
    Manufacturer = "[hardware-manufacturer-name]",
    ModelNumber = "[hardware-model-number]",
    FirmwareVersion = "[firmware-version]",
    HardwareVersion = "[hardware-version]",
    DeviceDescription = "simulator",
    Type = DeviceTypeEnum.Simulator,
    Timezone = "EST",
    Utcoffset = "UTC-5:00"
};

// add property extensions
manifest.Extensions.Add(
    new DeviceProperty("heartbeat", "30000"));
manifest.Extensions.Add(
    new DeviceProperty("birthdate", "10000"));
manifest.Extensions.Add(
    new DeviceProperty("customerId", customerProfile.id));
manifest.Extensions.Add(
    new DeviceProperty("teammateId", teammate.id));

// invoke the Create Manifest operation on the Device API
var uri = @"https://[apim-host].azure-
    api.net/dev/v1/device/manifests";
```

```
var uriBuilder = new UriBuilder(uri)
{
    Query = "subscription-key=[dev-key]"
};

var json = JsonConvert.SerializeObject(manifest);

Rest.Post(uriBuilder.Uri, json);
```

The API call will register the device with IoT Hub, add the IoT Hub hostname and symmetric key to the manifest, and store the manifest in DocumentDB.

■ **Tip**   The Bootstrap utility used in Chapter 2 to initialize the deployment of the Business in Real Time reference implementation is a good example of how an application can use the Device API to register devices. The Bootstrap utility can be found in the `utility/bootstrap` folder of the code repository.

To connect to IoT Hub, a device needs three pieces of information: (1) unique device ID, (2) IoT Hub hostname, and (3) the symmetric key generated when the device was registered. You can embed these values in the firmware. If any of these details change, however, a firmware update is required to refresh the device with the new information.

Another technique is to use a no-touch deployment technique where the IoT device calls an API at startup to retreive metadata. The only information that is embedded in the firmware is the unique device ID and the endpoint to the API that returns the device manifest.

Our implementation uses this no-touch API technique. Devices call the Device API at startup to retrieve their manifest. The manifest will have the additional two pieces of information—the hostname and symmetric key. This approach provides flexibility in that the IoT Hub location could be changed and the device, upon reboot or through a remote command, would reload its manifest and connect to the new IoT Hub instance without modification to the firmware.

Here is a Node.js code sample for a device that uses this startup process:

```
'use strict';

// refence the Azure IoT Hub SDK
var Client = require('azure-iot-device').Client;
var Protocol = require('azure-iot-device-mqtt').Mqtt;

var Manifest;
var Profile;
var DeviceClient;

// Add your unique device Id
var DeviceId = '[unique-device-id]';

var startup = function()
{
    var uri = 'https://[apim-host].azure-
        api.net/dev/v1/device/manifests/id/' + DeviceId;
```

```
ReST(uri, 'GET', function(data)
{
  Manifest = data;

  // create the IoT Hub connection string
  var connectionString = 'HostName=' + Manifest.Hub + ";" +
      "DeviceId=" + Manifest.SerialNumber + ";" +
      "SharedAccessKey=" + Manifest.Key.PrimaryKey

  // connect to IoT Hub
  DeviceClient = Client.fromConnectionString(
      connectionString, Protocol);

  DeviceClient.open(function(err)
  {
      if (err) {
          console.error('could not connect ' + err);
      } else {
          console.log('client connected to IoT Hub');

          // start sending telemetry
          sendTelemetry();
      }
  });
});
}
```

Configuring and Monitoring

Once the devices are registered and connected, the operations team will need the ability to adjust device configuration at the OS, firmware, and application levels and perform these operations remotely through a common operations dashboard.

To support ongoing configuration operations across your device ecosystem, IoT Hub provides these device management features:

- *Device Twin*: A virtual digital representation of the devices in the cloud that is kept synchronized with the physical device

- *Tags*: Properties of the device twin that allow you to set meta-information on devices so that devices can be queried by tag value and operations performed on the selected devices

- *Direct Methods*: The ability for cloud-hosted services to request device-level operations, such as reboot or firmware update, be performed using a request/response pattern

- *Queries*: Select a subset of devices or jobs based on device twin properties and tag values

- *Jobs*: As Device Twin, Tag, and Direct Method operations are performed across multiple devices, jobs track the progress and report status

Device Twin

A device twin is a JSON document that holds meta and configuration data. The twins are kept synchronized with connected physical devices. Twin metadata is used to perform queries and support long-running configuration operations such as firmware upgrades. Twins are managed by IoT Hub and are limited in size to 8K per property collection—Tags, Desired, and Reported—for a total of 24KB per twin. Device twins contain:

- *Tags*: Metadata attributes that can be used to drive device queries, e.g., "select all devices in building 3, floor 27". These values can only be read or written by the backend.

- *Desired Properties*: Properties that are used to make configuration requests by the backend.

- *Reported Properties*: Configuration properties as reported by the device.

Desired and reported properties are used together to communicate desired states by the backend and actual state by the device (see Figure 3-5).

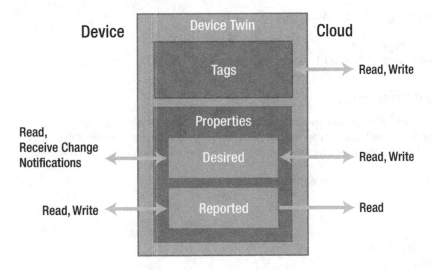

Figure 3-5. *Device twin model*

Tags

Tags are used to logically group devices based on organizational needs. To add a tag to a device twin, you create a JSON fragment with the following format:

```
var tags = '
    { "tags":
        { "tag-collection-name" :
            { "tag-name" : "tag-value", ... }
        }
    }'
```

For example:

```
var tags = '
    { "tags":
        { "location" :
            { "building" : "23", "floor" : "7" }
        }
    }'
```

To use the IoT Hub Service SDK, you reference the `Microsoft.Azure.Devices` NuGet package. You can use the `RegistryManager` object to retrieve the twin and apply the update:

```
using Microsoft.Azure.Devices;
...
var _registryManager =
    RegistryManager.CreateFromConnectionString(iothubconnstr);
...
// get the twin
var twin = await _registryManager.GetTwinAsync(myDeviceId);

// update the twin with new tags
_registryManager.UpdateTwinAsync(myDeviceId, tags, twin.ETag));
```

Desired and Reported Properties

Desired and reported properties can also be used to configure devices. Instead of sending specific commands or using direct methods, the backend can set a desired property. The device is notified that there is a new desired property and can act when appropriate. The device is in control of how and when it applies the configuration change.

To set a desired property, you create a JSON fragment with this format:

```
var property = '
    { "properties":
        { "desired" :
            { "propertyCollectionName" :
                { "property" : "value" , ... }
            }
        }
    }';
```

For example:

```
var properties = '
    { "properties":
        { "desired" :
            { "tempSensorConfig" :
                {
                    "configId" : "1",
                    "cadence" : "10000"
                }
            }
        }
    }';
```

This fragment defines a request to set the telemetry send message cadence for the temperature sensor to every 10 seconds. The backend service can update the device twin with this new desired property using the RegistryManager.

```
// get the twin
var twin = await _registryManager.GetTwinAsync(myDeviceId);

// update the twin's desired properties
_registryManager.UpdateTwinAsync(
    myDeviceId, properties, twin.ETag));
```

The device can use the device twin to report current property values and configure event handlers for property changes. This Node.js fragment would execute on the device to retrieve the device twin and updated a reported property.

```
client.getTwin(function(err, twin) {
  if (err) {
    console.error('could not get twin');
  } else {
    console.log('retrieved device twin');

  // reported temp sensor cadence
  twin.properties.reported.tempSensorConfig = {
    configId : "0",
    cadence : "30000",
  }

  // if a desired property is updated...
  twin.on('properties.desired', function(desiredChange) {
    console.log("received change");
    var currentTempSensorConfig=
        twin.properties.reported. tempSensorConfig ;

    // if the update is different than reported...
    if (desiredChange.tempSensorConfig.configId !==
            currentTempSensorConfig.configId) {

      // make the configuration change
      initConfigChange(twin);
    }
  });
}

var initConfigChange = function(twin) {

  // get the reported configuration for temp sensor
  var currentTempSensorConfig =
    twin.properties.reported.tempSensorConfig;

  // get the pending change
  currentTempSensorConfig.pendingConfig =
    twin.properties.desired.tempSensorConfig;
```

```javascript
    // report status
    currentTempSensorConfig.status = "Pending";

    var patch = {
        tempSensorConfig: currentTempSensorConfig
    };

    // report that an update is pending...
    twin.properties.reported.update(patch, function(err) {
      if (err) {
        console.log('Could not report properties');
      } else {
        console.log('Reported pending config change');

      setTimeout(function() {

        // complete the property update
        completeConfigChange(twin);}, 60000);
      }
    });
}

var completeConfigChange =  function(twin) {

  var currentTempSensorConfig =
    twin.properties.reported.tempSensorConfig;

  currentTempSensorConfig.configId =
    currentTempSensorConfig.pendingConfig.configId;

  currentTempSensorConfig.cadence =
    currentTempSensorConfig.pendingConfig.cadence;

  currentTempSensorConfig.status = "Success";

  delete currentTempSensorConfig.pendingConfig;

  var patch = {
      tempSensorConfig: currentTempSensorConfig
  };

  patch.telemetryConfig.pendingConfig = null;

  // complete the property update
  twin.properties.reported.update(patch, function(err) {
  if (err) {
    console.error('Error reporting properties: ' + err);
  } else {
    console.log('Reported completed config change');
  }
  });
};
});
```

Direct Methods

IoT Hub provides a command and control messaging mechanism that uses a store-and-forward pattern. Messages can be queued by the backend through IoT Hub. The device, if connected and listening, will receive the message asynchronously and can act on it when received. The sender of the message will be notified through a callback mechanism that the message arrived or failed to be delivered. The time-to-live on these command and control messages is from 1 to 48 hours and is configurable by the sender.

Direct methods provide a cloud application the ability to make a call to a device using a synchronous request/response pattern. These calls will either succeed or fail immediately. Direct methods leverage the ServiceClient object in the Microsoft.Azure.Devices NuGet package along with the CloudToDeviceMethod class, which provides the function name that the device will recognize and a timeout for request/response interaction.

For example, this code sample will send a reboot request to a device with a 30 second timeout:

```
using Microsoft.Azure.Devices;

ServiceClient _serviceClient;

_serviceClient = ServiceClient.CreateFromConnectionString(
    iothubconnstr);

var method = new CloudToDeviceMethod("reboot")
{
    ResponseTimeout = TimeSpan.FromSeconds(30)
};

_serviceClient.InvokeDeviceMethodAsync(myDeviceId, method));
```

In the following Node.js sample, we use the DeviceClient object to register the onReboot function to be called when the direct method named reboot is invoked. The onReboot function will send a response immediately, update the device twin with a reboot status, and then perform the reboot. The device updates the device twin so the backend can query for status of the reboot operation.

```
'use strict';

var Client = require('azure-iot-device').Client;
...
// register the reboot handler
DeviceClient.onDeviceMethod('reboot', onReboot);

// called when the reboot direct method is called
var onReboot = function(request, response) {

  // Respond to the cloud app that invoked the direct method
  response.send(200, 'Reboot started', function(err) {
    if (!err) {
      console.error('An error occurred ' + err.toString());
    } else {
      console.log('Response to method sent successfully.');
    }
  });
```

```
// Report the reboot before the physical restart
var date = new Date();
var patch = {
  iothubDM : {
    reboot : {
      lastReboot : date.toISOString(),
    }
  }
};

// Get device Twin
DeviceClient.getTwin(function(err, twin) {
  if (err) {
    console.error('could not get twin');
  } else {
    console.log('twin acquired');

    // update the twin's reported properties
    twin.properties.reported.update(patch, function(err) {
      if (err) throw err;
        console.log('Device reboot twin state reported')
    });
  }
});

// Add your device's reboot API for physical restart.
console.log('Rebooting!');
};
```

Queries

IoT Hub supports a SQL-like query language for retrieving collections of device twins and jobs. The IoT Hub device twin collection is called devices. For example, to select all device twins, you would use this query:

```
select * from devices
```

This next query will return all device twins for devices in building 23:

```
select * from devices where tags.location.building = '23'
```

It's also possible to query across tags and reported and desired properties. For example:

```
select * from devices where tags.location.region = 'US' and
properties.reported.connectivity IN ['Wi-Fi', 'Wired']
```

You can also define queries that return status for monitoring long-running operations. For example:

```
select properties.reported.firmwareUpgrade.status AS status,
    count() AS numberOfDevices
from devices
group by properties.reported.firmwareUpgrade.status
```

This query returns the following JSON:

```json
[
    {
        "status": "Success",
        "numberOfDevices": 3
    },
    {
        "status": "Pending",
        "numberOfDevices": 2
    },
    {
        "status": "Error",
        "numberOfDevices": 1
    }
]
```

To execute a query, use the `RegistryManager` class:

```csharp
var query = _registryManager.CreateQuery(
    "select * from devices", 100);

while (query.HasMoreResults)
{
    var page = await query.GetNextAsTwinAsync();
    foreach (var twin in page)
    {
        // perform configuration operation
    }
}
```

The second argument to `CreateQuery()` is the page size. The operations loop can cycle through the device twins a page at a time.

Jobs

Jobs can be used to update desired properties, update tags, and invoke direct methods. They can be executed on a single device or on a collection of devices. IoT Hub keeps track of all the job that have been or are being performed.

To schedule a job, the IoT Hub Service SDK provides the `JobClient`. You can use this object in conjunction with the definition of a direct method to kick off a job:

```csharp
CloudToDeviceMethod directMethod = new
    CloudToDeviceMethod("reboot", TimeSpan.FromSeconds(5),
    TimeSpan.FromSeconds(5));

JobResponse result = await
    jobClient.ScheduleDeviceMethodAsync(jobId,
      "deviceId='myDeviceId'", directMethod, DateTime.Now, 10);
```

You can use the query mechanism to query the status of jobs. Consider this query:

```
select * from devices.jobs
    where devices.jobs.deviceId = 'myDeviceId'
        and devices.jobs.jobType = 'firmwareUpgrade'
        and devices.jobs.status = 'completed'
        and devices.jobs.createdTimeUtc > '2016-09-01'
```

It will return all firmware upgrade jobs that completed successfully for the device with the unique ID myDeviceId.

Retiring

The process of retiring a device or collection of devices involves both the removal from the physical environment as well as the updates to the backend software services to either delete or archive the device metadata. The Real-Time Business reference implementation provides a delete function that removes the metadata from IoT Hub as well as from the DocumentDB collection as a feature of the Bootstrap utility. It uses the Device API to perform the operation across all registered devices.

EXERCISE SETUP

These exercises leverage the Azure services and microservices deployed in Chapter 2. In the following exercises, you configure a Device Management dashboard and a device simulator that implements the device management patterns covered in this chapter.

Both the dashboard and the device are built using Node.js. To run and test the device management features, you use Visual Studio, Visual Studio Code, and a utility called Device Explorer, which is part of the Azure IoT SDK.

■ **Tip** The Device Explorer can be found in the C# IoT SDK azure-iot-sdk-csharp\tools\DeviceExplorer folder.

To perform these operations, your development environment will require the following additions:

1. Download and install Node.js v6.9.x:

    https://nodejs.org/en/

2. Using a command shell window, navigate to the devices/device-node folder and run these commands to install the node packages for the device solution:

    ```
    C:> npm install azure-iot-device --save
    C:> npm install azure-iot-device-mqtt --save
    ```

3. Download and install the Visual Studio Node.js tools:

   https://visualstudio.com/vs/node-js/

4. Download and install the Visual Studio code:

   https://code.visualstudio.com

DEVICE MANAGEMENT DASHBOARD

Open the `dm.sln` solution in the folder `dashboards/dm`. This Visual Studio project is built using the Visual Studio Node.js Express 4 template, as shown in Figure 3-6, and leverages Jade, a high-performance HTML template engine, and Node to define an HTTP server that serves up the HTML-CSS-JavaScript based UI.

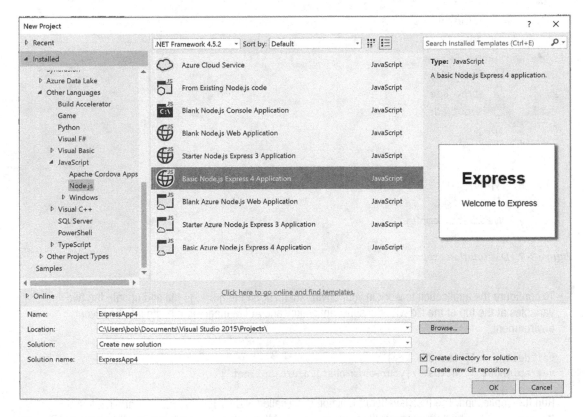

Figure 3-6. Visual Studio Node.js project templates

The Jade layout code is found in the `views/layout.jade` and `views/home.jade` file. The JavaScript that executes on the client is found in the `public/javascripts/home.js` file (see Figure 3-7).

Figure 3-7. *DM solution explorer*

To configure the application to work in your environment, open the `home.js` file and update the two variables at the top of the file with the subscription key and API Management hostname from your environment.

```
var devKey = '[your-dev-key]';
var apimHost = 'https://[your-apim-host].azure-api.net';
```

Run the application. The first JavaScript function to be called is `GetAllCompanies()`, and it's found in the `home.js` file. The code dynamically generates the HTML `SELECT` element by calling the Registry API and requesting all profiles of type `organization` (i.e., type = 1).

```
function GetAllCompanies()
{
  var selectContent =
   '<option value="">Select a company</option>';

  $.getJSON(
   apimHost +
   '/dev/v1/registry/profiles/type/1?subscription-key=' +
   devKey,
     function ( data ) {

       $.each( data.list, function ()
       {
         selectContent +=
          '<option value="' +
            this.id + '">' +
            this.companyname + '</option>';
       });

       $( '#companyList select' ).html( selectContent );
       $( document.getElementById(
           'companyList' ).selectedIndex = 0 );
   });
}
```

Select the WigiTech company and you will be presented with the devices that are registered to WigiTech employees (see Figure 3-8). The devices in our scenario are attached to employee's bodies and provide continuous biometric readings. The device heartbeat and telemetry message cadence settings are presented as editable fields, and there are command buttons for executing the Reboot, Update Firmware, and Configure Cadence commands.

Business in Real-Time

Manage Your Connected Team

Serial Number	Model	Heartbeat	Telemetry	Reboot	Upgrade	Configure
fb57e0a4-d3f7-443c-af10-310c7f09ccba	WT-SIM-001	30000	10000	Reboot Device	Update Firmware	Configure Cadence
21d5d6ca-9632-4a79-9caa-632c0cc78c32	WT-SIM-001	30000	10000	Reboot Device	Update Firmware	Configure Cadence
0f6a3116-63b9-4ac2-9961-e106846b76f7	WT-SIM-001	30000	10000	Reboot Device	Update Firmware	Configure Cadence
71abbd52-986f-44cb-a8dc-d6d07fee3322	WT-SIM-001	30000	10000	Reboot Device	Update Firmware	Configure Cadence
f0dd5745-11a7-48aa-9262-d7e220537e7c	WT-SIM-001	30000	10000	Reboot Device	Update Firmware	Configure Cadence
751c6d0c-a03f-4112-b7e7-77f7fe6f9eb3	WT-SIM-001	30000	10000	Reboot Device	Update Firmware	Configure Cadence
4b9f2d4b-e012-43cb-8262-66a53567ffbe	WT-SIM-001	30000	10000	Reboot Device	Update Firmware	Configure Cadence
4a061209-84ab-49ad-8f00-f3597b932590	WT-SIM-001	30000	10000	Reboot Device	Update Firmware	Configure Cadence
4abf70b7-e04d-4cbb-a9e6-8053916a6672	WT-SIM-001	30000	10000	Reboot Device	Update Firmware	Configure Cadence
54cc5c03-eb06-495d-ba2b-405bc79e6204	WT-SIM-001	30000	10000	Reboot Device	Update Firmware	Configure Cadence
c5ae7c45-d24c-4239-b4d8-a6a91f741043	WT-SIM-001	30000	10000	Reboot Device	Update Firmware	Configure Cadence
47ae5112-f50b-4a36-aa9c-9caea0808cdd	WT-SIM-001	30000	10000	Reboot Device	Update Firmware	Configure Cadence
caa19850-23f2-494a-a02e-684c7adb884c	WT-SIM-001	30000	10000	Reboot Device	Update Firmware	Configure Cadence
5a3600ca-ad6b-470e-9f2f-cdab1c1608d8	WT-SIM-001	30000	10000	Reboot Device	Update Firmware	Configure Cadence
9b16c815-230e-4d8d-93e7-a41e60946008	WT-SIM-001	30000	10000	Reboot Device	Update Firmware	Configure Cadence
1920dcc7-a92b-4e40-b124-a88bce85fa7a	WT-SIM-001	30000	10000	Reboot Device	Update Firmware	Configure Cadence
d1a41e4b-2600-4d83-98b7-dd734578a82f	WT-SIM-001	30000	10000	Reboot Device	Update Firmware	Configure Cadence

Figure 3-8. Device management dashboard

The Reboot and Update Firmware operations use the direct method mechanism to communicate with the device. Configure Cadence uses desired properties to request a configuration change to the device.

The data used to create this table comes from the manifests for each of the registered devices. When you select a company from the drop-down, the function GetDevices() is called. This function calls the "Get Manifests by Customer ID" API, returning a list of manifests that are associated with the company identified by customerId.

```
function GetDevices( select )
{
    var uri = apimHost +
        '/dev/v1/device/manifests/customer/' +
        select.value + '?subscription-key=' + devKey;

    $.getJSON( uri, function ( data ) {
        manifests = data.List;
...
```

The remainder of the code in this function goes on to dynamically build the device table using the manifest collection.

When you click the Reboot, Update Firmware, or Configure Cadence buttons, the associated JavaScript function is called. These functions call the Device API endpoints for performing device management and configuration tasks.

Let's examine the Reboot function. The function is passed the serial number of the device to be rebooted. It builds a JSON fragment for a JSON object called twinPropertyRequest. This class is passed to the Device API methods and contains the serial number, the name of the direct method, and a list of any parameters. The reboot direct method does not take any parameters, so the JSON fragment is only initialized with the serial number and the direct method name, as follows:

```
function Reboot( serialNumber )
{
    var command = {
        DeviceId: serialNumber,
        Name: 'reboot',
        Properties: []
    };
```

Next, the function calls the Device API endpoint for invoking a direct method passing in the twinPropertyRequest JSON.

```
    var twinPropertyRequest = JSON.stringify(command);

    var uri = apimHost +
        '/dev/v1/device/twin/properties/direct';

    $.ajax( {
        url: uri,
        type: "PUT",
        data: twinPropertyRequest,
```

```
        headers: {
            "Ocp-Apim-Trace": "true",
            "Ocp-Apim-Subscription-Key": devKey,
            "Content-Type":"application/json"
        },
        success: function ()
        {
          alert( "success" );
        },
        error: function ( xhr, status, error )
        {
          var err = eval( "(" + xhr.responseText + ")" );
          alert( status + ": " + err.Message );
        }
    });
}
```

The Device API accesses the `TwinPropertyRequest` from the request body and sets up a call to the direct method using the `CloudToDeviceMethod` and `ServiceClient` objects.

```
public void UpdateTwinPropertiesDirect(
    TwinPropertyRequest twinPropertyRequest)
{
    // Update Twin Properties using a Direct Method
    var method = new CloudToDeviceMethod(
        twinPropertyRequest.Name)
    { ResponseTimeout = TimeSpan.FromSeconds(30) };
...
    _serviceClient.InvokeDeviceMethodAsync(
        twinPropertyRequest.DeviceId, method));
```

■ **Note**   To review the complete implementation of the Device API, see the DeviceAPI solution in the `microservices/device` folder.

The `UpdateFirmware()` function also uses the direct method technique, but in addition to the firmware update command, it passes in a parameter that is the URI to the firmware image file.

```
function UpdateFirmware( serialNumber )
{
    var command = {
        DeviceId: serialNumber,
        Name: 'firmwareUpdate',
        Properties: [
            {
                Key: 'fwPackageUri',
                Val: 'https://[uri-to-firmware]'
            }
        ]
    };
```

```
    var twinPropertyRequest = JSON.stringify(command);

    var uri = apimHost +
        '/dev/v1/device/twin/properties/direct';
    $.ajax( {
        url: uri,
        type: "PUT",
        data: twinPropertyRequest,
        headers: {
            "Ocp-Apim-Trace": "true",
            "Ocp-Apim-Subscription-Key": devKey,
            "Content-Type": "application/json"
        },
        success: function ()
        {
            alert( "success" );
        },
        error: function ( xhr, status, error )
        {
          var err = eval( "(" + xhr.responseText + ")" );
          alert( status + ": " + err.Message );
        }
    });
}
```

It is common for devices to send heartbeat messages to signal that they are still working and able to communicate. The heartbeat cadence defines how long the device waits between sending heartbeat messages. Similarly, the telemetry cadence defines how long the device waits between sending telemetry messages.

The default settings for these values, 30 seconds for heartbeat and 10 seconds for telemetry, are stored in the device manifest and are used to initialize devices on startup. Through the Device Management application, we can update these settings while the device is running by sending a Device Twin Desired Property request change.

The Configure() function leverages the Desired Property technique to request a configuration change to the heartbeat and telemetry cadence settings. It uses the same TwinPropertyRequest data structure to pass in new values for the heartbeat and telemetry cadence settings.

```
function Configure( serialNumber, inputId ) {

    var hbInputId = 'hb' + String(inputId);
    var tlInputId = 'tl' + String(inputId);

    var heartbeat;
    var telemetry;

    $(heartbeat =
        document.getElementById( hbInputId ).value );
    $(telemetry =
        document.getElementById( tlInputId ).value);
```

```
var request = {
    DeviceId: serialNumber,
    Name: 'cadenceConfig',
    Properties: [
        {
            Key: 'heartbeat',
            Val: heartbeat
        },
        {
            Key: 'telemetry',
            Val: telemetry
        }
    ]
};

var twinPropertyRequest = JSON.stringify( request );

var uri = apimHost +
    '/dev/v1/device/twin/properties';

$.ajax( {
    url: uri,
    type: "PUT",
    data: twinPropertyRequest,
    headers: {
        "Ocp-Apim-Trace": "true",
        "Ocp-Apim-Subscription-Key": devKey,
        "Content-Type": "application/json"
    },
    success: function ()
    {
        alert( "success" );
    },
    error: function ( xhr, status, error )
    {
      var err = eval( "(" + xhr.responseText + ")" );
      alert( status + ": " + err.Message );
    }
});
}
```

In the next exercise, you define a device simulator to receive the direct method calls and desired property events.

Copy the serial number from the web page for the first device in the list and set it aside as you will need that to update the device simulator that will receive the commands coming from the console.

DEVICE SIMULATOR

To fully test the device management software services, you need a device. In this exercise, you modify the code for a device and, using the Device Management dashboard, test the Reboot, Firmware Upgrade, and Cadence Configuration commands.

Start Visual Studio Code and, using the open folder feature, open the root folder of the reference implementation code repository (see Figure 3-9).

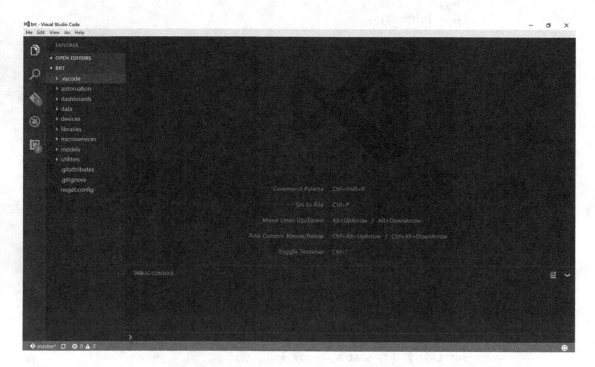

Figure 3-9. *Visual Studio code*

The device project is in `devices/device-node`. Navigate to that folder and open the `device.js` file.

Update the three variables at the top of the file with your API Management hostname, your API Management developer key, and the Device ID (serial number) that you copied from the Device Management dashboard in the previous exercise (see Figure 3-10).

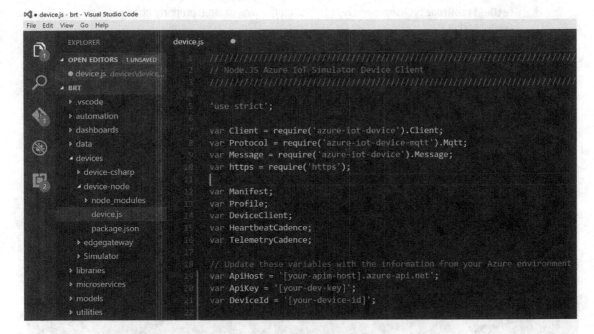

Figure 3-10. *Update the ApiHost, ApiKey, and DeviceId variables*

The `device.js` file is organized into the following sections:

- *Message Classes*: Define heartbeat and telemetry messages

- *Helper Functions*: Helper routines

- *Reboot Handler*: Code called when a reboot command is issued to the device

- *Firmware Update Handler*: Code called when the update firmware command is issued to the device

- *Desired Property Handler*: Code called when a desired property change event is received

- *Main*: Controller functions for each of the primary device operations

Let's first examine the `main()` function. This routine gives you control over each of the device's primary operations. These operations include:

- `getDeviceManifest()`: Calls Device API using device unique ID to retrieve the manifest

- `getUserProfile()`: Calls the Registry API to retrieve the user profile associated with this device

- `connectIoTHub()`: Connects to IoT Hub

- `setRebootHandler()`: Sets up the reboot direct method event handler

- `setFirmwareUpdateHandler()`: Sets up the firmware update direct method event handler

- setDesiredPropetyChangeHandler(): Sets up the twin desired property changed event handler

- sendHeartbeat(): Sends heartbeat messages

- sendTelemetry(): Sends telemetry messages

Most of the calls are commented out so that you can bring them online one at a time. Before you do that, let's set up Visual Studio Code for debugging.

Click the debug icon in the left-side gutter and then click the gear icon in the menu bar. Make sure that the program setting in the launch.json file points to the device.js file (see Figure 3-11).

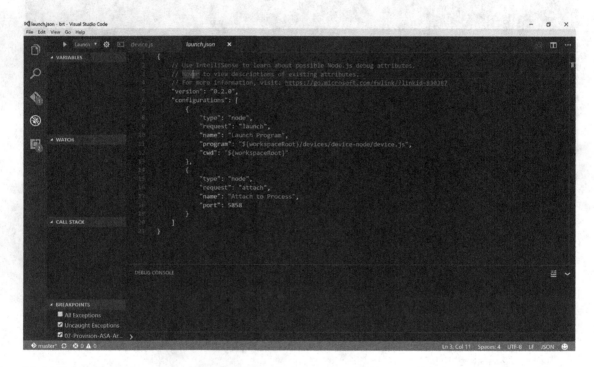

Figure 3-11. *Set up Launch.Json file for debugging*

Click the run button in the menu bar. Note the debugger controls along the top of the IDE. The device will retrieve its manifest, look up the user profile for the user assigned this device, and connect to IoT Hub (see Figure 3-12). The code uses the `console.log()` function of Node to output trace information to the debug console window.

Figure 3-12. *Launch the debugger*

Stop the debugger. Modify the `main()` function so that the `setRebootHandler()` function will be called the next time you run the application (see Figure 3-13).

Figure 3-13. *Activate the setRebootHandler() call*

Since we are going to activate the reboot event handler, you will also want to have the Device Management console application running so that you can test the reboot direct method.

The `setRebootHandler()` function uses the `DeviceClient` object to set up a direct method event handler. When the direct method called `reboot` is invoked, the callback function named `onReboot()` will be called.

```
var setRebootHandler = function (callback)
{
    callback();
    console.log('setHandlers --> reboot');
    DeviceClient.onDeviceMethod('reboot', onReboot);
}
```

As discussed earlier in this chapter, the function `onReboot()` will send an immediate response to the caller so that the cloud application knows whether the call succeeded. Next it updates the device twin with the reboot status and then starts the reboot process.

Run the application in the debugger. The debug console output will document that the `setRebootHandler()` is active. Using the Device Management dashboard, click the Reboot button for the device. The debug console will document that the direct method was successfully invoked (see Figure 3-14).

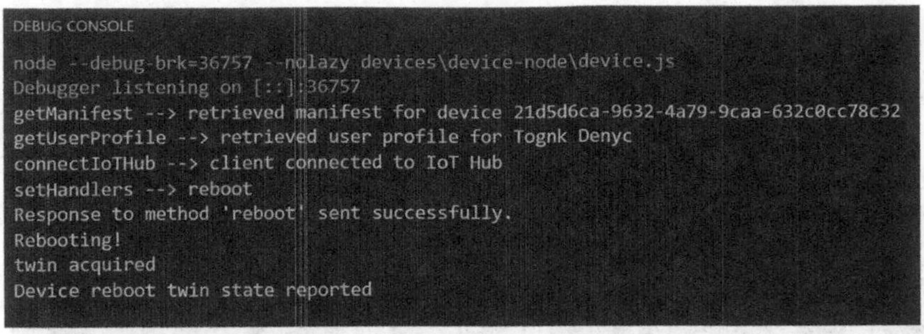

```
DEBUG CONSOLE
node --debug-brk=36757 --nolazy devices\device-node\device.js
Debugger listening on [::]:36757
getManifest --> retrieved manifest for device 21d5d6ca-9632-4a79-9caa-632c0cc78c32
getUserProfile --> retrieved user profile for Tognk Denyc
connectIoTHub --> client connected to IoT Hub
setHandlers --> reboot
Response to method 'reboot' sent successfully.
Rebooting!
twin acquired
Device reboot twin state reported
```

Figure 3-14. *Reboot direct method success*

Stop the debugger.

Uncomment the setFirmwareUpdateHandler() and run the device application again. Using the Device Management dashboard, click the Update Firmware button. Check the debug console output in Visual Studio Code to see that the direct method event was handled. Note how the device twin is updated as each step of the firmware update process is applied (see Figure 3-15).

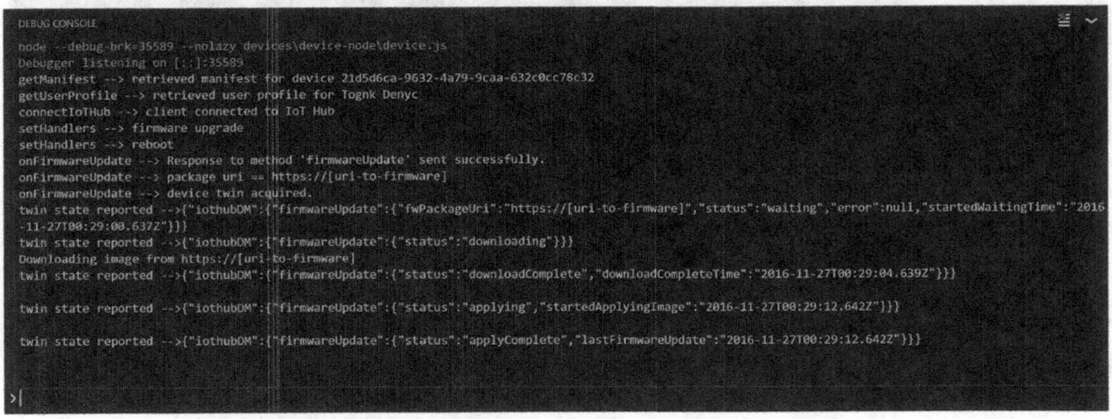

```
DEBUG CONSOLE
node --debug-brk=35589 --nolazy devices\device-node\device.js
Debugger listening on [::]:35589
getManifest --> retrieved manifest for device 21d5d6ca-9632-4a79-9caa-632c0cc78c32
getUserProfile --> retrieved user profile for Tognk Denyc
connectIoTHub --> client connected to IoT Hub
setHandlers --> firmware upgrade
setHandlers --> reboot
onFirmwareUpdate --> Response to method 'firmwareUpdate' sent successfully.
onFirmwareUpdate --> package uri == https://[uri-to-firmware]
onFirmwareUpdate --> device twin acquired.
twin state reported -->{"iothubDM":{"firmwareUpdate":{"fwPackageUri":"https://[uri-to-firmware]","status":"waiting","error":null,"startedWaitingTime":"2016
-11-27T00:29:00.639Z"}}}
twin state reported -->{"iothubDM":{"firmwareUpdate":{"status":"downloading"}}}
Downloading image from https://[uri-to-firmware]
twin state reported -->{"iothubDM":{"firmwareUpdate":{"status":"downloadComplete","downloadCompleteTime":"2016-11-27T00:29:04.639Z"}}}

twin state reported -->{"iothubDM":{"firmwareUpdate":{"status":"applying","startedApplyingImage":"2016-11-27T00:29:12.642Z"}}}

twin state reported -->{"iothubDM":{"firmwareUpdate":{"status":"applyComplete","lastFirmwareUpdate":"2016-11-27T00:29:12.642Z"}}}

>|
```

Figure 3-15. *Firmware update direct method success*

In this final test, uncomment the remainder of the main() function so that the desired property event handler is activated and the device will start sending heartbeat and telemetry messages.

Run the device application and, using the Device Management dashboard, change the heartbeat and telemetry cadence settings to 15000 and 5000, respectively (see Figure 3-16). The debug console will document:

- Messages are sent using the original cadence settings
- The desired property is received

- The device twin's reported properties are updated using the settings from the desired properties

- The device starts sending heartbeat and telemetry messages using the new cadence values

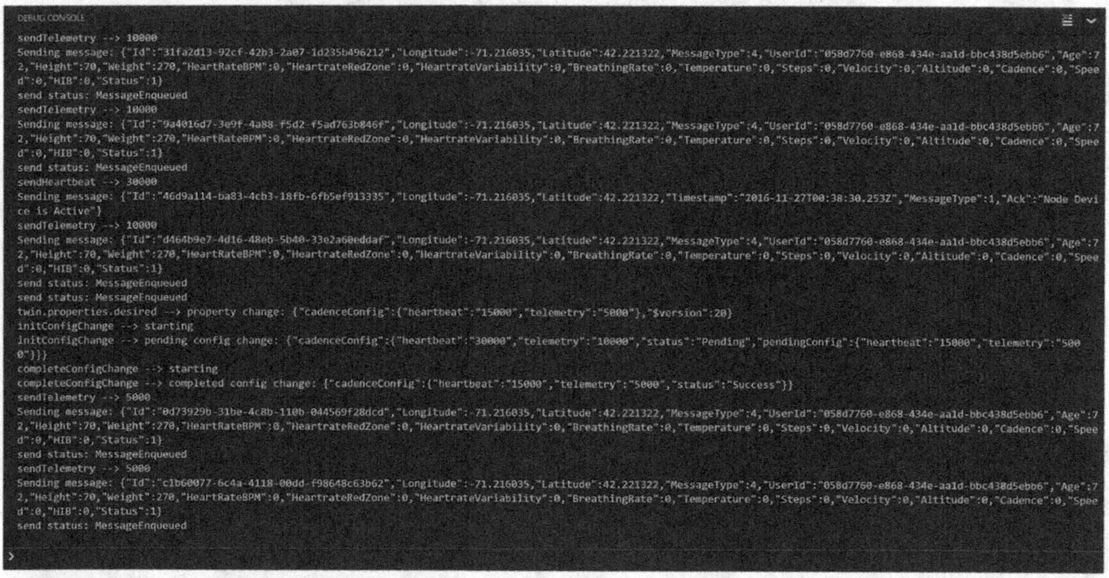

DEBUG CONSOLE

sendTelemetry --> 10000
Sending message: {"Id":"31fa2d13-92cf-42b3-2a07-1d235b496212","Longitude":-71.216035,"Latitude":42.221322,"MessageType":4,"UserId":"058d7760-e868-434e-aa1d-bbc438d5ebb6","Age":7
2,"Height":70,"Weight":270,"HeartRateBPM":0,"HeartrateRedZone":0,"HeartrateVariability":0,"BreathingRate":0,"Temperature":0,"Steps":0,"Velocity":0,"Altitude":0,"Cadence":0,"Spee
d":0,"HIB":0,"Status":1}
send status: MessageEnqueued
sendTelemetry --> 10000
Sending message: {"Id":"9a4016d7-3e9f-4a88-f5d2-f5ad763b846f","Longitude":-71.216035,"Latitude":42.221322,"MessageType":4,"UserId":"058d7760-e868-434e-aa1d-bbc438d5ebb6","Age":7
2,"Height":70,"Weight":270,"HeartRateBPM":0,"HeartrateRedZone":0,"HeartrateVariability":0,"BreathingRate":0,"Temperature":0,"Steps":0,"Velocity":0,"Altitude":0,"Cadence":0,"Spee
d":0,"HIB":0,"Status":1}
send status: MessageEnqueued
sendHeartbeat --> 30000
Sending message: {"Id":"46d9a114-ba83-4cb3-18fb-6fb5ef913335","Longitude":-71.216035,"Latitude":42.221322,"Timestamp":"2016-11-27T00:38:30.253Z","MessageType":1,"Ack":"Node Devi
ce is Active"}
sendTelemetry --> 10000
Sending message: {"Id":"d464b9e7-4d16-48eb-5b40-33e2a60eddaf","Longitude":-71.216035,"Latitude":42.221322,"MessageType":4,"UserId":"058d7760-e868-434e-aa1d-bbc438d5ebb6","Age":7
2,"Height":70,"Weight":270,"HeartRateBPM":0,"HeartrateRedZone":0,"HeartrateVariability":0,"BreathingRate":0,"Temperature":0,"Steps":0,"Velocity":0,"Altitude":0,"Cadence":0,"Spee
d":0,"HIB":0,"Status":1}
send status: MessageEnqueued
send status: MessageEnqueued
twin.properties.desired --> property change: {"cadenceConfig":{"heartbeat":"15000","telemetry":"5000"},"$version":20}
initConfigChange --> starting
initConfigChange --> pending config change: {"cadenceConfig":{"heartbeat":"30000","telemetry":"10000","status":"Pending","pendingConfig":{"heartbeat":"15000","telemetry":"500
0"}}}
completeConfigChange --> starting
completeConfigChange --> completed config change: {"cadenceConfig":{"heartbeat":"15000","telemetry":"5000","status":"Success"}}
sendTelemetry --> 5000
Sending message: {"Id":"0d73929b-31be-4c8b-110b-044569f28dcd","Longitude":-71.216035,"Latitude":42.221322,"MessageType":4,"UserId":"058d7760-e868-434e-aa1d-bbc438d5ebb6","Age":7
2,"Height":70,"Weight":270,"HeartRateBPM":0,"HeartrateRedZone":0,"HeartrateVariability":0,"BreathingRate":0,"Temperature":0,"Steps":0,"Velocity":0,"Altitude":0,"Cadence":0,"Spee
d":0,"HIB":0,"Status":1}
send status: MessageEnqueued
sendTelemetry --> 5000
Sending message: {"Id":"c1b60077-6c4a-4118-00dd-f98648c63b62","Longitude":-71.216035,"Latitude":42.221322,"MessageType":4,"UserId":"058d7760-e868-434e-aa1d-bbc438d5ebb6","Age":7
2,"Height":70,"Weight":270,"HeartRateBPM":0,"HeartrateRedZone":0,"HeartrateVariability":0,"BreathingRate":0,"Temperature":0,"Steps":0,"Velocity":0,"Altitude":0,"Cadence":0,"Spee
d":0,"HIB":0,"Status":1}
send status: MessageEnqueued

Figure 3-16. *Cadence properties applied*

Summary

Device management is a key component of an end-to-end IoT and advanced analysis solution. Device management provides complete lifecycle support for your device ecosystem through a set of cooperating software services for planning, provisioning, configuring, monitoring, and finally retiring deployed devices.

CHAPTER 4

■ ■ ■

Sensors, Devices, and Gateways

Chapters 2 and 3 focused on the core processes that must in place when embarking on an IoT and advanced analytics digital transformation journey, namely DevOps and Device Management. This chapter looks at the world of sensors, devices, and gateways. Although we won't be able to cover all the possible permutations of hardware and software, we will touch upon some of the more common scenarios we encounter and how they relate and work together to create a consistent, secure, and reliable network of connected things.

Sensors

The purpose of a sensor is to measure. Sensors take a measurement of a physical parameter and turn it into a value that can be read electrically using analog or digital circuitry. The physical shape, construction materials, and electronics are dependent on the application. There are many classes of sensors that are differentiated by accuracy, environmental resilience, range, resolution detail, ability to calibrate, and cost (see Figure 4-1).

| Temperature | Pressure | Heart Rate |

Figure 4-1. *Different types of sensors*

There is a robust industry of sensor manufacturers that provide sensor hardware solutions for collecting measurable qualities, including but not limited to:

- Position, proximity, dimension, distance, inclination, and motion

- Air quality, air pollution, levels of carbon dioxide, hydrocarbon, hydrogen, methane, and oxygen

- Electrical current, eddy current, electrical field, magnetic field, and voltage

- Weather conditions including temperature, humidity, dew point, heat flow, and smoke

© Bob Familiar and Jeff Barnes 2017
B. Familiar and J. Barnes, *Business in Real-Time Using Azure IoT and Cortana Intelligence Suite*,
DOI 10.1007/978-1-4842-2650-6_4

- Human and animal blood flow, blood glucose level, blood pressure, body temperature, and heart rate

- Acoustic parameters such as loudness, noise, resonance, ultrasound, and direction

- Fluid measurements including gauge pressure, mass, volume flow, bulk, and level

- vision and identification including image sensors, code detection, and object detection

- Optical and luminosity including radiation, light, turbidity, UV, and visible light

This list could go on and on. The key point is that the world of sensors is rich and wonderful, and the cost of these sensors along with the analog to digital converters and microprocessor hardware to connect and communicate has made IoT a ubiquitous commodity. We can measure anything and turn it into a floating-point number.

■ **Tip** When planning your IoT solution, document the properties and capabilities of each of the sensors, as those values have direct impact on your canonical message format and downstream analytics.

If you are using a Single-Board Computer (SBC) such as a Raspberry Pi, you can connect analog sensors using Analog-to-Digital (ADC) adapter shields. These adapters read the voltage coming from the analog sensor and turn that into a digital value. You can communicate with sensors through the UART, I2C, and GPIO interfaces as well.

It is not uncommon to connect your SBC to an intermediary device such as a Programmable Logic Controller (PLC). Sensors may be attached directly to the PLC, or the PLC may gather readings from sensor enabled hardware that is attached to the PLC. PLCs and single-board computers communicate using a serial interface or Ethernet. The SBC software uses a library such as Modbus or Ethernet/IP to communicate with the PLC.

■ **Note** Modbus is a serial communications protocol originally published by Schneider Electric in 1979 for use with its PLC products. Due to its ease of use and popularity, Modbus has become a de facto standard protocol for communicating with PLCs. Ethernet/IP is an industrial network protocol that adapts the Common Industrial Protocol (CIP) to standard Ethernet, and CIP is another popular protocol for industrial automation applications.

Programmable Logic Controllers

Programmable Logic Controllers (PLCs) play an important role in industrial IoT. PLCs are ruggedized computers that are used to provide a programmable interface to industrial machinery, cameras and sensors. A PLC may be used, for example, to control a valve on a chemical storage tank; it monitors the fluid level using a sensor and opens a valve to dispense when the sensor is triggered.

PLCs use special programming languages to customize how they control the machinery and attached sensors. There are five PLC programming approaches that are in use today:

- Function block diagram

- Ladder logic diagram

- Structured text
- Instruction list
- Sequential function chart

Here is an example of a PLC program that increments a counter each time a pulse generator fires (see Figure 4-2).

instruction list

LD	SM 0.1	On for One Scan
MOVW	# 0 , VW100	Put 0 in address VW100
MOVW	# 10 , VW110	Put 10 in address VW110
LD	SM 0.4	Pulse generator
EU		Raising edge
INCW	VW100	Increment VW100
DECW	VW110	Decrement VW110
		End programming
MEND		

ladder diagram

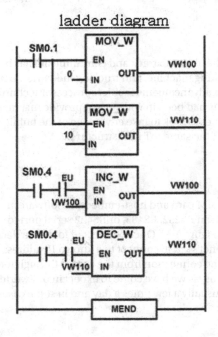

Figure 4-2. *Example PLC program from plcmanual.com*

PLCs are often used to connect light to heavy industrial equipment to a Supervisory Control And Data Acquisition (SCADA) system, a solution that provides process control for plants and factories. We encounter PLCs when working with clients who are looking to take advantage of IoT to connect their remote products, plants, and factories to the cloud to take advantage of predictive analytics to calculate mean-time-to-failure of their remote systems (see Figure 4-3). If you can predict mean-time-to-failure, you can reduce operating costs by optimizing scheduled maintenance.

Schneider Electric   ABB   Horner

Figure 4-3. *Examples of light and heavy industrial PLCs*

PLCs are not IoT-enabled by default. While it is common today to use an SBC to provide cloud connectivity and communication, GSM modems have been handling these duties for many years. Let's venture now into the world of devices by first looking at early versions of network capable devices and how they have evolved to what we now call smart devices.

Devices

As stated in Chapter 1, IoT is not new. For certain industries, the ability to track and communicate has been central to their businesses such as the shipping container, vending machine, and trucking industries. Before today's explosion of connected "things" that leverage the latest advancements in microprocessor technology and low-power wireless technology, the use of cellular modems had been in wide use to provide machine-to-machine (M2M) communication. It is common for companies to look to take advantage of the public cloud while also supporting their legacy M2M ecosystem using the same IoT infrastructure.

GSM Modems

GSM modems are cellular capable devices. They can accept a SIM card and host-embedded software and connect to a cellular provider such as ATT or Verizon. They use an RS232, RS485, or RS422 serial port to connect to a PLC that provides the data to be transmitted (see Figure 4-4). Once connected to the carrier, the embedded software uses a VPN connection to a corporate network to connect to a known IP address—a server—that accepts incoming data and provides responses. The connection from the carrier through the VPN to the server and the transmission of data is not continuous, as we have come to expect in our world of ubiquitous networking and connected things. The cadence is usually a few times a day and in some cases less often to control costs.

Figure 4-4. *Elementz engineers guild GSM modem*

To integrate a GSM modem with our Azure-hosted IoT sub-system, we need to provide a proxy that sits between the GSM modem and Azure IoT Hub. This proxy presents itself to the GSM modem as an IP addressable server sitting behind a secure VPN network and manages the interactions with the cloud. We refer to this proxy as a *protocol gateway* as its job is to translate from the legacy data formats and GSM modem commands supported by the modem's embedded software to the canonical message formats expected by our services.

Protocol Gateway

A *protocol gateway* is a cloud service deployed in the context of a VPN and made IP-addressable through cloud configuration. The protocol gateway provides a message and command-and-control translation layer between the GSM modem and Azure IoT Hub. The protocol gateway acts as a device management proxy as well, invoking the device startup process as outlined in Chapter 3, leveraging the device API to look up the device manifest and use that information to connect to IoT Hub on behalf of the GSM modem.

Microsoft provides the Azure Protocol Gateway as a starting point for a protocol gateway implementation. The Azure Protocol Gateway is a framework that enables bidirectional communication with Azure IoT Hub. The protocol gateway programming model also allows you to plug in custom components for specialized processing such as authentication, message transformations, compression, decompression, and encryption and decryption of traffic between the remote devices and IoT Hub. Since GSM modems are occasionally connected, this feature could be used to add a plugin for caching device management commands that are applied the next time the modem dials in (see Figure 4-5).

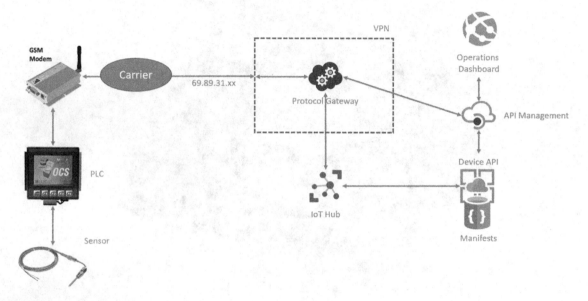

Figure 4-5. *GSM modem integration using a protocol gateway*

■ **Note**   For additional information on the Azure Protocol Gateway, see `https://github.com/Azure/azure-iot-protocol-gateway`.

GSM Modems and SMS

Since a GSM modem is essentially a mobile phone without the keyboard, screen, speakers, and headphone jack (is that still a thing?), and it can use Short Message Service (SMS) to send and receive messages. While this is not the most reliable communication option, it can still play a role in communicating small pieces of information for occasionally connected scenarios in a cost-effective way.

To support SMS communication, we can use a service such as Twilio to provide two-way communication with the GSM modem. To complete the communication chain, we can add an additional ReST service that provides an endpoint for Twilio and provides the protocol translation between the SMS messages coming from Twilio and our services. Let's call this service the SMS Gateway API.

The GSM modem sends SMS messages to Twilio which in turn forwards that message to the SMS Gateway API. The SMS Gateway follows the device startup process outlined in Chapter 3, invoking the device API to retrieve the manifest for the GSM modem and using that information to connect to IoT Hub (see Figure 4-6).

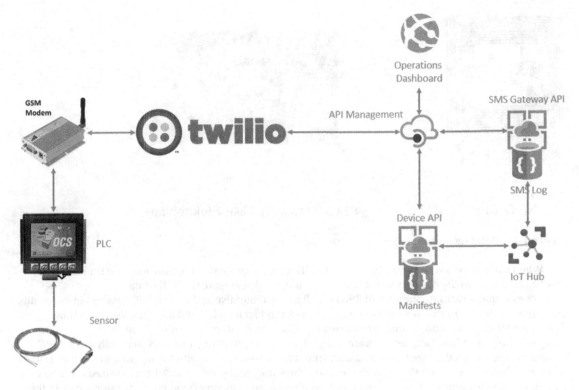

Figure 4-6. *GMS modem integration using Twilio and a custom SMS Gateway API*

RFID

Radio Frequency Identification (RFID) is a system that uses tags that are attached to or embedded in things. The tag can be passive or active. Active tags are battery powered and are activated when an RFID reader is within proximity. Tags contain a unique ID, a serial number, and application-specific data. For example, if the RFID tag were attached to a piece of clothing in a retail store, the tag would contain its unique serial number along with the product details for the clothing such as SKU number, name, color, size, etc.

To communicate with tags, two-way radio RFID readers send signals to the tags and receive the stored data in response (see Figure 4-7). Tags may be read-only or writable, i.e., the RFID readers can update the contents of the tag. RFID reader systems have a transmit/receive range anywhere from 1 to 2,000 feet. The range can be calibrated so that RFID tags are only read when they are within a well-defined zone around the reader. This is useful, for instance, if you want to set up a zone on a conveyor belt so that tags are read when they pass underneath the reader.

RFID Tag   RFID Reader by MikroElektronika

Figure 4-7. RFID tags and readers

When used in IoT scenarios, RFID tags and RFID readers are used in conjunction with smart devices that communicate to the cloud as well as transform, filter, and aggregate the RFID data.

For example, a clothing store could RFID tag all the merchandise and mount RFID readers in the ceiling to continually communicate with the RFID tags to track product location and SKU information. Using this information, you would be able to construct a real-time view of store inventory and product location using IoT services. While some retailers are using RFID, they are tracking inventory manually using RFID handheld devices and they are not coordinating the store inventory data with the inventory levels advertised on their web sites. A solution that provides real-time inventory and product location visualized through web and mobile applications for store management, employees, and customers would be transformative in the retail industry.

The smart device, in this scenario, would provide data filtering and transformation in addition to handling communication with the cloud services (see Figure 4-8).

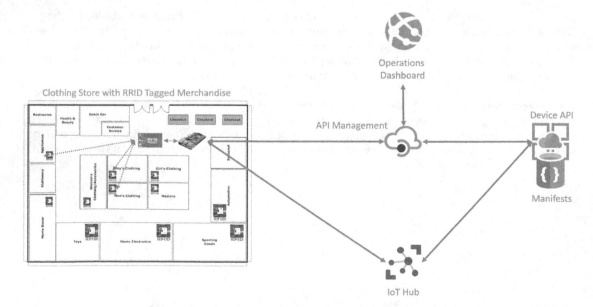

Figure 4-8. Clothing store using RFID to track real-time inventory and product location

Bluetooth Beacons

Bluetooth is a wireless technology standard for exchanging data over short distances. Bluetooth beacons are small, battery powered devices that can be attached to or embedded in things. Any Bluetooth enabled receiver such as a mobile phone or smart device with the Bluetooth stack installed can connect to and communicate with beacons when they are within range. Ranges vary by class of device from less than a meter to upwards of 100 meters (see Figure 4-9).

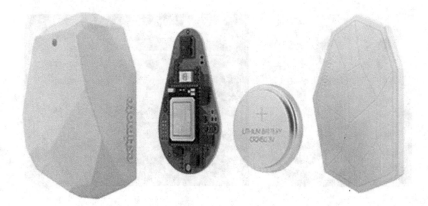

Figure 4-9. *A deconstructed Bluetooth beacon*

A common scenario is to use Bluetooth beacons positioned within a building along with a mobile phone application to provide location awareness. It is possible to use multiple Bluetooth beacons to perform triangulation and determine not only 2D coordinates within a space but also calculate height providing a 3D location (see Figure 4-10). In an assisted living space, this could be used to determine if someone is standing or lying down on the floor possibly needing assistance. An IoT solution could automatically alert first responders, turn off appliances, and unlock the door when first responders arrive.

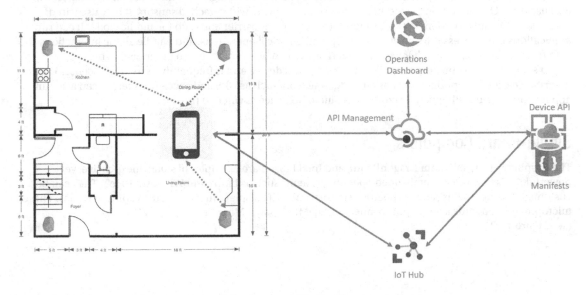

Figure 4-10. *Bluetooth beacons and mobile phone used for location awareness*

Get Smart

Both RFID and Bluetooth beacons are only useful when combined with a smart device. So, what is a smart device? Hollywood has done the bulk of visionary work in this field. One need only look to popular movies and TV to find the early prototypes of devices and technology we now use every day. Don Adams, who starred in the hit TV series *Get Smart* from 1965 to 1970, can be seen in Figure 4-11 demonstrating early versions of smart devices we now use every day.

The Mobile Phone   The Smart Watch   Skype for Business

Figure 4-11. *Visionary prototypes of smart devices (General Artists Corporation-GAC-management. Transferred from en.wikipedia to commons.)*

A smart device, such as a Single-Board Computer (SBC), consists of a credit-card sized microprocessor board with a powerful chipset, memory, storage, and I/O capabilities. It can connect to and read sensors using technologies such as Modbus for PLCs, radio signals for RFID tags, and Bluetooth for beacons. It can also use the I/O channels on the motherboard to communicate with attached sensors. It may use wired, wireless, or a cellular modem to connect to a local network or carrier and onto the public cloud. It can run applications that process the sensor data, apply mathematical operations, and handle all the interactions with the cloud and APIs. In other words, a smart device can be as smart as you program it to be.

It's important to note that a mobile phone is a smart device and is frequently used in IoT scenarios as described earlier. The phone itself has embedded sensors such as GPS and accelerometers. It can also run applications that use Bluetooth to connect to Bluetooth beacons when in proximity.

Single-Board Computers

The Raspberry Pi, Qualcomm DragonBoard, and Intel Edison are examples of small, inexpensive, yet powerful SBCs that can run embedded operating systems such as Linux and Windows 10 IoT. They can be customized using shields (add-on boards), sensors, and LCD displays that attach using pins or cables. These microprocessor boards also support connecting HDMI displays, MicroSD cards, and USB devices (see Figure 4-12).

Raspberry Pi   Intel Edison   Qualcomm DragonBoard

Figure 4-12. *Example SBCs with shields and sensor kits*

SBCs can be used to prototype your IoT hardware solution and even become the foundation of your device ecosystem. You may need to enclose your SBC in light to heavy industrial materials depending on the environmental conditions into which the device will be deployed (see Figure 4-13). Is the device indoors or outdoors or exposed to extreme heat or cold, dust, humidity, or vibration? This needs to be considered when designing your hardware solution.

- Plastic
  Enclosure

- Plastic and
  Metal Enclosure

- Metal
  Enclosure

Figure 4-13. *Examples of Raspberry Pi enclosures*

To develop the embedded microcontroller software, Microsoft provides IoT Device SDKs across several different programming languages, including Python, Node.js, Java, C, C++, and C#.

■ **Note**   For detailed information on the Azure IoT SDKs, see https://github.com/Azure/azure-iot-sdks.

Azure IoT Device SDKs can be used with a broad range of operating system (OS) platforms and devices. The minimum requirements are that the device platform:

- *Be capable of establishing an IP connection*: Only IP-capable devices can communicate directly with Azure IoT Hub.

- *Support Transport Layer Security (TLS)*: Required to establish a secure communication channel with Azure IoT Hub.

- *Support SHA-256*: Necessary to generate the secure token for authenticating the device with the service.

- *Have a Real-Time Clock or Implement Code to Connect to a Network Time Protocol (NTP) Server*: Necessary for establishing the TLS connection and for generating the secure token for authentication.

- *Have at Least 64KB of RAM*: The memory footprint of the SDK depends on the SDK and protocol used as well as the platform targeted. The smallest footprint is achieved using the C SDK targeting microcontrollers.

You can find an exhaustive list of the OS platforms the various SDKs have been tested against in the Azure Certified for IoT device catalog (see Figure 4-14). Note that you might still be able to use the SDKs on OS and hardware platforms that are not listed. All the SDKs are open source and designed to be portable. The *Azure-Certified IoT Device Catalog* is located at https://catalog.azureiotsuite.com/.

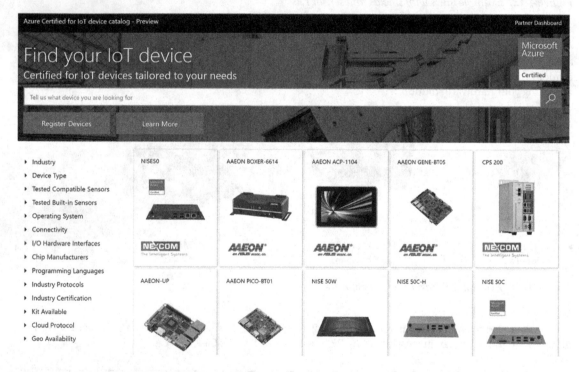

Figure 4-14. *Azure-certified IoT device catalog*

Microcontroller Software

Now that you have a small compact device that is running a modern, secure, embedded operating system, and full networking stack, you can leverage that power to implement the controller software that will read sensor data and integrate directly with IoT Hub and the ReST APIs.

There are three core messaging patterns employed by smart devices:

- *Heartbeat*: Send an occasional ping message at regular intervals

- *Telemetry*: Send telemetry at regular intervals often

- *Command and Control*: Receive incoming commands and data

As covered in Chapter 3, IoT Hub provides two additional message patterns that are variations of command and control:

- *Device Twin Events*: Receive device property change events

- *Direct Methods*: Provide function handlers for remote request/response invocations

Each of these operations is handled asynchronously, ensuring that the device is performant and no single operation blocks the others.

In addition to the device client SDK, we want to invoke our Device API to retrieve the device manifest. If you recall, the device manifest contains the URI to your instance of IoT Hub and the symmetric key for the device to authenticate. The following C# example demonstrates what the startup sequence would be for a device running Windows 10 IoT.

```csharp
// reference the Azure Devices Client SDK
using Microsoft.Azure.Devices.Client;
...
// device constants; Id, Device API and Dev Key
private const string DeviceSerialNumber = "[your-device-id]";
private const string DeviceApi =
    "https://[your-apim-host].azure-
        api.net/dev/v1/device/manifests/id/" + DeviceSerialNumber;
private const string SubscriptionKey =
    "subscription-key=[your-apim-devkey]";
...
// properties for manifest and IoT Hub client
private static Manifest _deviceManifest;
private static DeviceClient _deviceClient;
...
// invoke the Device API to retrieve the device manifest
_deviceManifest = await GetDeviceManifest();
// connect to IoT Hub
_deviceClient = DeviceClient.Create(
  _deviceManifest.Hub,
  AuthenticationMethodFactory.
    CreateAuthenticationWithRegistrySymmetricKey(
      _deviceManifest.SerialNumber,
      _deviceManifest.Key.PrimaryKey),
  TransportType.Amqp);
```

These few lines of code provide secure integration with your cloud services (see Figure 4-15). We examine this code in more detail later in this chapter as you create your own smart device-embedded software.

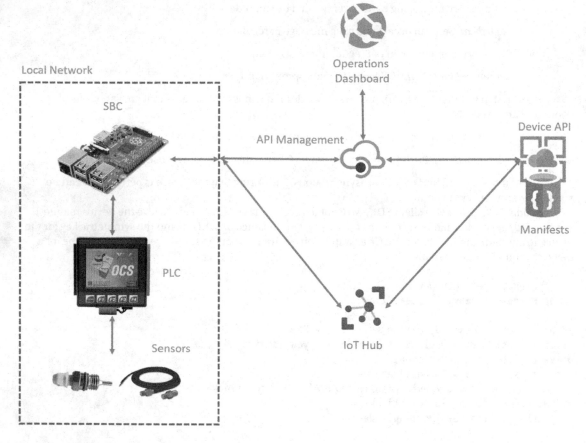

Figure 4-15. *Smart device integration to the cloud services*

Edge Gateways

Edge gateways are powerful smart devices that act as intermediaries between an ecosystem of devices and the cloud. By introducing this intermediary, you can apply more advanced operations on the sensor data locally before it is sent to the cloud. These local operations include but are not limited to:

- *Aggregation*: Build a collection of sensor readings

- *Logging*: Provide a transient store of the most recent events, collections, alerts, etc.

- *Analytics*: Apply mathematical operations to a collection of sensor readings such as average, standard deviation, Fast Fourier Transform, linear regression, etc.

- *Filtering*: Apply a filter to a collection of sensor readings

- *Rules*: Apply business rules defined by upper and lower thresholds defined by the sensor properties

- *Alerts*: Identify out-of-bounds readings and signal alerts using physical notifications such as flashing lights and whirring sirens or leveraging cellular capabilities to send text and voice messages

- *Windowing*: Collect telemetry and/or alert conditions over a defined period of time and only report when a windowing threshold has been exceeded, e.g., perform an alert when there are more than five errors every minute

The microcontroller software running on an edge gateway device defines a data pipeline for each type of telemetry it is responsible for. The data pipeline is made up of one or more modules that act on the data flowing through the pipeline. The order of operations matters, and you also want to be able to configure the modules at runtime.

Microsoft provides the Azure IoT Gateway SDK to assist in the development of edge gateways. This SDK provides a framework for defining pluggable modules that communicate through a message broker backbone. Each module you define and configure performs its operation on the oncoming message(s) and writes a possibly transformed message back to the broker for the next module.

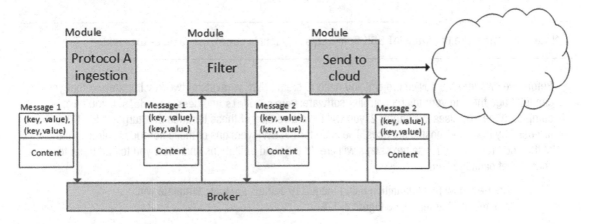

Figure 4-16. *Azure IoT gateway architecture*

■ **Note**   For more information on the Azure IOT Gateway SDK, see `https://azure.microsoft.com/en-us/services/iot-hub/iot-gateway-sdk/`.

In the following exercises, you learn how to create a simple smart device and deploy an application to an SBC. In addition, you will update the device simulator that is used to generate the biometric data for the IoT solution.

CREATE A SMART DEVICE

In this exercise, you create a basic smart device using the C# language and the Universal Windows Application (UWP) template. By using this template, the solution can run locally on your desktop providing you a simulator, and it can be deployed to an SBC running Windows 10 IoT.

Requirements for this exercise:

- Windows 10 Operating System

- Visual Studio 2015 with Update 3

- Windows 10 SDK

- Windows 10 Core IoT Visual Studio Templates

- Azure IoT SDK

■ **Note**   You can clone the Azure IoT SDK from `https://github.com/Azure/azure-iot-sdks`.

Before we dive into the device project, you need to create UWP versions of two key libraries so that you can leverage them in your microcontroller software: `DeviceModels` and `MessageModels`. If you have completed the exercises in Chapter 2, you will have a version of these libraries that target .NET 4.6 and are used by the cloud-hosted services. The code for the UWP versions of these libraries is already part of the code repository. These next steps will create the build definitions and allow you to add them to your NuGet package feed.

1. Create a new build definition using the `Build NuGet Package` template you created in Chapter 2 (see Figure 4-17).

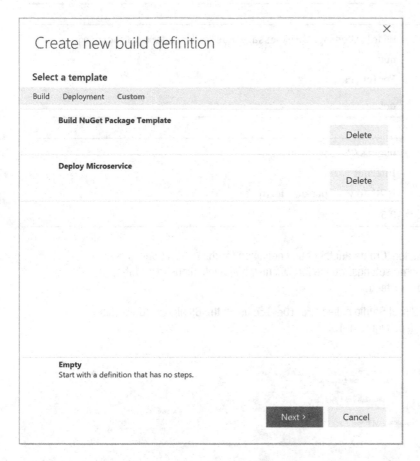

Figure 4-17. Create a build definition from the template

2. Fill out the build definition settings for the MessageModelUWP solution as shown in Table 4-1. This solution has been provided as part of the reference implementation repo.

Table 4-1. *Build MessageModelUWP NuGet Package Build Definition*

NuGet Installer Settings	
Path to solution	Models/Message/UWP/MessageModels.sln
Path to NuGet.Config	nuget.config
NuGet arguments	-outputdirectory packages
NuGet version	3.5

MSBuild Settings	
Path to solution	models/Message/UWP/MessageModels.sln
Configuration	debug

(continued)

Table 4-1. (*continued*)

NuGet Packager

Path to CSProj	models\Message\UWP\MessageModels\MessageModels.csproj
Package Folder	nugets
Include referenced projects	Yes (checked)
Configuration to package	debug

NuGet Publisher

Path to NuPkg	nugets/Message*.nupkg
Feed type	Internal
Internal feed URL	[URL to your package feed]
NuGet Version	3.5

3. Save the build definition. Create another build definition for the DeviceModelsUWP solution using the same settings. Queue the two new build definitions to add these NuGet packages to your feed.

4. Create a project in Visual Studio called SmartDevice using the Blank App (Universal Windows) template (see Figure 4-18).

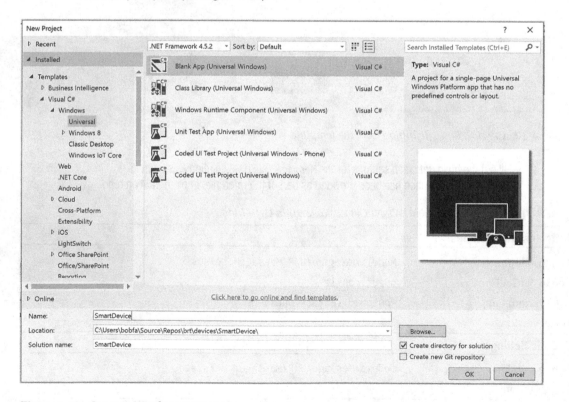

Figure 4-18. *Create a Windows universal app project*

You will be presented with a dialog box that informs you the target version and minimum version of Windows 10 that will be supported by the project (see Figure 4-19). Select the defaults.

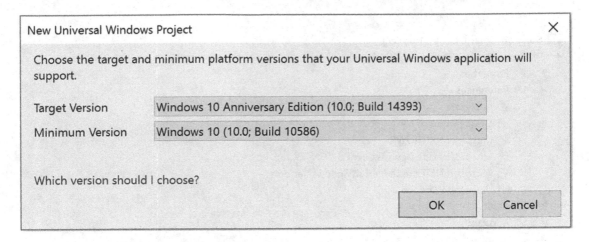

Figure 4-19. *New universal Windows project*

5. After the project has finished initializing, right-click on the References node in the Solution Explorer and select Manage NuGet Packages from the menu.

Select NuGet.org as the package source location and search for Azure.Devices. Add a reference to the Microsoft.Azure.Devices.Client NuGet package. Also add a reference to the Newtonsoft.Json NuGet package.

Select your NuGet feed as the package source and add a reference to the DeviceModelUWP and MessagesModelUWP NuGet packages that you just created. When complete, your solution references should appear as depicted in Figure 4-20.

Figure 4-20. *SmartDevice references*

6. Open the `MainPage.xaml.cs` file and add these `using` statements at the top.

```
using Microsoft.Azure.Devices.Client;
using brt.Models.Message;
using brt.Models.Device;
using Newtonsoft.JSON;
```

You will need a unique ID for your smart device. We registered several devices using the Bootstrap utility in Chapter 2. You can use the Device Explorer utility that is part of the Azure IoT SDK to look up a registered device Id in IoT Hub to use for your smart device.

■ **Tip**   The Device Explorer can be found in the C# IoT SDK `azure-iot-sdk-csharp\tools\DeviceExplorer` folder.

---

7. Open the Device Explorer solution in another instance of Visual Studio and run the app (see Figure 4-21).

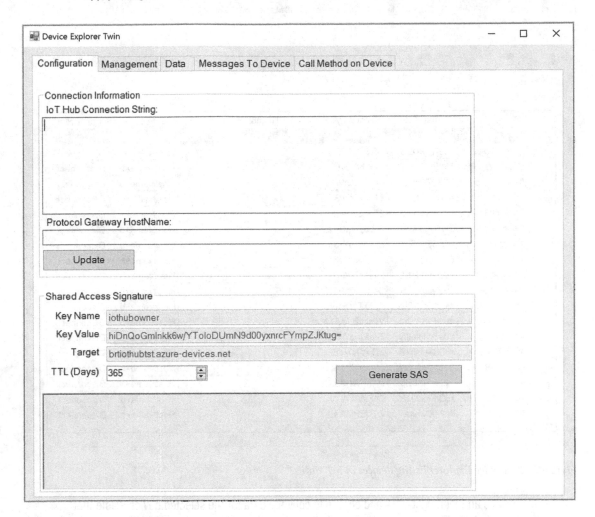

Figure 4-21. *Device Explorer*

Enter the connection string to your instance of IoT Hub on the Configuration tab and click the Update button. Navigate to the Management tab and click List (see Figure 4-22).

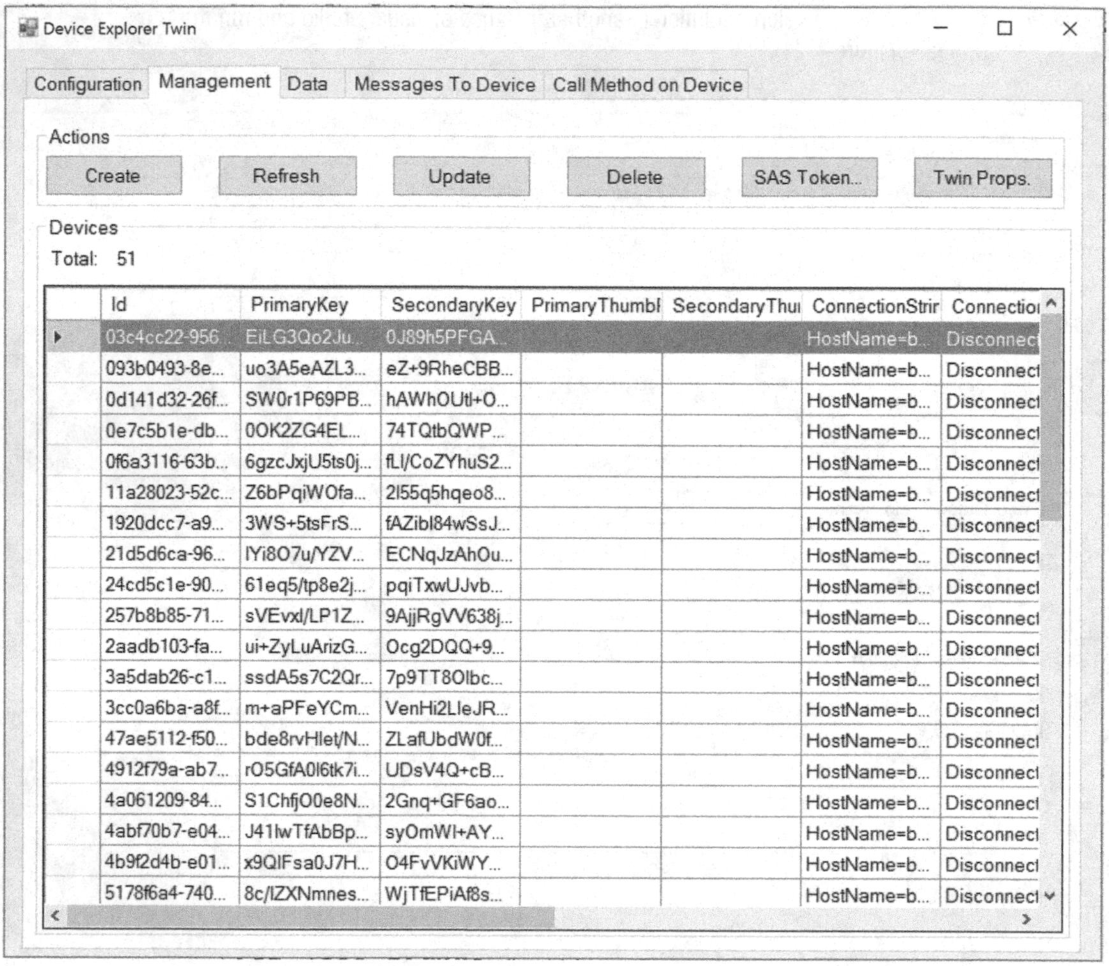

Figure 4-22. *Device Explorer listing devices in IoT Hub*

Select a device and then right-click and choose to copy the data for the selected device. Paste that information into Notepad so that you can access the unique ID to use as the smart device serial number.

You will also need your API Management hostname and developer key to initialize the properties that define device identity. You can retrieve those settings from the API Management Developer portal.

8. Add the following class variables to the MainPage class in your UWP solution. Use the device ID that you copied from the Device Explorer to use as the device serial number. Update the API URIs to use your APIM hostname and subscription key.

```
// Device Identity
private const string DeviceSerialNumber = "[device-id]";
private const string DeviceApi = "https://[your-apim-
    host].azure-api.net/dev/v1/device/manifests/id/" + DeviceSerialNumber;
```

```
private const string SubscriptionKey =
    "subscription-key=[your-apim-devkey] ";
private static Manifest _deviceManifest;
private static DeviceClient _deviceClient;

// Thread Management
private static Task _heartbeatTask;
private static Task _telemetryTask;
```

9. Open the `MainPage.xaml` file and add a `MainPage_OnLoaded()` event handler to the `<Page>` element. The handler is defined in the XAML file and the function is generated in the `MainPage.xaml.cs` file.

```
<Page
...
    Loaded="MainPage_OnLoaded">
...
</Page>
```

10. Add the `async` keyword to the method signature of `MainPage_OnLoaded()`.

```
private async void MainPage_OnLoaded(
  object sender, RoutedEventArgs e)
{
  throw new System.NotImplementedException();
}
```

11. In the `Mainpage.Xaml` file, replace the `<Grid>` element section with this XAML code:

```
<Grid Background="{ ThemeResource
    ApplicationPageBackgroundThemeBrush}">
  <Grid.RowDefinitions>
    <RowDefinition Height="50*"/>
    <RowDefinition Height="50*"/>
  </Grid.RowDefinitions>

  <TextBlock Grid.Row="0"
          HorizontalAlignment="Center"
          VerticalAlignment="Center"
          FontSize="24">
      Windows 10 IoT Device
  </TextBlock>
  <StackPanel Grid.Row="1" Margin="10,10,10,10">
  <TextBox x:Name="Status"
          Margin="10"
          IsReadOnly="True"
          TextAlignment="Center" />
  </StackPanel>
</Grid>
```

12. Add two `private static` method stubs for the code that will handle the background messaging threads.

```
private static void StartHeartbeat()
{
}

private static void StartTelemetry()
{
}
```

13. Add a `private static` method called `GetDeviceManifest()` that invokes the Device API to retrieve the device manifest.

```
private static async Task<Manifest> GetDeviceManifest()
{
  var client = new HttpClient();
  var uriBuilder = new UriBuilder(DeviceApi)
  {
    Query = SubscriptionKey
  };

  var json = await client.GetStringAsync(uriBuilder.Uri);
  var deviceManifest =
    JsonConvert.DeserializeObject<Manifest>(json);

  return deviceManifest;
}
```

14. Replace the body of the `MainPage_OnLoaded()` event handler with this code.

```
Status.Text = "Main Page Loaded";

// get the device manifest
_deviceManifest = await GetDeviceManifest();

try
{
  // connect to IoT Hub
  _deviceClient = DeviceClient.Create(
    _deviceManifest.Hub,
    AuthenticationMethodFactory
      .CreateAuthenticationWithRegistrySymmetricKey(
        _deviceManifest.SerialNumber,
        _deviceManifest.Key.PrimaryKey),
    TransportType.Amqp);

  Status.Text = $"{_deviceManifest.SerialNumber}
    Connected to Azure IoT Hub";
}
```

CHAPTER 4 ■ SENSORS, DEVICES, AND GATEWAYS

```
catch (Exception connectionErr)
{
    Status.Text = connectionErr.Message;
}


StartHeartbeat();
StartTelemetry();
```

This code will invoke the Device API to retrieve the device manifest and connect to IoT Hub using properties of the device manifest. If successful, a status message is displayed on the application user interface.

To implement the heartbeat message pattern, we will start a background task and within that task continuously send heartbeat messages based on the cadence setting, which is defined as an extension property in the device manifest. The heartbeat message is defined in the `MessageModelsUWP` library. It is a simple message that contains an acknowledgement string, the device serial number, and the longitude and latitude of the device.

15. Add the following code to the body of the `StartHeartbeat()` method.

```
var cadence = Convert.ToInt32(
    _deviceManifest.Extensions["heartbeat"]);

_heartbeatTask = Task.Factory.StartNew(async () =>
{
  while (true)
  {
    // create a heartbeat message
    var heartbeat = new Heartbeat
    {
      Ack =
       $"{_deviceManifest.SerialNumber} is functioning",
      Longitude = _deviceManifest.Longitude,
      Latitude = _deviceManifest.Latitude,
      DeviceId = _deviceManifest.SerialNumber
    };

    var json = JsonConvert.SerializeObject(heartbeat);

    var message = new Message(
        Encoding.ASCII.GetBytes(json));

    await _deviceClient.SendEventAsync(message);

    await Task.Delay(cadence);
  }
});
```

16. To test your smart device, start the Device Explorer utility, select the Data tab, and begin monitoring for messages arriving from your device by selecting its ID from the drop-down.

Start your Smart Device application. It will begin sending a heartbeat message every 30 seconds (see Figure 4-23).

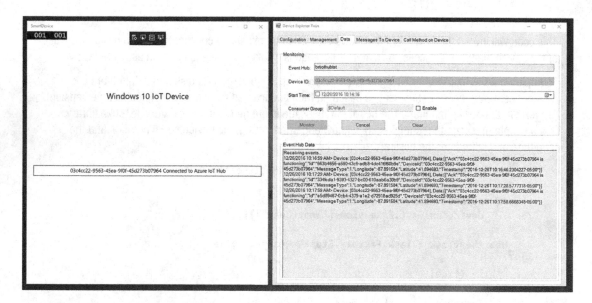

Figure 4-23. *Smart device sending heartbeat messages*

At this point we do not have any connected sensors. We will simulate taking a temperature with an expected range of values between 60 and 70. These readings will be sent more often than heartbeat messages. We will use the `SimpleSensorReading` class as defined in the `MessageModelsUWP` library. Like the heartbeat message, it will contain the device serial number and the longitude and latitude. In addition, it will contain a floating point reading for the simulated temperature.

17. Add the following code to the `StartTelemetry()` method.

```
var cadence = Convert.ToInt32(
  _deviceManifest.Extensions["telemetry"]);

var random = new Random();

_telemetryTask = Task.Factory.StartNew(async () =>
{
  while (true)
  {
    // the temperature will be simulated
    // it will be a value between 60 and 70
```

```
var sensorReading = new SimpleSensorReading
{
  Longitude = _deviceManifest.Longitude,
  Latitude = _deviceManifest.Latitude,
  DeviceId = _deviceManifest.SerialNumber,
  Reading = random.Next(60, 70)
  };

var json =
  JsonConvert.SerializeObject(sensorReading);

var message = new Message(
  Encoding.ASCII.GetBytes(json));

await _deviceClient.SendEventAsync(message);

await Task.Delay(cadence);
}
});
```

18. Run the Smart Device application and review the incoming messages in IoT Hub using the Device Explorer. You should see multiple telemetry messages arriving and an occasional heartbeat (see Figure 4-24).

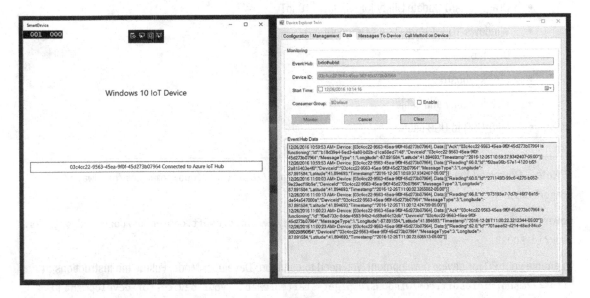

Figure 4-24. *Heartbeat and telemetry arriving in IoT Hub*

DEPLOY YOUR SMART DEVICE APP TO AN SBC

Now that we have a functioning Smart Device simulator application, we can deploy it to an SBC. In this exercise, you will update your Smart Device app to use a temperature sensor attached to a Qualcomm DragonBoard. Note that this exercise is not a requirement for going through the other exercises in the book. It is provided here for completeness.

■ **Note**   To do this exercise, you need a Qualcomm DragonBoard and the 96Boards Linker Starter Kit.

To purchase a Qualcomm DragonBoard, visit `https://www.arrow.com/en/products/dragonboard410ciotsdk/arrow-development-tools`.

To purchase the 96Board Linker Starter Kit, visit `https://www.arrow.com/en/products/96boards-starter-kit/linksprite-technologies-inc`.

The requirements for this exercise are as follows:

- DragonBoard 410c
- 96Boards Linker Starter Kit
- DragonBoard Update Utility for Windows 10 IoT
- Windows 10 IoT Core OS for DragonBoard
- USB mouse
- USB keyboard
- HDMI display and cable
- Mini-USB to USB cable

■ **Note**   Download the DragonBoard Update utility at `https://developer.qualcomm.com/hardware/dragonboard-410c/tools`.

Download Windows 10 IoT Core for DragonBoard at `https://www.microsoft.com/en-us/download/details.aspx?id=50038`.

To enable your PC for device development, you need to configure Developer Mode. Follow the instructions at `https://msdn.microsoft.com/windows/uwp/get-started/enable-your-device-for-development` to configure your PC.

The DragonBoard 410c is a single-board computer built around a Qualcomm® Snapdragon™ 400 series processor. It features advanced processing power, Wi-Fi, Bluetooth, and GPS, all packed into a board the size of a credit card. Based on the 64-bit capable Snapdragon 410E processor, the DragonBoard 410c is designed to support Linux- or Windows-based software development (see Figure 4-25).

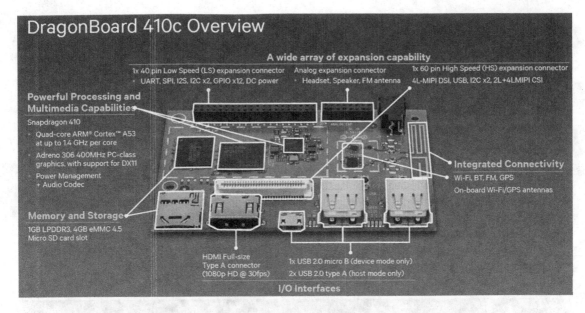

Figure 4-25. *DragonBoard 410c overview*

1. Set up your hardware as depicted in Figure 4-26. The DragonBoard is connected to an HDMI display and to your development laptop using a mini-USB cable. There is also a USB mouse and USB keyboard attached to the DragonBoard.

Figure 4-26. *DragonBoard setup*

■ **Note** It is recommended that whenever you make changes to the hardware configuration of the board, that you power down the DragonBoard and remove the power cable.

2. Flash the DragonBoard with the Windows 10 Core IoT operating system.

    ● Plug the HDMI adapter, the USB keyboard, and mouse into the DragonBoard.

    ● Use the mini-USB to USB adapter to connect the board to your PC.

■ **Note** The detailed instructions on how to flash the DragonBoard using the DragonBoard Update Utility and Windows 10 IoT Core are located at https://developer.microsoft.com/en-us/windows/iot/Docs/ GetStarted/dragonboard/GetStartedStep1.htm.

Once the device has been flashed and connected to your wireless network, you can manage the device using the Windows Device portal. The Windows Device portal is an application that is part of Windows 10 IoT Core and is running locally on the DragonBoard. This application is accessible from your PC by using a browser and navigating to the home page of the application running on the device. You will need the IP address of your device on you network. The DragonBoard home screen will display the device IP address, as shown in Figure 4-27.

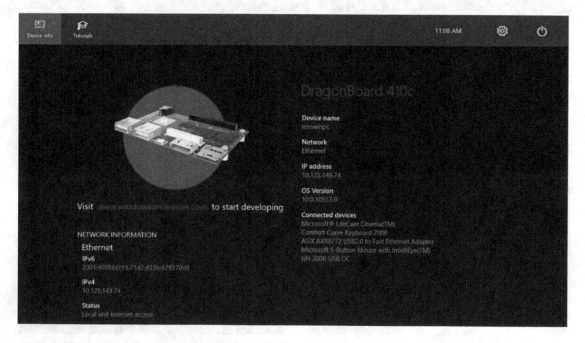

Figure 4-27. *DragonBoard home screen*

3. Using a browser, navigate to http://[deviceIP]:8080 and log in to the device portal using the default username and password:

    Username: Administrator
    Password: p@ssw0rd.

Using this application, you can manage the device name, administrator password, and many other features of the device by navigating through the menu on the left side of the user interface (see Figure 4-28).

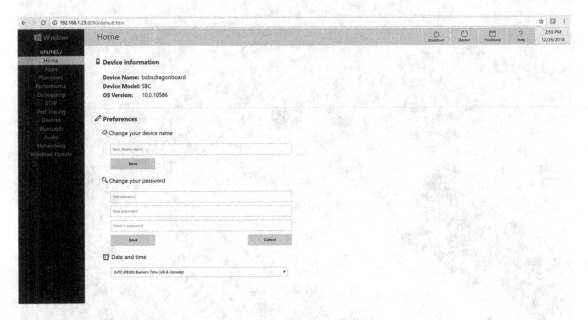

Figure 4-28. *Windows device portal*

All the Linker kit sensors can be added to the DragonBoard through the Linker mezzanine card. The Linker mezzanine card has eight connectors supporting Analog, UART, I2C, and GPIO, and two channels of analog input using the MCP3004 ADC chip. There are bidirectional voltage-level translators, which allow for low-voltage bidirectional translation between any of the 1.2-V,1.5-V, 1.8-V, 2.5-V, 3.3-V, and 5-V voltage nodes. It is compatible with 3.3V or 5V modules and makes connecting peripherals easy. You can select the appropriate voltage by placing a jumper on the JP9 voltage selector. We will be using the mezzanine in 5-V mode as that is what is required by the sensors we are going to attach.

4. Power down the device and remove the keyboard and mouse. Set the voltage to 5V using the JP9 jumper, as shown in Figure 4-29.

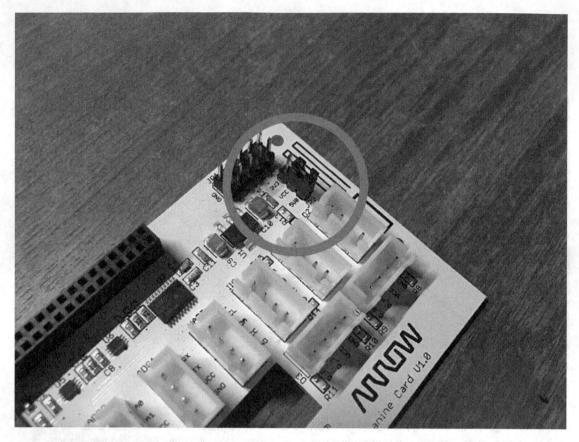

Figure 4-29. *Set the voltage jumper to 5V*

5. Stack the mezzanine board on top of the DragonBoard and carefully insert the general-purpose I/O (GPIO) prongs into the GPIO connectors on the DragonBoard (see Figure 4-30).

Figure 4-30. *Before and after stacking the mezzanine*

6. Attach the red LED sensor and the thermal sensor as shown in Figure 4-31.

   - Using an adapter cable, attach one end to the red LED module and the other to the connector labeled DC2 on the Linker mezzanine.

   - Using a second adapter cable, attach one end to the thermal sensor and the other to the connector labeled ADC1 on the Linker mezzanine.

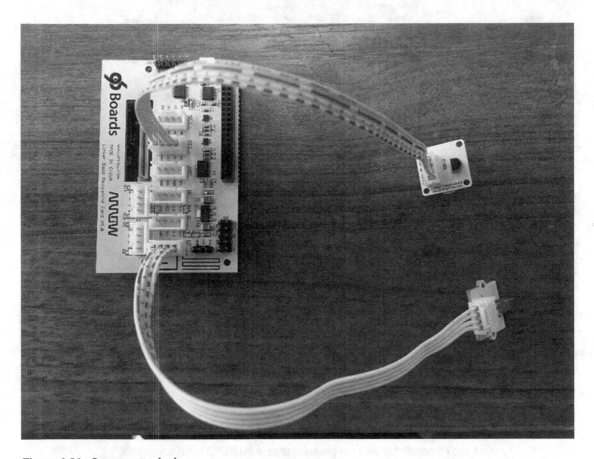

Figure 4-31. *Sensors attached*

7. Attach the keyboard, mouse, and HDMI monitor to the power cable. You are now ready to test the full hardware configuration.

8. Add a reference to the Windows IoT Extensions for UWP to your Smart Device solution. This library will provide high-level classes for working with single-board computers.

Right-click on the References node in the Solution Explorer and select Add Reference. Select Universal Windows ➤ Extensions in the left menu. Check the box next to the Windows IoT Extensions for the UWP for version 10.0.14393 and then click OK (see Figure 4-32).

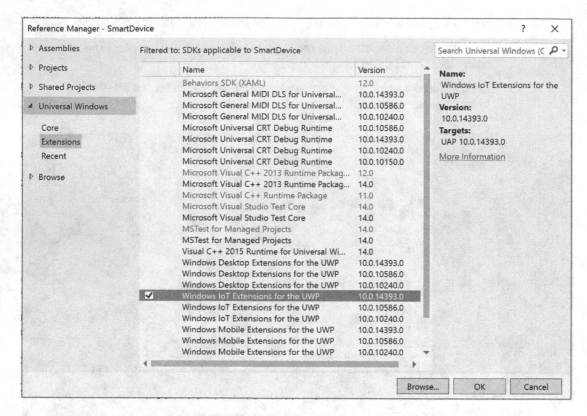

Figure 4-32. *Add a reference to the Windows IoT extensions*

9. Add the following `using` statements at the top of the `MainPage.xaml.cs` file:

```
using Windows.Devices.Gpio;
using Windows.Devices.Spi;
using Windows.Devices.Enumeration;
```

10. Add the following `private` variables to the `MainPage` class. These are used to connect and communicate with the general-purpose I/O (GPIO) interface and the serial peripheral interface (SPI) bus.

```
// GPIO
private static GpioPinValue _value;
private const int LedPin = 13;
private static GpioPin _led;

// SPI
private static byte[] _readBuffer =
    new byte[3] { 0x00, 0x00, 0x00 };
private static byte[] _writeBuffer =
    new byte[3] { 0x01, 0x80, 0x00 };
```

```
private const string SpiControllerName = "SPI0";
private const int SpiChipSelectLine = 0;
private static SpiDevice _spiDisplay;
```

11. Add a `private static` method to initialize the GPIO. The GPIO interface will be used to turn the red LED on and off.

```
private static void InitGPIO()
{
  _led = GpioController.GetDefault().OpenPin(LedPin);
  _led.Write(GpioPinValue.Low);
  _led.SetDriveMode(GpioPinDriveMode.Output);
}
```

12. Add an asynchronous `private static` method to turn the LED on and off. This is done by setting the value of the LED pin location to high (on), sleeping for some number of milliseconds, and then setting the pin to low (off). This will cause the LED light to blink on and then off.

```
public static async void BlinkLED(int duration)
{
  _led.Write(GpioPinValue.High);
  await Task.Delay(duration);
  _led.Write(GpioPinValue.Low);
}
```

13. Add a `private static` method to initialize the SPI. The SPI will be used to communicate with the temperature sensor using the analog-to-digital converter on the mezzanine board.

```
private static async void InitSPI()
{
  try
  {
    var settings =
      new SpiConnectionSettings(SpiChipSelectLine)
    {
      ClockFrequency = 500000,
      Mode = SpiMode.Mode0
    };

    var spiAqs = SpiDevice.GetDeviceSelector(
      SpiControllerName);
    var deviceInfo = await
      DeviceInformation.FindAllAsync(spiAqs);

    _spiDisplay = await SpiDevice.FromIdAsync(
      deviceInfo[0].Id, settings);
  }
```

```
  catch (Exception ex)
  {
    throw new Exception("SPI Initialization Failed", ex);
  }
}
```

14. Add a `private static` helper method to convert the byte array returned from the sensor into a floating-point value.

```
public static double ConvertToDouble(byte[] data)
{
  int result = 0;
  int i = Convert.ToInt32("1100000000", 2);
  result = (data[1] << 8) & i;
  result |= (data[2] & 0xff);
  return result;
}
```

15. Update the `StartTelemetry()` method to use the SPI interface to read the temperature sensor and set that as the temperature reading of the simple sensor message. This replaces the use of the random number generator.

```
// get the temperature setting from the sensor
_spiDisplay.TransferFullDuplex(
  _writeBuffer, _readBuffer);

// convert the value to Fahrenheit
var temperature = ConvertToDouble(_readBuffer);
temperature = (((temperature * 5.0) /
  (1023 - 0.5)) * 100);

var sensorReading = new SimpleSensorReading
{
  Longitude = _deviceManifest.Longitude,
  Latitude = _deviceManifest.Latitude,
  DeviceId = _deviceManifest.SerialNumber,
  Reading = temperature
};
```

16. Add a call to the `BlinkLED()` method right after sending the temperature message to IoT Hub. Pass in a value of 500ms for the duration of the blink.

```
await _deviceClient.SendEventAsync(message);
BlinkLED(500);
```

17. Update the start of the `MainPage_OnLoaded()` method to call the `GPIOInit()` and `SPIInit()` methods.

```
Status.Text = "Main Page Loaded";
InitGPIO();
Status.Text = "GPIO Initialized";
InitSPI();
Status.Text = "SPI Initialized";
```

That's it. We are now ready to test our smart device.

18. To deploy the application to the device, set the Build Target to ARM and then select Remote Machine, as shown in Figure 4-33.

Figure 4-33. *Configure Visual Studio to build and deploy a solution to a remote device*

The first time you do this Visual Studio will request the IP address of the device. Provide the IP address from the DragonBoard home screen, as shown in Figure 4-34, and click Select.

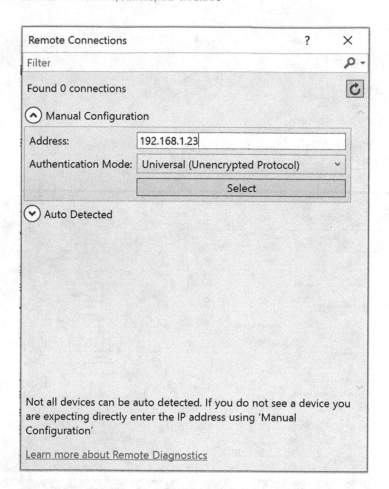

Figure 4-34. *Setting the IP address of your SBC in Visual Studio*

19. Run the application using the Visual Studio debugger. The applications will be built and deployed to your DragonBoard. You will see the UI on your HDMI display and you can track the incoming heartbeat and temperature messages on your PC using the Device Explorer utility, as shown in Figure 4-35.

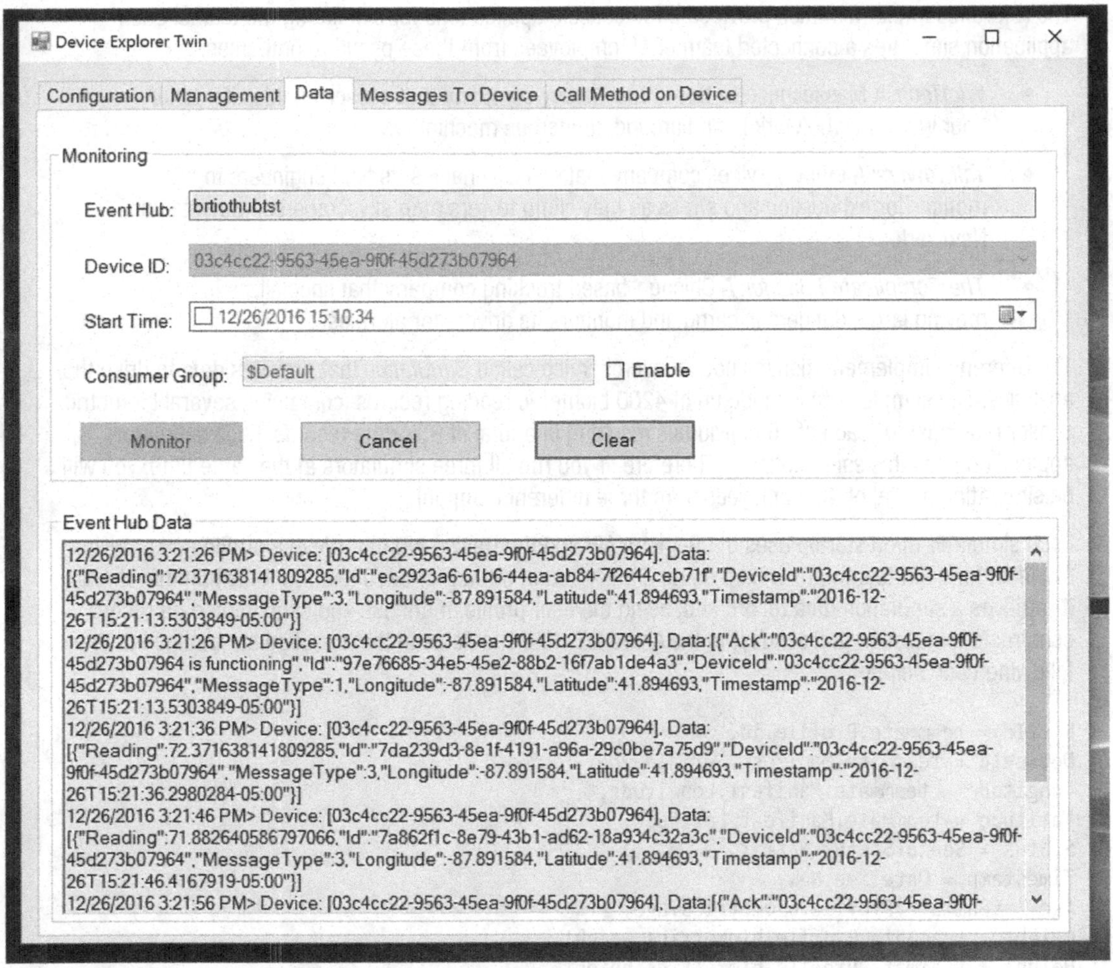

Figure 4-35. DragonBoard sending heartbeat and temperature sensor messages to IoT Hub

---

■ **Note** You can use Visual Studio to set breakpoints and do remote debugging using this configuration.

MODIFY THE TEAM SIMULATORS

The Real-Time Business reference implementation is a multi-tenant solution. It provides a common set of platform services that can be used by many customers at the same time, providing secure access to data for each customer.

In our scenario, each company has defined groups of employees called *teams,* where each member of the team is connected to the cloud using a sensor-enabled vest. Companies can monitor biometric readings from individual employees, which are then routed to advanced analytics services to identify exhaustion and stress levels and provide real-time data visualization, alerts, and notifications.

The reference implementation provides three console applications for simulating the teams. Each application simulates a connected team of 15 employees from these pseudo-companies:

- *WigiTech*: A Massachusetts-based technology company that sensor-enables its factory floor workers who work in and around dangerous machinery.

- *Tall Towers*: A utility services company that sensor-enables its field engineers to monitor for exhaustion and stress as they climb towers atop skyscrapers in downtown New York.

- *The Complicated Badger*: A Chicago-based trucking company that specializes in moving large, dangerous cargo and monitors its drivers for alertness.

The reference implementation includes a microservice called *Simulation* that provides data to drive the analytics. The sample data is made up of 4200 biometric reading records (containing several biometric sensor readings) for each of 15 individuals resulting in a total of 63K data records. Each simulator application uses this same data set. Therefore, if you run all three simulators at the same time, you will be simulating a total of 45 employees from three different companies.

Each simulator upon startup uses the Registry API and the Device API to retrieve a profile and a device manifest for each teammate. Next it starts a background thread for each teammate. Within that thread, it retrieves a simulation data record and, using the user profile, manifest, and simulation data record, constructs a message and sends it to the Azure IoT Hub. The fields in the message are outlined in the following code snippet.

```
UserId = teammate.Profile.id,
DeviceId = teammate.Manifest.SerialNumber,
Longitude = teammate.Manifest.Longitude,
Latitude = teammate.Manifest.Latitude,
Status = SensorStatus.Normal,
Timestamp = DateTime.Now,
Age = teammate.Profile.biometrics.age,
Weight = teammate.Profile.biometrics.weight,
Height = teammate.Profile.biometrics.height,
BreathingRate = datarow.columns[0].dataValue,
Ventilation = datarow.columns[1].dataValue,
Activity = datarow.columns[2].dataValue,
HeartRateBPM = datarow.columns[3].dataValue,
Cadence = datarow.columns[4].dataValue,
Velocity = datarow.columns[5].dataValue,
Speed = datarow.columns[6].dataValue,
HIB = datarow.columns[7].dataValue,
HeartrateRedZone = datarow.columns[8].dataValue,
HeartrateVariability = datarow.columns[9].dataValue,
Temperature = datarow.columns[10].dataValue
```

To use the simulators, you need to make some minor updates to each of the three simulator applications so that they use the managed APIs that you deployed using the exercises in Chapter 2. The team simulators are in the `devices/device-teamsim` folder. There you will find a simulator for each pseudo-company.

1. Navigate to the `devices/device-teamsim/wigitech` folder and open the WigiTechSim solution.

2. Open the `App.config` file and update the following configuration settings:

   `<add key="DeviceAPI" value="https://`**`[your-apim-host]`**`.azure-api.net/ dev/v1/device/manifests" />`

   `<add key="RegistryAPI" value="https://`**`[your-apim-host]`**`.azure-api.net/ dev/v1/registry/profiles" />`

   `<add key="SimulationAPI" value="https://`**`[your-apim-host]`**`.azure-api.net/ dev/v1/simulation/datasets" />`

   `<add key="SubscriptionKey" value="subscription-key=`**`[your-dev-key]`**`" />`

3. Do this for each of the other simulator applications as well.

4. Start the Device Explorer and each of the three simulator applications. Once they are connected to IoT Hub and are sending data, you can use the Device Explorer to check the messages coming from the devices associated with each of the simulators (see Figure 4-36).

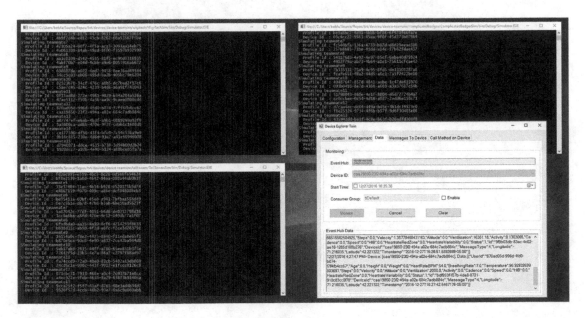

Figure 4-36. *Three simulators and the Device Explorer*

Each of the device serial numbers is displayed in the console window so that you can easily correlate them to the Device Explorer.

Summary

This chapter examined the rich and wonderful world of sensors and devices and the various ways different configurations can connect to Azure IoT Hub. It examined GSM modems, single-board computer smart devices, and edge gateways. You learned about the Protocol Gateway SDK and how you can use that to provide a translation layer between legacy devices and the new cloud services. You examined the architecture of edge gateways and the IoT Gateway SDK and how to use these devices to provide aggregation, filtering, and analytics at the edge.

Through the exercises, you learned how to implement the microcontroller software that runs on your remote devices, reads sensors, and sends messages to IoT Hub. Finally, you configured the team simulators so you can drive a feature-rich set of advanced analytics provided by the reference implementation.

The next set of chapters turns to those advanced analytics and leverages the data coming from the simulators. They cover stream analytics, data factory, data lake, and Machine Learning.

CHAPTER 5

∎ ∎ ∎

Real-Time Processing Using Azure Stream Analytics

This chapter examines the use of Microsoft Azure Streaming Analytics to create jobs to process the incoming data streams from various sensors, perform data transformations and enrichment, and finally, to provide output results into various data formats.

It has been said that the cloud represents a *once-in-a-generation technology transformation*. Certainly, one of the cornerstones of this key transformation is the ability to efficiently ingest, process, and report on massive amounts of data at scale.

The Lambda Architecture

In today's modern data analytics, a new stream processing strategy has been proposed—the "Lambda" architecture—and has been widely attributed to Nathan Marz, the creator of Apache Storm.

The fundamental essence of the Lambda architecture is that it's designed to ingest massive quantities of incoming data by taking advantage of batch and stream processing methodologies. Additional attributes of the Lambda architecture include the following:

- Ability to process a vast array of workloads and scenarios.

- High throughput characterized by low-latency reads with frequent writes and updates.

- Retaining the incoming data in the original format. This is the notion of a "data lake".

- Modeling data transformations as a series of materialized stages from the original data.

- Highly scalable, nearly linear, scale-out infrastructure to provide scale up/down.

Figure 5-1 depicts the Lambda architecture.

© Bob Familiar and Jeff Barnes 2017
B. Familiar and J. Barnes, *Business in Real-Time Using Azure IoT and Cortana Intelligence Suite*,
DOI 10.1007/978-1-4842-2650-6_5

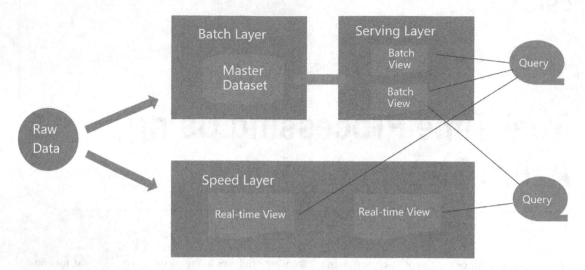

Figure 5-1. *The Lambda architecture*

By merging batch and stream processing in the same architecture, the result is an optimized data analytics engine that is capable of not just processing the data, but also of delivering the right data at the right time.

It should be noted that this new just-in-time (JIT) data that can now be surfaced with streaming analytics (via the Lambda architecture) can often become the source of many types of competitive advantages for a business or enterprise that knows how to exploit this type of information across a wide array of use cases.

The real magic comes in knowing how to recognize the hidden opportunities buried deep inside the data and from there take action to explore, develop, fail-fast, and finally succeed in evoking true transformational changes in a business or industry. This is basically the essence of this book and the guiding light for our own reference implementation.

Microsoft has recognized the need for streaming analytics at scale as part of today's modern Internet-of-Things (IoT) solutions and has incorporated streaming capabilities into several popular architectures, such as Cortana Analytics along with the IoT Suite offerings shown in Figure 5-2.

Azure IoT Suite Architecture

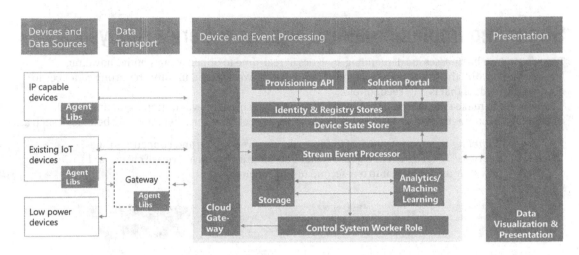

Figure 5-2. *Azure IoT suite architecture*

What Is Streaming Analytics?

One of the real advantages of a great streaming analytics engine is the ability to provide real-time analytics and outputs so that data becomes actionable with a minimum of delay.

To provide context to the challenges involved in developing streaming analytics solution, the best canonical example is a scenario of counting the number of red cars in a parking lot versus counting the number of red cars that pass by any major freeway (assuming it's not rush hour) for every 10 minute interval in a one-hour period (see Figure 5-3).

Figure 5-3. *Challenges of streaming analytics*

The essence of this scenario is "data in motion" versus "data at rest". The key difference here is the element of "time" and the ability to capture and analyze periodic "slices" of data across potentially millions of events in order to detect patterns and anomalies in the massive amounts of streaming data.

Real-Time Analytics

Real-time analytics is all about the ability to process data coming from literally millions of connected devices or applications, with the inherent ability to ingest and process potentially millions of events per second. A key component of this scenario is integration with a highly-scalable publish/subscribe pattern. Another key requirement is for simplified processing capabilities on continuous streams of data that allow a solution to transform, augment, correlate, and perform temporal (time-based) operations.

171

Correlating streaming data with reference data is also a core requirement in many cases, as the incoming data often needs to be matched with a corresponding host record.

Streaming Implementations and Time-Series Analysis

Today's modern businesses are demanding analytics in real-time to obtain a competitive advantage; they have moved beyond the "old school" method of hourly, daily, weekly, and monthly reporting cadences to now relying on data that is only seconds old.

In order to make streaming analytics and reporting all the more relevant, support for time-window calculations becomes even more imperative. To this end, a set of time-series windows are beneficial such as:

- *Tumbling Windows*: A series of fixed-sized, non-overlapping and contiguous time intervals. The diagram in Figure 5-4 illustrates a stream with a series of events and how they are mapped into ten-second tumbling windows.

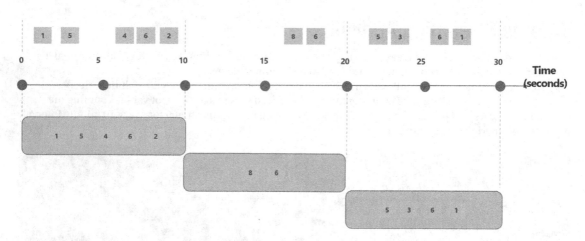

Figure 5-4. *An example of tumbling windows in streaming analytics*

- *Hopping Windows*: Model scheduled overlapping windows. A hopping window specification consist of these parameters:

  - A time unit.

  - A window size, how long each window lasts

  - A hop size, how much each window moves forward relative to the previous one

  - <Optional> Offset size, an optional fourth parameter.

The illustration in Figure 5-5 shows a stream with a series of events. Each box represents a hopping window and the events that are counted as part of that window, assuming that the hop is 5, and the size is 10.

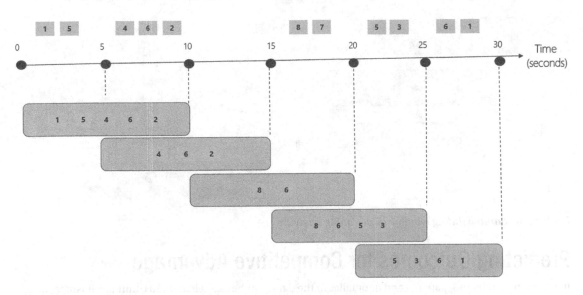

Figure 5-5. *An example of hopping windows in streaming analytics*

- *Sliding Windows*: When using a sliding window, the system is asked to logically consider all possible windows of a given length and output events only for those points in time when the content of the window actually changes, in other words when an event entered or exists the window. Figure 5-6 illustrates a sliding window.

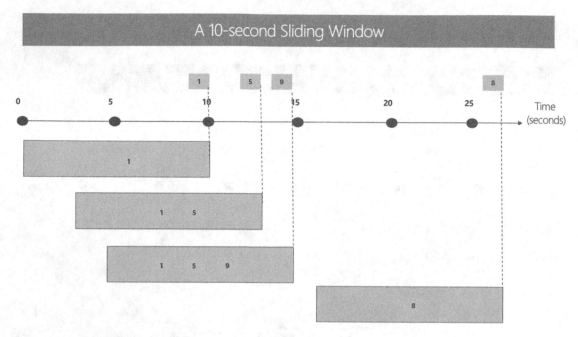

Figure 5-6. *Sample sliding window in streaming analytics*

Predicting Outcomes for Competitive Advantage

In addition to detecting patterns and anomalies in the data, another key element to running a business at Internet speed is the ability to shape new business outcomes by predicting what may happen in the future. This is exactly the problem domain for predictive analytics and Machine Learning, which can use historical data combined with modern data science algorithms to predict a future outcome.

One of the key methods to accelerating business and building a competitive advantage is the ability to automate, supplement, or accelerate key business decision-making processes through the use of predictive analytics and Machine Learning. In today's business world, decisions are made every day, often without all the facts and data, so any additional insights can often result in a huge competitive advantage.

Across many industries and verticals, many bottlenecks can be found today where there is lack of *actionable data*. This is a key area where Azure Stream Analytics and Machine Learning can help reduce friction and accelerate results.

A recent new feature of Azure Streaming Analytics is the ability to directly invoke Azure Machine Learning Web Services as streaming data is processed in order to enrich the incoming data stream or predict outcomes that might in turn, require triggering a notification or alert. This is certainly a key feature and capability and so we will cover this in all in detail in Chapter 8.

Stream Processing: Implementation Options in Azure

When using Microsoft Azure, there are several choices available for implementing a Stream Processing layer, as illustrated in Figure 5-7 with an IoT architecture.

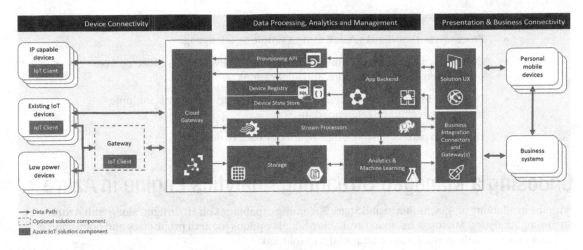

Figure 5-7. Stream processing layer in an IoT architecture

With Microsoft Azure, there are many options available for creating a steam processing layer. The choices range from using Open Source Software (OSS) packages on Linux Virtual Machines to leveraging fully managed Platform-as-a-Service, such as Azure HDInsight.

Here are the basic options for running a stream processing engine in Azure:

Streaming Options: Virtual Machines - (Infrastructure-as-a-Service):

- **Virtual machines (running Windows or Linux)**

  - Open Source Software Distributions:

  - Hortonworks

  - Cloudera

  - Roll your own: Apache Storm/Spark, Apache Samza, Twitter Heron, Kafka Streams, Apache Flink, Apache Beam (data processing workflows), Apache Mesos (project myriad).

  - Note that these options will also work for on-premise stream processing applications.

Azure Managed Services (Platform-as-a-Services – PaaS) Options:

- **Azure HDInsight: Managed Spark / Storm**

  - Essentially managed 100% compatible Hadoop in Azure.

  - HBase as a columnar NoSQL transactional database running on Azure blobs.

  - Apache Storm as a streaming service for near real-time processing.

  - Hadoop 2.4 support for 100x query gains on Hive queries.

  - Mahout support for Machine Learning and Hadoop.

  - Graphical user interface for hive queries.

- **Azure Streaming Analytics**
  - Process real-time data in Azure using a simple SQL language.
  - Consumes millions of real-time events from IoT or Event Hubs collected from devices, sensors, infrastructure, and applications.
  - Performs time-sensitive analysis using SQL-like language against multiple real-time streams and reference data.
  - Outputs to persistent stores, dashboards, or back to devices.

Choosing a Managed Streaming Analytics Engine in Azure

With the availability of Apache Storm and Spark Streaming capabilities on HDInsight, along with Azure Streaming Analytics, Microsoft has made available multiple options for both proprietary and open source technologies for implementing a streaming analytics solution.

It should be noted that both Azure managed analytics platforms provide the benefits of a managed PaaS solution, however, there are a few key distinct capabilities that differentiate them and should be considered when determining your final streaming architecture solution.

Ultimately, the final choice will be narrowed down to a few key considerations, which are highlighted in Table 5-1.

Table 5-1. *Comparison Between Azure Streaming Analytics and HDInsight*

Feature	Azure Stream Analytics	HDInsight Apache Storm
Input Data formats	Supported input formats are Avro, JSON, and CSV.	Any format may be implemented via custom code.
SQL Query Language	An easy-to-use SQL language support is available with the same syntax as ANSI SQL.	No, users must write code in Java C# or use Trident APIs.
Temporal Operators	Windowed aggregates and temporal joins are supported out-of-the-box.	Temporal operators must be implemented via custom code.
Custom Code Extensibility	Available via JavaScript user-defined functions.	Yes, there is availability to write custom code in C#, Java, or other supported languages on Storm.
Support for UDFs (User Defined Functions)	UDFs can be written in JavaScript and invoked as part of a real-time stream processing query.	UDFs can be written in C#, Java, or the language of your choice.
Pricing	Stream Analytics is priced by the number of streaming units required. A unit is a blend of compute, memory and throughput.	For Apache Storm on HDInsight, the unit of purchase is cluster-based, and is charged based on the time the cluster is running, independent of jobs deployed.
Business Continuity / High Availability Services with guaranteed SLAs	SLA of 99.9% uptime. Auto-recovery from failures. Recovery of state-full temporal operators is built-in.	SLA of 99.9% uptime of the Storm cluster. Apache Storm is a fault-tolerant streaming platform. Customers' responsibility to ensure their streaming jobs run uninterrupted.

(*continued*)

Table 5-1. (*continued*)

Feature	Azure Stream Analytics	HDInsight Apache Storm
Reference data	Reference data available from Azure Blobs with max size of 100MB of in-memory lookup cache. Refreshing of reference data is managed by the service.	No limits on data size. Connectors available for HBase, DocumentDB, SQL Server and Azure. Unsupported connectors may be implemented via custom code. Refreshing of reference data must be handled by custom code.
Integration with Machine Learning	Via configuration of published Azure Machine Learning models as functions during Azure Streaming Analytics job creation.	Available through Storm Bolts.

■ **Note**   Refer to the following link for additional information regarding choosing a managed streaming analytics platform in Azure:

Choosing a streaming analytics platform: Apache Storm comparison to Azure Stream Analytics:

`https://azure.microsoft.com/en-us/documentation/articles/stream-analytics-comparison-storm`

It should be noted that HDInsight supports both Apache Storm and Apache Spark Streaming. Each of these frameworks provide streaming capabilities and these capabilities may be worthy of further analysis depending on your specific implementation requirements.

See the following link for additional information:

Apache Spark for Azure HDInsight; `https://azure.microsoft.com/en-us/services/hdinsight/apache-spark/`

Here is an additional comparison of the three managed streaming implementations (via HDI and ASA) that are possible on Microsoft Azure:

Feature	Storm on HDI	SparkStreaming on HDI	Azure Streaming Analytics
Programming Model	Java, C#	Scala, Python, Java	SQL Query Language
Delivery Guarantee	At-least-once (Exactly once w/ Trident)	Exactly Once.	At least once
State Management	Yes	Yes	Yes
Processing Model	Event at-a-time	Micro-batching	Real-time event processing
Scaling	Manual	Manual	Automatic
Open Source	Yes	Yes	NA

Streaming Technology Choice: Decision Considerations

When evaluating a managed streaming analytics platform in Azure, additional consideration should be given to the factors in order to make a better educated decision regarding your choice of Azure managed streaming platforms:

- Development team expertise and background
- Expertise in writing SQL queries versus writing code
- Required skill levels: Analyst versus a developer for queries
- Development effort and velocity
- Using OOB connectors versus using OSS components
- Troubleshooting and diagnostics
- Custom logging, Azure operation logs
- Scalability, adjustability, and pricing

Pain Points with Other Streaming Solutions

Regardless of your choice of managed streaming analytics platforms in Azure, there are many advantages to choosing a platform that runs in Azure versus a one-off solution.

The implementation options with other streaming analytics engines can leave a lot to be desired when it comes to providing a holistic and easily managed solution. A few key points are listed here that should be taken into consideration when evaluating a streaming analytics platform for your solution, include the following:

- *Depth and breadth*: Levels of development skills required.
- *Completeness*: Typically not end-to-end solutions.
- *Expertise*: Need for special skills to set up and maintain.
- *Costs*: Development, testing, and production environments and licensing.

Reference Implementation Choice: Azure Streaming Analytics

In our reference implementation and throughout the remaining chapters of this book, we will be using Azure Streaming Analytics to implement the reference solution. Azure Streaming Analytics is a fully managed cloud service for real-time analytics on streams of data using a SQL-like query language with built-in temporal semantics. It's a perfect "fit" for the solution requirements.

Advantages of Azure Streaming Analytics

Choosing the right streaming analytics platform is a critical decision that will have major impacts on the overall performance, reliability, scalability, and overall operation of your solution.

For that reason, it is helpful to document the specific reasons for choosing Microsoft Azure Streaming Analytics and share these for future solution architecture considerations.

No Challenges with Deployment

Azure Streaming Analytics is a fully managed PaaS service in the cloud, so you can quickly configure and deploy from the Azure Portal or via PowerShell deployment scripts.

- No hardware acquisition and maintenance

- Bypasses requirements for deployment expertise

- Up and running in a few clicks (and within minutes)

- No software provisioning or maintenance

- Easily expand your business globally

Mission Critical Reliability

- Achieve mission-critical reliability and scale with Azure Streaming Analytics

- Exactly once delivery guarantee up to the output adapter that writes the output events

- State management for auto recovery

- Guaranteed not to lose events or incorrect output

- Preserves event order on per-device basis

- Guaranteed 99.9% availability SLA

See the following link for additional details:

Event Delivery Guarantees (Azure Stream Analytics)

https://msdn.microsoft.com/en-us/library/azure/mt721300.aspx

How to achieve exactly-once delivery for SQL output:

https://blogs.msdn.microsoft.com/streamanalytics/2017/01/13/how-to-achieve-exactly-once-delivery-for-sql-output/

Business Continuity

- Stream Analytics processes data at a high throughput with predictable results and no data loss

- Guaranteed uptime (three nines of availability)

- Auto-recovery from failures

- Built-in state management for fast recovery

No Challenges with Scale:

Scale to any volume of data while still achieving high throughput, low-latency, and guaranteed resiliency.

- Elasticity of the cloud for scale up or scale down
- Spin up any number of resources on demand
- Scale from small to large when required
- Distributed, scale-out architecture
- Scale using slider in Azure Portal and not writing code

Low Startup Costs

Azure Stream Analytics lets you rapidly develop and deploy low-cost solutions to gain real-time insights from devices, sensors, infrastructure, and applications.

- Provision and run streaming solutions for as low as $25/month
- Pay only for the resources you use
- Ability to incrementally add resources
- Reduce costs when business needs change

Rapid Development

Reduce friction and complexity and use fewer lines of code when developing analytic functions for scale-out of distributed systems. Describe the desired transformation with SQL-based syntax, and Stream Analytics automatically distributes it for scale, performance, and resiliency.

- Decrease bar to create stream processing solutions via SQL-like Language
- Easily filter, project, aggregate, join streams, add static data with streaming data, and detect patterns or lack of patterns with a few lines of SQL
- Built-in temporal semantics

Development and Debugging Experience Through Azure Portal

Queries in Azure Stream Analytics are expressed in a SQL-like query language. In Azure Stream Analytics, operational logging messages can be used for debugging purposes such as viewing job status, job progress, and failure messages to track the progress of a job over time; from start to processing, to output.

- Manage out-of-order events and actions on late arriving events via configurations

Scheduling and Monitoring Built-In

The Azure Management Portal and Azure Portal both surface key performance metrics that can be used to monitor and troubleshoot your query and job performance.

- Built-in monitoring
- View your system's performance at a glance
- Help you find the cost-optimal way of deployment

Why Are Customers Using Azure Stream Analytics?

The previous section outlines some of the key advantages of utilizing Azure Streaming Analytics. By leveraging Microsoft Azure Streaming Analytics for quick infrastructure provisioning along with the low-maintenance aspects of running on a completely managed streaming analytics platform, you can avoid the usual complications listed next:

- Monitoring and troubleshooting the solution.

- Develop solutions and infrastructure that can scale at pace with business growth.

- Develop solutions to manage resiliency, such as infrastructure failures and geo-redundancy.

- Develop solutions to integrate with other components like Machine Learning, BI, etc.

- Develop solution (code) for ingestion, temporal processing, and hot/cold egress operations.

- Infrastructure procurement: avoid long hardware delays and provision in minutes.

Focus on building solutions, not on the solution infrastructure, and get the applications developed and deployed faster so you can truly work at Internet speed.

It should be noted that in addition to the many benefits outlined for individual Azure customers, Azure Streaming Analytics is also a core technology that makes up several other Microsoft Azure-based solution offerings, such as:

- *Azure IoT Suite*: Microsoft provides Azure IoT Suite as part of its preconfigured IoT solutions built on the Azure platform and makes it easy to connect devices securely and ingest events at scale.

- *Cortana Intelligence Suite*: A fully managed Big Data and advanced analytics suite to transform your data into intelligent action.

Key Vertical Scenarios to Explore for Azure Stream Analytics

There are many use cases for leveraging streaming analytics across industry verticals. Some of the more popular applications are listed here:

- Financial Services:

  - Fraud detection

  - Asset tracking

- Healthcare:

  - Patient monitoring

- Government:

  - Surveillance and monitoring

- Infrastructure, Energy, and Utilities:

  - Operations management in oil and gas

  - Smart buildings

- Manufacturing:
  - Predictive maintenance
  - Remote monitoring
- Retail:
  - Real-time customer engagement and marketing
  - Inventory optimization
- Telco/IT:
  - IT Infrastructure and cellular network monitoring
  - Location-based awareness
- Transportation and Logistics:
  - Container monitoring
  - Perishables shipment tracking

Our Solution: Leveraging Azure Streaming Analytics

In our reference solution, we use Azure Stream Analytics, which is a fully managed, cost effective, real-time, event processing engine that can help us unlock deep insights from our data. Azure Stream Analytics makes it easy to set up real-time analytic computations on data streaming from devices, sensors, web sites, social media, applications, infrastructure systems, and more. It's perfect for our solution.

Before we begin the walk-through of our specific reference architecture implementation, we will explore the overall workflow of creating Streaming Analytics jobs in Microsoft Azure. Stream Analytics leverages years of Microsoft Research work in developing highly tuned streaming engines for time-sensitive processing, as well as SQL language integration for intuitive specifications of streaming jobs.

With a few clicks in the Azure Portal, you can author a Stream Analytics job specifying the three major components of an Azure Streaming Analytics Solution. These three components are inputs, outputs, and U-SQL queries.

Streaming Analytics Jobs: INPUT definitions

The first task in setting up an Azure Streaming Analytics job is to define the inputs for the new streaming job. The input definitions are related to the source of the incoming streaming data.

Note that, at the time of this writing, there are only two data format types supported:

- *JSON*: Streaming message payloads in the JavaScript-Object-Notation format.

- *CSV*: Streaming data in the Comma-Separated-Value text format. Header rows are also supported (and recommended) to provide additional column naming functionality.

When specifying data stream inputs, there are two definition types—Data Streams and Reference Data:

- *Data Streams*: A data stream is denoted as an unbounded series of events flowing over time. Stream Analytics jobs must include at least one data stream input to be consumed and transformed by the job. Stream Analytics jobs must include at least one data stream input to be consumed and transformed by the job. The supported data stream input sources include the following input types: (at the time of this writing):

    - **IoT Hub Streams:**

        - Azure IoT Hub is a highly scalable publish-subscribe event ingestion platform optimized for IoT scenarios.

        - Used for device-to-cloud and cloud-to-device messaging streams.

        - Optimized to support millions of simultaneously connected devices.

        - Can be used to send inbound and outbound messages to IoT devices.

    - **Event Hub Streams:**

        - Enables inbound (only) event message streams for device-to-cloud scenarios.

        - Supports a more limited number of simultaneous connections.

        - Event Hubs enables you to specify the partition for each message sent for increased scalability.

    - *Blob Storage*: Used as an input source for ingesting bulk data as a stream. For scenarios with large amounts of unstructured data to store in the cloud, blob storage offers a cost-effective and scalable solution.

■ **Note** See the following link for more information concerning the differences between Azure IoT Hubs and Event Hubs:

Comparison of IoT Hub and Event Hubs:

https://azure.microsoft.com/en-us/documentation/articles/iot-hub-compare-event-hubs

---

- *Reference Data*: Stream Analytics supports a second type of auxiliary input called reference data. As opposed to data in motion, reference data is static or slowing changing.

    - It is typically used for performing lookups and correlations with other data streams to enrich a dataset.

    - At the time of this writing, Azure blob storage is currently the only supported input source for reference data. Reference data source blobs are currently limited to 100MB in size.

Streaming Analytics Jobs: OUTPUT Definitions

We have defined our input sources for a new Azure Streaming Analytics job, so the next step is to define the output formats for the job. In order to enable a variety of application patterns, Azure Stream Analytics has different options for storing output and viewing analysis results. This makes it easy to view job outputs and provides flexibility in the consumption and storage of the job output for data warehousing and other purposes.

Note that any output configured in the job must exist before the job is started and events start flowing. For example, if you use blob storage as an output, the job will not create a storage account automatically. It needs to be provisioned by the user before the Streaming Analytics job is started.

The Output formats for Azure Streaming Analytics include the following storage options (at the time of this writing):

- *SQL Database*: Azure SQL Database can be used as an output for data that is relational in nature or for applications that depend on content being hosted in a relational database. The one requirement for this Stream Analytics output option is that the destination be an existing table in an Azure SQL Database. Consequently, the table schema must exactly match the fields and their types being output from the streaming analytics job.

- *Azure SQL Data Warehouse*: Note that an Azure SQL Data Warehouse can also be specified as an output via the SQL Database output option. This feature is currently in preview mode at the time of this writing.

- *Blob Storage*: Blob storage offers a cost-effective and scalable solution for storing large amounts of unstructured data in the cloud.

- *Event Hubs*: A highly scalable publish-subscribe event ingestion construct. Event Hubs are highly scalable and can handle ingestion of millions of events per second. Note that a key reason for using an Event Hub as an Output of a Stream Analytics job is so that the data can become the input of another streaming job. In this way, you can "chain" multiple streaming jobs together to complete an application scenario, such as providing real-time alerts and notifications.

- *Table Storage*: A NoSQL key/attribute store that can be leveraged for structured data with minimal schema constraints. Table storage provides highly available, massively scalable storage, so that an application can automatically scale to meet user demand.

- *Service Bus Queue*: Provides a First-In, First-Out (FIFO) message delivery to one or more consumers. Messages are then set up to be received and processed by the receivers in the date/time order in which they were added to the queue, and each message is received and processed by only one message consumer.

- *Service Bus Topic*: While service bus queues provide a one-to-one communication pattern from sender to receiver, service bus topics provide a one-to-many form of communication where many applications can subscribe to a topic.

- *DocumentDB*: A fully-managed NoSQL document database service that offers query and transactions over schema-free data, predictable, and reliable performance, as well as rapid development.

- *Power BI*: Can be used as an output for a Stream Analytics job to provide for rich visualizations for analytical results. This capability can be used for operational dashboards, report generation, and metric driven reporting.

- *Data Lake Store*: This output option enables you to store data of any size, type and ingestion speed for operational and exploratory analytics. At this time, creation and configuration of Data Lake Store outputs is supported only in the Azure Classic Portal.

Planning Streaming Analytics Outputs

The *output* stage of the streaming analytics process requires a little upfront, advanced planning, as some thought must be given to how the data will be delivered and consumed. This is where the real value of the modern Lambda architecture comes into play with the notion of "hot", "warm", and "cold" data paths.

Proper analysis and exploitation of these key reporting capabilities can mean the difference between creating a true competitive advantage and just creating a noisy data overload scenario. The fortunes of many businesses can rise and fall on the timeliness and accuracy of key operational data. Choose your outputs carefully.

Hot Path

The processing pathway for urgent data, for example, data that is sent from field devices to an IoT system. This data typically requires immediate analysis. It is frequently used for raising alerts and other critical notifications. The "hot path" output option(s) for Azure Streaming Analytics include:

- *Power BI*: For real-time streaming integration along with rich, visual dashboards.

- *Event Hubs*: For integrating with other Streaming Analytics jobs and outbound Notification hubs.

- *Service Bus Queues*: For integration with other publisher/subscriber notification systems.

- *Service Bus Topics*: For integration with one-to-many notification scenarios.

Warm Path

The processing path for device data that is not urgent but typically has a limited lifetime before it becomes stale. This data should be considered to have an "expiration date" and consequently should be processed in a specified period of time.

This data can also be used to augment the results generated by hot path processing to provide additional context. Examples of warm path data include diagnostic information for performance analysis, troubleshooting, or A/B testing. The data may need to be held in storage that is relatively quick to access (and therefore possibly more expensive than that required for the cold path), but the storage capacity is likely to be much less, as this data has a limited life span and is unlikely to be retained for an extended period.

The "warm path" output option(s) for Azure Streaming Analytics include:

- *Azure SQL Database*: For near-real-time, relational data queries

- *DocumentDB*: For near-real-time, NOSQL data queries

Cold Path

The processing pathway for data that is stored and processed later. For example, this data can be pulled from storage for processing at a later time in batch mode. The data can be held in relatively cheap, high capacity, storage due to its potential high volume and historical nature. The data is commonly used to provide statistical information, to generate analytical reports, and for auditing purposes.

The "cold path" output option(s) for Azure Streaming Analytics include:

- *Blob Storage*: For low cost, high-scale, generic data storage

- *Table Storage*: For low cost, high-scale, key-value-pair data storage

- *Data Lake Store*: For unlimited, low cost, high-scale, historical data storage platform with deep analytical processing capabilities.

- *Power BI*: For real-time streaming integration along with rich, visual dashboards.

- *Event Hubs*: For integrating with other Streaming Analytics jobs and outbound Notification hubs.

- *Service Bus Queues*: For integration with other publisher/subscriber notification systems.

- *Service Bus Topics*: For integration with one-to-many notification scenarios.

Power BI for Real-Time Visualizations

Power BI can be used as an output for a Stream Analytics job to provide for a real-time, rich visualization experience of analysis results. This capability can be used for operational dashboards, dynamic report generation, and other forms of real-time, metric-driven reporting and analysis.

■ **Note**   See the following link for more information on specifying Streaming Analytics Outputs:

`https://azure.microsoft.com/en-us/documentation/articles/stream-analytics-define-outputs`

Streaming Analytics Jobs: Data Transformations via SQL Queries

After the Azure Streaming Analytics job input and output definitions have been created, the next task is creating the *data transformations*. This is where all the pieces start to come together and a complete solution can finally be configured based on the previously defined inputs and outputs.

Azure Stream Analytics offers a SQL-like query language for performing transformations and computations over incoming streams of event data. Stream Analytics query language is a subset of the standard Transaction-SQL (T-SQL) syntax for performing simple and complex streaming analytics computations.

Azure Streaming Analytics SQL: Developer Friendly

Since most developers today may already possess a good working knowledge of T-SQL, this feature makes it very approachable to become very productive in a very short amount of time when using Azure Streaming Analytics.

This portion of the Streaming Analytics job setup is where the actual processing will occur and we will map, enrich, and transform the incoming streaming data input into one or more pre-defined streaming outputs. Note that it is possible in a single Streaming Analytics job to send processed data from a single input to multiple output destinations by chaining the SQL statements together in the job.

Azure Streaming Analytics (ASA): SQL Query Dialect Features

The SQL language in ASA is very similar to T-SQL, which is the primary database language for modern SQL database application engines such as Microsoft SQL Server, IBM DB2, and Oracle Database server.

It should be noted that Azure Streaming Analytics (ASA) SQL also contains a superset of functions that support advanced analytics capabilities as "temporal" (date/time) operations such as applying sliding, hopping, or tumbling time windows to the event stream in order to get time-boxed, summarized data directly from the incoming event stream.

All this is accomplished eloquently and effortlessly using familiar T-SQL statements. To assist you in further understanding the features of the ASA SQL Query language, the following is a short synopsis of the primary capabilities available with the Azure Streaming Analytics SQL Query language.

SQL Query Language

- All data transformation jobs are written declaratively as a series of T-SQL-like query language statements.

- There is no additional programming required and no code compilation required.

- The SQL scripts are easy to author and deploy.

Supported Data Types

The following data types are supported in the ASA SQL language:

- *Bigint*: Integers in the range -2^63 (-9,223,372,036,854,775,808) to 2^63-1 (9,223,372,036,854,775,807).

- *Float*: Floating-point numbers in the range - 1.79E+308 to -2.23E-308, 0, and 2.23E-308 to 1.79E+308.

- *Datetime*: Defines a date that is combined with a time of day with fractional seconds that is based on a 24-hour clock and relative to UTC (time zone offset 0).

- *nvarchar (max)*: Text values made up of Unicode characters.

- *record*: A set of name/value pairs. Values must be of supported data type.

- *array*: An ordered collection of values. Values must be of supported data type.

Data Type Conversions

CAST

Data type conversions in types in Stream Analytics query language are accomplished via the CAST function. This function converts an expression of one data type to another data type in the supported types in Stream Analytics query language.

Proper care should be taken when using the CAST function over inconsistent data streams, as a failure will cause the streaming analytics job to stop if the conversion cannot be performed.

As a good example of what not to do—the ASA SQL statement in Listing 5-1 will result in an Azure Streaming Analytics job failure.

Listing 5-1. An Example of the CAST Operator Usage That Will Result in a Job Failure in an ASA SQL Statement

```
CAST ('Test-String' AS bigint)
```

TRY_CAST

To avoid a catastrophic job failures due to a data type conversion failure, it is highly recommended that the TRY_CAST SQL operation be used instead. This version returns either a value cast to the specified data type if the cast succeeds or else, the call returns null.

The SQL transformation job will gracefully continue no matter the result of the TRY_CAST call. Listing 5-2 illustrates the TRY_CAST call.

Listing 5-2. An Example of the TRY_CAST Operator in an ASA SQL Statement

```
SELECT TweetId, TweetTime
FROM Input
WHERE TRY_CAST( TweetTime AS datetime) IS NOT NULL
```

Temporal Semantic Functionality

All ASA SQL operators are compatible with the temporal properties of event streams. Additional functionality is added to the ASA SQL language via new operators such as:

- TumblingWindow
- HoppingWindow
- SlidingWindow

Built-In Operators and Functions

- The ASA SQL language supports other key T-SQL constructs such as filters, projections, joins, windowed (temporal) aggregates, and text and date manipulation functionality.

- Advanced event stream queries can be composed via these powerful query extensions.

User Defined Functions: Azure Machine Learning Integration

- The ASA SQL language now supports direct calls to Azure Machine Learning (ML) via user defined functions.

- User-defined functions provide an extensible way for a streaming job to transform input data to output data using an externally defined function and accessed as part of the SQL query.

- A Machine Learning function in stream analytics can be used like a regular function call in the stream analytics query language.

- This functionality provides the ability to score individual events of streaming data by leveraging a Machine Learning model hosted in Azure and accessed via a web service call.

- At the time of this writing, Azure Machine Learning Request-Response Service (RRS) is the only supported UDF framework and is in currently in "preview" mode.

- This capability allows you easily build applications for scenarios such as real-time Twitter sentiment analytics, as illustrated in Listing 5-3. The Azure Machine Learning user-defined function named `sentiment` is easily incorporated into an ASA SQL query. This capability provides a powerful mechanism to leverage predictive analytics to enrich the incoming event stream data and turn it into actionable data.

Listing 5-3. Example of an Azure Machine Learning User-Defined Function

```
WITH subquery AS (
     SELECT text, sentiment(text) as result from input
  )
SELECT text, result.[Scored Labels]
INTO output
FROM subquery
```

Event Delivery Guarantees Provided in Azure Stream Analytics

The Azure Stream Analytics query language provides extensions to the T-SQL syntax to enable complex computations over incoming streams of events. With Azure Streaming Analytics, the following concepts related to event delivery are noteworthy to review:

- Exactly once delivery
- Duplicate records

Exactly Once Delivery

An "exactly once" delivery guarantee means all input events are processed exactly once by the streaming analytics system. In this way, the results are also guaranteed to be complete with no duplicate outputs. In terms of Azure Service Level Agreements (SLAs), Azure Stream Analytics guarantees exactly once delivery up to the output adapter that writes the output events.

Duplicate Records

When a Stream Analytics job is running, duplicate records may occasionally occur within the output data. These duplicate records are expected, due to the fact that Azure Stream Analytics output adapters do not write the output events in a complete transactional manner.

See the following link for more information:

How to achieve exactly-once delivery for SQL output:

https://blogs.msdn.microsoft.com/streamanalytics/2017/01/13/how-to-achieve-exactly-once-delivery-for-sql-output/

Time Management Functions

The Azure Stream Analytics SQL query language extends the T-SQL syntax to enable complex computations over streams of events. Stream Analytics provides language constructs to deal with the temporal aspects of the data. For example, it is possible to assign custom timestamps to the stream events, specify time window for aggregations, specify allowed time difference between two streams of data for JOIN operation, etc.

- *System.Timestamp*: A system property that can be used to retrieve an event's timestamp.

- *Time Skew Policies*: Provides policies for out-of-order and late arrival events.

- *Aggregate Functions*: Used to perform a calculation on a set of values from a time window and return a single value.

- *DATEDIFF*: Allowed in the JOIN predicate and allows the specification of time boundaries for JOIN operations.

- *Date and Time Functions*: Azure Stream Analytics provides a variety of date and time functions for use in creating time-sensitive streaming analytics queries.

- *TIMESTAMP BY*: Allows specifying custom timestamp values.

The Importance of the TIMESTAMP BY Clause

In Azure Streaming Analytics, all incoming events have a well-defined timestamp. If a solution is required to use the application time, they can use the TIMESTAMP BY keyword to specify the column in the payload which should be used to timestamp every incoming event to perform any temporal computation like windowing functions (Hopping, Tumbling, Sliding), Temporal JOINs, etc.

Note that it is recommended to use the TIMESTAMP BY clause over an "arrival time" as a best practice since the TIMESTAMP BY clause can be used on any column of type "datetime" and all ISO 8601 formats are supported. In comparison, the System.timestamp value can only be used in the SELECT clause.

Listing 5-4 illustrates a TIMESTAMP BY example that uses the TweetTime column as the application time for all incoming events.

Listing 5-4. The TIMESTAMP BY Clause

```
SELECT TweetId, TweetTime
FROM TweetInput
TIMESTAMP BY TweetTime
```

Azure Stream Analytics: Unified Programming Model

As we have seen in the previous sections covering the superset of features, functions, and capabilities that extend the Azure Streaming Analytics SQL dialect, the end result is an extremely powerful, yet easily approachable, SQL-based programming model that brings together event streams, reference data, and Machine Learning extensions to create a comprehensive solution.

Azure Stream Analytics: Examples of the SQL Programming Model

The Simplest Example

Listing 5-5 is a very simple example of a streaming SQL Query that will copy *all* the fields in the input named iothub-input into an output named blob-output.

Listing 5-5. The Simplest ASA SQL Query Possible

```
select * into blob-output from iothub-input
```

In many cases, the Azure Streaming Analytics SQL queries will be more complex and will usually incorporate various temporal semantics in order to surface the data related to the sliding, hopping, or tumbling timeframe windows from the event stream. As mentioned previously, this is where the real power of Azure Streaming Analytics really shines, as it is very easy to accomplish via the superset of functionality that Microsoft has added to the familiar T-SQL dialect.

To illustrate, the following temporal window examples will make the assumption that we are reading from an input stream of tweets from Twitter.

Tumbling Windows: A 10-Second Tumbling Window

Tumbling windows can be defined as a series of fixed-sized, non-overlapping, and contiguous time intervals taken from a data stream. The ASA SQL in Listing 5-6 seeks to answer the following question:
   "Tell me the count of tweets per time zone every 10 seconds"

Listing 5-6. Sample Tumbling Window SQL Statement

```
SELECT TimeZone, COUNT(*) AS Count
FROM TwitterStream TIMESTAMP BY CreatedAt
GROUP BY TimeZone, TumblingWindow(second,10)
```

Hopping Windows: A 10-Second Hopping Window with a 5-Second "Hop"

Hopping windows are designed to model scheduled overlapping windows. The ASA SQL in Listing 5-7 seeks to answer the following question:
   "Every 5 seconds give me the count of tweets over the last 10 seconds"

Listing 5-7. Sample Hopping Window SQL Statement

```
SELECT Topic, COUNT(*) AS TotalTweets
FROM TwitterStream TIMESTAMP BY CreatedAt
GROUP BY Topic, HoppingWindow(second, 10 , 5)
```

Sliding Windows: A 10-Second Sliding Window

With a sliding window, the system is asked to logically consider all possible windows of a given length and output events for cases when the content of the window actually changes, for example, when an event was detected that entered or existed the window. The ASA SQL in Listing 5-8 seeks to answer the following question:

"Give me the count of tweets for all topics which are tweeted more than 10 times in the last 10 seconds"

Listing 5-8. A Sample Sliding Window SQL Statement

```
SELECT Topic, COUNT(*) FROM TwitterStream
TIMESTAMP BY CreatedAt
GROUP BY Topic, SlidingWindow(second, 10)
HAVING COUNT(*) > 10
```

Joining Multiple Streams

Similar to standard T-SQL language, the JOIN clause in the Azure Stream Analytics query language is used to combine records from two or more input sources. However, the JOIN clause in Azure Stream Analytics SQL are temporal in nature. This means that each JOIN must provide limits on how far the matching rows can be separated in time. The ASA SQL in Listing 5-9 seeks to answer the following question:

"List all users and the topics on which they switched their sentiment within a minute"

Listing 5-9. JOINing Multiple Streams in ASA SQL

```
SELECT TS1.UserName, TS1.Topic
FROM TwitterStream TS1 TIMESTAMP BY CreatedAt
JOIN TwitterStream TS2 TIMESTAMP BY CreatedAt
                ON TS1.UserName = TS2.UserName AND TS1.Topic = TS2.Topic
                AND DateDiff(second, TS1, TS2) BETWEEN 1 AND 60
WHERE TS1.SentimentScore != TS2.SentimentScore
```

Detecting the Absence of Events

This SQL query pattern can be extremely useful as it will provide the ability to determine if a stream has no value that matches a certain criteria. For example, Listing 5-10 is a sample ASA SQL query that will seek to provide the real-time answers for the question.

"Show me if a topic is not tweeted for 10 seconds since it was last tweeted."

Listing 5-10. Detecting the Absence of Data in ASA SQL

```
SELECT TS1.CreatedAt, TS1.Topic
FROM TwitterStream TS1 TIMESTAMP BY CreatedAt
LEFT OUTER JOIN TwitterStream TS2 TIMESTAMP BY CreatedAt
ON TS1.Topic = TS2.Topic
AND DATEDIFF(second, TS1, TS2) BETWEEN 1 AND 10
WHERE TS2.Topic IS NULL
```

■ **Note**   The following link provides guidance for common Stream Analytics Usage Patterns:

Query examples for common Stream Analytics usage patterns:

https://azure.microsoft.com/en-us/documentation/articles/stream-analytics-stream-analytics-query-patterns

---

The Reference Implementation

Now that we have covered all the basics related to the configuration and setup of Azure Streaming Analytics, it is time to walk through the actual configuration steps for our reference implementation solution. In this next section, we walk through the configuration of our streaming analytics job via the Azure Portal in order to implement various data pathways for our incoming IoT data streams. As part of the configuration, we will create and configure the following artifacts in Azure:

- Azure Streaming Analytics Job.
    - *Inputs*: For our Azure Streaming Analytics Job. In this case, we will be using two inputs. The first one is for the incoming data stream from the IoT Hub, the second input is for reference data. In this example, we will read from a reference .CSV file in Azure blob storage to match a team member's personal health information with their real-time health sensor information readings.
    - *Functions*: Consisting of references to Azure Machine Learning Web Services. To help enrich the data with predictive analytics. In this example, we will check to see if a team member is fatigued to the point of exhaustion.
    - *Outputs*: For output of results from the Azure Streaming Analytics Job into various storage formats: Hot, Warm, and Cold (from the Lambda architecture).
    - *ASA SQL Query Language*: Will combine all of the previous configurations to process the incoming data streams and send computed results to various output destinations.

Business Use Case Scenario

As you may recall, the use case scenario for our reference implementation involves monitoring workers health during strenuous activities. To that end, IoT sensors are being worn and by the members of the various work teams and their sensor readings are being transmitted to the Azure cloud via an IoT Hub configuration.

The next critical step in the process is where Azure Streaming Analytics is utilized to quickly and efficiently process the incoming data streams. Figure 5-8 denotes the use of Azure Streaming Analytics as the primary ingestion processing engine in the overall architecture.

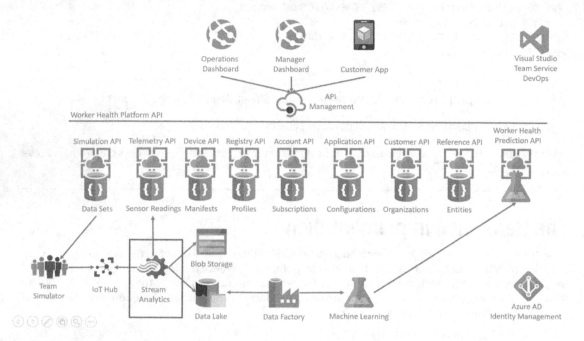

Figure 5-8. *Worker Health and Safety Reference solution*

AZURE SETUP: CREATE AZURE STREAMING ANALYTICS JOB

The first step in the process is to create a new Azure Streaming Analytics job. To do this, we will assume that you have an Azure subscription and have already deployed the Azure IoT suite infrastructure components covered in Chapters 1-4 of this book.

Start by adding a new resource to your existing Azure resource group and searching for Stream Analytics Job, as depicted in Figure 5-9.

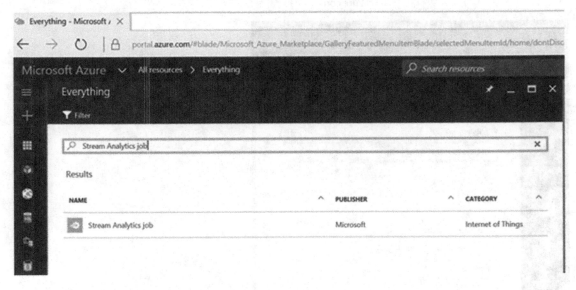

Figure 5-9. *Adding a stream analytics job to an Azure resource group*

After clicking on Stream Analytics job, you will be asked to fill in the parameters for creating the Azure Stream Analytics job, as shown in Figure 5-10.

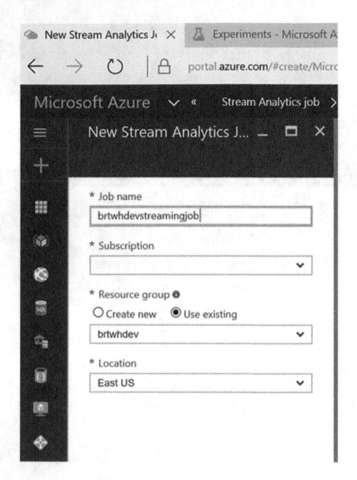

Figure 5-10. *Adding Stream Analytics job parameters*

Fill in your parameter choices for the corresponding values:

- Job Name
- Subscription
- Resource Group
- Location

Once you are done, click on the Create button at the bottom of the screen. Your input will then be validated and the new Azure Streaming Analytics job will be created after a brief period of time. It took less than one minute via the portal.

Once you have configured an Azure Streaming Analytics job, you can add and configure additional components of the job, such as the following:

- *Inputs*: For defining incoming data streams and reference data in our Azure Streaming Analytics Job.

- *Functions*: For defining references to Azure Machine Learning Web Service calls. In our example, we will check to see if a team member is fatigued to the point of exhaustion.

- *Outputs*: For defining the output of results from our Azure Streaming Analytics Job into various storage formats and delivery platforms: Hot, Warm, and Cold (from the Lambda architecture).

- *SQL Query*: Will combine all of the previously defined inputs, functions, and outputs in a series of SQL statements to process the incoming data stream and send computed results to various output destinations and delivery/notification methods.

Figure 5-11 displays a screen capture of a newly created Streaming Analytics job and the corresponding inputs, query, and outputs.

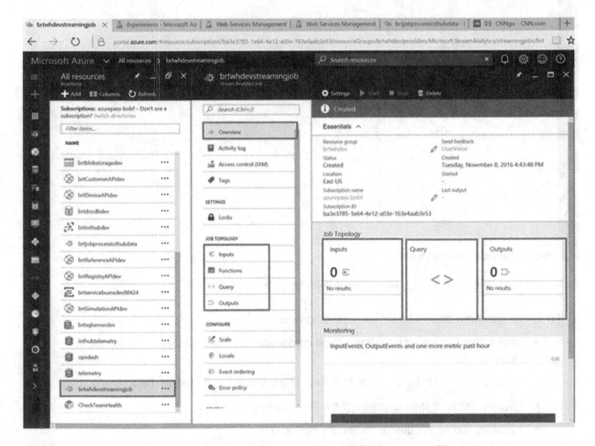

Figure 5-11. *Stream Analytics job: add input(s), function(s), query(s), and output(s)*

AZURE SETUP: STREAMING ANALYTICS JOB AND INPUT IOT HUB DATA STREAM

Let's start with configuring the input definition for describing our incoming data stream, which arrives via an IoT Hub configuration in Azure.

IoT Hub is an event processing service that enables event and telemetry ingress to the cloud at massive scale, with low latency and high reliability.

Start by clicking on the inputs image and then + Add, as shown in Figure 5-12.

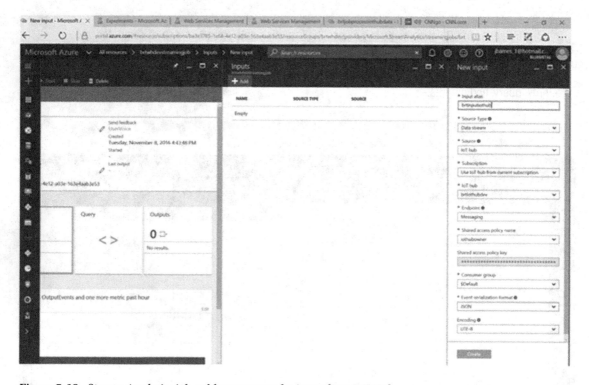

Figure 5-12. *Stream Analytics job, add parameters for input from IoT Hub*

Fill in your parameter choices for the corresponding values:

- *Input Alias*: This will be the primary name used in any SQL Queries to refer to this input stream.

- *Source Type*: Set to Data Stream. Note the additional option for Reference Data.

- *Source*: Detected input sources that are Data Streams.

- *Subscription*: Azure Subscription for this input source.

- *IoT Hub*: Select the appropriate choice for your environment.

- *Endpoint*: Select Messaging. Other option includes Operations Monitoring.

- *Shared Access Policy Name*: For delegated and shared access to resources.

- *Consumer Group*: All event consumers read the event stream through partitions in a consumer group.

- *Event Serialization Format*: Specify JSON. Other options include Avro and CSV.

- *Encoding*: Specify UTF-8.

Once you are done, click on the Create button at the bottom of the screen. Your input will then be validated and the new Azure Streaming Analytics input definition will be created after a brief period of time.

AZURE SETUP: STREAMING ANALYTICS JOB INPUT REFERENCE DATA

After we have configured the primary input data path from the IoT Hub, we will next define a secondary type of input definition that will be used for reference data.

Reference data is defined as more static or slower changing data, which can often be refreshed on longer time intervals. A prerequisite for this step is to have a reference data file uploaded into an Azure blob storage container in CSV, JSON, or Avro format.

For our reference implementation, we will upload a .CSV formatted file that contains team member reference data with more static attributes like name, height, weight, gender, e-mail, etc.

This reference data can then be used in JOIN statements in the Azure Streaming Analytics SQL Query language to enrich the data output and provide more meaningful and actionable business results.

Reference data is stored in Azure blob storage and is modeled as a sequence of blobs in ascending date/time order. It only supports adding to the end of the sequence by using a date/time greater than the one specified by the last blob in the sequence.

Currently, Azure Stream Analytics jobs look for the blob refresh only when the machine time advances to the time encoded in the blob name.

For example, our job will look for our pattern named TeamReferenceData{date}{time}.csv. It will then find this file: TeamReferenceData2016-11-1217-30.csv and will process it as soon as possible but no earlier than 5:30 PM on November 13th 2016 UTC time zone. It will never look for a file with an encoded time earlier than the last one that is discovered.

■ **Note**   See the following link for more information about refreshing reference data for Azure Streaming Analytics jobs using Azure Data Factory:

Refreshing reference data with Azure Data Factory for Azure Stream Analytics Jobs

https://azure.microsoft.com/en-us/blog/refreshing-reference-data-with-azure-data-factory-for-azure-stream-analytics-jobs-3

INPUT Reference Data: Sample SQL Usage

The inclusion of reference data as a potential input for a streaming analytics job means that you can utilize a SQL JOIN (INNER or LEFT OUTER) between streams and reference data sources to enrich your incoming data model.

Note that "reference" data appears as just another input in the ASA SQL query in Listing 5-11.

Listing 5-11. SQL JOIN of Reference Data with Incoming Streaming Data

```
SELECT myRefData.Name, myStream.Value
FROM myStream
JOIN myRefData
                ON myStream.myKey = myRefData.myKey
```

Configure the Streaming Analytics INPUT: Reference Data Definition

To get started, navigate to your Streaming Analytics job in the Azure Portal that was previously defined in this chapter and select the Inputs option on the left-side navigation pane.

Click + Add at the top of the page to add a new input definition. You will need to provide configuration options for the following parameters:

- *Input Alias*: A unique name to reference this input definition.
- *Source Type*: Select Reference Data.
- *Subscription*: Azure subscription for this input source.
- *Storage account*: Your storage account (brtblobstoragedev in this case).
- *Storage account key*: Copied from subscription
- *Container*: ref-data-team
- *Path pattern*: TeamReferenceData{date}{time}.csv
- *Date format*: YYY-MM-DD.
- *Time format*: HH-mm.
- *Event Serialization Format*: Specify CSV. Other options include JSON and Avro.
- *Delimiter*: Comma (,).
- *Encoding*: Specify UTF-8.

Click on the Create button at the bottom of the screen to create the input definition.

The screenshot in Figure 5-13 denotes the input parameters for the input reference definition.

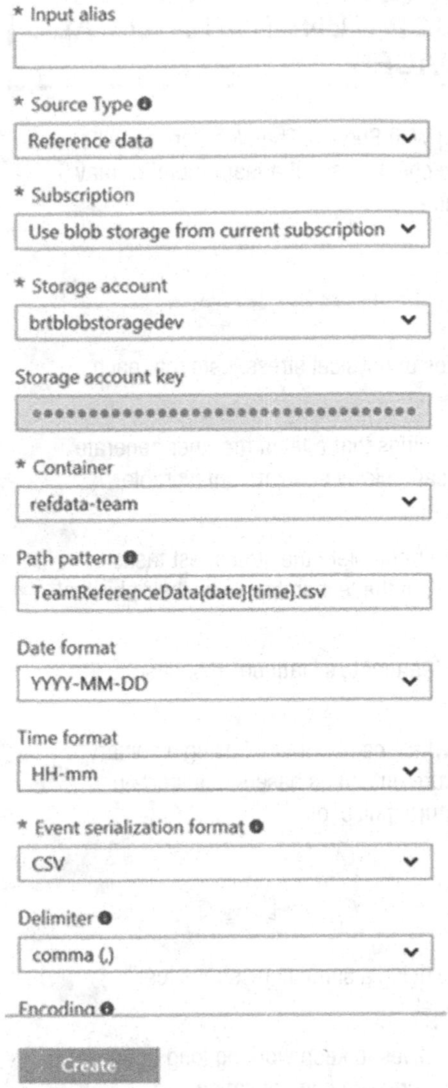

* Input alias

```
[                                    ]
```

* Source Type ❶

```
[ Reference data                  ∨ ]
```

* Subscription

```
[ Use blob storage from current subscription ∨ ]
```

* Storage account

```
[ brtblobstoragedev               ∨ ]
```

Storage account key

```
[ •••••••••••••••••••••••••••••••••••• ]
```

* Container

```
[ refdata-team                    ∨ ]
```

Path pattern ❶

```
[ TeamReferenceData{date}{time}.csv ]
```

Date format

```
[ YYYY-MM-DD                      ∨ ]
```

Time format

```
[ HH-mm                           ∨ ]
```

* Event serialization format ❶

```
[ CSV                             ∨ ]
```

Delimiter ❶

```
[ comma (,)                       ∨ ]
```

Encoding ❶

```
[ Create ]
```

Figure 5-13. Stream Analytics job: add parameters for input for Reference data

After the new input for our reference data is created and tested (this process takes only about one minute), you can then use this new input definition as part of the SQL query to JOIN the "reference data" with the incoming sensor data from the IoT Hub.

Typically, IoT sensor data is transformed to be very "lean" when transmitted over networks, so no additional information other than what is the minimal necessary to keep packet sizes small and transmission costs efficient.

By matching the incoming data streams with more complete profile data from our reference data, we can provide more complete data profiles for the various entities being measured. This capability also allows for finer-grained decision support mechanisms, as additional meaningful attributes may now unlocked and utilized to predict better outcomes.

AZURE SETUP: STREAMING ANALYTICS JOB, FUNCTIONS TO CALL AZURE ML WEB SERVICES

The next step is to define an alias for an Azure Machine Learning Web Service. The Web Service will be used to call out from the processing SQL script and is used to check to see if a team member may displaying symptoms that he/she may be near physical exhaustion.

Azure Machine Learning: Predicting a Team Member's Health

The Azure Machine Learning predictive model is based on a series of physical stress tests that each team member must undergo each quarter (every three months).

The purpose of the stress tests is to track all the same sensor readings that a team member generate while working, but in a simulated, stress-test, environment that can quickly simulate unfavorable working conditions to induce physical fatigue and mental exhaustion.

At any point that a team member feels that they cannot continue or complete the stress test tasks at hand safely, they simply press a Fatigued button on their vest to stop the test and register their physical attributes at the point of exhaustion.

In this way, key physical sensor readings are correlated with the teammate's "fatigue" response to the stress tests.

This allows us to create a predictive analytics "training" model, which can be trained using a "binary classification" Machine Learning algorithm in order to predict future outcomes based upon certain attributes such as breathing, heart rate, speed, velocity, temperature, pulse, etc.

Obtaining Unbiased Machine Learning Training Data

It should also be noted that there is another distinct advantage to using a simulated "stress test" environment as training data to create the Machine Learning model.

This is due to the fact that the team members have financial incentives to keep working long hours under adverse conditions in order to attain financial rewards and increased compensation.

For this reason, team members may be disinclined to signal fatigue while working on the real production-line jobs in order to maximize their financial compensation. However, by measuring the team's stress test responses outside of the production work environment—where there are no financial incentives involved—more accurate results can be obtained.

The key to success is to obtain unbiased and accurate training data that more closely resembles the key indicators of fatigue and stress that can be measured, recorded, and utilized to train the Azure Machine Learning Model.

Configure the Streaming Analytics Function Definition

To get started, navigate to your Streaming Analytics job in the Azure Portal that was previously defined in this chapter and select the Functions option on the left-side navigation pane.

Click the + Add at the top of the page to add a new function definition. You will need to provide the following:

- *Function Alias*: A unique name to reference this function definition.

- *Function Type*: Defaults to Azure ML. Note: the function option is currently restricted to only refer to Azure Machine Learning Web Service definitions. It is anticipated that Microsoft may open-up this capability to reference "Azure Functions" in the near future. This new functionality would dramatically expand the capabilities of the Azure Streaming Analytics SQL Query language by incorporating function callouts to custom code modules.

- *Subscription*: The Azure subscription to be used for the function definition.

- *URL*: Refers to the Azure Machine Learning Web Service deployment name.

- *Key*: The security key for access to the Azure Machine Learning Web Service deployment.

Click on the Create button at the bottom of the screen to create the function definition. The screenshot in Figure 5-14 denotes the function definition parameters for the reference implementation.

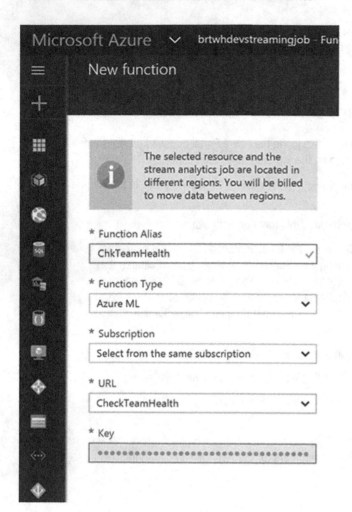

Figure 5-14. *Add parameters to the streaming job for function reference to desired Azure Machine Learning Web Service*

After the function is created and tested (this process takes only about 1 minute), we can then use this new function definition as part of our SQL Query to call our Azure Machine Learning Web Service to predict whether a team member is at risk of being physically exhausted to the point that it could cause an unsafe work environment.

The screenshot in Figure 5-15 depicts the newly defined function that we created.

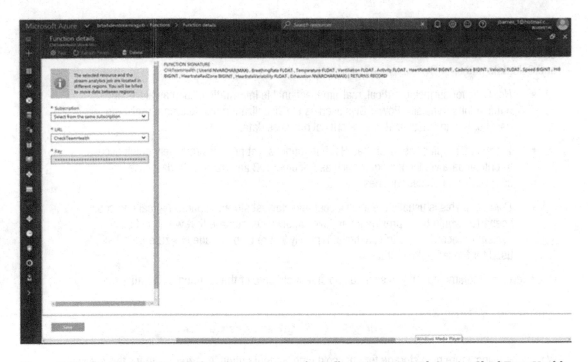

Figure 5-15. *Stream Analytics job: function parameters for Calling Azure ML Web Service CheckTeamHealth*

Also shown is the function signature, which shows all 13 parameters and various field types that must be configured correctly in order to make the function call from the Streaming Analytics SQL query.

We will cover the implementation details of the Azure Machine Learning Web Service called CheckTeamHealth in Chapter 8.

As part of the Chapter 8 background, we cover the creation of an Azure ML training model based on stress test results and utilize a "Binary Classification" algorithm to create a predictive model that can correctly determine if a team member is nearing the point of physical exhaustion. We will also cover the mechanics of deploying, testing, and managing the Azure ML Web Service.

AZURE SETUP: STREAMING ANALYTICS JOB OUTPUTS

Now that we have created the inputs and functions for our Azure Streaming Analytics job, it is time to create the various outputs for our streaming job.

This is a critical step in the process, as we will be creating multiple outputs from a single input stream coming from the IoT Hub.

One key set of decisions around defining the streaming job outputs is the notion of the Lambda architecture that we reviewed earlier in the chapter. Azure Streaming Analytics provides the ability to define various output formats and storage options that can directly relate to the notion of Hot, Warm, and Cold data paths:

- *Hot Path*: for surfacing critical, real-time, actionable information, such as alerts and notifications. Typically, Power BI is used as the visualization tool to create real-time dashboards and visualizations for critical business data.

- *Warm Path*: Typically slower than Hot Path options, yet provides relatively quick access to critical data via technologies such as DocumentDB and Azure SQL database via canned or ad hoc user queries.

- *Cold Path*: This is usually the lowest cost and slowest storage option. Typical use case scenarios would be to provide an archive capability or storage that would act as a system of record for all transactions. Typically, Azure blob storage or Azure Data Lake is used for these implementations.

Our reference implementation will seek to implement all three of the Lambda data pathways.

Streaming Analytics Job: Cold Path Output Blob Storage

We will be using Azure blob storage for our "cold path" output option. A prerequisite for this step is to create an Azure Storage account and a container in the storage account to hold our data.

■ **Note**   Refer to the following link for more information:

About Azure storage accounts

`https://azure.microsoft.com/en-us/documentation/articles/storage-create-storage-account`

A handy tool for navigating Azure Storage is the "Azure Storage Explorer," which can be downloaded from `http://azurestorageexplorer.codeplex.com`. Since it is on CodePlex, it's also great to have the source code, to see how the Azure Storage API's are called from .NET.

Once you have created an Azure Storage Account and a container in the storage account, you will need the storage account access keys for the next step.

To get started with our first output definition, navigate (via the Azure Portal) to the Azure Streaming Analytics job we defined earlier in the chapter:

Select Outputs:

- Click on the + Add to add a new output definition.

- Under the Sink parameter, select Blob Storage from the drop-down list. This action will properly set the remaining fields for you to populate:

- *Output Alias*: A name for this output definition that will be used in our SQL query.

- *Sink*: Refers to the selected output destination; in this case, select blob storage.

- *Subscription*: The Azure subscription to be used for this output definition.

- *Storage Account*: The name of the Azure Storage account that was created as a prerequisite for this output definition.

- *Storage Account Key*: The corresponding Account key for the storage account.

- *Container*: The name of the storage account repository or folder that will contain our output data.

- *Path Pattern*: Denotes the file path used to locate your blobs within the specified container. Within the path pattern definition, you can choose to use the keywords {date} and {time} to help create a logical representation of the data output. For our implementation, we will use [date]/[time] to keep the data separated by date and time. This will provide a file structure within the blob container similar to the path "year/month/day/time".

- *Date Format*: The default format is YYYY/MM/DD. Accept the default.

- *Time Format*: The default format is HH. Accept the default.

- *Event Serialization Format*: The choices are JSON, CSV, and Avro. We will use JSON for our output definition, especially since the incoming data stream is in the same format (JSON).

The screenshot in Figure 5-16 depicts the parameter options for defining an output definition for blob storage.

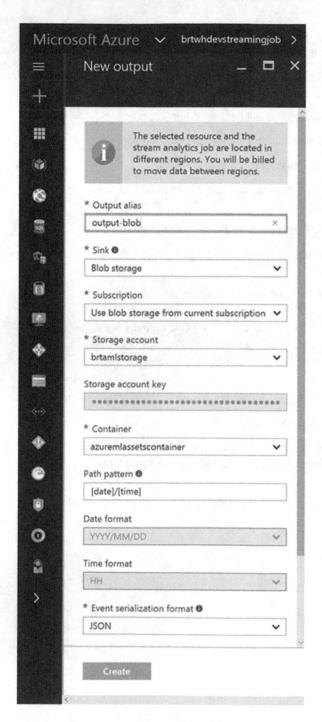

Figure 5-16. *Stream Analytics job: cold path output definition parameters using blob storage*

Once you have entered all the required parameters, click on the Create button at the bottom of the screen and the new output definition will be quickly tested and added to the Azure Streaming Analytics job.

Streaming Analytics Job: Warm Path Output: Azure SQL Database

For our "warm path" we will be using Azure SQL database for our output option. A mandatory prerequisite for this step is to create an Azure database server, an Azure database, and an Azure table to store the data.

■ **Note** Refer to the following link for more information on creating an Azure SQL database:

SQL Database tutorial: Create a SQL database in minutes by using the Azure portal:

https://azure.microsoft.com/en-us/documentation/articles/sql-database-get-started/

Listing 5-12 is a Transact-SQL script that will create an Azure SQL database table named IotHubSensorReadings.

Listing 5-12. SQL Table Definition for [IotHubSensorReadings]

```
CREATE TABLE [dbo].[IotHubSensorReadings](
    [UserId] [char](256) NOT NULL,
    [Age] [float] NOT NULL,
    [Height] [float] NOT NULL,
    [Weight] [float] NOT NULL,
    [HeartRateBPM] [float] NOT NULL,
    [BreathingRate] [float] NOT NULL,
    [Temperature] [float] NOT NULL,
    [Steps] [float] NOT NULL,
    [Velocity] [float] NOT NULL,
    [Altitude] [float] NOT NULL,
    [Ventilization] [float] NOT NULL,
    [Activity] [float] NOT NULL,
    [Cadence] [float] NOT NULL,
    [Speed] [float] NOT NULL,
    [HIB] [float] NOT NULL,
    [HeartRateRedZone] [float] NOT NULL,
    [HeartrateVariability] [float] NOT NULL,
    [Status] [int] NOT NULL,
    [Id] [char](256) NOT NULL,
    [DeviceId] [char](256) NOT NULL,
    [MessageType] [int] NOT NULL,
    [Longitude] [float] NOT NULL,
    [Latitude] [float] NOT NULL,
    [Timestamp] [datetime2](7) NOT NULL,
    [EventProcessedUtcTime] [datetime2](7) NOT NULL,
    [PartitionId] [int] NOT NULL,
    [EventEnqueuedUtcTime] [datetime2](7) NOT NULL
)
```

Note that the column names in the `IotHubSensorReadings` table exactly match the column names of our input data stream. This is not a necessary step, but as you will soon see, this helps make it very easy when it comes time to write the SQL query statements. To fix any column name mismatches, we can simply use the T-SQL `AS` clause to rename an incoming column to a destination column in our `SELECT` statements.

Once the prerequisite Azure SQL Database artifacts (Server, Database, and Table) have been created, you will need to gather the credentials for the database (username and password) for the next step in the configuration process—creating the streaming job output definition.

To create the Azure Streaming Analytics job output definition for the "warm" data path, start by navigating (via the Azure Portal) to the previously defined streaming job definition and selecting Outputs.

Click on + Add to add a new output definition:

- Under the Sink parameter, select SQL database from the drop-down list. This action will properly set the remaining fields for you to populate:

- *Output Alias*: A name for this output definition that will be used in our SQL query.

- *Sink*: Refers to the selected output destination; in this case, select SQL database.

- *Subscription*: The Azure subscription to be used for this output definition.

- *Database*: The name of the Azure SQL database we created as a prerequisite earlier in the chapter.

- *Server Name*: The name of the Azure SQL Server we created as a prerequisite earlier in the chapter. Note that the naming convention should follow the following format:

- `<Your Server Name>.database.windows.net`

- **Username:** The username credential for the Azure SQL database server.

- **Password:** The password credential for the Azure SQL database server.

- **Table:** The name of the Azure SQL database table we created as a prerequisite earlier in the chapter. Our reference implementation example used the table named `IotHubSensorReadings`.

The screenshot shown in Figure 5-17 depicts the parameter options for defining an output definition for a SQL database.

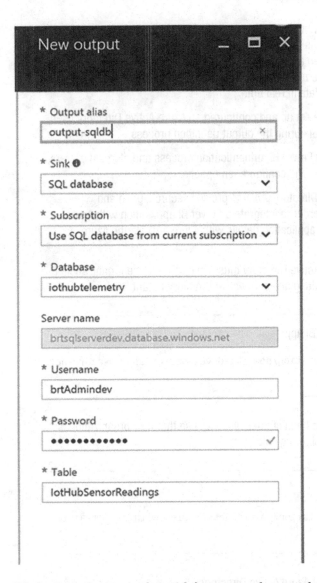

Figure 5-17. *Stream Analytics job for warm path output definition parameters using SQL database*

Once you have entered all the required parameters, click on the Create button at the bottom of the screen and the new output definition will be quickly tested and added to the Azure Streaming Analytics job.

Streaming Analytics Job: Hot Path OUTPUT Power BI

For our "hot path" we will be using Power BI for our output option. As stated previously, Power BI is a rich data visualization tool that allows you to create rich, real-time, dashboards and visualizations for critical business data.

Power BI displays dashboards that are interactive and can be created and updated from many different data sources in real time. In a later chapter of this book, we will be using Power BI as a real-time operational dashboard just like a dashboard in an automobile. It displays critical information about vehicles, such as its speed, its fuel level, or oil temperature. In our reference application, we will be monitoring team member's health and activity data in real time.

A mandatory prerequisite for this step is to have set up and configured an Azure Active Directory user that we can use to authenticate against Power BI during the output definition process.

Azure Active Directory is a foundational piece of Power BI Authentication process and stores the users, groups, and domains in addition to other settings and configuration options.

Power BI apps are integrated with Azure Active Directory (AAD) to provide secure sign in and authorization for your Power BI applications. In order to integrate a Power BI application with Azure Active Directory, you would need to register the application details with Azure AAD via the Azure Management Portal.

To sign up for the Power BI service, your Azure Active Directory must have at least one organizational user. See the following link for details about creating an Azure Active Directory tenant:

Create an Azure Active Directory tenant for a Power BI app:

https://powerbi.microsoft.com/en-us/documentation/powerbi-developer-create-an-azure-active-directory-tenant

---

Once a tenant and a user within that tenant have been created, you can use that new organizational user to sign up for the Power BI service at the following link:

Sign up for the Power BI service:

https://powerbi.microsoft.com/en-us/documentation/powerbi-admin-free-with-custom-azure-directory

---

See the following link for more information about Azure Active Directory:

Azure Active Directory: http://azure.microsoft.com/en-us/services/active-directory

---

Once the prerequisites for the Power BI Output option have been configured (Azure Active Directory user/password and registration on the Power BI site), the next step is start the creation of the Power BI output option.

The creation of a Power BI output option is basically a two-step process:

1. Authenticate against Power BI. While doing this step, Azure Streaming Analytics is generating and saving those credentials for when the job is running and pushing real-time data to your Power BI dashboard applications.

2. Provide the necessary details for the output definition.

To create the Azure Streaming Analytics job output definition for the "hot" data path, start by navigating (via the Azure Portal) to the previously defined streaming job definition. Select Outputs.

Click on + Add to add a new output definition:

-   *Under the Sink Parameter.* Select Power BI from the drop-down list. This action will properly set the remaining fields for you to populate.

-   *Output Alias.* A name for this output definition that will be used in our SQL Query.

-   *Sink.* Refers to the selected output destination; in this case, select Power BI.

-   *Authorize Connection.* By clicking on the Authorize button, you will be presented with an authorization screen for you to authenticate against the Power BI service.

As mentioned previously, these credentials are cached and used for real-time access to push new data into your Power BI dashboard.

Figure 5-18 displays a screenshot of the required parameters for the first step.

Figure 5-18. *Stream Analytics job: hot path output definition parameters, Power BI authentication*

After clicking on the Authorize button, you will see a screen similar to the one in Figure 5-19 for you to enter your Power BI credentials.

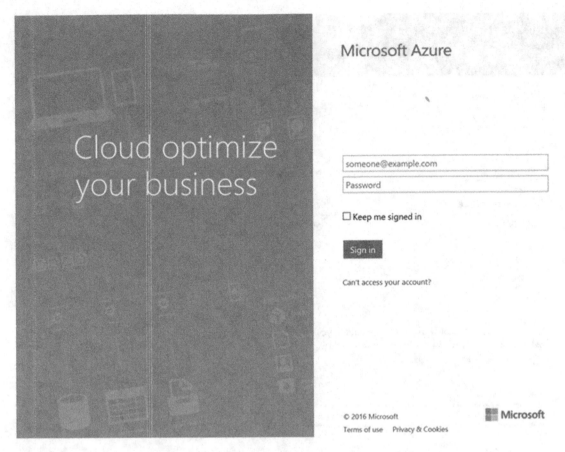

Figure 5-19. Stream Analytics job: hot path output definition parameters Power BI AAD Authentication screen

After you have authenticated against Power BI with your AAD credentials, you will then gain access to the remaining configuration parameters required to complete the output definition.

- *Output Alias*: A name for this output definition that will be used in our SQL query.

- *Sink*: Refers to the selected output destination; in this case, select Power BI.

- *Group Workspace*: Refers to a workspace in your Azure Power BI tenant under which the output dataset will be created.

- *Dataset Name*: A descriptive dataset name for the Power BI output that will be used to reference when creating Power BI dashboards and visualizations.

- *Table Name*: A descriptive table name in a dataset for the Power BI output that will be used to reference when creating Power BI dashboards and visualizations.

Figure 5-20 depicts the additional configuration parameters that are visible once the Power BI connection has been authenticated.

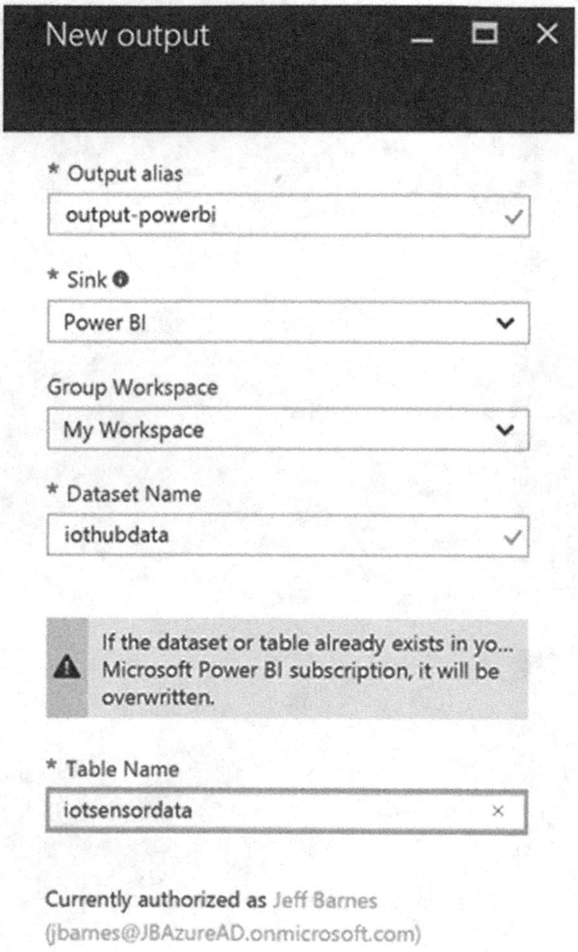

Figure 5-20. *Stream Analytics job: hot path output definition parameters Power BI additional parameters after authentication*

Once you have entered all the required parameters, click on the Create button at the bottom of the screen and the new output definition will be quickly tested and added to the Azure Streaming Analytics job.

We will explore in greater detail the use of Power BI in Chapter 9.

Azure Streaming Analytics Job: Inputs and Outputs

At this point, you have created the following components of the Azure Streaming Analytics job:

- *Inputs:*
  - IoT Hub
  - Reference data

- *Functions*:
  - Azure ML Web Service – `ChkTeamHealth()`
- *Outputs*:
  - Blob storage
  - Azure SQL database
  - Power BI

At this point, your Azure Streaming Analytics job should look like the screenshot in Figure 5-21.

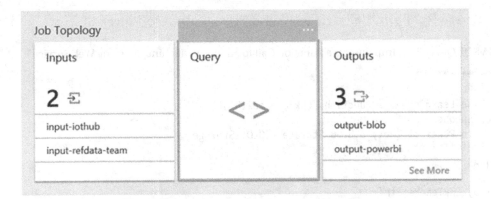

Figure 5-21. *Stream Analytics job: two input definitions and three output definitions*

AZURE SETUP: STREAMING ANALYTICS JOB SQL QUERY

Now that we have created the inputs, functions, and outputs for our Azure Streaming Analytics job, it is time to pull it all together using the ASA SQL Query language.

In the reference implementation, we will make use of most of the options and features available with Azure Streaming Analytics in order to help illustrate how easy it becomes to put together a high-performance ingestion engine that can easily be enhanced to add capabilities to turn massive volumes of data into real-time, actionable data.

The SQL queries that you will implement will allow you to combine the two input definitions along with the Azure ML function definition and then populate three separate output data path destinations for our streaming data. The three paths will correlate to our Lambda architecture guidance for Hot, Warm, and Cold data paths:

- *Hot Path*: We defined an output definition using Power BI, which will allow us to update real-time dashboards and visualizations with the sensor data plus the results of the Azure Machine Learning Web Service calls via the function definition.

- *Warm Path*: We will target Azure SQL database which will allow us to add, update, and query data from many clients.

- *Cold Path*: We will use Azure blob storage to archive the data in its original format plus the additional results of the JOIN on the INPUT with the reference data definition for team member reference health data.

To create the Azure Streaming Analytics job SQL Query definition, start by navigating (via the Azure Portal) to the previously defined streaming job definition. Select Query.

- You will be presented with a SQL Query Editor window.

- Enter the SQL Query text as shown in Figure 5-14 to implement the "hot path" output to Power BI. Note the call to ChkTeamHealth(). This calls the Azure ML Web Service to predict the team member's exhaustion level.

SQL Query Hot Path: Call Azure ML and Then Output to Power BI

Listing 5-13. ASA SQL Query That Implements a Function Call to an Azure Machine Learning Web Service

```
-- ************************
-- * HOTPATH
-- * Invoke Machine Learning As a Function "ChkTeamHealth()"
-- * Via ASA SQL Subquery
-- * then output to Power BI (Hot) & BLOB Storage (COLD) Storage
-- ************************
WITH [subquery] AS
(
    SELECT UserId, ChkTeamHealth(
        UserId,
        BreathingRate,
        Temperature,
        Ventilization,
        Activity,
        HeartRateBPM,
        Cadence,
        Velocity,
        Speed,
        HIB,
        HeartrateRedZone,
        HeartrateVariability,
        "N")
    as result from [input-iothub]
    TIMESTAMP BY [Timestamp]
)
SELECT UserId,
        result.[BreathingRate],
        result.[Temperature],
        result.[Ventilization],
        result.[Activity],
        result.[HeartRateBPM],
        result.[Cadence],
        result.[Velocity],
        result.[Speed],
```

```
        result.[HIB],
        result.[HeartrateRedZone],
        result.[HeartrateVariability],
        result.[Scored labels],
        result.[Scored Probabilities],
        result.[Timestamp]
INTO [output-powerbi]
FROM subquery
```

> ■ **Note**   If there are no red squiggly lines, you can click on the Save button in the top-left navigation pane in the Azure Portal to save the SQL query.

It is highly recommended that you resolve any grammatical errors in your SQL script before progressing. The most common issues are misspellings between your input/function/output definitions and the ones in the reference implementation scripts provided as sample code with this book.

SQL Query Warm Path: Output to Azure SQL Database

Enter the SQL query text as shown in Listing 5-14 to implement the "warm path" output to Azure SQL database.

> ■ **Note**   The field names in the SQL table definition were matched to the incoming JSON column names to expedite development efforts.

Listing 5-14. ASA SQL Query that Outputs to Azure SQL Database

```
-- ***************************
-- * WARM Path
-- * OUTPUT to Azure SQL DB
-- ***************************
SELECT
    UserId,
    Age,
    Height,
    Weight,
    HeartRateBPM,
    BreathingRate,
    Temperature,
    Steps,
    Velocity,
    Altitude,
    Ventilization,
    Activity,
    Cadence,
    Speed,
```

```
    HIB,
    HeartRateRedZone,
    HeartrateVariability,
    Status,
    Id,
    DeviceId,
    MessageType,
    Longitude,
    Latitude,
    [Timestamp],
    EventProcessedUtcTime,
    PartitionId,
    EventEnqueuedUtcTime
INTO [output-sqldb]

FROM [input-iothub]
TIMESTAMP BY [Timestamp]
```

SQL Query Cold Path: Output to Azure SQL Database

Enter the SQL Query text shown in Listing 5-15 to implement the "cold path" output to Azure blob storage.

■ **Note**   The incoming sensor data from IoT Hub is JOINed with the team member's reference data.

Listing 5-15. ASA SQL Query that JOINS with Reference Data and Outputs to Azure Blob Storage

```
-- ************************
-- * COLD Path
-- * OUTPUT ALL incoming fields into to Azure BLOB Storage
-- * JOIN on Reference Data
-- ************************
SELECT
    IH.UserId,
    IH.Age,
    IH.Height,
    IH.Weight,
    IH.HeartRateBPM,
    IH.BreathingRate,
    IH.Temperature,
    IH.Steps,
    IH.Velocity,
    IH.Altitude,
    IH.Ventilization,
    IH.Activity,
    IH.Cadence,
```

```
    IH.Speed,
    IH.HIB,
    IH.HeartRateRedZone,
    IH.HeartrateVariability,
    IH.Status,
    IH.Id,
    IH.DeviceId,
    IH.MessageType,
    IH.Longitude,
    IH.Latitude,
    IH.[Timestamp],
    IH.EventProcessedUtcTime,
    IH.PartitionId,
    IH.EventEnqueuedUtcTime,
    RF.healthInformation__age,
    RF.healthInformation__height,
    RF.healthInformation__weight,
    RF.healthInformation__gender,
    RF.healthInformation__race

INTO
    [output-blob]
FROM
    [input-iothub] IH
TIMESTAMP BY [Timestamp]

JOIN
[input-refdata-team] RF
    ON IH.UserId = RF.id
```

Click on the Save button in the top-left navigation pane in the Azure Portal to save the SQL query.

AZURE SETUP: STREAMING ANALYTICS JOB, START JOB

Now that the last remaining step to completing the Azure Streaming Analytics job has been completed, it is time to start our streaming Analytics job and view the expected output results.

Navigate to the streaming analytics job you created previously and click on the |> Start button on the top-center of the Azure Portal, as shown in Figure 5-22.

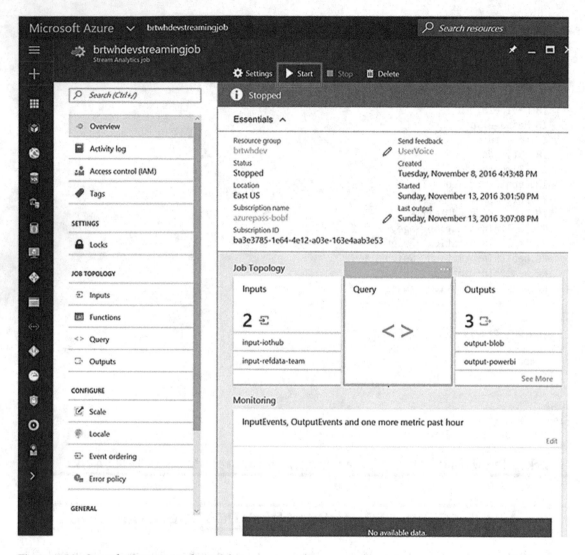

Figure 5-22. *Start the Stream Analytics job*

■ This step will normally take a few minutes (three to five) for the Azure Streaming Analytics job to fully start.

Using the Device Simulator to Test the Azure Streaming Analytics Job Stream

Once the Azure streaming job is running, you can run the C# Device Simulator code from the GitHub repository to test the Azure Streaming Analytics job.

Once downloaded, you will find a Visual Studio Solution in the \brt\devices\Simulator folder. This is a simple C# .NET Console application that creates a comprehensive dataset of sensor information and sends it into the Azure IoT Hub connection.

Once you locate the solution in the repository, you can then load, build, and run the solution (`Simulator.sln`). You will see a console window similar to the one in Figure 5-23.

```
Simulating teammate1
  Profile Id : 058d7760-e868-434e-aa1d-bbc438d5ebb6
  Device Id  : 339810bc-e868-4ff7-b648-72ee1a161695
Simulating teammate2
  Profile Id : c3ec2fe4-6789-4d3e-8446-852856ce025c
  Device Id  : 9369763c-39a8-4e6b-9795-5683b62938a1
Simulating teammate3
  Profile Id : 663d1c24-9afd-4550-8d57-7d869b0918ca
  Device Id  : 94697898-627f-447f-93f7-b55a76edfae9
Simulating teammate4
  Profile Id : 7809cfad-5cc0-4ce1-97ca-d4ed261a8e94
  Device Id  : 542f805c-e2fa-454e-9e50-33428ffd5a30
Simulating teammate5
  Profile Id : 2d49b721-e157-4dcd-ba50-4de2f0323489
  Device Id  : d6a8aee0-0b95-43ba-a663-d0116dbc02f6
Simulating teammate6
  Profile Id : 8b3ac2c9-807b-4470-9611-1ec362250654
  Device Id  : 59ba9390-ac3e-4512-a2b3-e4781abf763d
Simulating teammate7
  Profile Id : 42105a24-00f7-4f5a-aca3-3001aa14eb75
  Device Id  : 8d9a836a-96f1-4960-a009-6e3c02adfee3
Simulating teammate8
  Profile Id : aa1c0209-d542-4535-81f5-ec90d0316935
  Device Id  : c48a7162-501d-4cde-bca9-f36062f4e701
Simulating teammate9
  Profile Id : 698607de-a022-4ed7-9458-8ee36ad49144
  Device Id  : 67226a07-7490-4cf8-b13d-eec8d653ca18
Simulating teammate10
  Profile Id : 82923b70-34cf-476c-a8b5-dc7bed2f17c6
  Device Id  : e8f3e93b-568e-468b-a7a4-937744f52fc2
Simulating teammate11
  Profile Id : 0f15ad8d-272e-4981-9829-b34a284a526a
  Device Id  : 87995524-7c7f-420e-a7bf-f94c6fe06f4e
Simulating teammate12
  Profile Id : 870ad05d-996d-4fd0-b074-f7ff4fb4cc67
  Device Id  : 130879df-8cae-40c2-940f-1bc682c806c9
Simulating teammate13
  Profile Id : a87747ef-e6ab-4b3f-a9b1-0889299a92f9
  Device Id  : b2aac61e-3dd7-435d-ae79-65b76bc36f0e
Simulating teammate14
  Profile Id : ce177590-df50-43f4-bfc0-7c54c53ba9e9
  Device Id  : 7002b8a9-5317-4d6e-950f-357495c72cad
Simulating teammate15
  Profile Id : d7940971-ddce-4535-b738-3d94b00d2b24
  Device Id  : 563cc9bd-a061-499f-8362-78511fe959a3
```

Figure 5-23. *C# .NET Console Device Simulator output*

You should also start to see the data flowing into the various output destinations as defined in the Azure Streaming Analytics job.

Verify the Azure Streaming Analytics job Output: Azure Blob Storage

You can easily check and verify the Azure blob output destination using tools like the Cloud Explorer in Visual Studio 2015 or by using the "Azure Storage Explorer," which can be downloaded from `http://azurestorageexplorer.codeplex.com`.

Figure 5-24 provides an example screenshot of the Azure blob output results when viewed with the Visual Studio Cloud Explorer tool.

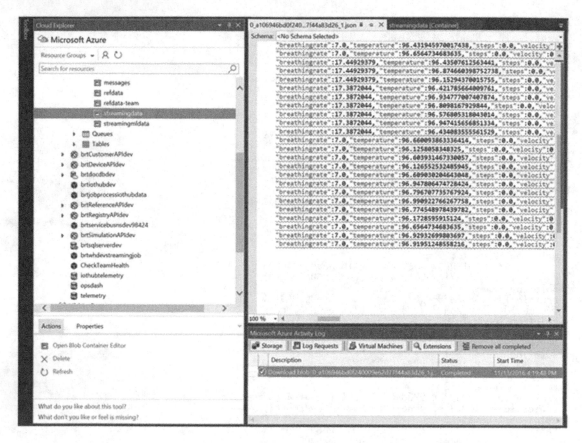

Figure 5-24. *Visual Studio 2015 Cloud Explorer Tool to verify Azure blob output results from THE Streaming Analytics job*

Verify the Azure Streaming Analytics job Output: Azure SQL Database

To verify the Azure SQL database output results from the Azure Streaming Analytics job, YOU can use tools like SQL Server Management Studio (SSMS). You can download it from the following link:

Download SQL Server Management Studio (SSMS)

https://msdn.microsoft.com/en-us/library/mt238290.aspx

Figure 5-25 provides an example screenshot of the Azure SQL database output results when a SELECT statement is executed against the output SQL table and viewed within the SQL Server Management Studio Query window.

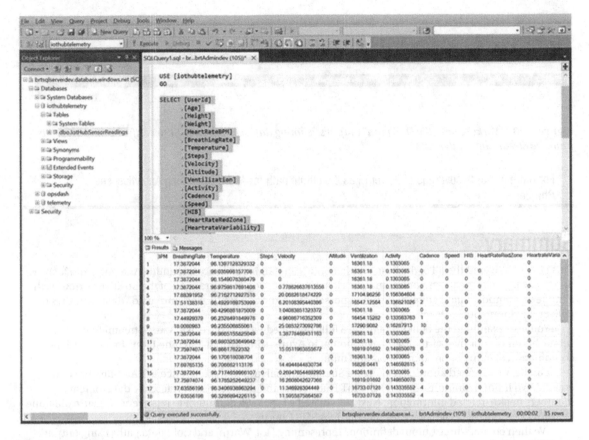

Figure 5-25. *Using SQL Server Management Studio to verify Azure SQL database output results from THE Streaming Analytics job*

Verify the Azure Streaming Analytics job Output: Power BI

To verify the Streaming Analytics job output to Power BI, you can sign in to THE Power BI web site at the following link using your Azure Active Directory organizational ID: https://powerbi.microsoft.com/en-us.

Once you have signed in to the Power BI Web Portal, you can navigate down the left-side navigation pane to the topic area named Datasets and select the option for Streaming Datasets.

After clicking on the link, you should see a list of available streaming datasets. Look for one named iothubdata, which represents the output from THE Azure Streaming Analytics job, as shown in Figure 5-26.

Figure 5-26. *Working with the "hot path" output streaming dataset for Power BI to verify the output results from the Streaming Analytics job*

For more in-depth coverage of Power BI as the output path for Azure Streaming Analytics, see Chapter 9.

Summary

This chapter covered the all of the basic fundamental capabilities of Azure Streaming Analytics. You learned how you can easily create streaming analytics jobs that allow you to leverage all of the positive attributes that a modern, Lambda data architecture should possess, including "hot", "warm", and "cold" data pathways to deliver maximum business results.

You also examined the benefits of using a fully managed PaaS service like Azure Streaming Analytics, versus building your own virtualized environment in Azure using Virtual Machine Linux images and the combination of many open source tools and utilities.

Finally, you applied knowledge of Azure Streaming Analytics to the reference IoT Architecture and created two input definitions—one for the IoT Hub events and the second for reference data for team members health-related information. Next, we created a FUNCTION definition to represent an Azure Machine Learning Web Service call that we used in our ASA SQL Query.

We then created three output definitions representing Hot, Warm, and Cold data paths using output definition parameters to update corresponding Azure data platforms—Power BI for "Hot", Azure SQL Database for "Warm", and Azure blob STORAGE for "Cold" storage.

As can easily be seen from this chapter, Azure Streaming Analytics can play a key role in the ingestion, organization, and orchestration of IoT sensor transactions. The environment makes it easy to get started yet is extremely powerful and flexible and can easily scale to handle millions of transactions per second. A powerful stream analytics engine is critical to success for the modern enterprise seeking to operate a business at Internet speed.

■ ■ ■

## CHAPTER 6

Batch Processing with Data Factory and Data Lake Store

This chapter examines the use of Azure Data Factory and Azure Data Lake, including where, why, and how these technologies fit in the capabilities of a modern business running at Internet speed. It first covers the basic technical aspects and capabilities of Azure Data Factory and Azure Data Lake. Following that, the chapter implements three major pieces of functionality for the reference implementation:

- Update reference data that we used for the Azure Stream Analytics job. As you may recall, we used the reference data in an ASA SQL JOIN query for gathering extended team member health data.

- Re-train the Azure Machine Learning Model for predicting team member health and exhaustion levels. This data will be based on updated medical stress tests that are administered to team members on a periodic basis.

- Move data from Azure blob storage to Azure Data Lake. This step prepares the reference implementation Data Lake analytics, which is the topic of Chapter 7.

Azure Data Factory Overview

Azure Data Factory fulfills a critical need in any modern Big Data processing environment. It can be seen as the backbone of any data operation, as Data Factory provides the critical core capabilities required to perform enterprise data transformation functions. This includes:

- *Data Ingestion and Preparation*: From multiple sources; any combination of on-premise and cloud-based data sources.

- *Transformation and Analysis*: Schedule, orchestrate, and manage the data transformation and analysis processes.

- *Publish and Consumption*: Ability to transform raw data into finished data that is ready for consumption by BI tools or mobile applications.

- *Monitoring and Management*: Visualize, monitor, and manage data movement and processing pipelines to quickly identify issues and take intelligent action. Alert capabilities to monitor overall data processing service health.

- *Efficient Resource Management*: Saves you time and money by automating data transformation pipelines with on-demand cloud resources and management.

© Bob Familiar and Jeff Barnes 2017
B. Familiar and J. Barnes, *Business in Real-Time Using Azure IoT and Cortana Intelligence Suite*,
DOI 10.1007/978-1-4842-2650-6_6

Azure Data Factory is a cloud-based data integration service that orchestrates and automates the movement and transformation of data. You can create data integration solutions using Azure Data Factory that can ingest data from various data stores (handles both on-premise and cloud-based), transform and process the data, and then publish the processing results to various output data stores.

The Azure Data Factory service is a fully managed cloud-based service that allows you to create data processing "pipelines" that can move and transform data. Data Factory has the capability to perform highly advanced and customizable ETL (Extract-Transform-Load) functions on the data as it moves through the various stages in a processing pipeline.

These data processing "pipelines" can then be run either on a specified schedule (such as hourly, daily, weekly, etc.) or on-demand to provide a rich batch processing capability for data movement and analytics at enterprise scale.

Azure Data Factory also provides rich visualizations to display the history, versions, and dependencies between your data pipelines, as well as monitor all your data pipelines from a single unified view. This allows you to easily detect and pinpoint any processing issues and set up appropriate monitoring alerts.

Figure 6-1 provides an illustration of the various data processing operations performed by Azure Data Factory, such as data ingestion, preparation, transformation, analysis, and finally publication. This data can be easily consumed by the key users of the data.

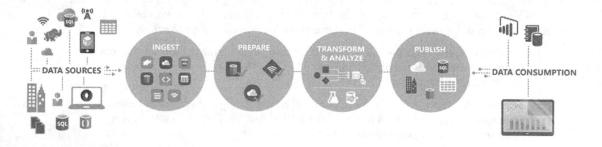

Figure 6-1. *Azure Data Factory can ingest data from various data sources*

Pipelines and Activities

In a normal Azure Data Factory solution, one or more data processing pipelines are typically utilized. A Data Factory pipeline is a logical grouping of activities. It's used to group activities into a unit that together performs a single task.

Activities

Azure Data Factory *activities* define the actions to perform on your data. For example, you may use a *copy* activity to copy data from one data store to another. Similarly, you may use a *hive* activity, which runs a hive query on an Azure HDInsight cluster to transform or analyze your data. Data Factory supports two types of activities:

- *Data Movement Activities*: This includes the copy activity, which copies data from a source data store to a sink data store. Data Factory supports the following data stores:
  - *Azure:*
    - Azure blob storage
    - Azure Data Lake Store
    - Azure SQL database

- Azure SQL data warehouse
- Azure table storage
- Azure DocumentDB
- Azure Search Index

- *Databases:*
  - SQL Server*
  - Oracle*
  - MySQL*
  - DB2*
  - Teradata*
  - PostgreSQL*
  - Sybase*
  - Cassandra*
  - MongoDB*
  - Amazon Redshift

- *File Systems:*
  - File System*
  - HDFS*
  - Amazon S3
  - FTP

- *Other Systems:*
  - Salesforce
  - Generic ODBC*
  - Generic OData
  - Web Table (table from HTML)
  - GE Historian*

- Note: Data stores denoted with a * can exist either on-premises or on an Azure Virtual Machine (IaaS). This option requires that you install the Data Management Gateway on either an on-premises or Azure Virtual Machine.

▪ **Note**   See the following link for more information on the Data Management Gateway.

Move data between on-premises sources and the cloud with Data Management Gateway: `https://docs.microsoft.com/en-us/azure/data-factory/data-factory-move-data-between-onprem-and-cloud`.

- *Data Transformation Activities*: Azure Data Factory supports the following transformation activities that either can be added to pipelines individually or chained together with another activity.

Data Transformation Activity Environment	Compute Environment
Hive	HDInsight [Hadoop]
Pig	HDInsight [Hadoop]
MapReduce	HDInsight [Hadoop]
Hadoop Streaming	HDInsight [Hadoop]
Machine Learning activities	Azure VM
Stored Procedure	Azure SQL, Azure SQL Data Warehouse, or SQL Server in VM
Data Lake Analytics U-SQL	Azure Data Lake Analytics
Dot Net	HDInsight [Hadoop] or Azure Batch

If you need to move data to or from a data store that the Azure Data Factory Copy Activity doesn't support, or you need to transform data using custom logic, you can always create a custom .NET activity.

■ **Note** For details on creating and using a custom activity, see the "Use custom activities in an Azure Data Factory pipeline" link at `https://docs.microsoft.com/en-us/azure/data-factory/data-factory-use-custom-activities`.

Linked Services

Linked services define the information needed for Azure Data Factory to connect to external data resources (for example: on-premises SQL Server, Azure Storage, and HDInsight running in Azure). Linked services are used for two primary purposes in Azure Data Factory:

- *To represent a data store*: Such as an on-premise SQL Server, Oracle database, file share, or an Azure blob storage account.

- *To represent a compute resource*: One that can host the execution of an activity. As an example, the HDInsight hive activity runs on an HDInsight Hadoop cluster and can be used to perform data transformations.

Datasets

In the larger scheme of things, linked services link the data stores to an Azure Data Factory job. Datasets represent data structures within those data stores.

As an example, an "Azure SQL linked service" might provide connection information for an Azure SQL database. An Azure SQL dataset would then specify the specific table that would contain the data for Azure Data Factory to process.

Additionally, an "Azure storage linked service" would provide connection information for Azure Data Factory to be able to connect to an Azure Storage account. From there, an Azure blob dataset would specify the container for the blob and the folder in the Azure Storage account from which the pipeline should read the incoming data.

Pipelines

An Azure Data Factory pipeline is a grouping of logically related activities. A pipeline is used to group activities into a logical unit that performs a task.

Activities define the specific actions to perform on the data. Each pipeline activity can take zero or more datasets as an input and can produce one or more datasets as output.

For example, a copy activity can be used to copy data from one Azure data store to another data store. Alternatively, one could use an HDInsight hive activity to run a hive query on an Azure HDInsight cluster in order to transform the data stream.

Azure Data Factory provides a wide range of data ingestion, movement, and transformation activities. Developers also have the freedom to choose to create a custom .NET activity to run their own custom code in an Azure Data Factory pipeline.

Scheduling and Execution

At this point, we have examined what Data Factory pipelines and activities are and how they are composed to create holistic data processing work streams in Azure Data Factory. We will now examine the scheduling and execution engine in Azure Data Factory.

It is important to note that an Azure Data Factory pipeline is active only between its start time and end time. Consequently, it is not executed before the start time or after the end time. If the pipeline is in the "paused" state, it will not get executed at all, no matter how the start and end times are set.

Note that it is not the pipeline that gets actually gets executed. Rather, it is the set of activities within the Data Factory pipeline that actually get executed. However, they do so in the overall context of the Data Factory pipeline.

The Azure Data Factory service allows you to create data pipelines that move and transform data, and then run those pipelines on a specified operational schedule (hourly, daily, weekly, etc.).

Data Factory also provides rich visualizations to display the history, version, and dependencies between data pipelines, and allows you to monitor all your data pipelines from a single unified view. This provides an easy management tool to help pinpoint issues and set up monitoring alerts.

Pipeline Copy Activity End-to-End Scenario

In this section, we examine a complete end-to-end example of creating an Azure Data Factory pipeline to copy data from Azure blob storage to an Azure SQL database. Along the way, we emphasize the major features and capabilities that you can exploit to make the most out of Azure Data Factory for your requirements.

■ **Note**   See this link for detailed steps to accomplish this Data Factory scenario:

Copy data from blob storage to SQL database using Data Factory: `https://docs.microsoft.com/en-us/azure/data-factory/data-factory-copy-data-from-azure-blob-storage-to-sql-database`

Scenario Prerequisites

Before you can create an Azure Data Factory pipeline or activities, you need the following:

- *Azure Subscription*: If you don't already have a subscription, you can start for free at https://azure.microsoft.com/en-us/free/?b=16.46.

- *Azure Storage Account*: You use the blob storage as a "source" data store in this scenario.

- *Azure SQL Database*: You use an Azure SQL database as a destination data store in this tutorial.

- *SQL Server Management Studio or Visual Studio*: You use these tools to create a sample database and destination table, and to view the resultant data in the database table.

JSON Definition

If you have walked through the Azure Data Factory link to "Copy Data from Blob Storage to SQL Database Using Data Factory," you may have noticed that there are a variety of tools that you can use to define an Azure Data Factory pipeline or activity:

- Copy Wizard

- Azure Portal

- Visual Studio

- PowerShell

- Azure Resource Manager template

- ReST API

- .NET API

No matter what the tool is used to create the initial Azure Data Factory job, ultimately, Azure Data Factory utilizes JavaScript Object Notation (JSON) to define and persist the definitions that you create via the tools.

JSON is a lightweight data-interchange format that makes it easy for humans to read and write as well as easy for machines to parse and generate. One distinct advantage of this approach is that the specific JSON configuration parameters can be finely tweaked and tuned for the scenario at hand in order to provide complete control over the configuration and run options for the Data Factory job.

To get started, navigate (via the Azure Portal) to your Azure Data Factory job created in the link and click on the Author and Deploy option, as shown in Figure 6-2.

Author and deploy
Copy data (PREVIEW)
Monitor & Manage
Sample pipelines
Diagram
Metrics and operations

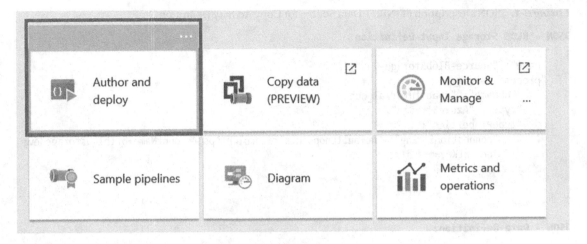

Figure 6-2. *Azure Portal Data Factory: Author and Deploy options*

Once you have clicked on the Author and Deploy option, you will see a screen similar to the one in Figure 6-3, where you can navigate thru each step of a Data Factory pipeline job that was created and see the corresponding JSON for each step of the process.

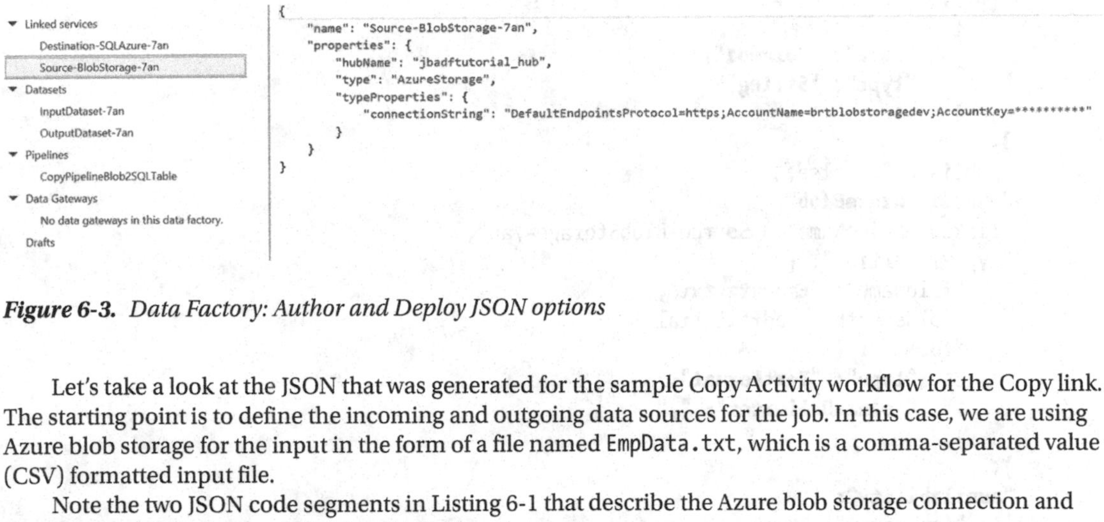

Linked services
Destination-SQLAzure-7an
Source-BlobStorage-7an
Datasets
InputDataset-7an
OutputDataset-7an
Pipelines
CopyPipelineBlob2SQLTable
Data Gateways
No data gateways in this data factory.
Drafts
{
"name": "Source-BlobStorage-7an",
"properties": {
"hubName": "jbadftutorial_hub",
"type": "AzureStorage",
"typeProperties": {
"connectionString": "DefaultEndpointsProtocol=https;AccountName=brtblobstoragedev;AccountKey=**********"
}
}
}

Figure 6-3. *Data Factory: Author and Deploy JSON options*

Let's take a look at the JSON that was generated for the sample Copy Activity workflow for the Copy link. The starting point is to define the incoming and outgoing data sources for the job. In this case, we are using Azure blob storage for the input in the form of a file named `EmpData.txt`, which is a comma-separated value (CSV) formatted input file.

Note the two JSON code segments in Listing 6-1 that describe the Azure blob storage connection and the corresponding dataset definition for the input source.

Listing 6-1. JSON Description of INPUT Data Source for Copy Activity Definition

```
JSON - BLOB Storage Input Definition
{
    "name": "Source-BlobStorage-7an",
    "properties": {
        "hubName": "jbadftutorial_hub",
        "type": "AzureStorage",
        "typeProperties": {
            "connectionString": "DefaultEndpointsProtocol=https;AccountName=brtblobstoragedev;
            AccountKey=**********"
        }
    }
}


JSON - Data Definition:
{
    "name": "InputDataset-7an",
    "properties": {
        "structure": [
            {
                "name": "Column0",
                "type": "String"
            },
            {
                "name": "Column1",
                "type": "String"
            }
        ],
        "published": false,
        "type": "AzureBlob",
        "linkedServiceName": "Source-BlobStorage-7an",
        "typeProperties": {
            "fileName": "EmpData.txt",
            "folderPath": "adftutorial",
            "format": {
                "type": "TextFormat",
                "columnDelimiter": ","
            }
        },
        "availability": {
            "frequency": "Day",
            "interval": 1
        },
        "external": true,
        "policy": {}
    }
}
```

Note in the two JSON code segments that these two definitions completely describe the data input source even down to the field definitions within the CSV text file in Azure blob storage. This interface in the Azure Portal also allows you to easily override the standard parameters by simply editing the JSON directly.

Listing 6-2 shows sample JSON output for a Data Factory Copy Operation.

Listing 6-2. Data Factory Copy Operation JSON Parameters

Data Factory - JSON Copy Pipeline Operations
```json
{
    "name": "CopyPipelineBlob2SQLTable",
    "properties": {
        "description": "CopyPipelineBlob2SQLTable",
        "activities": [
            {
                "type": "Copy",
                "typeProperties": {
                    "source": {
                        "type": "BlobSource",
                        "recursive": false
                    },
                    "sink": {
                        "type": "SqlSink",
                        "writeBatchSize": 0,
                        "writeBatchTimeout": "00:00:00"
                    },
                    "translator": {
                        "type": "TabularTranslator",
                        "columnMappings": "Column0:FirstName,Column1:LastName"
                    }
                },
                "inputs": [
                    {
                        "name": "InputDataset-7an"
                    }
                ],
                "outputs": [
                    {
                        "name": "OutputDataset-7an"
                    }
                ],
                "policy": {
                    "timeout": "1.00:00:00",
                    "concurrency": 1,
                    "executionPriorityOrder": "NewestFirst",
                    "style": "StartOfInterval",
                    "retry": 3,
                    "longRetry": 0,
                    "longRetryInterval": "00:00:00"
                },
                "scheduler": {
                    "frequency": "Day",
                    "interval": 1
                },
                "name": "Blobpathadftutorial->dbo_emp"
            }
```

```
    ],
    "start": "2016-11-22T15:06:22.806Z",
    "end": "2099-12-31T05:00:00Z",
    "isPaused": false,
    "hubName": "jbadftutorial_hub",
    "pipelineMode": "Scheduled"
  }
}
```

The JSON definition in Listing 6-2 allows you to have full control over the parameters, the mapping between the CSV file and the SQL table, and run behavior of this pipeline Copy job.

Additionally, note that within the scheduler section of the activity JSON code sample, you can specify a recurring schedule for a pipeline activity. For example, you can schedule a Data Factory pipeline copy activity to run every hour by modifying the JSON as follows:

JSON Code Fragment - Scheduler
```
"scheduler": {
    "frequency": "Hour",
    "interval": 1
},
```

■ **Note**   See the following link for a complete overview of the JSON options for a Data Factory pipeline Copy operation:

Move data to and from Azure blob using Azure Data Factory: `https://docs.microsoft.com/en-us/azure/data-factory/data-factory-azure-blob-connector#azure-storage-linked-service`.

As can be seen from the composable architecture that the JSON definitions provided, Azure Data Factory is an extremely powerful and flexible tool to help manage all the critical aspects of managing Big Data in the cloud. Aspects such as data ingestion (either on-premise or in Azure), preparation, transformation, movement, and scheduling are all required features for running an enterprise-grade data management platform.

Monitoring and Managing Data Factory Pipelines

The Azure Data Factory service provides a rich monitoring dashboard capability that helps to perform the following tasks:

- Assess pipeline health data from end-to-end
- Identify and fix any pipeline processing issues
- Track the history and ancestry of your data
- View relationships between data sources
- View full historical accounting of job execution, system health, and job dependencies

You can easily monitor the state of an Azure Data Factory pipeline job by navigating to your Data Factory job in the Azure Portal and then clicking on the Diagram option, as shown in Figure 6-4.

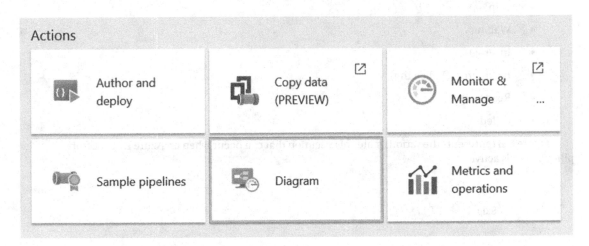

Figure 6-4. *Azure Portal: Data Factory job, diagram view*

Next, you will see a visual diagram of your Data Factory pipeline job, as shown in Figure 6-5. By clicking on either one of the Input or Output definitions, you can see the history and status of each "slice" of data that was created, along with what is scheduled to occur next.

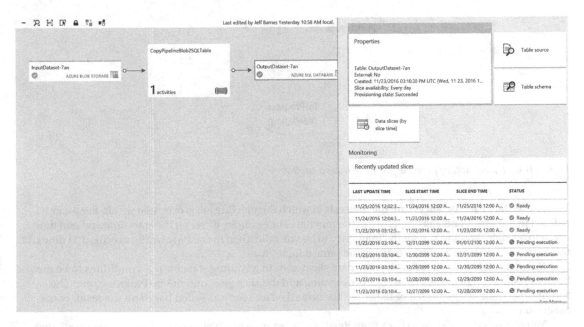

Figure 6-5. *Monitoring an Azure Data Factory job by viewing the output segment history*

Note that the status for each pipeline activity in Azure Data Factory can cycle among many potential execution states, as follows:

- Skip

- Waiting

- In-Progress

- In-Progress (Validating)

- Ready

- Failed

Figure 6-6 represents the various states of execution that can occur when an Azure Data Factory pipeline job is active.

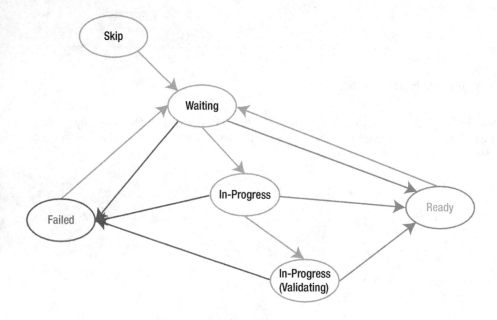

Figure 6-6. *Data Factory pipeline job state transition flow*

Azure Data Factory "slices" are the intervals in which the pipeline job is executed within the period defined in the start and end properties of the pipeline. For example, if you set the start time and end time to occur in a single day, and you set the frequency to be one hour, then the activity will be executed 24 times. In this case, you will have 24 slices, all using the same data source.

Normally, in Azure Data Factory, the data slices start in a Waiting state for pre-conditions to be met before executing. Then, the activity starts executing and the slice goes into the In-Progress state. The activity execution may succeed or fail. The slice is marked as Ready or Failed based on the result of the execution.

You can reset the slice to go back from Ready or Failed state to a Waiting state. You can also mark the slice state to Skip, which prevents the activity from executing and will not process the slice.

■ **Note**   See this link for more information: "Monitor and Manage Azure Data Factory Pipelines": https://docs.microsoft.com/en-us/azure/data-factory/data-factory-monitor-manage-pipelines.

Data Factory Activity and Performance Tuning

Another key set of factors to consider when choosing a cloud data analytics processing system is performance and scalability. Azure Data Factory provides a secure, reliable, and high-performance, data ingestion, and transformation platform that can run at massive scale. Azure Data Factory can enable enterprise scenarios where multiple terabytes of data are moved and transformed across a rich variety of data stores, both on-premise and in Azure.

The Azure Data Factory copy activity offers a highly optimized data loading experience that is easy to install and configure. Within just a single pipeline copy activity, you can achieve load speeds similar to the following:

- Load data into Azure SQL data warehouse at 1.2 GB per second.

- Load data into Azure blob storage at 1.0 GB per second.

- Load data into Azure Data Lake Store at 1.0 GB per second.

Parallel Copy

Azure Data Factory also has the ability to run copy activities from a source or write data to a destination in parallel operations executed in a Copy Activity run. This feature can have a dramatic impact on the throughput of a copy operation and can also reduce the time it takes to perform data transformation and movement functions.

You can use the JSON "parallel copies" property to indicate the parallelism that you want copy activity to use. You can think of this property as the maximum number of threads in the copy activity that can read from your source or write to your sink data stores in parallel.

Listing 6-3.   JSON Snippet of Pipeline Copy Activity Showing the parallelCopies Property

```
JSON Pipeline Copy Activity - "parallelCopies" Property
"activities":[
    {
        "name": "Sample copy activity",
        "description": "",
        "type": "Copy",
        "inputs": [{ "name": "InputDataset" }],
        "outputs": [{ "name": "OutputDataset" }],
        "typeProperties": {
            "source": {
                "type": "BlobSource",
            },
            "sink": {
                "type": "AzureDataLakeStoreSink"
            },
            "parallelCopies": 8
        }
    }
]
```

For each copy activity run, Azure Data Factory determines the number of parallel copies to utilize to copy data from the source data store to the destination data store. The default number of parallel copies that are used is dependent on the type of data source and the data sink that is used.

Cloud Data Movement Units (DMUs)

A Cloud data Movement Unit (DMU) is a Data Factory measurement that represents the relative power (a combination of CPU, memory, and network resource allocation) of a single unit in Azure Data Factory. A DMU might be used in a cloud-to-cloud copy operation, but not in a hybrid copy from an on-premise data store.

By default, Azure Data Factory uses a cloud DMU to perform a single pipeline copy activity execution. To override the default, specify a value for the cloudDataMovementUnits property, as shown in the code segment in Listing 6-4.

Listing 6-4. Sample JSON snippet showing the cloudDataMovementUnits Property

```
Data Factory - JSON Property for "cloudDataMovementUnits"
"activities":[
    {
        "name": "Sample copy activity",
        "description": "",
        "type": "Copy",
        "inputs": [{ "name": "InputDataset" }],
        "outputs": [{ "name": "OutputDataset" }],
        "typeProperties": {
            "source": {
                "type": "BlobSource",
            },
            "sink": {
                "type": "AzureDataLakeStoreSink"
            },
            "cloudDataMovementUnits": 4
        }
    }
]
```

Note that you can achieve higher throughput by leveraging more data movement units (DMUs) than the default maximum DMUs, which is eight for a cloud-to-cloud copy activity run. As an example, you can copy data from Azure blob to Azure Data Lake Store at the rate of 1 gigabyte per second if you are set to use (100) DMUs. In order to request more DMUs than the default of eight for your subscription, you need to submit a support request via the Azure Portal.

■ **Note** For more detailed information concerning performance and tuning for Azure Data Factory jobs, visit the "Copy Activity Performance and Tuning Guide" at https://docs.microsoft.com/en-us/azure/data-factory/data-factory-copy-activity-performance.

Azure Data Lake Store

Azure Data Lake Store is a hyper-scale repository and processing environment for today's modern Big Data analytical workloads.

Azure Data Lake enables you to persist data of any size, data type, and ingestion speed, in a single location, for use in operational and data analytics research.

Hadoop Access

Azure Data Lake Store can be accessed from Hadoop and Azure HDInsight using the WebHDFS-compatible ReST APIs. The `hadoop-azure-datalake` module provides support for integration with the Azure Data Lake Store. The JAR file is named `azure-datalake-store.jar`.

■ **Note**   For Hadoop Azure Data Lake Support, visit `https://hadoop.apache.org/docs/r3.0.0-alpha1/` `hadoop-azure-datalake/index.html`.

Note that there is a distinction to be made around the meaning of the term *Azure Data Lake*. There are potentially two different meanings in Microsoft Azure. It is typically used to refer to a storage subsystem in Azure more commonly referred to as "Azure Data Lake Store" or "ADLS".

The other variation of the term is "Azure Data Lake Analytics" or "ADLA," which is an Azure-based analytics service where you can easily develop and run massively parallel data transformation and processing programs in a variety of languages such as U-SQL, R, Python, and .NET. Azure Data Lake Analytics are covered in detail in Chapter 7. For now, we will cover the basics of Azure Data Lake Store.

ADLS is specifically designed to enable analytics on the data stored in Azure Data Lake. The Data Lake storage subsystem is fine-tuned specifically for high performance for data analytics scenarios.

As a completely managed service offering from Microsoft, Azure Data Lake Store includes all the enterprise-grade capabilities one would expect from a cloud-based repository with massive scalability. The key "abilities" provided by Azure Data Lake Store include: security, manageability, scalability, reliability, and availability. All of the characteristics are essential for real-world enterprise use cases.

With Azure Data Lake Store, you can now explore and harvest value from all your unstructured, semi-structured, and structured enterprise data by running massively parallel analytics over literally any amount of data. Azure Data Lake Store has no artificial constraints on the amount of data, number of files, or the size of individual files that can be stored. At the time of this writing, ADLS can store individual files that can be as large as petabytes in size, which is at least 200x larger than any other cloud storage service available today.

Security Layers

Azure Data Lake Store has security features that are "built-in" from the ground up. As can be seen in Figure 6-7, Azure Data Lake Store has a number of Azure security features and capabilities layered in to help provide the highest confidence in the security of the data, whether the data is at rest or in transit.

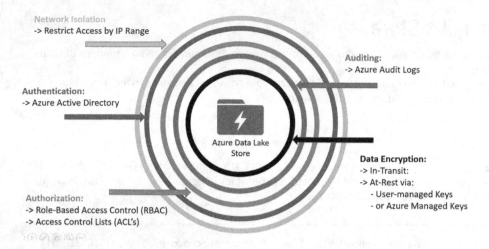

Figure 6-7. *Layered security in Azure Data Lake Store*

Figure 6-7 illustrates the various security layers involved in protecting your data in the Azure Data Lake Store. Here is a quick re-cap of these "built-in" security features:

- *Network Isolation*: Azure Data Lake Store allows you to establish firewalls and define an IP address range for your trusted clients. With an IP address range, only clients that have an IP in the defined range can connect to Azure Data Lake Store.

- *Authentication*: Azure Data Lake Store has Azure Active Directory (AAD) natively integrated to help manage users and group access and permissions. AAD also provides full lifecycle management for millions of identities, integration with on-premise Active Directory, single sign-on support, multi-factor authentication, and support for industry standard open authentication protocols such as OAuth.

- *Authorization*: Azure Data Lake Store (ADLS) provides Role-Based Access Control (RBAC) capabilities via Access Control Lists (ACLs) for managing access to the data files in the Data Lake store. These capabilities provide fine-grained control over file access and permissions (at scale) to all data stored in an Azure Data Lake.

- *Auditing*: Azure Data Lake Store provides rich auditing capabilities to help meet today's modern security and regulatory compliance requirements. Auditing is turned on by default for all account management and data access activities. Audit logs from Azure Data Lake Store can be easily parsed as they are persisted in JSON format. Additionally, since the audit logs are in an easy-to-consume format such as JSON, you can you a wide variety of Business Intelligence (BI) tools to help analyze and report on ADLS activities.

- *Encryption*: Azure Data Lake Store provides built-in encryption for both "at-rest" and "in-transit" scenarios. For data at-rest scenarios, Azure administrators can specify whether to let Azure to manage your Master Encryption Keys (MEKs) or you can use bring-your-own MEKs. In either case, the MEKs will be stored and managed securely in Azure Key Vault, which can utilize FIPS 140-2 Level 2 validated HSMs (Hardware Security Modules). For data in-transit scenarios, the Azure Data Lake Store data is always encrypted, by using the HTTPS (HTTP over Secure Sockets Layer) protocol.

Note that in Azure Data Lake Store, you can choose to have your data encrypted or have no encryption at all. If you choose encryption, all data stored in the Azure Data Lake Store is encrypted prior to persisting the data in the store. Alternately, ADLS will decrypt the data prior to retrieval by the client. From a client perspective, the encryption is transparent and seamless. Consequently, there are no code changes required on the client side to view or encrypt/decrypt the data.

ADLS Encryption Key Management

For encryption key management, Azure Data Lake Store provides two modes for managing your Master Encryption Keys (MEKs). These keys are required for encrypting and decrypting any data that is stored in the Azure Data Lake Store.

You can either let Data Lake Store manage the master encryption keys for you or choose to retain ownership of the MEKs using your Azure Key Vault account. You can specify the mode of key management while creating a new Azure Data Lake Store account.

■ **Tip**   Get started with Azure Data Lake Analytics using the Azure Portal: `https://docs.microsoft.com/en-us/azure/data-lake-analytics/data-lake-analytics-get-started-portal`.

Implementing Data Factory and Data Lake Store in the Reference Implementation

Now that you have a solid background of the features and capabilities in Azure Data Factory and Azure Data Lake Store, you will put your knowledge to use by implementing a few more key pieces of the reference implementation in the remainder of this chapter. As a quick refresher, you will implement the following three pieces of functionality that are required for the reference implementation:

- Update Reference data that you used for the Azure Stream Analytics job. You will use an Azure Data Factory copy job to copy team members' profile data from Azure DocumentDB to a text-based CSV file in Azure Blob storage. As you may recall, you used this reference data in an ASA SQL JOIN query for gathering extended team member health data. We want to make sure that this reference data is updated periodically via a scheduled copy job.

- Re-train the Azure Machine Learning model for predicting team member health and exhaustion levels. We implemented a function in Chapter 5 (StreamAnalytics) to call an Azure Machine Learning Web Service. We want to update the predictive model that runs behind this service using updated medical stress data from tests that are administered to team members on a periodic basis.

- Move data from Azure blob storage to Azure Data Lake. This job will copy the data that originally came from the IoT Hub and was saved into Azure blob storage by the Azure Stream Analytics job in Chapter 5. We want to move this data from Azure blob Storage to Azure Data Lake Store.

UPDATE REFERENCE DATA INPUT FILE FOR AZURE STREAM ANALYTICS JOBS

In this section, we walk through the steps necessary to create an Azure Data Factory copy pipeline job that will copy data from an Azure DocumentDB "NoSQL" database to a text-based CSV file that is persisted in Azure blob storage.

Note that the CSV file will implement a specific file naming convention so that the Azure Stream Analytics job knows to utilize the latest version of the file for use in stream analytics jobs that require this reference data. Figure 6-8 illustrates the INPUT REFERENCE DATA parameter for the Azure Stream Analytics job that describes the file naming convention.

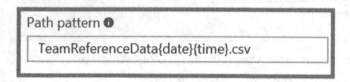

Figure 6-8. *Stream Analytics reference data file naming convention*

By utilizing this file naming convention, the reference data used as input in Azure Stream Analytics job will always reflect the most recent version of the data. Another advantage of using this approach is that future reference data updates can be easily made without adversely impacting any stream analytics jobs currently in process.

The next job that runs simply locates and ingests the latest reference data file that exists in Azure blob storage, based on the file naming convention. In this simple, but very effective, way, the stream analytics job will always use the latest version of the reference data at runtime.

Create Azure Data Factory Job

To get started, navigate to the resource group for your deployment via the Azure Portal. Click on the + Add button and search for Data Factory, as shown in Figure 6-9.

Figure 6-9. *Searching and adding a Data Factory job to a resource group*

After selecting Azure Data Factory, click on the next screen to create the new job, as shown in Figure 6-10.

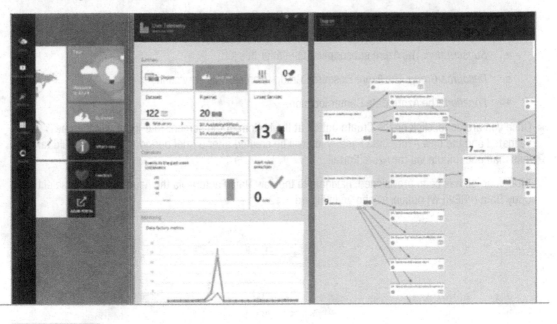

Create

Figure 6-10. *Create Data Factory job*

The next screen allows you to enter the specific parameters for creating a new Azure Data Factory job, as shown in Figure 6-11.

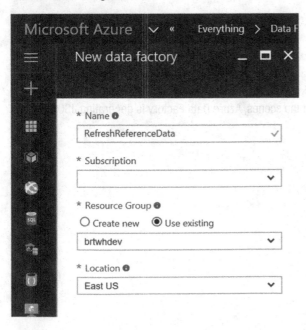

Figure 6-11. *Data Factory create job parameters*

Fill in your choices for the corresponding parameter values:

- *Name*: Enter a unique name for your new Data Factory. Note that the name of the Azure Data Factory must be globally unique.

- *Subscription*: The Azure subscription to use for this job.

- *Resource Group*: The Azure Resource Group to create this service in.

- *Location*: The Azure Data Center location.

Once you are done, click on the Create button at the bottom of the screen. Your input will then be validated and the new Azure Data Factory job will be created after a brief period of time. It should take less than one minute via the Azure Portal.

After your job has been provisioned, navigate to the new Data Factory via the Azure Portal and select the Copy Data (PREVIEW) option, as shown in Figure 6-12.

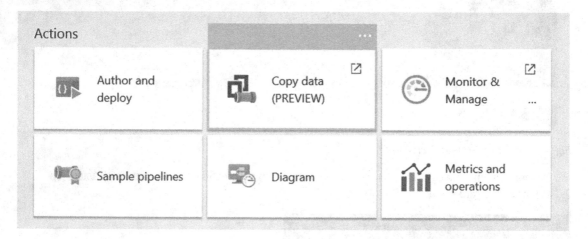

Figure 6-12. *Data Factory: Copy Data Wizard*

This will invoke the Azure Data Factory Copy Data Wizard to launch and will walk you through the steps necessary to create a basic copy pipeline. Behind the scenes, Azure Data Factory is generating JSON files to reflect your choices in the Copy Wizard.

Figure 6-13 depicts the first screen of the Copy Data Wizard and allows you to specify the properties for the copy job.

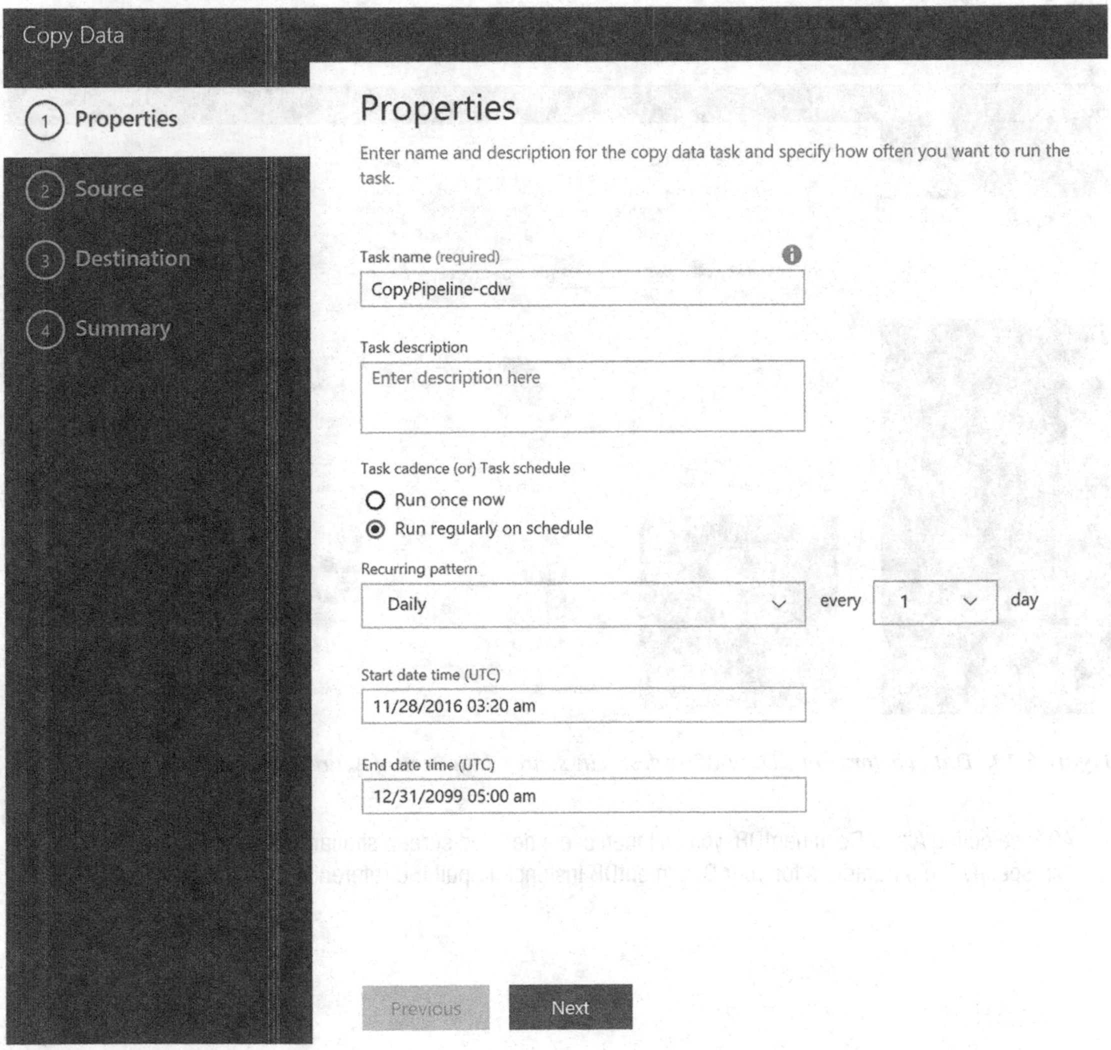

Figure 6-13. *Data Factory Copy Data Wizard: specify properties*

For this example, enter a task name of `CopyReferenceData` and keep the remaining defaults for the schedule, stat, and end dates. Click Next to advance to the next step.

Figure 6-14 depicts the Source Data screen, where you select Azure DocumentDB for the reference implementation scenario.

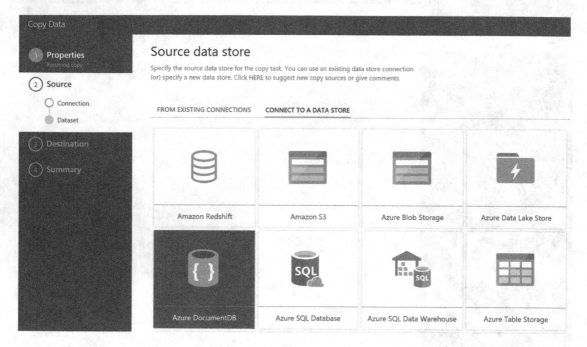

Figure 6-14. *Data Factory Copy Data Wizard: specify source data store of Azure DocumentDB*

After selecting Azure DocumentDB, you will then see a detailed screen similar to Figure 6-15, where you can specify the parameters for your DocumentDB instance to pull the reference data from.

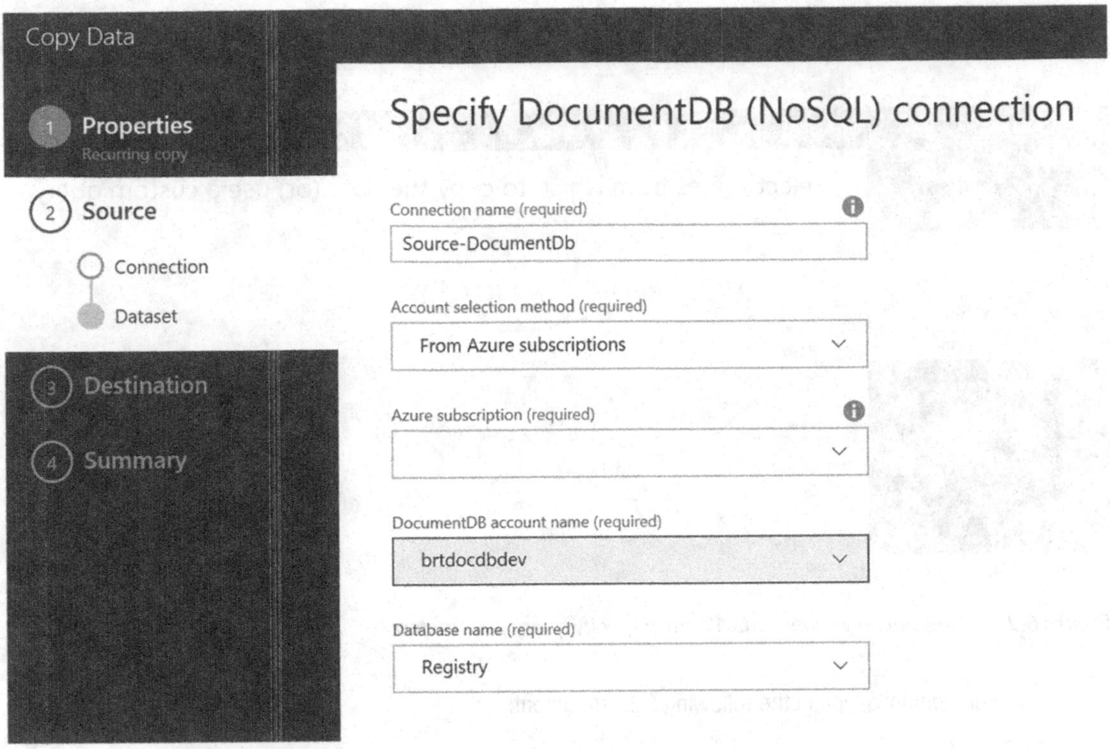

Figure 6-15. *Data Factory Copy Data Wizard: specify Azure DocumentDB parameters*

Click the Next button after entering the DocumentDB parameters. You will see a screen similar to Figure 6-16.

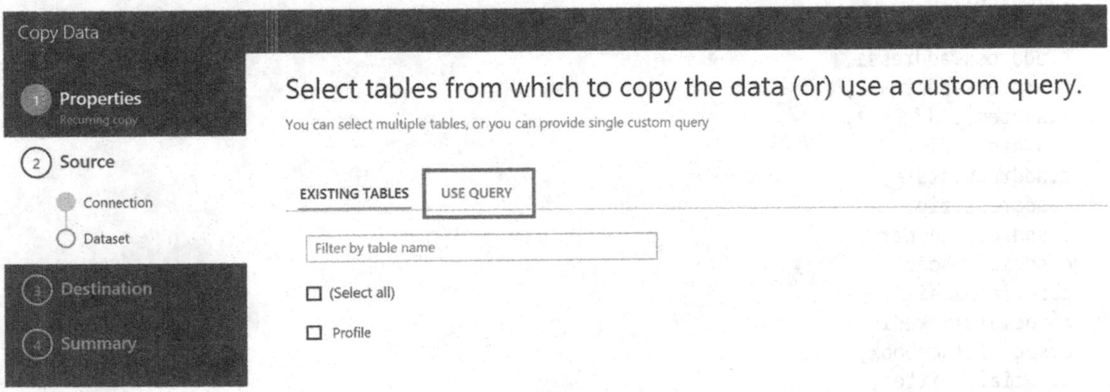

Figure 6-16. *Data Factory Copy Data Wizard: specify copy from tables or query*

Click on the option to Use Query instead of the existing tables. You want to dynamically select the fields you need from the DocumentDB table. You will see a screen similar to Figure 6-17.

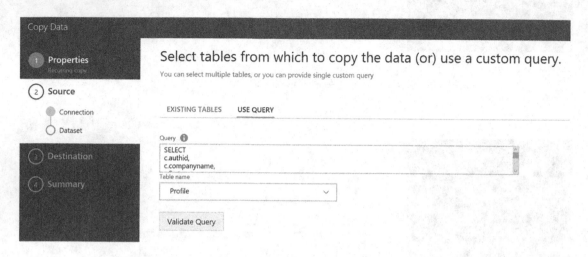

Figure 6-17. *Data Factory Copy Data Wizard: specify query parameters*

In the Query window, type in the following SQL statement:

```
SELECT
c.authid,
c.companyname,
c.firstname,
c.lastname,
c.username,
c.imageUrl,
c.type,
c.address.address1,
c.address.address2,
c.address.address3,
c.address.city,
c.address.state,
c.address.zip,
c.address.country,
c.social.phone,
c.social.email,
c.social.linkedin,
c.social.facebook,
c.social.twitter,
c.social.blog,
c.healthInformation.age,
c.healthInformation.height,
c.healthInformation.weight,
c.healthInformation.gender,
c.healthInformation.race,
```

```
c.location.longitude,
c.location.latitude,
c.id,
c.cachettl,
c._rid,
c._self,
c._etag,
c._attachments,
c._ts
FROM
c
WHERE
c.type <> 1
```

For the table name, select Profile. Then click on Validate Query to test your SQL syntax. If there are no errors, the button will transition from Validating… back to Validate Query.

Click on the Next button to advance to the next screen where you will specify the destination data store, as shown in Figure 6-18.

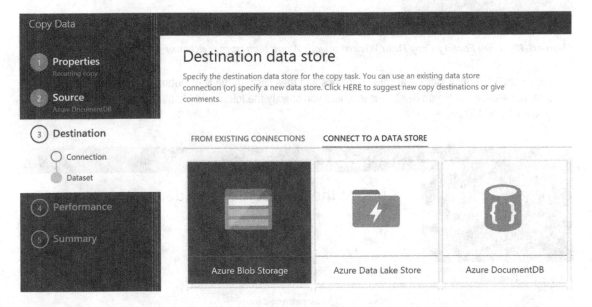

Figure 6-18. *Data Factory Copy Data Wizard: specify destination data store*

Select Azure Blob Storage and then click on the Next button to advance to the next screen. The next will ask for your Azure blob storage account specifics, as shown in Figure 6-19.

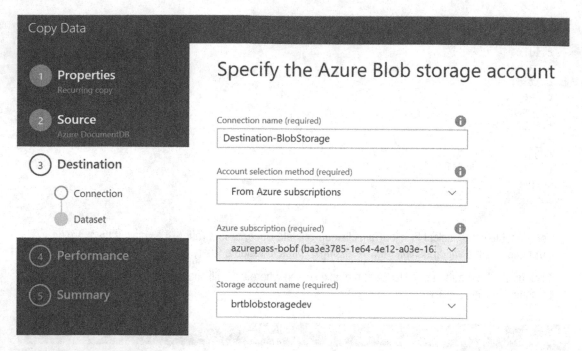

Figure 6-19. *Data Factory Copy Data Wizard: specify Azure blob storage account properties*

Enter your Azure blob storage account specifics and then click on the Next button to advance to the next screen, as shown in Figure 6-20. This is where you specify the folder and file names for the destination in Azure blob storage.

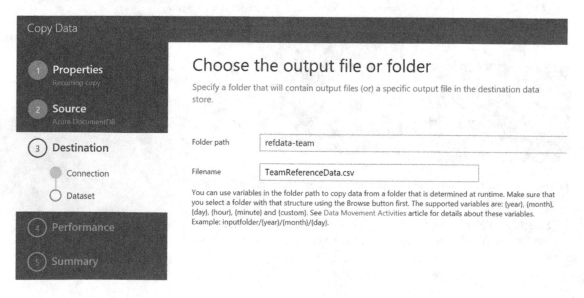

Figure 6-20. *Data Factory Copy Data Wizard: specify output file or folder properties*

Enter `refdata-team` as the folder path and `TeamReferenceData.csv` as the file name for the destination outputs. Then click on the Next button to advance to the next screen, as shown in Figure 6-21, where you will specify the file format settings.

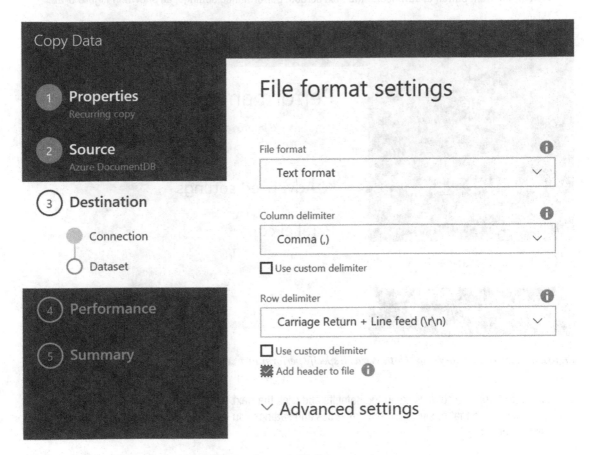

Figure 6-21. Data Factory Copy Data Wizard: specify file format settings

Keep the defaults for the file format settings options, but be sure to check the option for Add Header to File so that the column names are preserved.

Click on the Next button to advance to the next screen, performance settings, as shown in Figure 6-22.

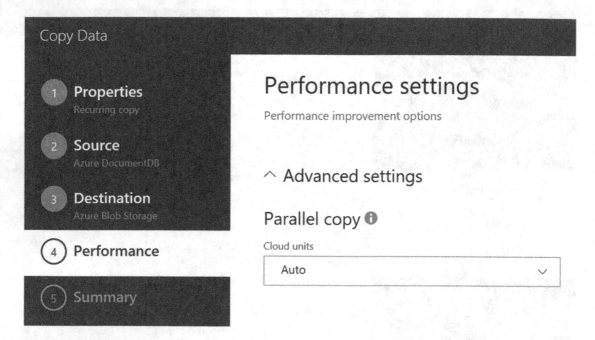

Figure 6-22. Data Factory Copy Data Wizard: specify performance settings

For the performance settings, keep the defaults and click the Next button. At this point, you will see a summary page that recaps all of the properties and settings you specified for this new copy job, as shown in Figure 6-23.

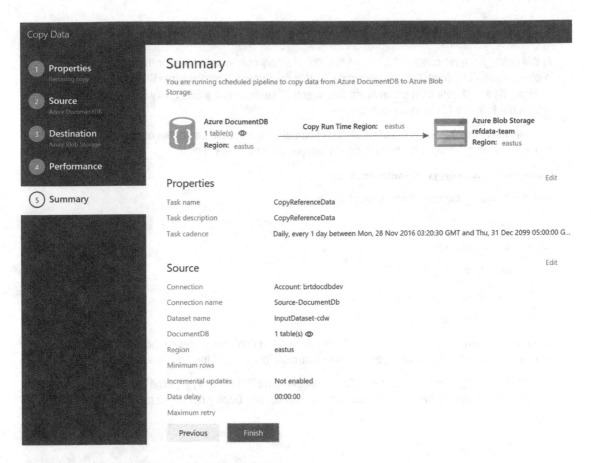

Figure 6-23. *Data Factory Copy Data Wizard summary page*

If all of the settings look good, click on the Finish button. The new Data Factory copy job will be validated and deployed. When that's complete, you will see a screen similar to Figure 6-24.

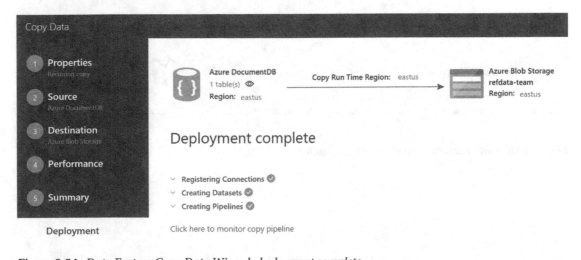

Figure 6-24. *Data Factory Copy Data Wizard, deployment complete*

Modify JSON Parameters for Copy Job

At this point, you have created the basic Azure Data Factory copy pipeline job for the reference implementation to refresh the reference data used in the Stream Analytics job in Chapter 5. This copy pipeline will select data from of the Azure DocumentDB database (via a SQL query statement) and then write it out to a CSV file in Azure blob storage.

The only minor change left is to tweak the JSON output parameters to create the output file name in Azure blob storage using a file naming convention pattern as the one shown:

`TeamReferenceDatayyyy-MM-ddhh-mm.csv`

Note the following the date/time naming format:

- yyyy = Year
- MM = Month
- dd = Day
- hh = Hour
- mm = Minute

This naming convention change is crucial to ensure that you don't try to update the file while it is in use and may be locked. It also allows you to build a historical inventory of the previous versions.

To make the change, you need to the JSON of the new Azure Data Factory pipeline job, navigate to the new pipeline job via the Azure Portal, and select the Author and Deploy option, as shown in Figure 6-25.

Figure 6-25. *Data Factory, Author and Deploy option*

After you select this option, you will see a screen similar to Figure 6-26. Here, you can click on each of the components of the pipeline and expand the parameters underneath each section.

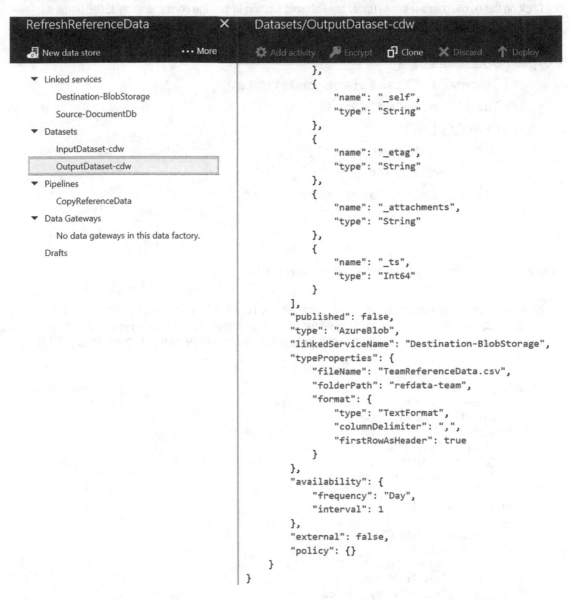

Figure 6-26. *Data Factory, view data factory components*

As you click on each section, you will see the corresponding JSON template and parameters on the right side of the Azure Portal web page.

Click on the OutputDataset-cdw under the Datasets section to see the corresponding JSON. Scroll all the way down to the bottom and you should see a section of code similar to Figure 6-27.

```
"typeProperties": {
    "fileName": "TeamReferenceData.csv",
    "folderPath": "refdata-team",
    "format": {
        "type": "TextFormat",
        "columnDelimiter": ",",
        "firstRowAsHeader": true
    }
},
```

Figure 6-27. *Data Factory: default output file naming in JSON*

Note the fileName parameter, which is set to the value of TeamReferenceData.csv. This will be the section of JSON code you will modify to meet the file naming convention of TeamReferenceData" + "yyyy-MM-ddhh-mm.csv". To do this, find and replace the previous JSON code with the following JSON code:

```
"typeProperties": {
    "fileName": "TeamReferenceData{slice}.csv",
    "folderPath": "refdata-team",
    "format": {
        "type": "TextFormat",
        "columnDelimiter": ",",
        "firstRowAsHeader": true
    },
    "partitionedBy": [
        {
            "name": "slice",
            "value": {
                "type": "DateTime",
                "date": "SliceStart",
                "format": "yyyy-MM-ddhh-mm"
            }
        }
    ]
},
```

Note that the JSON code you replaced will use a dynamic file naming convention based on the Date and Time attributes for the specific processing slice that is created from the Data Factory pipeline job.

After you make this update to the JSON, the Deploy option will become available, as shown in Figure 6-28.

Figure 6-28. *Data Factory: deploy updated JSON*

After selecting the option to deploy your updated pipeline JSON data to Azure, the JSON will be saved, validated, and then deployed to the Azure Data Factory service.

Run Data Factory Copy Job On-Demand and Check Results

To run this new Azure Data Factory pipeline job, navigate to the job via the Azure Portal and select the Monitor & Manage option, as shown in Figure 6-29.

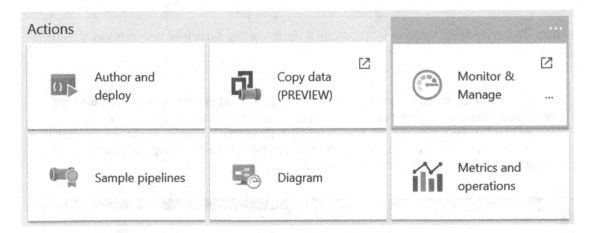

Figure 6-29. *Data Factory's Monitor & Manage option*

After selecting this option, a new tab will open in your browser. The Data Factory Resource Explorer App will open and display your Data Factory jobs and their corresponding pipeline definitions and activities, as shown in Figure 6-30.

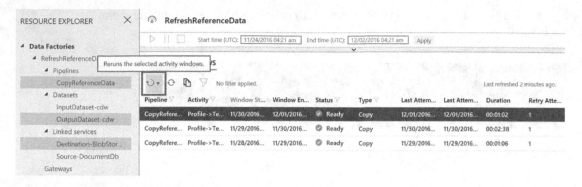

Figure 6-30. *Data Factory, re-run job activity*

To run this updated copy pipeline job "on demand," do the following:

- Select the latest pipeline activity.

- Click on the Rerun icon, as highlighted in red in Figure 6-30.

- Choose either Rerun or Rerun with Upstream Data.

■ **Note**   When you select the Rerun with Upstream in Pipeline option, it reruns all upstream activity windows as well.

After a few minutes, the copy pipeline job will run to completion. At this point, you can check the Azure blob output destination container `refdata-team` and look for a file with a naming convention that follows `TeamReferenceDatayyyy-MM-ddhh-mm.csv`. The screenshot in Figure 6-31 displays successful output of several Team Reference Data CSV files over a period of three days using the Visual Studio Cloud Explorer tool to view the output blob container.

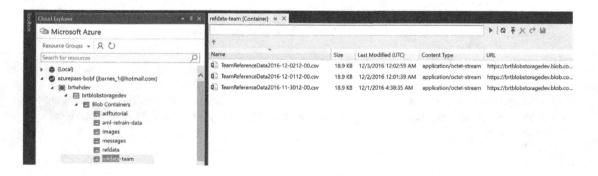

Figure 6-31. *Data Factory: successful daily outputs of team reference data CSV output files*

To summarize this exercise, you just walked through all the steps necessary to update the reference data that you used for the Azure Stream Analytics job in Chapter 5.

IMPLEMENTING THE DATA FACTORY AZURE ML UPDATE RESOURCE ACTIVITY

In this next section, we tackle the second objective for the Azure Data Factory pipeline tasks, which is to re-train the Azure Machine Learning model via an Azure Data Factory pipeline job. The updates to the Azure Machine Learning model will come from the results of medical stress tests that are administered to team members on a periodic basis and then uploaded into Azure blob storage for re-training the model.

We cover the detailed specifics of implementing the Azure Machine Learning model and associated Web Services in Chapter 9.

For this exercise, we assume that the Azure ML predictive model has already been extended with an additional web service endpoint. The additional endpoint will allow for re-training the model (in batch mode) based on recently updated training data.

Data Factory AML Retraining: High-Level Design

At a high level, we are going to create a Data Factory pipeline job that will accomplish two objectives in order to fully re-train our Azure ML model:

1. Process the updated Machine Learning training data and produce an .iLearner ML output file. This file then becomes the input to the Update Resource activity in the next step.

2. Add a second Update Resource Activity to the pipeline to update the existing Azure ML Web Service with the updated trained model via the .iLearner ML output file.

Create Data Factory Job to Retrain Azure ML Model

To get started, navigate to the resource group for your deployment via the Azure Portal. Click on the + Add button and search for Data Factory, as shown in Figure 6-32.

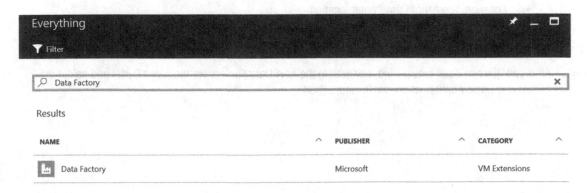

Figure 6-32. *Searching for and adding a Data Factory job to a resource group*

After selecting Azure Data Factory, you will see a Data Lake overview screen. Click on the Create button to create the new Data Factory job.

The next screen allows you to enter the specific parameters for creating a new Azure Data Factory job, as shown in Figure 6-33.

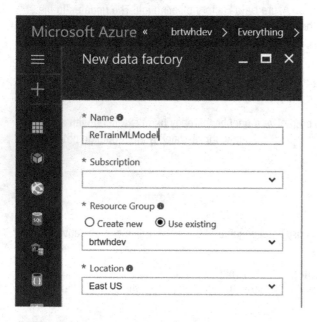

Figure 6-33. *Data Factory create job parameters*

Fill in your choices for the corresponding parameter values:

- *Name*: Enter a unique name for your new Data Factory. Note that the name of the Azure Data Factory must be globally unique. We use ReTrainMLModel.

- *Subscription*: The Azure subscription to use for this job.

- *Resource Group*: The Azure Resource Group to create this service in.

- *Location*: The Azure Data Center location.

Once you are done, click on the Create button at the bottom of the screen. Your input will then be validated and the new Azure Data Factory job will be created after a brief period of time.

After your job has been provisioned, navigate to the new Data Factory via the Azure Portal and select the Author and Deploy option, as shown in Figure 6-34.

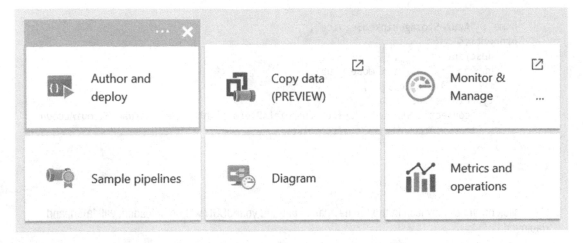

Figure 6-34. *Data Factory Author and Deploy option*

Next, you are going to build the Data Factory pipeline components using just JSON to define the individual elements of the Data Factory Azure ML re-training pipeline job.

Define Linked Service: Azure Storage

To define the Linked Service for Azure Storage, click on the New Data Store icon in the top navigation bar and then select Azure Storage, as shown in Figure 6-35.

Figure 6-35. *Data Factory: add a new data store*

After your new linked service has been created, replace the default JSON with the JSON code shown here. Note that you need to have your specific Azure blob storage credentials to fill in.

```json
{
    "name": "AzureStorageLinkedService",
    "properties": {
        "description": "",
        "hubName": "retrainmlmodel_hub",
        "type": "AzureStorage",
        "typeProperties": {
            "connectionString": "DefaultEndpointsProtocol=https;AccountName=<YourAccoun
            tName>;AccountKey=<YourAccountKey>"
        }
    }
}
```

Next, click on the Deploy icon in the top navigation bar and your JSON will be uploaded, validated, and deployed.

Define Input Dataset: Updated Azure ML Training Data

To define a new dataset, click on the …More icon and then click on the New Dataset icon, as shown in Figure 6-36.

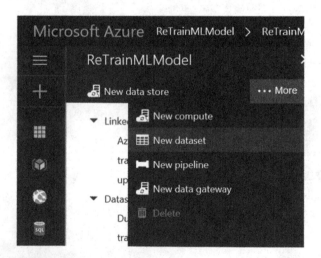

Figure 6-36. *Data Factory: add new dataset, training data*

Next, select the option for Azure Blob Storage, as shown in Figure 6-37.

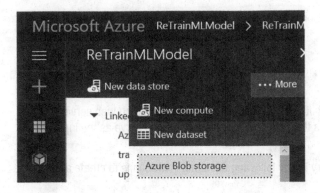

Figure 6-37. *Data Factory: add new dataset, Azure blob storage option*

After your new dataset has been created, replace the default JSON with the JSON code shown here.

```
{
    "name": "trainingData",
    "properties": {
        "published": false,
        "type": "AzureBlob",
        "linkedServiceName": "AzureStorageLinkedService",
        "typeProperties": {
            "fileName": "RETRAIN_Teammates_AML_Training_Data.csv",
            "folderPath": "aml-retrain-data",
            "format": {
                "type": "TextFormat"
            }
        },
        "availability": {
            "frequency": "Week",
            "interval": 1
        },
        "external": true,
        "policy": {
            "externalData": {
                "retryInterval": "00:01:00",
                "retryTimeout": "00:10:00",
                "maximumRetry": 3
            }
        }
    }
}
```

Make sure the `fileName` and `folderPath` parameters are set for your environment. Note that the frequency will be once per week.

Next, click on the Deploy icon in the top navigation bar and your JSON will be uploaded, validated, and deployed to the Data Factory definition.

Define Output Dataset: Updated Azure ML Training Model

This dataset definition will represent the output .iLearner file from the Azure ML training web service. The Azure ML Batch Execution Activity produces this dataset. This dataset will also serve as the input file for the Azure ML Update Resource activity.

Create an additional dataset for our Data Factory job by following the same instructions to create a new dataset and summarized here:

- Click on the ...More icon and then click on the New Dataset icon.

- Select the option for Azure Blob Storage.

After your new dataset has been created, replace the default JSON with the JSON code shown here.

```
{
    "name": "trainedModelBlob",
    "properties": {
        "published": false,
        "type": "AzureBlob",
        "linkedServiceName": "AzureStorageLinkedService",
        "typeProperties": {
            "fileName": "model.ilearner",
            "folderPath": "aml-retrain-data",
            "format": {
                "type": "TextFormat"
            }
        },
        "availability": {
            "frequency": "Week",
            "interval": 1
        }
    }
}
```

Make sure the `folderPath` parameter is set correctly for your environment.

When finished, click on the Deploy icon in the top navigation bar and your JSON will be uploaded, validated, and deployed to the Data Factory definition.

Define Linked Service: Azure ML Training Endpoint

Next, you will create a linked service that points to the default endpoint of the Azure ML training web service.

To get started, click on the ...More icon and then click on the New Compute icon. Then select the Azure ML option, as shown in Figure 6-38.

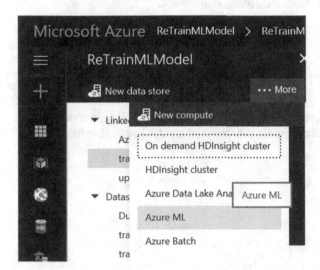

Figure 6-38. *Data Factory: add new compute Azure blob storage option*

After your new linked service has been created, replace the default JSON with the JSON code shown here. Note that you will need to have your specific Azure ML URL endpoint and API key to fill in the parameters:

```
{
    "name": "trainingEndpoint",
    "properties": {
        "hubName": "retrainmlmodel_hub",
        "type": "AzureML",
        "typeProperties": {
            "mlEndpoint": "<YourEndPointURL>",
            "apiKey": "<YourAPIKey>"
        }
    }
}
```

Next, click on the Deploy icon in the top navigation bar and your JSON will be uploaded, validated, and deployed.

Define Linked Service: Azure ML Updatable Scoring Endpoint

Next, you will create a linked service that defines an Azure Machine Learning linked service that points to the non-default updatable endpoint of the scoring Azure ML Web Service.

■ **Note**   Before creating and deploying an Azure ML linked service, follow the steps in this link to create a second (non-default and updatable) endpoint for the Azure ML Scoring Web Service.

https://docs.microsoft.com/en-us/azure/machine-learning/machine-learning-create-endpoint.

To get started, click on the …More icon and then click on the New Compute icon. Then select the Azure ML option, as shown in Figure 6-38.

After your new linked service has been created, replace the default JSON with the JSON code shown here. Note that you will need to have your specific Azure ML URL endpoint and API key to fill in the parameters:

```
{
    "name": "updatableScoringEndpoint2",
    "properties": {
        "hubName": "retrainmlmodel_hub",
        "type": "AzureML",
        "typeProperties": {
            "mlEndpoint": "<YourMLRetrainingEndpoint>",
            "apiKey": "<YourMLRetrainingAPIKey>",
            "updateResourceEndpoint": "<YourMLRetrainingURLEndpoint>"
        }
    }
}
```

Next, click on the Deploy icon in the top navigation bar and your JSON will be uploaded, validated, and deployed.

Define Output Dataset: Dummy Azure Blob Output

At the time of this writing, when you include an Azure ML Update resource activity in a Data Factory pipeline job, it does not generate any output.

However, Azure Data Factory requires an output dataset in order to drive the schedule of a pipeline. Therefore, we will implement a dummy/placeholder Azure blob dataset to handle this use case.

To define a new Dataset, click on the …More icon and then click on the New Dataset icon, as shown in Figure 6-39.

Figure 6-39. *Data Factory: add new dataset, dummy output data*

Next, select the option for Azure Blob Storage, as shown in Figure 6-40.

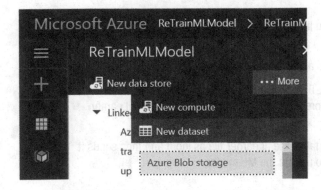

Figure 6-40. *Data Factory: add new dataset, Azure blob storage option*

After your new dataset has been created, replace the default JSON with the JSON code shown here.

```
{
    "name": "DummyPlaceholderBlob",
    "properties": {
        "published": false,
        "type": "AzureBlob",
        "linkedServiceName": "AzureStorageLinkedService",
        "typeProperties": {
```

```
                "fileName": "dummyfile.csv",
                "folderPath": "aml-retrain-data",
                "format": {
                    "type": "TextFormat"
                }
            },
            "availability": {
                "frequency": "Week",
                "interval": 1
            }
        }
    }
}
```

Make sure the `fileName` and `folderPath` parameters are set for your environment. Note that the frequency will be once per week.

Next, click on the Deploy icon in the top navigation bar and your JSON will be uploaded, validated, and deployed to the Data Factory definition.

Define Data Factory Pipeline Job with Two Activities

Now, you will combine all the previously defined linked services and dataset definitions as you define a new Data Factory pipeline job.

The new Data Factory pipeline job will have two activities defined:

- *AzureMLBatchExecution*: The Azure ML Batch Execution activity takes the updated team health training data from Azure blob storage as input, and then produces an .iLearner file as an output.

- *AzureMLUpdateResource*: This activity takes the .iLearner file as input and then sends it to the Azure ML Training web service to update the ML model.

■ **Note:** The `placeholderBlob` is just a dummy output dataset that is required by the Azure Data Factory service to run the pipeline.

To define the new pipeline, right-click on the Pipelines section of the left navigation bar of the Authoring pane and then select New Pipeline, as shown in Figure 6-41.

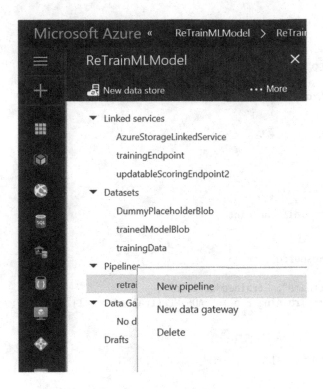

Figure 6-41. *Data Factory: add new pipeline*

After your new pipeline has been created, replace the default JSON with the JSON code shown here.

```json
{
    "name": "retrainmlpipeline",
    "properties": {
        "activities": [
            {
                "type": "AzureMLBatchExecution",
                "typeProperties": {
                    "webServiceInput": "trainingData",
                    "webServiceOutputs": {
                        "output1": "trainedModelBlob"
                    },
                    "webServiceInputs": {},
                    "globalParameters": {}
                },
                "inputs": [
                    {
                        "name": "trainingData"
                    }
                ],
                "outputs": [
                    {
                        "name": "trainedModelBlob"
```

```json
                }
            ],
            "policy": {
                "timeout": "02:00:00",
                "concurrency": 1,
                "executionPriorityOrder": "NewestFirst",
                "retry": 1
            },
            "scheduler": {
                "frequency": "Week",
                "interval": 1
            },
            "name": "retraining",
            "linkedServiceName": "trainingEndpoint"
        },
        {
            "type": "AzureMLUpdateResource",
            "typeProperties": {
                "trainedModelDatasetName": "trainedModelBlob",
                "trainedModelName": "Training Exp for ADF ML [trained model]"
            },
            "inputs": [
                {
                    "name": "trainedModelBlob"
                }
            ],
            "outputs": [
                {
                    "name": "DummyplaceholderBlob"
                }
            ],
            "policy": {
                "timeout": "01:00:00",
                "concurrency": 1,
                "retry": 3
            },
            "scheduler": {
                "frequency": "Week",
                "interval": 1
            },
            "name": "AzureML Update Resource",
            "linkedServiceName": "updatableScoringEndpoint2"
        }
    ],
    "start": "2016-02-13T00:00:00Z",
    "end": "2016-02-14T00:00:00Z",
    "isPaused": false,
    "hubName": "retrainmlmodel_hub",
    "pipelineMode": "Scheduled"
    }
}
```

Make sure the `fileName` and `folderPath` parameters are set for your environment. Note that the frequency will be once per week.

Next, click on the Deploy icon in the top navigation bar and your JSON will be uploaded, validated, and deployed to the Data Factory definition.

At this point, you have manually created a complete Data Factory pipeline job (described via JSON) to update the Azure ML training service.

The Data Factory pipeline is composed of the following components, as shown in Figure 6-42.

- Three linked services
- Three datasets
- One pipeline

Figure 6-42. *Data Factory pipeline components*

In order to get a visual representation of the Azure Data Factory and components you have created, navigate to your Data Factory job in the Azure Portal and select the Diagram option, as shown in Figure 6-43.

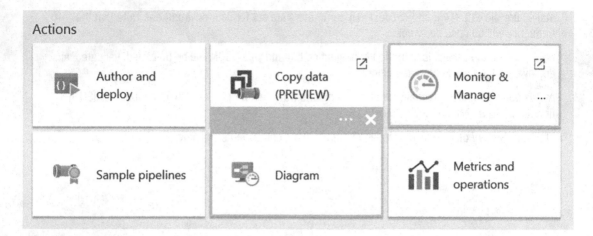

Figure 6-43. *Data Factory Diagram view*

After clicking on the Diagram icon, you will see a representation of your Data Factory pipeline, as shown in Figure 6-44.

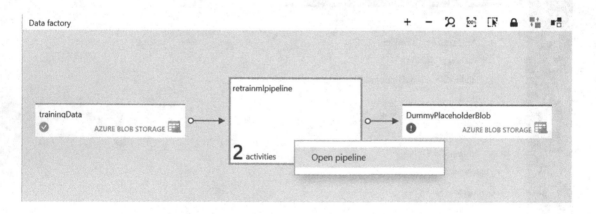

Figure 6-44. *Data Factory diagram, open pipeline option*

However, you will notice that this view is still collapsed, as the pipeline icon states it has two activities. To expand the pipeline, right-click on the pipeline icon and select Open Pipeline, as shown in Figure 6-44.

When you click on the Open Pipeline option, the screen will expand to auto-fit the viewing window in order to reveal the entire pipeline. Figure 6-45 illustrates the new view.

Figure 6-45. *Data Factory diagram, open pipeline view*

Note that this view is extremely helpful when assembling multi-step pipeline jobs using Azure Data Factory. You can also adjust the zoom levels and drill down into individual components.

To summarize, in this section, you created a new Data Factory pipeline job to automatically update the Machine Learning Web Service using the following JSON definitions:

- *Linked Service*: Azure Storage
- *Linked Service*: Azure ML Training Endpoint
- *Linked Service*: Azure ML Updatable Scoring Endpoint
- *Input Dataset*: Updated Azure ML Training Data
- *Output Dataset*: Updated Azure ML Training Model
- *Output Dataset*: Dummy Azure Blob Output
- *Data Factory Pipeline* Job: With two Activities

This piece of the reference implementation provides a completely automated method of retraining the Azure Machine Learning Web Service.

The updates are based on updated team health data that is generated from periodic stress test results administered to team members. This creates a "full lifecycle" solution to maintaining an updated Azure ML training models based on physical data updates.

■ **Note**   See the following link for more details about configuring an Azure Data Factory pipeline job to retain an Azure ML Web Service:

https://docs.microsoft.com/en-us/azure/data-factory/data-factory-azure-ml-batch-execution-activity#updating-azure-ml-models-using-the-update-resource-activity.

MOVE DATA FROM BLOB STORAGE TO DATA LAKE

The third and last Data Factory job we will implement in this chapter focuses on moving data from Azure blob storage to Azure Data Lake.

This Data Factory will prepare the reference implementation data for the next subject covered in Chapter 7.

As a refresher, the data in Azure blob storage that you will move to Azure Data Lake was created as an output result of the Azure Stream analytics job created in Chapter 5.

You will move this data to Azure Data Lake for several reasons, including the following:

- *Data Archival*: Keep the data in its original form as when it was received from the IoT Hub.

- *Deep Analytics*: Azure Data Lake is both a powerful storage and powerful analytics platform, as we will explore more in Chapter 7.

- *Regression Analysis*: Oftentimes, there is value in being able to re-run Big Data analysis over historical data to evaluate alternative outcomes or make other make other (historical) improvements.

Create Azure Data Lake Store Account

Before you can copy your data from Azure blob storage to Azure Data Lake, you need to create an Azure Data Lake Store account.

To get started, navigate to the resource group for your deployment via the Azure Portal. Click on the + Add button and search for Data Lake, as shown in Figure 6-46.

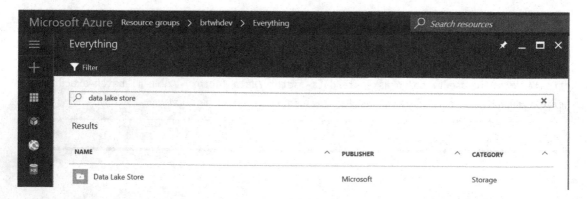

Figure 6-46. *Searching for and adding a Data Lake Store to a resource group*

Next, you will see an overview page about Azure Data Lake Store. Click on the Create button to advance to the next screen.

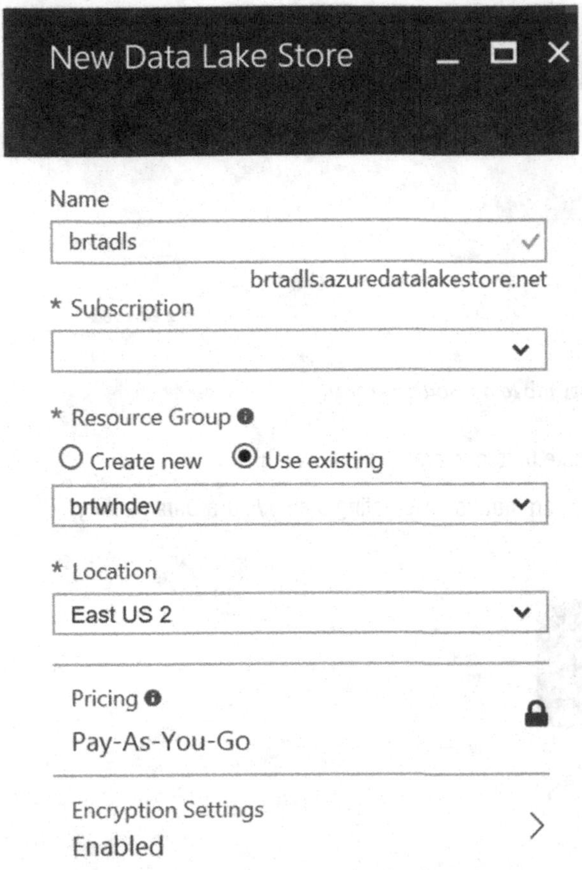

New Data Lake Store _ ☐ ✕

Name

brtadls ✓

brtadls.azuredatalakestore.net

* Subscription

[⌄]

* Resource Group ❶

○ Create new   ◉ Use existing

brtwhdev   ⌄

* Location

East US 2   ⌄

Pricing ❶   🔒
Pay-As-You-Go

Encryption Settings   ＞
Enabled

Figure 6-47. *Parameters for creating a new Data Lake Store*

Fill in your choices for the corresponding parameter values:

- *Name*: Enter a unique name for your new Data Lake Store.

- *Subscription*: The Azure subscription to use for this job.

- *Resource Group*: The Azure Resource Group to provision this resource in.

- *Location*: The Azure Data Center location.

Once you are done, click on the Create button at the bottom of the screen. Your input will then be validated and the new Azure Data Lake Store will be created in a few minutes at most.

Create Data Factory Job: Copy from Azure Blob to Data Lake

To get started, navigate to the resource group for your deployment via the Azure Portal. Click on the + Add button and search for Data Factory, as shown in Figure 6-48.

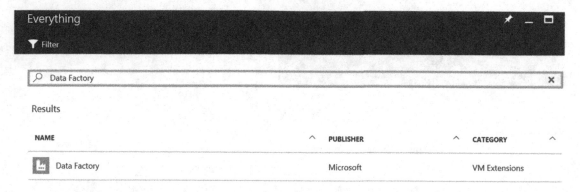

Figure 6-48. *Searching for and adding a Data Factory job to a resource group*

After selecting Azure Data Factory, click on the Create button to create the new job.

The next screen will allow you to enter the specific parameters for creating a new Azure Data Factory job, as shown in Figure 6-49.

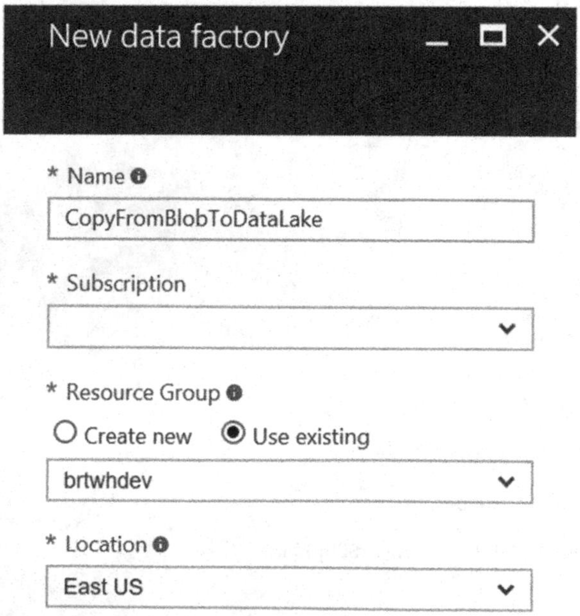

Figure 6-49. *Data Factory create job parameters*

Fill in your choices for the corresponding parameter values:

- *Name*: Enter a unique name for your new Data Factory job. Note that the name of the Azure Data Factory must be globally unique.

- *Subscription*: The Azure subscription to use for this job.

- *Resource Group*: The Azure Resource Group to create this service in.

- *Location*: The Azure Data Center location.

Once you are done, click on the Create button at the bottom of the screen. Your input will then be validated and the new Azure Data Factory job will be created after a brief period of time. It should take less than one minute via the Azure Portal.

After your job has been provisioned, navigate to the new Data Factory via the Azure Portal and select the Copy Data (PREVIEW) option, as shown in Figure 6-50.

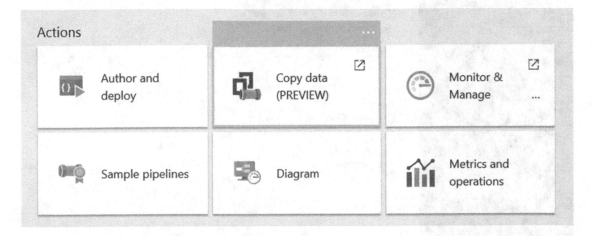

Figure 6-50. *Data Factory Copy Data Wizard*

This will invoke the Azure Data Factory Copy Data Wizard to launch and will walk you through the steps necessary to create a basic copy pipeline. Behind the scenes, Azure Data Factory is generating JSON files to reflect your choices in the Copy Wizard.

Figure 6-51 depicts the first screen of the Copy Data Wizard and allows you to specify the properties for the copy job.

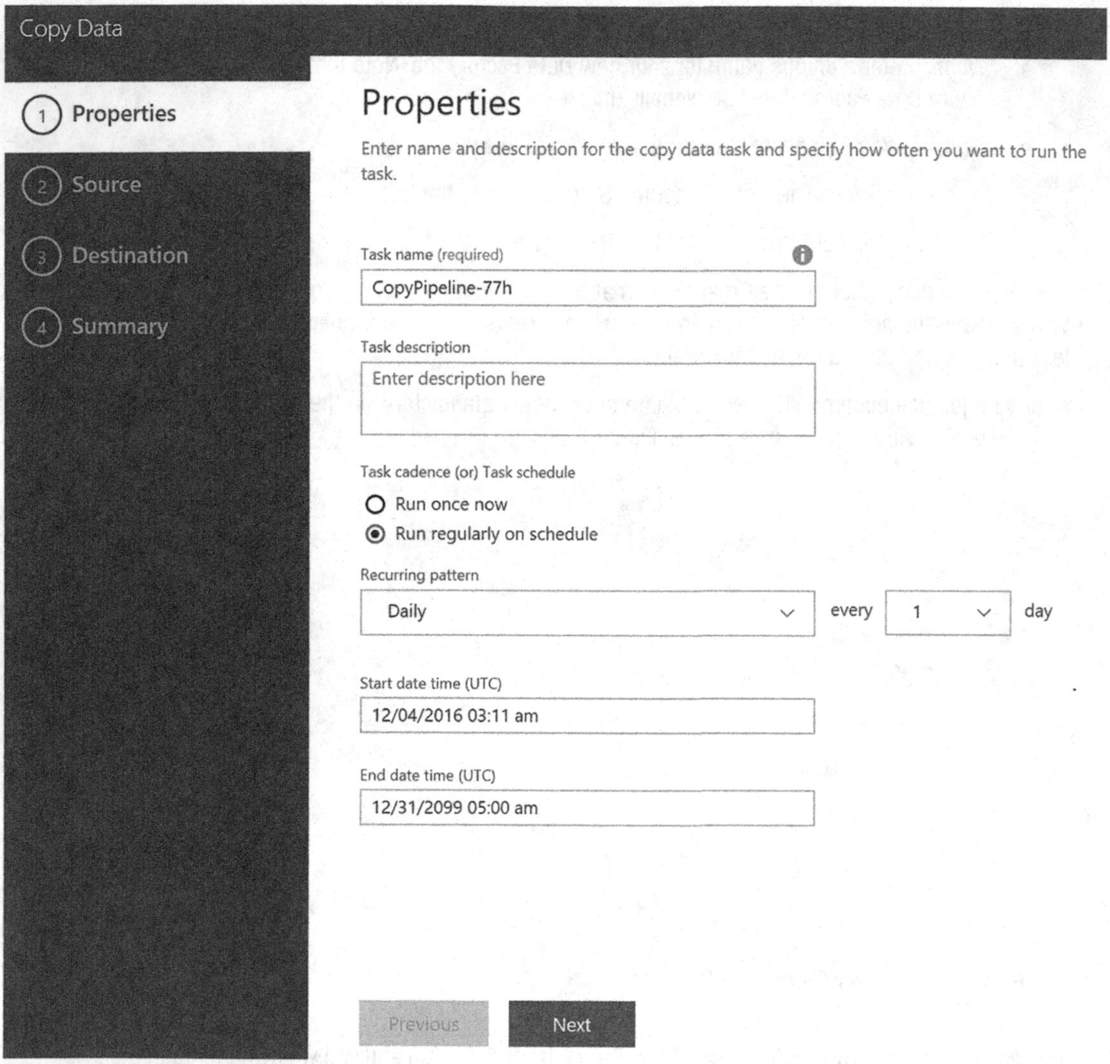

Copy Data

① **Properties**

② Source

③ Destination

④ Summary

Properties

Enter name and description for the copy data task and specify how often you want to run the task.

Task name (required) ⓘ

CopyPipeline-77h

Task description

Enter description here

Task cadence (or) Task schedule

○ Run once now
◉ Run regularly on schedule

Recurring pattern

Daily ∨   every 1 ∨ day

Start date time (UTC)

12/04/2016 03:11 am

End date time (UTC)

12/31/2099 05:00 am

Previous   Next

Figure 6-51. Data Factory Copy Data Wizard: specify properties

For this example, enter a task name of CopyBlobToDataLake and keep the remaining defaults for the schedule, stat, and end dates. Click Next to advance to the next step.

Figure 6-52 depicts the Source Data screen, where you should select Azure Blob Storage for the reference implementation scenario.

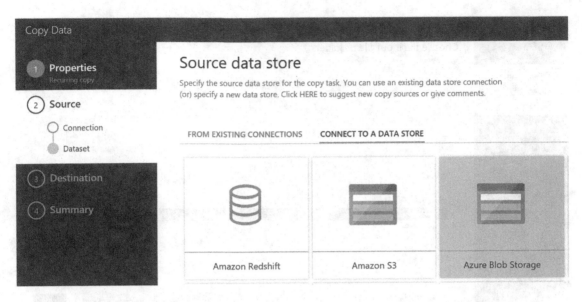

Figure 6-52. Data Factory Copy Data Wizard: specify source data store for Azure blob storage

Next, specify the Source Data Store properties for Azure blob storage, as shown in Figure 6-53.

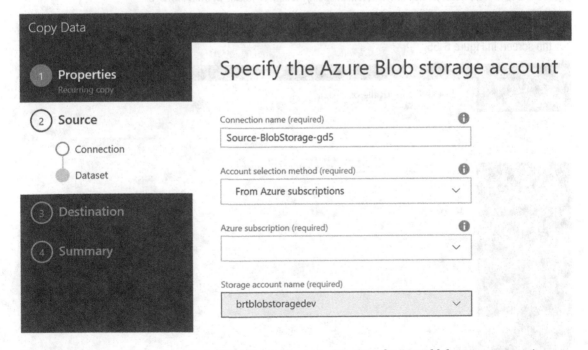

Figure 6-53. Data Factory Copy Data Wizard: specify source data store for Azure blob storage properties

Next, choose the folder in Azure blob storage that will contain the source dataset, as shown in Figure 6-54.

281

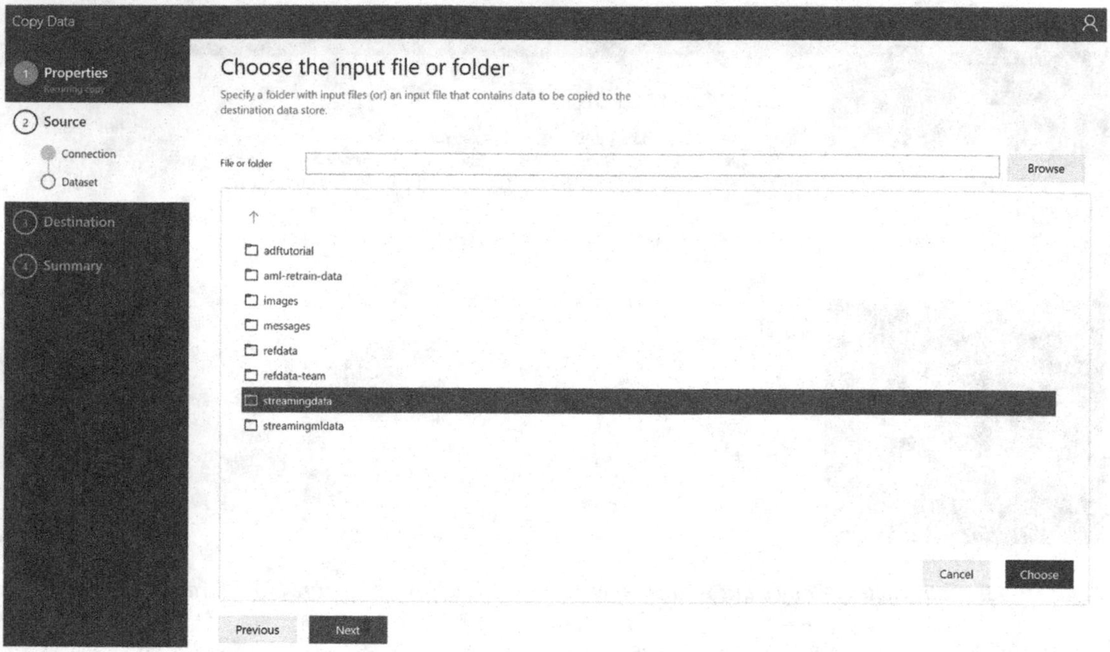

Figure 6-54. Data Factory Copy Data Wizard: specify a source folder in blob storage

After selecting the streamingdata folder and clicking on Choose, click on the Next button. You will see the screen in Figure 6-55.

Figure 6-55. Data Factory Copy Data Wizard: specify a source folder and an option for copying files recursively

Select the option to Copy Files Recursively, as shown in Figure 6-55, then click on the Next button.

At this point, the Data Factory Copy Wizard will attempt to connect to the Azure blob storage folder and automatically detect the file format of the files in blob storage, as shown in Figure 6-56.

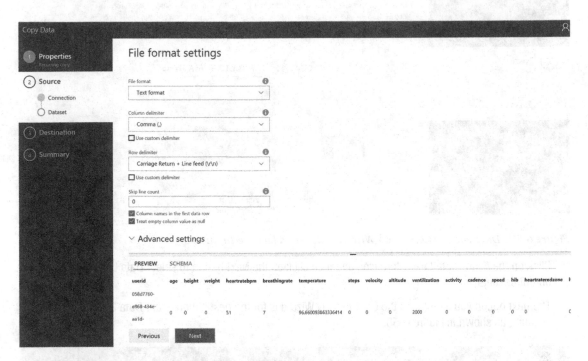

Figure 6-56. *Data Factory Copy Data Wizard: file format settings*

If the settings do not match, you may need to review the Azure blob storage output from the Stream Analytics job defined in Chapter 5.

If the file format settings match your expected inputs, click on the Next button to select the destination data store, as shown in Figure 6-57.

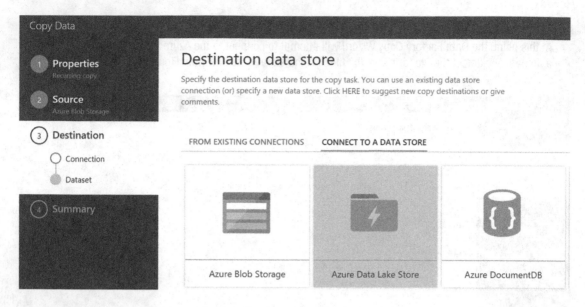

Figure 6-57. *Data Factory Copy Data Wizard: select Data Lake destination*

Click on the Azure Data Lake Store icon and then click on the Next button to select Data Lake as the output destination.

The next option you'll define in the Copy Activity Wizard is for the destination Azure Data Lake Store account, as shown in Figure 6-58.

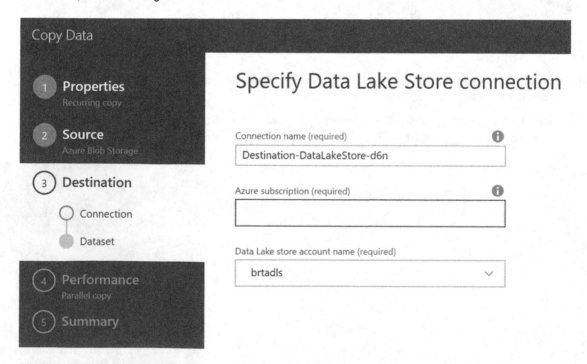

Figure 6-58. *Data Factory Copy Data Wizard: select Data Lake destination*

Select your Azure subscription and Azure Data Lake Store Name and then click on the Next button.

The next screen in the Copy Wizard will allow you to select the output destination folder and file path for the destination data in Azure Data Lake.

Set the Filename parameter to the value of inputfolder/{year}/{month}/{day}, as shown in Figure 6-59.

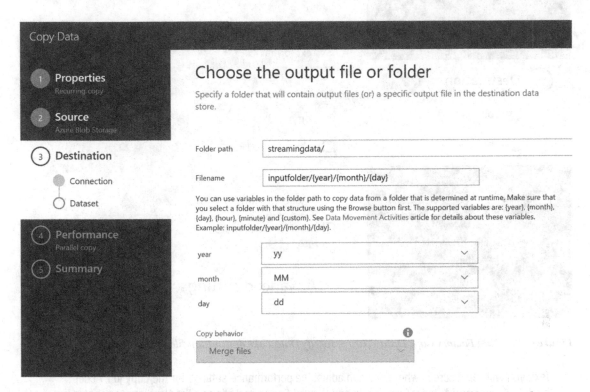

Figure 6-59. *Data Factory Copy Data Wizard: select a Data Lake Destination folder and file name values*

Click on the Next button to advance to the next screen in the Copy Wizard. Here, you will see options for specifying the file format settings. Select the option for Add Header to File, as shown in Figure 6-60.

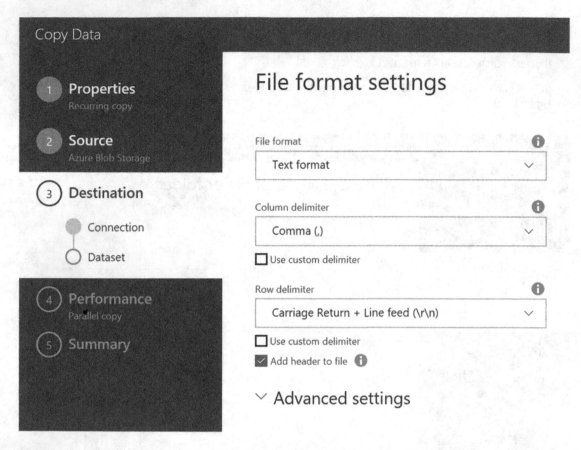

Figure 6-60. *Data Factory Copy Data Wizard: specify Data Lake destination file format values*

Next, you will see a screen where you can adjust the performance settings for the copy job. Accept the default values of Auto for Cloud Units and Parallel Copies and click on the Next icon, as shown in Figure 6-61.

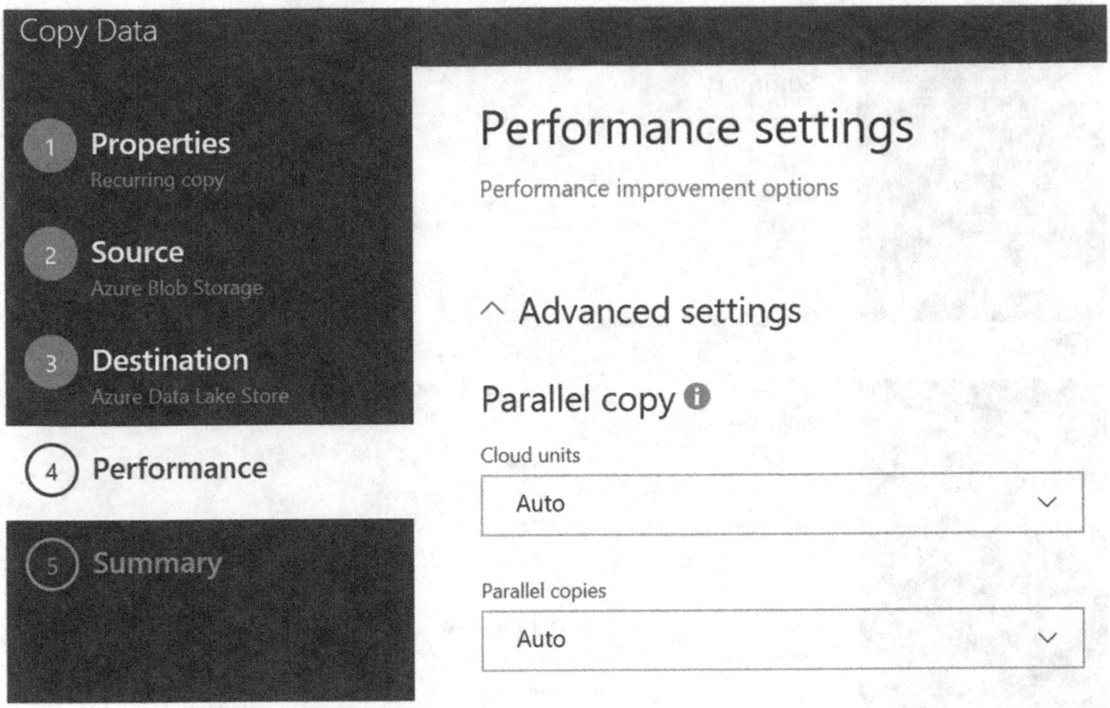

Copy Data

1 **Properties**
Recurring copy

2 **Source**
Azure Blob Storage

3 **Destination**
Azure Data Lake Store

4 **Performance**

5 **Summary**

Performance settings

Performance improvement options

∧ Advanced settings

Parallel copy ⓘ

Cloud units

Auto ∨

Parallel copies

Auto ∨

Figure 6-61. *Data Factory Copy Data Wizard: specify Data Lake destination file format values*

The last screen in the Copy Wizard is the summary screen, as shown in Figure 6-62.

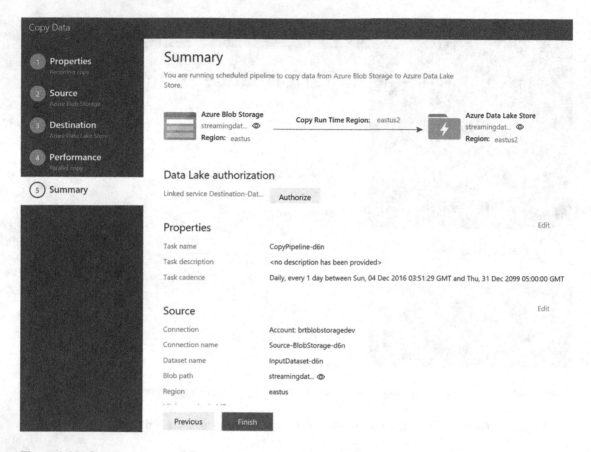

Figure 6-62. Summary screen of the Data Factory Copy Data Wizard

First, click on the Authorize button, as shown in Figure 6-62 so that you can sign in to the Azure subscription again and the copy job can capture the credentials.

Finally, click on the Finish button to create the new Data Factory pipeline job.

After a brief period of time, the new Data Factory copy job will be registered and deployed, as shown in Figure 6-63.

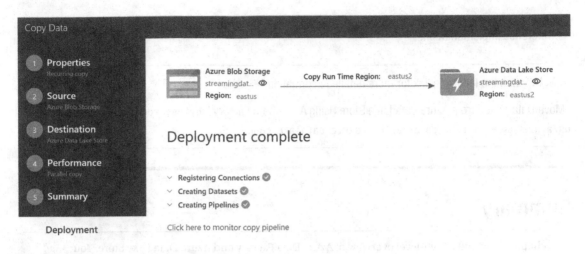

Figure 6-63. *Deployment complete*

After your new pipeline job has been deployed, it will run and you can check for the output in your destination Azure Data Lake Store.

Figure 6-64 depicts an example of the updated Data Lake Store copy results using the Visual Studio Cloud Explorer to view the destination output in the Data Lake Store folder.

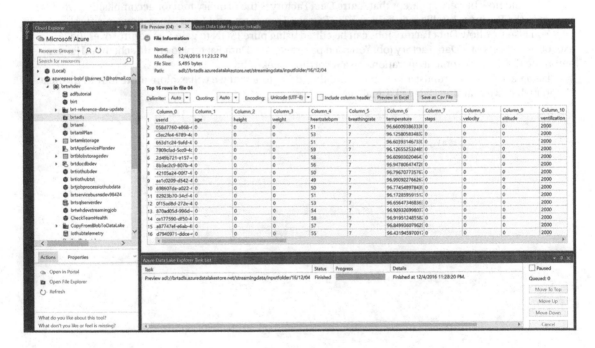

Figure 6-64. *Visual Studio Cloud Explorer: view Data Lake Store*

At this point, you have now completed the third and final Data Factory use case scenario for the reference implementation.

■ **Note**   See the following link for more detailed information.

"Move Data to and from Azure Data Lake Store Using Azure Data Factory": `https://docs.microsoft.com/en-us/azure/data-factory/data-factory-azure-datalake-connector`.

Summary

This chapter provided a high-level overview of Azure Data Factory and Azure Data Lake Store. You implemented three Data Factory jobs to accomplish the corresponding use case scenarios for the reference implementation:

- Update reference data
- Re-train the Azure Machine Learning model
- Move data from Azure blob storage to Azure Data Lake Store

It should now be very apparent that Azure Data Factory is the primary tool for accomplishing what is known in the Business Intelligence field as ETL (Extract, Transform, and Load) operations in Azure.

You also saw how Data Factory jobs can be edited using pure JSON to gain fine control over the execution aspects of a Data Factory job. You used parameters in Data Factory to create scheduled jobs to automate the data movement operations on a recurring, weekly, basis.

Data Lake Store is a robust and virtually limitless data store that we will explore more fully in the next chapter when we examine Data Lake analytics.

CHAPTER 7

■ ■ ■

Advanced Analytics with Azure Data Lake Analytics

This chapter examines the use of Azure Data Lake Analytics (ADLA), which is Microsoft's new "Big Data" toolset that runs on top of Azure Data Lake.

The ADLA tools and capabilities help make it easier and more efficient to solve today's modern business analysis and reporting problems than with traditional, on-premise solutions. It is more efficient because it offers virtually unlimited storage, with immediate access to that storage for running analytical operations directly on top of it. There is no need for additional provisioning or acquisition; the resources are immediately available on-demand.

Data Lake offers the ability to persist the raw data in its native form and then run transformational and analytical jobs to create new analyses, summarizations, and predictions—across structured and un-structured data—all based on the original data. All this adds up to a "faster time-to-value" for a modern business seeking to maximize its true potential.

The key advantage is that you do not need to perform any ETL (Extract-Transform-Load) operations on the data in Azure Data Lake to run the analytical operations. This offers a huge advantage when dealing with large amounts of data, particularly when historical and regression analysis requirements come into play.

The ADLA service can handle jobs of virtually any scale instantly; you simply specify how much compute power you need when you submit your job. You can specify both the job's priority and the number of Analytical Units (AU) for your job. AU'sallow you to specify how many computational resources your job can use. A single AU is roughly equivalent to two CPU cores and 6 GB of RAM. You only pay for your job while it is running, making it more cost-effective than with traditional on-premise approaches, where you must pay for the infrastructure whether it is utilized or not.

In this chapter, we begin by providing a wide-angle view of the features and capabilities of ADLA. We then apply this knowledge to the reference implementation and put all the pieces together as we walk through building the complete working solution. Figure 7-1 illustrates the role that ADLA plays in the reference implementation.

© Bob Familiar and Jeff Barnes 2017
B. Familiar and J. Barnes, *Business in Real-Time Using Azure IoT and Cortana Intelligence Suite*,
DOI 10.1007/978-1-4842-2650-6_7

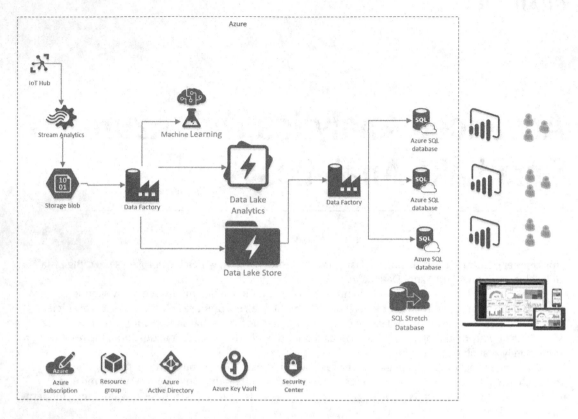

Figure 7-1. *Azure Data Lake Analytics in the reference implementation architecture*

We draw upon our key lessons from Chapter 5 (Stream Analytics) and Chapter 6 (Data Factory) to continue with the data movement activities in this chapter.

Specifically, we process the data that was moved to Azure Data Lake from Azure Blob storage (via Data Factory); that data represents the incoming IoT streaming data. We then join this raw, IoT data with the results of the Azure Machine Learning Web Service calls that were made "real-time" during the Stream Analytics ingestion job and then persist the data to Azure storage. Let's get started with a brief technical overview of Azure ADLA capabilities and features.

Azure Data Lake Analytics

ADLA is a recent new Microsoft Azure distributed analytics service built on top of Apache YARN. YARN stands for "Yet Another Resource Negotiator" and is a cluster management technology for Apache Hadoop. ADLA was built with the primary goal of making Big Data analytics easy and more efficient. ADLA lets you focus on writing, running, and managing analytical jobs, rather than operating distributed computing infrastructure.

Some of the core capabilities of the ADLA service include the following:

- *Dynamic Scaling*: ADLA has been architected at its core for cloud scale and performance. ADLA can dynamically provision resources and will allow you do analytics on extremely large datasets, such as terabytes or even exabytes of data. When a job completes, it winds down resources automatically, and you pay only for the processing power used for your job run. As you increase or decrease the size of data stored or the amount of compute used, you don't have to rewrite any code. This lets you focus on your business logic only and not on how you process and store large datasets.

- *U-SQL*: ADLA includes U-SQL, a query language that combines a familiar SQL-like declarative language with the extensibility and programmability provided by C#, for creating custom processors and reducers. U-SQL also provides the ability to query and combine data from a variety of data sources, including Azure Data Lake Storage, Azure Blob Storage, Azure SQL DB, Azure SQL Data Warehouse, and SQL Server instances running in Azure Virtual Machines.

- *Develop, Debug, and Optimize Faster Using Visual Studio*: ADLA has deep integration with Visual Studio, so that you can use familiar tools to run, debug, and tune your analytics job code. Additionally, ADLA provides handy visualizations of your U-SQL jobs. These visualizations allow you to examine how your code runs at scale, which makes it easier to identify performance bottlenecks early and thereby optimize performance (and costs).

- *Big Data Analytics for the Masses*: ADLA provides the tooling and framework so that even new developers can easily develop and run massively parallel data transformation and processing programs in U-SQL, R, Python, and .Net over petabytes of data. All your data can be analyzed with ADLA and U-SQL including unstructured, semi-structured, and structured data.

- *Integration with Existing IT Investments*: ADLA can use your existing IT investments for identity, management, security, and data warehousing. ADLA is integrated with Azure Active Directory for user management and permissions. It also comes with built-in monitoring and auditing capabilities.

- *Cost Effective*: ADLA becomes a very cost-effective solution for running Big Data workloads when you look at the details of how it is priced and scaled. With ADLA, you pay on a "per-job" basis only when your data is processed. The system automatically scales up or down as the job starts and completes, so you never pay for more than what you need. No additional hardware, licenses, or service-specific support agreements are required.

- *Optimized for Data Lake*: It should be noted that ADLA is specifically designed and optimized to work together with Azure Data Lake Store to provide the highest levels of performance, throughput, and parallelization for your most demanding Big Data workloads.

- *Simplified Management and Administration*: ADLA can be easily managed via the Azure Portal. Additionally, PowerShell can be used to automate analytics jobs and perform related ADLA tasks. The Azure Portal blades for ADLA also offer the ability to secure your analytics environment with Role-Based Access Control (RBAC) tools that are integrated with Azure Active Directory. Monitoring and alerting capabilities are also built into the Azure Portal for fulfilling operations and administration requirements.

Getting Started with Azure Data Lake Analytics

It is easy to get started with ADLA. There is a three-step process to get up and running:

1. Create an ADLA account in your Azure Subscription/Resource group. This is a one-time setup and allows you to start exploring your data along with running analytics jobs on that data.

2. Write and submit an ADLA job with U-SQL. You can create, submit, and monitor jobs from many different sources, such as the Azure Portal, Visual Studio, and PowerShell commands.

3. Examine the job results. At their core, ADLA jobs basically read and write data from storage in a highly distributed and massively parallel manner. For easy access, the storage sources can be from many various locations such as Data Lake Store, Azure blob storage, or data from other SQL servers on other platforms or services. And all the data can be analyzed "in-place" without any delay for extraction, preparation, or loading.

Next, we walk through these steps in more detail so that you can see how easy it is to get started with processing Big Data using ADLA.

Create an ADLA Account

To get started, in the Azure Portal navigate to the resource group for your deployment. Click on the + Add button and search for Data Lake Analytics, as shown in Figure 7-2.

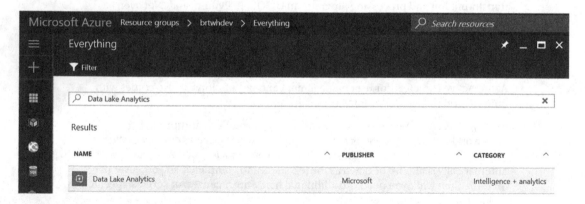

Figure 7-2. Adding Data Lake Analytics to a resource group

After selecting the option for Data Lake Analytics, click on the next screen to create the new Data Lake Analytics account, as shown in Figure 7-3.

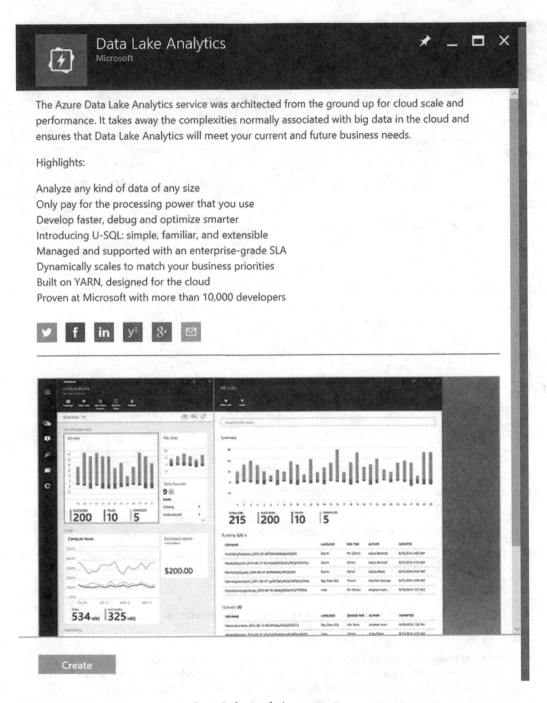

Figure 7-3. *Creating a new Azure Data Lake Analytics account*

The next screen allows you to enter the specific parameters for creating a new ADLA account, as shown in Figure 7-4.

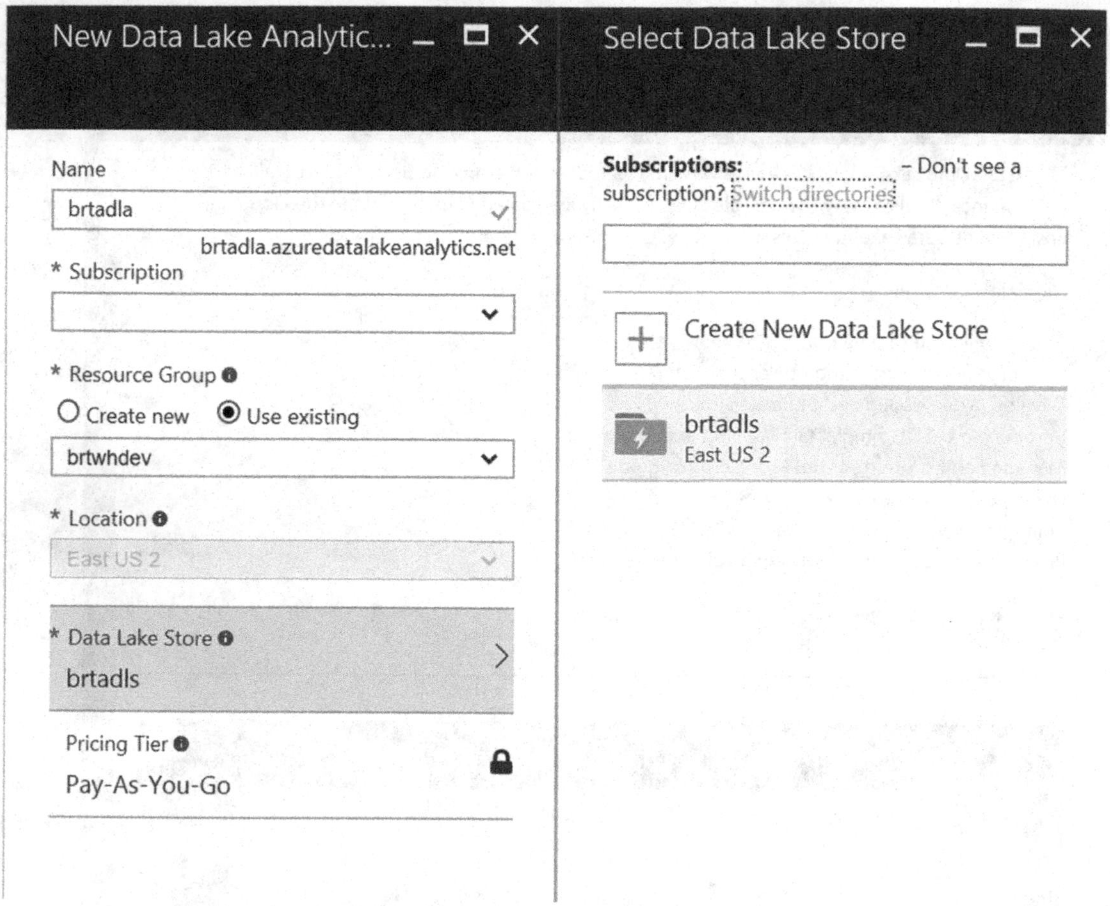

Figure 7-4. *Creating a new Azure Data Lake Analytics account*

Fill in your choices for the corresponding parameter values:

- *Name*: Enter a unique name for your new ADLA account. Note that the name of the ADLA must be globally unique.

- *Subscription*: The Azure subscription to use for this job.

- *Resource Group*: The Azure Resource Group to create this service in.

- *Location*: The Azure Data Center location.

- *Data Lake Store*: The Azure Data Lake Store that will be the primary location for analyzing your data. Note that each ADLA account has a dependent Data Lake Store account. The ADLA account and the dependent Data Lake Store account must be located in the same Azure data center.

Once you are done, click on the Create button at the bottom of the screen. Your input will then be validated and the new Azure Data Lake account will be created after a brief period of time (typically less than one minute).

After your new ADLA account has been provisioned, navigate to the account via the Azure Portal. Your ADLA screen should appear similar to Figure 7-5.

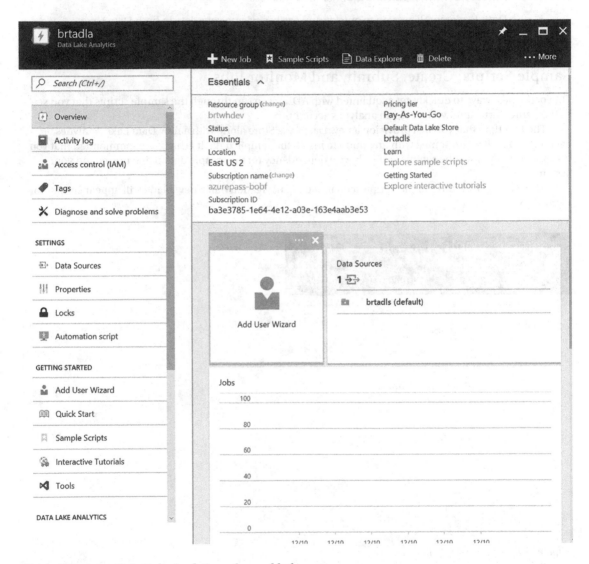

Figure 7-5. *Azure Data Lake Analytics web page blade*

When working with ADLA via the Azure Portal, note that you will primarily use two of the navigation options shown at the top of the screen in Figure 7-5:

- *+ New Job*: Allows you to create, submit, and monitor your ADLA jobs. This option allows you to create, upload, and download U-SQL scripts. When you are ready, you can submit them to run and monitor their progress.

- *Data Explorer*: Allows you to quickly and easily navigate your data in both Data Lake Storage and ADLA database structures that contain tables and schemas.

Sample Scripts: Create, Submit, and Monitor Jobs

One of the best ways to quickly get acquainted with ADLA is to run through the sample scripts that you see in the Azure Portal after you create an analytics account.

The first time that you first provision a new Data Lake Store along with a new Data Lake Analytics account, you will be presented with an option to install the sample data. It is highly recommended that you do so, especially since the sample scripts have a dependency on the sample data being present on your system.

After you click on the Sample Scripts icon in the top navigation bar, a new blade will appear similar to Figure 7-6.

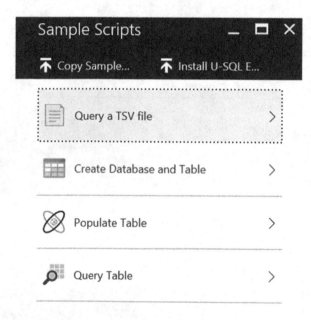

Figure 7-6. *Sample script options*

Click on the Query a TSV File option, as shown in Figure 7-6, and the New U-SQL Job window will appear, as shown in Figure 7-7.

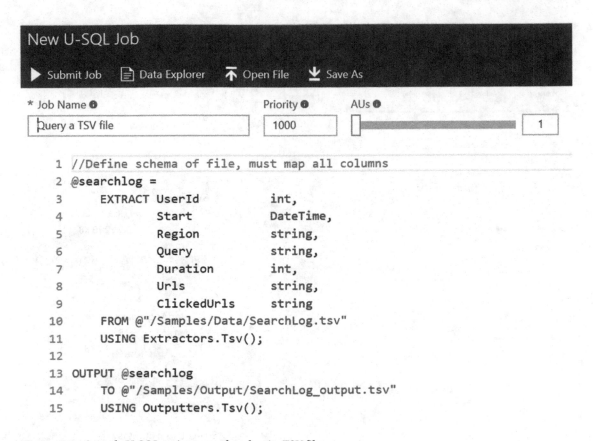

Figure 7-7. Sample U-SQL script to read and write TSV files

From this initial sample script, you can identify several key aspects of the U-SQL language and operations:

- U-SQL queries can be expressed in familiar SQL syntax.

- Extractors and outputters are the keys to working with semi-structured and unstructured data.

- U-SQL can easily extract tab-separated-value data from one flat file and then write it out to another flat file.

- Values read from flat files can be assigned to different variable types.

Click on the Submit Job icon, as shown in the top-left side of Figure 7-7. Next, you will see a Job Summary screen similar to one shown in Figure 7-8.

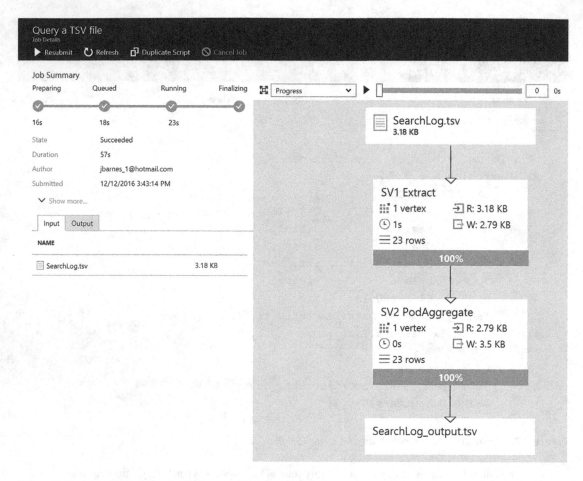

Figure 7-8. Azure Data Lake Analytics: sample job results

This screen provides information as the job goes through the four stages of ADLA job execution: Preparing, Queued, Running, and Finalizing. Note that you can (and often will) use the Refresh command to manually refresh the screen to see an updated status of your job real-time in the dashboard.

Note that you can also browse both the input and the output files related to the analytics job execution, as shown on the left side of Figure 7-8.

The right side of the screen provides information pertaining to the execution details of the job. Figure 7-8 illustrates graphs that are provided to help visualize the job's execution information: Progress, Data Read, Data Written, Execution Time, Average Execution Time per Node, Input Throughput, and Output Throughput.

By leveraging this rich job execution information, you can tune and tweak your Big Data analytical queries to optimize both your results and your costs. Note that you can also click on Replay (arrow icon) in the top navigation bar to visually replay your job (logically without actually running the job) and see how it consumes resources as it runs. See Figure 7-9 for the Replay button.

Figure 7-9. *The Azure Data Lake Analytics Replay button helps you visualize your job after it runs*

Close this blade and you will return to the job submission blade, where you can click on the Data Explorer option in the top navigation bar (see Figure 7-10).

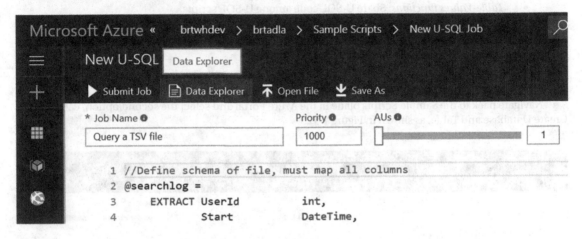

Figure 7-10. *Data Explorer icon*

Next, you will see a view of the Data Explorer screen similar to the one shown in Figure 7-11.

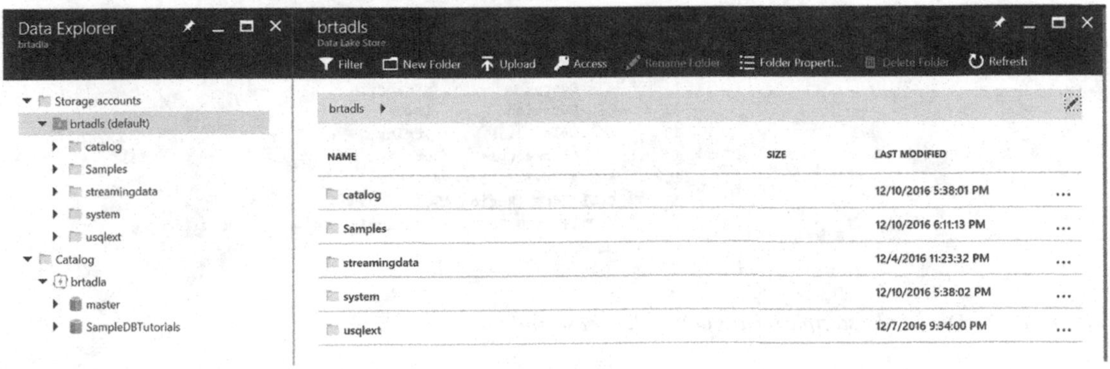

Figure 7-11. *The Data Lake Analytics Data Explorer view*

A few items are noteworthy in Figure 7-11:

- *Top-left of the screen*: You will see that you have a view into the contents of your Azure Data Lake Store. The contents appear as a file system with folders and files. This is the location where you will primarily work with any kind of unstructured data or "flat files".

- *Bottom-Left of the screen*: Includes the "Catalog" which represents a "structured" view of your data in ADLA, similar to a SQL Server database store. This catalog is used to hold structured data and code so that they can both be shared by U-SQL scripts. Each catalog can contain one or more additional databases.

A U-SQL database contains the following:

- *Assemblies*: Share .NET code among U-SQL scripts.

- *Table-Values functions*: Share U-SQL code among U-SQL scripts.

- *Tables*: Share data among U-SQL scripts.

- *Schemas*: Share table schemas among U-SQL scripts.

The next sample script explores this concept further, as you will create a database and a table in U-SQL script.

Navigate back to the Sample Scripts blade in the Azure Portal and select the second option, called Create Database and Table, as shown in Figure 7-12.

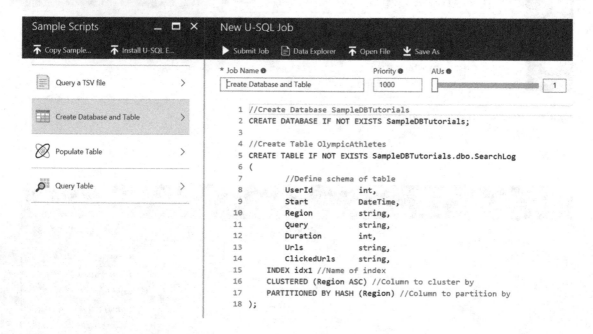

Figure 7-12. *Data Lake sample scripts create database and table*

Here, you see familiar SQL-like syntax statements that allow you to easily declare a new ADLA database and corresponding table. Additionally, we have declared a clustered index partitioned by a hash on the region. This could potentially provide a huge performance boost when dealing with large numbers of records.

Another observation is that the ADLA environment allows for an optimized mixture of storage and SQL commands that summarize, aggregate, transform, extract, and output meaningful business data at scale.

Click on the Submit Job icon in the top navigation bar and your job will be placed in the queue to eventually create a new database and table.

By now, it should be clear that there are many similarities in ADLA to the manner in which older generation "legacy" computer systems were designed to run. Batch environments have always been most efficient at dividing up computational workloads, running the workloads on distributed nodes, monitoring and gathering the results, and finally producing an output.

This next section demonstrates the U-SQL capabilities in action as you populate the sample database using the sample CSV input file.

Navigate back to the Sample Scripts blade and select the third option to populate the table, as shown in Figure 7-13.

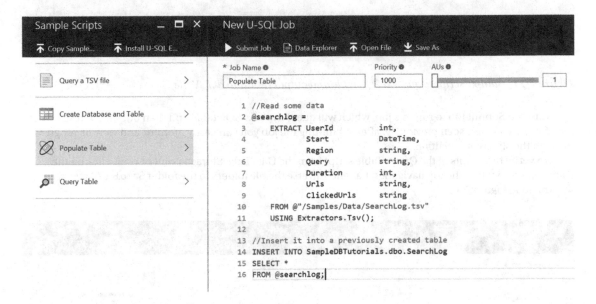

Figure 7-13. *Sample script to populate SQL table*

This SQL script will read from the (semi-structured) .TSV file named SearchLog.tsv as the input source. It will then output the results into a new SQL table that you created with the previous script. Click on Submit Job and run the job to populate the new SQL table.

The last sample script step allows you to verify the results of the previous script by outputting the data from the SQL table you just populated back into a .TSV file.

Navigate back to the Sample Scripts blade and select the fourth and last option called Query Table, as shown in Figure 7-14.

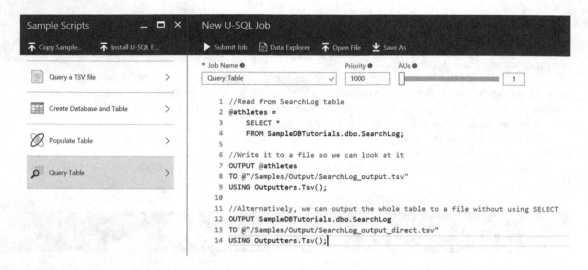

Figure 7-14. *Sample script to query a SQL table and output results to a .TSV file*

Click on Submit Job to run this job, which will query the new SQL table and then output the results to a .TSV file. As you have seen previously, after submitting the job you can easily monitor and view its progress through the stages of execution.

To verify the results of the Query Table script from the Data Lake Storage point of view, click on the Data Explorer icon in the top navigation bar and traverse the file folders to the folder `Samples/Output`, as illustrated in Figure 7-15.

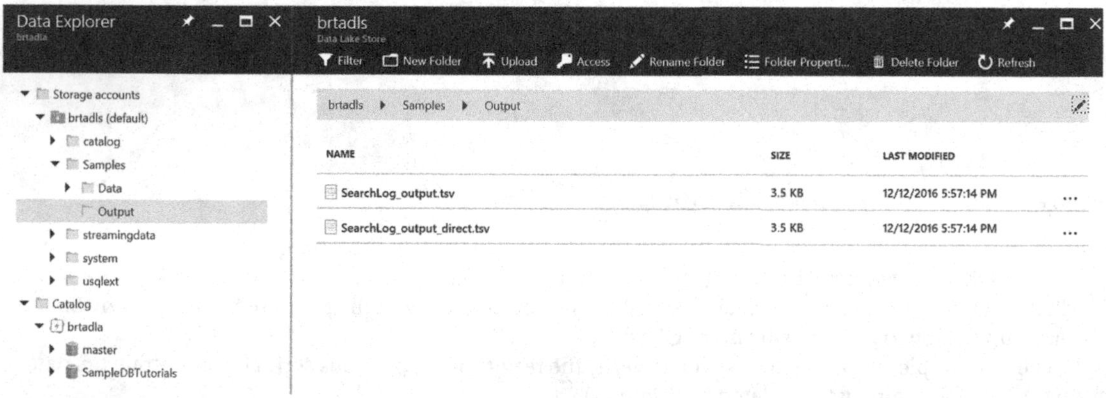

Figure 7-15. *Verify SQL-to-File job output files using the Data Explorer*

You can click on each file to see the contents and verify that they originated from the file that you used to populate the Data Lake SQL table in Sample Script #3 (Populate Table).

Note that there is currently no way to interactively query or view the results of ADLA SQL query. That is due to the fact that ADLA is primarily based on a batch processing architecture.

To account for this reality, the easiest way to verify the contents of SQL queries is to declare an output file and write to that destination, as shown in Figure 7-14. Then you can use the Data Explorer to verify the results.

By running through the sample U-SQL scripts that come with ADLA, you have explored some of the more commonly used capabilities and features of the service. Although everything you accomplished in this quick tour of the samples was via the Azure Portal, Microsoft also provides additional tools for working with U-SQL in Visual Studio.

■ **Tip** When developing ADLA scripts in the Azure Portal, it is often a good idea to have multiple browser tabs or windows open. One window would normally contain the Data Explorer view, and the other window would be used for editing scripts and submitting analytics jobs.

Azure Data Lake Tools for Visual Studio

Azure Data Lake Tools for Visual Studio is a free plug-in that works with Visual Studio (2015/2017) to enable easy authoring, debugging, and tuning of ADLA U-SQL scripts and queries.

In addition to handling all the basic operations available via the Azure Portal such as authoring, submitting, and monitoring ADLA jobs, there are many additional tools, utilities, and functionality you can leverage with Azure Data Lake Tools for Visual Studio, such as:

- *Unit Tests*: Visual Studio Tools includes a new project template for creating U-SQL unit test scripts. This is invaluable for being able to run automated testing and regression scenarios.

- *IntelliSense*: For help with prompting for Data Lake catalog entities such as databases, schemas, tables, User Defined Objects (UDOs), etc. Since you can only have one master catalog per ADLA account, the entities are all related to your specific compute account.

- *Auto-Formatting*: When creating ADLA jobs, Visual Studio makes it easier to visual your U-SQL code and thereby improve readability and maintain-ability. All the formatting rules are configurable under Tools ➤ Options ➤ Text Editor ➤ SIP ➤ Formatting.

- *Go-To Definition and Find All References*: These help you pinpoint code segments and determine code paths.

- *Heat Map*: The VS Data Lake Tools provide user-selectable, color overlays on the job view to indicate: Progress, Data I/O, Execution time, and I/O throughput of each stage. This feature allows users to determine potential issues and distribution of job properties visually and intuitively.

- *Run U-SQL Locally*: This capability alone with Data Lake Tools for Visual Studio can provide a U-SQL developer a huge boost in productivity. These tools allow developers to take advantage of all of the following rich development capabilities, all locally:

  - Run U-SQL scripts, along with C# assemblies.

  - Debug scripts and C# assemblies. Create/delete/view local databases, assemblies, schemas, and tables in Server Explorer, in exactly the same manner as you would do for an ADLA service.

The combination of the Visual Studio tools and tooling on top of the Azure Data Lake Store and Analytics provides a rich and powerful environment to develop, run, and mange a Big Data analytics environment.

A deeper detailed discussion of the features and capabilities of Data Lake Tools for Visual Studio is beyond the scope of this book. You are strongly advised to refer to the following links and resources for additional information.

■ **Note** Download Azure Data Lake Tools for Visual Studio: `https://www.microsoft.com/en-us/download/details.aspx?id=49504`.

■ **Tip** Develop U-SQL scripts using Data Lake Tools for Visual Studio: `https://docs.microsoft.com/en-us/azure/data-lake-analytics/data-lake-analytics-data-lake-tools-get-started`.

ADLA U-SQL Features and Benefits

Regardless of whether you are creating U-SQL jobs using the Azure Portal or using the Data Lake Tools for Visual Studio, there are some huge benefits in leveraging this service for your Big Data processing needs.

U-SQL is a new language from Microsoft for processing Big Data jobs in Azure. U-SQL combines the familiar syntax of SQL with the expressiveness of custom code written in C#, on top of a scale-out runtime that can handle virtually any size of data. Some of the many features and benefits of leveraging U-SQL include the following:

- Handles all types of data: unstructured, semi-structured, and structured.

- Allows you to declare and use domain-specific, user-defined types using C#.

- You can run U-SQL queries over Data Lake Store and Azure blobs.

- You can also run federated queries over operational and data warehouse SQL stores, reducing the complexity of ETL operations.

- Allows developers to leverage their existing skills with SQL and .NET. U-SQL developers are productive from day one.

- Easy to scale and performance tune without the need to manually configure the environment.

- Easy to use built-in connectors for common data formats.

- Simple and rich extensibility model for adding customer–specific data transformations.

- No limits on scale. Scales on-demand with no changes required to the code.

- Automatically parallelizes U-SQL queries and custom code.

- Designed to process petabytes of data.

- Built-in aggregation functions that can be extended with custom C# aggregation functions.

- Uses built-in extractors to read CSV and TSV files or create custom extractors for different data file formats.

- Enterprise grade tools and execution environment.

- Includes tools for managing, securing, sharing, and discovery of familiar data and code objects (tables, functions etc.)

- Provides role-based authorization of catalogs and storage accounts using Azure Active Directory (AAD) security.

- Provides auditing for catalog objects such as databases, tables, etc.

- Sample SQL Table DDL (Data Definition Language) commands:

  - CREATE TABLE

  - CREATE CLUSTERED INDEX

  - CREATE TABLE w/ CLUSTERED INDEX

  - INSERT

  - TRUNCATE

  - DROP

  - Tables are registered in the metadata catalog and are discoverable by others via the catalog/metadata APIs.

■ **Note** You can insert data into a table *only* if it has a clustered index.

Types of U-SQL User-Defined Operators

The U-SQL language allows for the following User-Defined Operators (UDOs) that can be extended:

- Extractors (called with Extract syntax)

- Processors (called with Process syntax)

- Appliers (called with Apply syntax)

- Combiners (called with Combine syntax)

- Reducers (called with Reduce syntax)

- Outputters (called with Output syntax)

See the following link for more detailed information:

U-SQL programmability guide: `https://docs.microsoft.com/en-us/azure/data-lake-analytics/data-lake-analytics-u-sql-programmability-guide#use-user-defined-extractors`.

As of this writing, ADLA comes out-of-the-box with three extractors:

- Comma-Separated-Value (CSV) delimited text
- Tab-Separated-Value (TSV) delimited text
- General-purpose extractor for delimited text

See the following link for U-SQL samples, libraries, and tools for extending U-SQL.

■ **Note** The U-SQL GitHub Repository is found at `https://github.com/Azure/usql`.

See the following link for a more detailed walkthrough of using Azure Data Analytics from the Azure Portal.

■ **Tip** Get started with Azure Data Lake Analytics using Azure Portal: `https://docs.microsoft.com/en-us/azure/data-lake-analytics/data-lake-analytics-get-started-portal`.

U-SQL Windowing Functions

U-SQL contains a powerful construct called "windowing functions," which are defined by the use of the OVER clause and represent those values that are computed from multiple rows instead of just the current row. U-SQL adopts a subset of the ANSI Standard SQL Window functions that were introduced into the language in 2003.

The window functions are categorized into the following general areas:

- *Reporting Aggregation Functions*: Includes SUM and AVG.
- *Ranking Functions*: Includes DENSE_RANK, ROW_NUMBER, NTILE, and RANK.
- *Analytic Functions*: Includes cumulative distribution or percentiles and accessing data from a previous row (in the same result set) without using a self-join.

As you learned in Chapter 5, these types of aggregates can be especially crucial to the analysis of real-time streaming data over a period of time. In addition to the obvious benefits of gathering aggregates in real-time over fast moving data streams, there can also be value in performing these same types of aggregate analysis over historical datasets for "what-if" analyses and regression testing scenarios.

Figure 7-16 presents a sample U-SQL script that demonstrates the use of the OVER keyword with the PARTITION BY clause to refine the "window" to list all the employees, the department, and the total salary for the department. Note that the PARTITION BY clause is added to the OVER clause to create this summarization effect.

```
@employees =
    SELECT * FROM ( VALUES
        (1, "Nick",   "IT Department", 100, 10000),
        (2, "Sheryl","IT Department", 100, 20000),
        (3, "Jim",    "IT Department", 100, 30000),
        (4, "Claire","Human Resources",200, 10000),
        (5, "Jason", "Human Resources",200, 10000),
        (6, "Becky", "Human Resources",200, 10000),
        (7, "Scott", "Exec Management",  300, 50000),
        (8, "Anna",    "Sales & Marketing",  400, 15000),
        (9, "Eric",  "Sales & Marketing",  400, 10000) )
    AS T(EmpID, EmpName, DeptName, DeptID, Salary);

@result=
SELECT
    EmpName, DeptName,
    SUM(Salary) OVER( PARTITION BY DeptName ) AS SalaryByDept
FROM @employees;

OUTPUT @result TO "/DepartmentSummary.csv"
    USING Outputters.Csv();
```

Figure 7-16. Sample U-SQL script demonstrating the windowing capabilities of ADLA using OVER and PARTITION BY

Note that in Figure 7-16 the sample input data stream for employees was created entirely in code rather than read from a file or SQL table. Because we are working with a batch service, we still need to output our results to a CSV file (`DepartSummary.csv`) using the built-in CSV outputter format option. Figure 7-17 depicts that output.

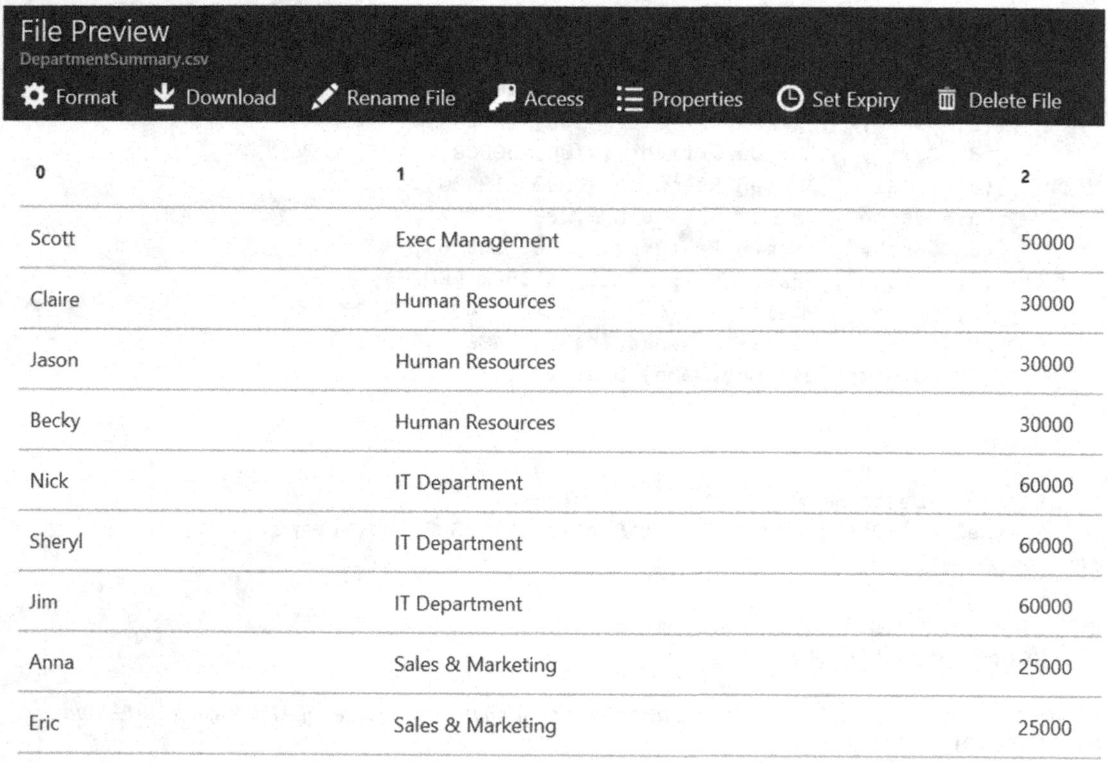

File Preview
DepartmentSummary.csv

⚙ Format   ⬇ Download   ✎ Rename File   🔑 Access   ☰ Properties   🕐 Set Expiry   🗑 Delete File

0	1	2
Scott	Exec Management	50000
Claire	Human Resources	30000
Jason	Human Resources	30000
Becky	Human Resources	30000
Nick	IT Department	60000
Sheryl	IT Department	60000
Jim	IT Department	60000
Anna	Sales & Marketing	25000
Eric	Sales & Marketing	25000

Figure 7-17. *Results of the sample U-SQL script demonstrating the windowing capabilities*

Each row of the output results also contains the total salary for each department (the pre-aggregated sum of all salaries in that department) and is broken down by department.

Reporting Aggregation Functions

ADLA window functions support the following aggregates as part of the U-SQL language:

- COUNT
- SUM
- MIN
- MAX
- AVG
- STDEV
- VAR

Ranking Functions

ADLA window functions support the following ranking functions as part of the U-SQL language:

- RANK
- DENSE_RANK
- NTILE
- ROW_NUMBER

Analytical Functions

ADLA window functions support the following analytical functions as part of the U-SQL language:

- CUME_DIST
- PERCENT_RANK
- PERCENTILE_CONT
- PERCENTILE_DISC

See the following link for a more detailed walkthrough of using Azure Data Analytics window functions:

■ **Note** Visit "Using U-SQL window functions for Azure Data Lake Analytics Jobs" at https://docs. microsoft.com/en-us/azure/data-lake-analytics/data-lake-analytics-use-window-functions.

ADLA Federated Queries: Querying the Data Where It Lives

One of the most powerful features of ADLA is that it allows you to easily query data residing in multiple Azure data stores, with the added benefit of not having to first move the data into a single data store before executing the query.

There are many additional benefits to the approach of querying the data from "where it lives"; here are just a few:

- Avoids moving large amounts of data across the network between data stores. This can result in drastically reduced bandwidth and latency issues over the network.

- Provides a single view of data without regard to the underlying physical location of the remote data store. Reference or master data can now live in its "natural habitat" where it normally resides.

- Minimizes data proliferation issues caused by maintaining multiple copies. This was yesterday's IT solution to handling the master data problem. It was usually accomplished by attempting to centralize the data stores, and that usually meant making multiple copies of the data.

- Utilizes a single query language (U-SQL) for all data queries. In addition to being a "unifying" and "singular" programming language, it is also the most familiar to developers and therefore fastest to adopt and leverage based on existing skillsets. This can amount to a huge advantage in terms of developer productivity, code maintainability, and agility.

- Each data store can maintain its own sovereignty. Because the data can reside in its original location, it can be queried "in-place" and with only a subset (the query results) returned over the network to the ADLA query results. This allows the data to always reside in its home location and thereby adhere to all the rules governing the domain and movement of the data.

There is one important point to make when it comes to the implementation of this feature. When you specify a U-SQL query to work with data from other external sources in Azure, such as Azure SQL database or SQL data warehouse, you will need to specify the following information as part of the query statement:

- *DATA SOURCE*: Represents a remote data source such as Azure SQL Database. Requires that you specify all the details (connection string, credentials, etc.) required to connect and issue SQL statements.

- *EXTERNAL TABLE*: A local ADLA SQL table, with columns defined as C# data types, that redirects queries issued against it to the remote table that it is based on. U-SQL handles the data type conversions automatically.

  - ADLA's implementation of external tables allows you impose a specific schema against the remote data, which would help to shield you from remote schema changes. This capability allows you to issue queries that join external tables with local tables, allowing for some creative Big Data processing scenarios.

- *PASS THROUGH Queries*: The U-SQL queries are issued directly against the remote data source in the syntax of the remote data source. An example would be that Transact SQL would be issued against the remote data source for Azure SQL database queries.

- *REMOTABLE_TYPES*: For every external data source, you have to specify the list of "remoteable types". This list constrains the types of queries that will be remoted. Ex: REMOTABLE_TYPES = (bool, byte, short, ushort, int, decimal).

- *LAZY METADATA LOADING*: Here the remote data is schematized only when the query is actually issue to the remote data source. Your program must be able to deal with remote schema changes.

These implementation requirements result in a few key lessons that are worthy of a deeper technical walkthrough. This is necessary to fully demystify for the reader how this feature is implemented in Azure Data Lake Analytics.

Federated Queries: Overview of Steps Required to Query External Tables

It is important to note that there are several steps required to successfully implement an ADLA Federated query. We walk through each of the steps required starting with the prerequisites.

Confirm U-SQL Federated Query: Prerequisites Installed and Configured

Note that most of the prerequisites are required and will cause significant connectivity and access issues that can be difficult to diagnose.

- Azure Subscription

- Azure Data Lake Store (ADLS) account

- Azure Data Lake Analytics (ADLA) account

- Azure SQL Database or Azure SQL Data warehouse with SQL login/password credentials

- Visual Studio 2015 (Optional). To create and execute U-SQL queries. U-SQL scripts can also be developed and deployed via the Azure Portal.

- Azure Data Lake Tools for Visual Studio 2015. (Optional) works with Visual Studio 2015.

  - Download: `https://www.microsoft.com/en-us/download/details.aspx?id=49504`

- Azure PowerShell (Optional)

  - Download: `http://aka.ms/webpi-azps`

Verify "Read/Execute" Permissions on Your Azure Data Lake Store Account

This is required to create the catalog secret via a PowerShell command in a later step. To verify your permissions:

1. Navigate to your ADLS account in Azure Portal.

2. Click on the Data Explorer icon in the top navigation bar.

3. Click on the Access icon in the top navigation bar.

4. Validate you have Read/Execute permissions.

The screenshot in Figure 7-18 illustrates the proper permissions for an authorized user.

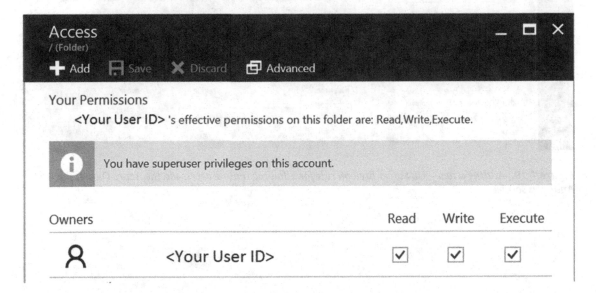

Figure 7-18. Azure Data Lake Store: user permissions view via the Azure Portal

Configure Access to the Remote Azure SQL Database: Allow IP Range in the SQL Server Firewall for the ADLA Services That Execute the U-SQL Queries

This step grants access to the ADLA service to access your Azure SQL Server and its related Azure SQL databases.

Navigate to the targeted Azure SQL Database Server instance via the Azure Portal:

1. Click on the SQL Server icon to get to the settings page.

2. Click on the Firewall icon on the left navigation blade.

3. Create a new rule with range 25.66.0.0 to 25.66.255.255.

4. Click on the Save icon on the top navigation bar to save these changes.

The screenshot in Figure 7-19 depicts the Azure SQL Server Firewall configuration screen and a new firewall rule added for ADLA access.

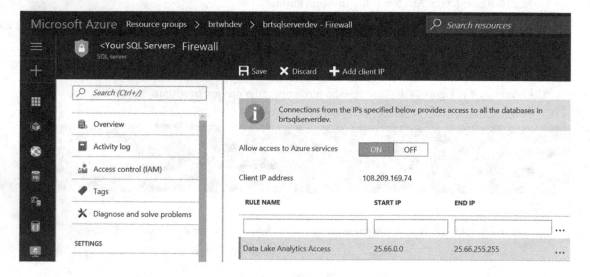

Figure 7-19. Adding a new SQL Server firewall rule for allowing remote access via the Azure Data Lake Analytics service

Create a *New ADLA SQL Database* and SQL table via U-SQL Query

The next step is to create an ADLA SQL Database and SQL table. To do this, navigate to your ADLA account via the Azure Portal and then select the +New Job icon to submit a new U-SQL job. Enter this U-SQL code to create an ADLA SQL database and table:

```
//Create Table
CREATE DATABASE IF NOT EXISTS SearchMaster;

//Create Table
CREATE TABLE IF NOT EXISTS SearchMaster.dbo.SearchLog
(
        //Define schema of table
        UserId          int,
        Start           DateTime,
        Region          string,
        Query           string,
        Duration        int,
        Urls            string,
        ClickedUrls     string,
    INDEX idx1 //Name of index
    CLUSTERED (Region ASC) //Column to cluster by
    PARTITIONED BY HASH (Region) //Column to partition by
);
```

Use PowerShell to Create a New Catalog Secret in the ADLA Database

This secret contains the password for the SQL login and connection string for the Azure SQL database.:

```
#Login (Microsoft Azure Login screen will appear):
Login-AzureRmAccount

#Show your available Azure Subscriptions:
Get-AzureRmSubscription

#Connect to Azure Subscription that contains the ADLA Database:
Set-AzureRMContext -SubscriptionId 00000000-0000-0000-0000-000000000000

New-AzureRmDataLakeAnalyticsCatalogCredential -AccountName "ContosoADLAAccount" `
-DatabaseName "ContosoADLADB" `
-CredentialName "ContosoAzureSQLDB_Secret" `
-Credential (Get-Credential) `
-DatabaseHost "ContosoSQLSVR.database.windows.net" -Port 1433
```

You can verify that these PowerShell commands created a new credential object in your ADLA SQL database by navigating to your SQL database using the ADLA Data Explorer. Start by expanding the node for your database and then expanding the Credentials node, as shown in Figure 7-20.

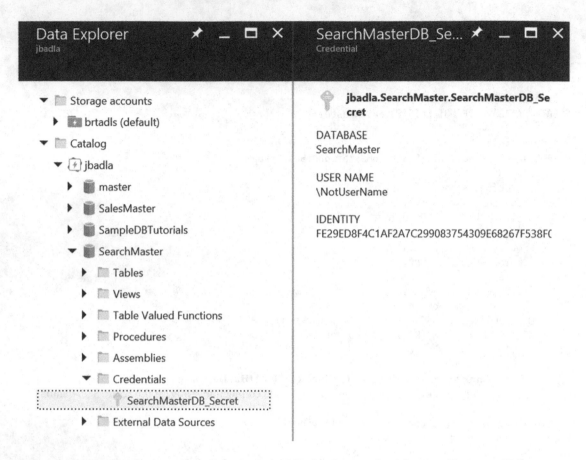

Figure 7-20. Viewing the Azure Data Lake Analytics SQL database credentials created by PowerShell

Create a CREDENTIAL with an IDENTITY that matches the AzureRmDataLakeAnalyticsCatalogCredential Name

This is used in the PowerShell script (`ContosoAzureSQLDB_Secret`) in the ADLA Database using this U-SQL query:

```
//Connect to ADLA Database
USE DATABASE YourADLADatabaseName;
//Create CREDENTIAL
//IDENTITY: ADLA SQL Catalog Secret, MUST MATCH name chosen in prior PowerShell script ->
"ContosoAzureSQLDB_Secret"
CREATE CREDENTIAL IF NOT EXISTS [ContosoAzureSQLDB_Secret] WITH USER_NAME = "
YourAzureSQLDB_Username ", IDENTITY = " YourAzureSQLDB_Secret";
```

Create Data Source in ADLA Database with a Reference to the Azure SQL Database
Use this U-SQL query:

```
// Create External Data Source on ADLA SQL DB
CREATE DATA SOURCE IF NOT EXISTS [ASQL_YOURDB]
FROM AZURESQLDB
WITH (PROVIDER_STRING = "Initial Catalog= YourASQLDB;Trusted_Connection=False;Encrypt=True",
    CREDENTIAL = [ContosoAzureSQLDB_Secret],
    REMOTABLE_TYPES = (bool, byte, sbyte, short, ushort, int, uint, long, ulong, decimal,
    float, double, string, DateTime)
    );
```

Create an External Table in ADLA SQL Database Based on the Remote Data Source
Use this U-SQL query. Note that the ADLA SQL table schema needs to match the remote table schema with corresponding field types.

```
// CREATE EXTERNAL TABLE in ADLA SQL database to represent the remote database table.

CREATE EXTERNAL TABLE DailySales  (
        OrderID     int?,
        SalesDate   DateTime?,
        Customer    string,
        Street      string,
        City        string,
        Region      string,
        State       string,
        Zip         string,
        SubTotal    decimal?,
        SalesTax    decimal?,
        SalesTotal  decimal?
) FROM [ASQL_YOURDB] LOCATION "dbo.DailySales";
```

Query the New Federated External Azure SQL Database Table
Output the results to a text (.CSV) file using this U-SQL query statement:

```
@query = SELECT * FROM DailySales;

OUTPUT @query
TO "/Output/TestFederatedfile.csv"
USING Outputters.Csv();
```

At this point, you have successfully configured your environment according to the setup procedures and prerequisites. You should now be able to issue U-SQL job queries against the remote external data store (an Azure SQL database in this case) .

The ADLA Federated Query capability offers a huge advantage in productivity as it allows you to query and compute remote data that lives virtually anywhere and then join that data with multiple additional cloud sources.

At the time of this writing, the following external data sources are allowed in an ADLA Federated Query:

- *AZURESQLDB*: Specifies that the external source is a Microsoft Azure SQL Database instance.

- *AZURESQLDW*: Specifies that the external source is a Microsoft Azure SQL Data warehouse instance.

- *SQLSERVER*: Specifies that the external source is a Microsoft SQL Server instance running in an accessible Microsoft Azure VM. Only SQL Server 2012 and newer versions are supported.

Combining Row Sets

The Azure Data Lake U-SQL language provides a number of operators to combine row sets from various data sources. Here are the current operators supported in the ADLA U-SQL programming language:

- `LEFT OUTER JOIN`
- `LEFT INNER JOIN`
- `RIGHT INNER JOIN`
- `RIGHT OUTER JOIN`
- `FULL OUTER JOIN`
- `CROSS JOIN`
- `LEFT SEMI JOIN`
- `RIGHT SEMI JOIN`
- `EXCEPT ALL`
- `EXCEPT DISTINCT`
- `INTERSECT ALL`
- `INTERSECT DISTINCT`
- `UNION ALL`
- `UNION DISTINCT`

Azure Portal Integration

As you have seen in this brief overview of ADLA, there are many tasks that can be accomplished right in the Azure Portal. For example, you can accomplish all of these tasks right from the Azure Portal in order to be (immediately) highly productive:

- Create a New ADLA account.
- Author U-SQL scripts. Open/Save.
- Submit U-SQL jobs.
- Cancel running jobs.
- Provision users who can submit ADLA jobs.
- Visualize usage statistics (compute hours).
- Visualize job management charts.

These tasks comprise the full lifecycle of U-SQL job execution from creation, to submission, to monitoring, and finally to analyzing job results.

Of course, for the hard-core ADLA developers, Visual Studio and the Data Lake Tools for Visual Studio may be a better fit. To get an idea of the capabilities of the Data Lake Tools for Visual Studio, take a look at the following link.

■ **Note** Develop U-SQL scripts using Data Lake Tools for Visual Studio at this link: `https://docs.microsoft.com/en-us/azure/data-lake-analytics/data-lake-analytics-data-lake-tools-get-started`

Big Data Jobs: Simplified Management and Administration

In addition to the web-based management capabilities available in the Azure Portal, there are additional management and monitoring capabilities available for Azure Data Lake Store and Analytics.

- *Task Automation via PowerShell Scripts*: They enable you to create a highly automated, Big Data data processing environment.

- *Role-Based Access Control (RBAC) with Azure Active Directory (AAD)*: Provides seamless user authentication and authorization integration services.

- *Monitoring for Service Operations and Activity*

  - *Job Management*: The total number of jobs submitted as well as the number that succeeded, failed, or were cancelled

  - *Job Compute Usage*: The number of compute hours consumed by the jobs

U-SQL: Optimization Is Built-In

The ADLA U-SQL language is truly unique in that it has the following powerful optimization capabilities built-in:

- Automatic "in-lining" of U-SQL expressions, which means that the whole U-SQL script leads to a single execution model.

- Execution plan that is optimized "out-of-the-box" and without any user intervention required.

- Automatic per-job and user-driven parallelization optimizations.

- Detailed visibility into the U-SQL job execution steps, for debugging and optimization purposes.

- Heat map functionality to help identify performance bottlenecks.

Implementing ADLA in the Reference Implementation

Now that you have a solid background of the features and capabilities of ADLA and the U-SQL programming language, you will put this knowledge to use by implementing a few more key pieces of the reference implementation.

As a quick refresher, Figure 7-21 illustrates the "big picture" when it comes to the reference implementation and the role that ADLA plays in the implementation of this architecture.

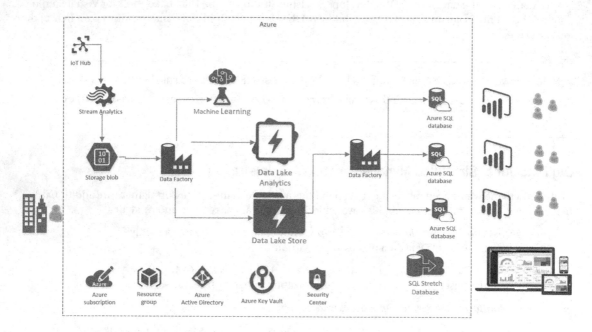

***Figure 7-21.** Data Lake Analytics role in the reference implementation architecture*

As can be seen in Figure 7-21, you'll draw upon our key lessons from Chapter 6 (Data Factory) and Chapter 7 (Data Lake Analytics) to continue with the data movement and transformation activities for the reference application in this chapter.

Specifically, in this next section, you will be processing the data that was moved to the Azure Data Lake Store from Azure Blob storage (via an Azure Data Factory job), which represents the incoming IoT streaming data.

You will then join this raw, incoming, IoT data with the results of the Azure Machine Learning Web service calls that were made real-time during the Stream Analytics ingestion job and then persisted to Azure Blob storage. This is the persisted copy of the "hot" data path that checked the team member's health. The "hot" output path destination defined in Chapter 5 was for Power BI; we also persisted the output to Azure blob Storage for a more permanent record of the real-time streaming results that were processed with Machine Learning Web Service calls.

PLANNING THE DATA SOURCES IN AZURE DATA LAKE

The goal in this section is to identify the input files (.CSV) necessary to create a consolidated SQL Azure Data Lake Analytics (ADLA) table that combines the following data sources:

1. Historical IoT Hub Streaming Data.

    a. JOIN Keys: userid, timestamp.

2. Historical IoT Hub Machine Learning Web Service Call Results.

   a. JOIN Keys: userid, timestamp.

3. Reference Data Team Member Company Affiliation.

   a. JOIN Keys: userid, id.

In the existing reference implementation, all three of these files were created in Chapters 5 and 6 when we covered the topics of Azure Stream Analytics and Azure Data Factory.

The JOIN Keys under each file represent the keys that we will use to create logical JOINs between these two tables of data in order to combine the records together and thereby enrich and enhance the data by combining these data sources together.

The JOIN with the reference data is critical so that we can match the records (by user ID) with the appropriate business entity based on the contents of the "companyname" column. We will then use this data to create individual outputs that will, in turn, be used to populate individual Azure SQL Databases by business entity.

By exposing the data as an Azure SQL database to each Business Entity, we can fully enable a "self-service" Business Intelligence (BI) experience. An additional benefit is that the Azure SQL database data is completely separated and can be further secured to reduce the legal risks of accidental data exposure to other Business Entities.

Note that in this scenario, our goal is to create a very "wide" data record that is highly denormalized to help improve the read performance. This can also enable a much easier and richer reporting experience, as there is no need for many joins on supplemental tables.

The first two files (`Historical IOT Hub*.csv`) were created as the result of the Stream Analytics job that persisted the incoming data streams into hot, warm, and cold data output storage paths.

The Historical IoT Hub Streaming Data files were captured as part of the "cold path" that output all of the sensor event messages sent to the IoT Hub in real time. The Stream Analytics job persisted this output directly to files in an Azure blob storage container.

The Historical IoT Hub Machine Learning Web Service Call results files were generated as part of the "hot path" that also populated a Power BI dataset for exposing real-time dashboard monitoring of team members health while on the job. This data contains all of the input parameters and associated Machine Learning (ML) Web Service Call results that were returned in real time, as each team member's sensor data was being processed by the Azure Stream Analytics job.

The purpose of the Machine Learning Web Service calls is to predict (in real-time) if a team member was at a point of physical exhaustion or fatigue that could result in a higher chance of a work-related accident. We cover the details behind developing the Machine Learning model and exposing it as an easily consumable web service in the next chapter.

The Reference Data files were created as the result of the Azure Data Factory Job to update the Reference data, which, in turn, was used by the Azure Stream Analytics job as an "input" for reference data that could be joined to the incoming streaming data.

OVERVIEW OF TASKS TO ACCOMPLISH

In this section, we outline the tasks that you will need to accomplish. The goal is to populate an individual Azure SQL Database (by Business Entity) with the combined information from the previous files. These data represent the historical view of all of the sensor data recorded for a business entity's individual team members along with the results of Machine Learning Web Service calls.

The data could be used for several purposes, including:

- *Enhance Team Member Feedback*: Provide historical analysis to help create an additional feedback loop (based on the physical sensor readings) to help infer and correlate "causality" surrounding daily events. Positive outcomes include noting any health-related improvement plans or behavior modifications.

- *Operations Auditing*: As a means of providing further operational, legal, or medical background and analysis. This data could be considered highly critical and would be analogous to a "black box" recorder: in the unlikely event that an incident should occur.

- *Prediction Model Enhancement*: To help provide a feedback loop to further enhance the Machine Learning prediction model for future model refinements and enhancements based on real-world data updates.

The tasks you will accomplish in the next section include the following:

1. Modify Data Factory job called `CopyFromBlobToDataLake` to include the three files to be moved into Data Lake.

2. Create and test new Azure Data Lake CSV Extract Scripts. Test extraction logic for all three files for proper field parsing and field type assignments.

   - *Test Extract 1*: IoT Hub streaming data

   - *Test Extract 2*: IoT Hub streaming Machine Learning Web Service results data

   - *Test Extract 3*: Team reference data

3. Create a new Azure Data Lake Analytics (ADLA) database and table. Populate a new table based on JOIN results from the three extract files.

4. Create separate extract files (one for each business entity) to hold the data extracted from the newly populated ADLA Database table.

5. Create separate Azure SQL databases (one for each business entity) to hold the data extracted from the ADLA database.

6. Create an Azure Data Factory job to automatically populate the Azure SQL databases based on SQL extracts (by business entity) from the ADLA database.

Now that we have outlined the plan, it's time to get started.

MODIFY AZURE DATA FACTORY JOB: "COPYFROMBLOBTODATALAKE"

In this section, we walk through modifying the existing Data Factory pipeline named CopyFromBlobToDataLake.

Basically, we need to add two more copy activities to the pipeline in order to move these two files to Azure Data Lake:

- Historical IoT Hub Streaming Data Machine Learning Web Service Call Results from "hot" path.

- Team Member Reference Data Team Member Company Affiliation.

The easiest way to do this is to navigate to the existing Azure Data Factory Job, called CopyFromBlobToDataLake, and then select the option for Copy Data (PREVIEW) as shown in Figure 7-22.

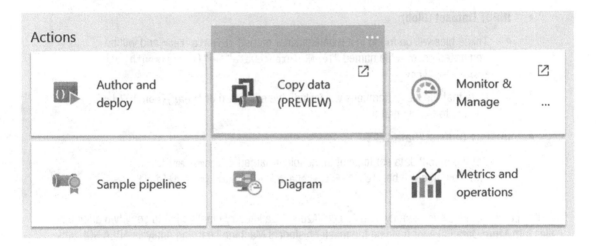

Figure 7-22. Azure Data Factory Copy Data option

Selecting this option will allow you to easily add copy functionality to the existing Data Factory Pipeline Copy job.

Walk through the steps in the Azure data Factory Copy Data PREVIEW Wizard to create the copy job for the first additional file we need—the Historical IoT Hub Streaming Data Machine Learning Web Service Call Results. Here is a high-level outline of the input and outputs that are required to create this new copy pipeline.

New Copy Job: Historical IoT Hub Streaming Data Machine Learning Web Service Call Results:

- **INPUT Dataset (Blob):**

  - These files will be found in a Blob container named `streamingmldata` and will be generated under a folder structure of Year/Month/Day/Hour.

- **OUTPUT Dataset (Data Lake):**

  - Set the output data set to point to the file name of the form `StreamingMLResults DataFile{year}{month}{day}{hour}.csv`.

Next, add another copy job to the existing Azure Data Factory Pipeline job to copy the second data file, the Team Member Reference Data .CSV file.

Again, we will use the Copy Data Wizard to make it fast and easy. Refer to the following input and output dataset guidance for locating and replicating your data according to the reference implementation.

Here is a high-level outline of the input and outputs that are required to create this new "copy" pipeline.

New Copy Job: Team Member Reference Data:

- **INPUT Dataset (Blob):**

  - These files will be found in a Blob container named `refdata-team` and will be generated under a file named `"TeamReferenceData"` + `"{year}{month}{day}{hour}"`+ `".csv"`.

  - Note that the file generations will include the extension of `{year}{month}{day}{hour}` to the file name.

- **OUTPUT Dataset (Data Lake):**

  - Set the output data set to point to the folder named `streamingmldata`. The file name will be `"TeamReferenceData"` + `"{year}{month}{day}{hour}"` + `".csv"`.

At this point, we have successfully modified our Azure Data Factory Pipeline job to copy two additional files into Azure Data Lake for building the master historical Machine Learning Analysis ADLA SQL table.

The last step is to run the updated Data Factory Copy jobs and actually move the data files from Azure Blob Storage to Azure Data Lake.

CREATE AND TEST NEW AZURE DATA LAKE CSV EXTRACT SCRIPTS FOR THREE INPUT FILES

This section focuses on reading the three .CSV files we copied into Azure Data Lake from Azure Blob Storage.

In order to simplify the development experience, we will create a separate ADLA job for individually testing the extraction of each of the three files. For each file, we will simply test our parsing logic by simply reading the file and then outputting it.

To get started, navigate to your Azure Data Lake Account in the Azure Portal, and then click on the + New Job icon.

Create Extract #1: READ Streaming Data Input .CSV Files

At this point, you can name your new job "TEST EXTRACT of STREAMING DATA CSV File" and then paste the contents of this code into that file.

```
@streamingdata =
    EXTRACT
            userid          string,
            age             int,
            height          int,
            weight          int,
            heartratebpm    int,
            breathingrate   double,
            temperature     double,
            steps           int,
            velocity        double,
            altitude        int,
            ventilization   double,
            activity        double,
            cadence         double,
            speed           int,
            hib             double,
            heartrateredzone        double,
            heartratevariability    double,
            status          int,
            id              string,
            deviceid        string,
            messagetype     int,
            longitude       double,
            latitude        double,
            timestamp       string,
            eventprocessedutctime   string,
            partitionid     int,
            eventenqueuedutctime string,
            firstname       string,
            lastname        string,
            username        string,
            utype           int,
            phone           string,
            email           string,
            gender          int,
            race            int
    FROM "/streamingdata/2016/StreamingResultsDailyFile{*}.csv"
    USING Extractors.Csv();

OUTPUT @streamingdata
    TO "/output/TESTStreamingResultsDailyFile20161222.csv"
    USING Outputters.Csv();
```

325

Note that the purpose of this script is for testing purposes only; it's okay if some aspects are hard-coded. Select Save As to download a copy locally and save the script. Submit the job and check for the expected outputs. Correct any errors and re-submit the job until you have success.

When working with ADLA U-SQL scripts, it is often better to break things up into smaller chunks of code, rather than attempt to debug a larger and often more complicated script.

Make sure the first file extract is working correctly before advancing to coding the next two file extractions.

■ **Tip**   Depending on how your environment is configured, you may notice quite a few .CSV files that are uniquely generated and stored under recursive folder structures.

The key to processing this type of scenario is to use a "wildcard" extension when naming the input file. In ADLA U-SQL scripts that is accomplished by using the {*} notation. For example, you can use the file name of DailySales{*}.csv to include *all* files that start with the name DailySales and end with a .CSV file extension.

Create Extract #2: READ Streaming ML Data Input .CSV Files

At this point, you can rename your existing job "TEST EXTRACT of STREAMING ML DATA CSV File" and then paste this code into the file.

```
// @streamingMLdata
@streamingmldata =
    EXTRACT
            userid        string,
            timestamp     string,
            eventprocessedutctime    string,
            partitionid int,
            eventenqueuedutctime string,
            breathingrate    double,
            temperature double,
            ventilization string,
            activity      double,
            cadence       double,
            heartratebpm int,
            velocity      double,
            speed         int,
            hib           double,
            heartrateredzone      double,
            heartratevariability      double,
            scored_labels    string,
            scored_prob      double

    FROM "/streamingmldata/2016/StreamingMLResultsDataFile{*}.csv"
    USING Extractors.Csv();

OUTPUT @streamingmldata
 TO "/output/TESTStreamingMLResultsDataFile20161222.csv"
 USING Outputters.Csv();
```

Select Save As to download a copy locally and save the script. When you are ready, submit the job and check for the expected output results. Correct any errors and re-submit the job until you can generate a complete output file.

Create Extract #3: READ Team Member Reference Data

For this job, you can rename your existing job "TEST EXTRACT of TEAM REFERENCE DATA CSV File" and then paste this code into the new file.

```
// @ refdatateamdata
@refdatateamdata =
    EXTRACT
        authid          string,
        companyname     string,
        firstname       string,
        lastname        string,
        username        string,
        imageUrl        string,
        utype           string,
        address1        string,
        address2        string,
        address3        string,
        city            string,
        state           string,
        zip             string,
        country         string,
        phone           string,
        email           string,
        linkedin        string,
        facebook        string,
        twitter         string,
        blog            string,
        age             int,
        height          double,
        weight          double,
        gender          int,
        race            int,
        longitude       double,
        latitude        double,
        id              string,
        cachettl        string,
        _rid            string,
        _self           string,
        _etag           string,
        _attachments    string,
        _ts             string

    FROM "/refdata-team/TeamReferenceData{*}.csv"
    USING Extractors.Csv();
```

```
OUTPUT @refdatateamdata
    TO "/output/TESTTeamReferenceData20161222.csv"
    USING Outputters.Csv();
```

Select Save As to download a copy locally and save the script. When you are ready, submit the job and check for the expected output results. Correct any errors and re-submit the job until you can generate a complete output file.

At this point, you have successfully verified the three input files, and you are now ready to JOIN them to populate an ADLA database and table.

CREATE NEW AZURE DATA LAKE ANALYTICS (ADLA) DATABASE AND POPULATE NEW TABLE BASED ON JOIN RESULTS FROM THE THREE EXTRACTED FILES

This step involves creating a new U-SQL job that will combine the three test extract scripts you created in the previous step to create a series of JOINs among the datasets. The job will then create an Azure Data Lake database, and then you will then automatically populate a new ADLA SQL table with the results of the JOIN operations.

Note that at the time of this writing, there is no UPDATE or MERGE support available in the ADLA U-SQL language for updating SQL tables. Therefore, you will usually issue DROP and CREATE U-SQL commands against your ADLA SQL tables in order to accomplish UPDATE and MERGE operations.

Note also that U-SQL provides common join operators such as INNER JOIN, LEFT/RIGHT/FULL OUTER JOIN, and SEMI JOIN to join not only ADLA SQL tables but also *any* row sets (even those produced from files) or external federated data sources.

For reference purposes, here are the most common types of JOIN operations and the underlying logic for matching records that they employ:

- *LEFT JOIN*: Return all rows from the left table and the matched rows from the right table.

- *RIGHT JOIN*: Return all rows from the right table and the matched rows from the left table.

- *INNER JOIN*: Return all rows when there is at least one match in both tables.

- *FULL JOIN*: Return all rows when there is a match in one of the tables.

For this job, you can rename your existing job to "EXTRACT All 3 Files and JOIN into ADLA Table". This task results in a rather long script.

You'll start by consolidating the three previous U-SQL extract scripts into a single script.

You will then paste the following code to implement the JOIN operations, create the ADLA database, and then output the JOIN into a new ADLA SQL table.

```
//(1) JOIN the streaming data with the ML Results data
@joindata1 =
    SELECT
            s.userid,
            s.age,
            s.height,
            s.weight,
            s.heartratebpm,
            s.breathingrate,
            s.temperature,
            s.steps,
            s.velocity,
            s.altitude,
            s.ventilization,
            s.activity,
            s.cadence,
            s.speed,
            s.hib,
            s.heartrateredzone,
            s.heartratevariability,
            s.status,
            s.id,
            s.deviceid,
            s.messagetype,
            s.longitude,
            s.latitude,
            s.timestamp,
            s.eventprocessedutctime,
            s.partitionid,
            s.eventenqueuedutctime,
            s.firstname,
            s.lastname,
            s.username,
            s.utype,
            s.phone,
            s.email,
            s.gender,
            s.race,
            m.mluserid,
            m.mltimestamp,
            m.scoredlabels,
            m.scoredprob

    FROM @streamingdata AS s
        LEFT JOIN @streamingmldata AS m
                ON s.timestamp == m.mltimestamp
                AND s.userid == m.mluserid;
```

```
//(2) JOIN the NEW streaming data + ML data by USER to GET the Associated COMPANY
@joindata2 =
    SELECT
                j.userid,
                j.age,
                j.height,
                j.weight,
                j.heartratebpm,
                j.breathingrate,
                j.temperature,
                j.steps,
                j.velocity,
                j.altitude,
                j.ventilization,
                j.activity,
                j.cadence,
                j.speed,
                j.hib,
                j.heartrateredzone,
                j.heartratevariability,
                j.status,
                j.id,
                j.deviceid,
                j.messagetype,
                j.longitude,
                j.latitude,
                j.timestamp,
                j.eventprocessedutctime,
                j.partitionid,
                j.eventenqueuedutctime,
                j.firstname,
                j.lastname,
                j.username,
                j.utype,
                j.phone,
                j.email,
                j.gender,
                j.mluserid,
                j.mltimestamp,
                j.scoredlabels,
                j.scoredprob,
                j.race,
                r.companyname,
                r.rid

    FROM @joindata1 AS j
        LEFT JOIN @refdatateamdata AS r
                    ON j.userid == r.rid;

OUTPUT @joindata2
    TO "/output/SQLJoinTestResults.csv"
    USING Outputters.Csv();
```

```
DROP DATABASE IF EXISTS IOTStreamingDataMLHistoryDB;
CREATE DATABASE IOTStreamingDataMLHistoryDB;
USE DATABASE IOTStreamingDataMLHistoryDB;

CREATE TABLE StreamingDataMLHistory(
                INDEX sl_idx CLUSTERED (userid ASC)
                PARTITIONED BY HASH (userid) )
                AS SELECT * FROM @joindata2 AS S; // Note: Automatic Table Schema
                generation
```

As before, select Save As to download a copy of the U-SQL script locally and then save the script.

When you are ready, submit the job and check for the expected output results in the ADLA SQL database. Correct any errors and re-submit the job until you can generate a successfully populated ADLA SQL table.

Note that the last statement in the U-SQL script issues a CREATE TABLE command that is populated from a SELECT statement.

The huge benefit here is that the ADLA Table Schema is implicitly inferred (column names and types) from the prior U-SQL .csv data file extraction code. This negates the need to predefine the ADLA SQL table layout before it is populated.

CREATE SEPARATE EXTRACT FILES (ONE FOR EACH BUSINESS ENTITY) TO HOLD THE DATA EXTRACTED FROM THE NEWLY POPULATED AZURE DATA LAKE ANALYTICS DATABASE TABLE

In this step, you simply create separate .CSV file exports (one per business entity) from the newly populated ADLA database table.

To get started, navigate to your Azure Data Lake account in the Azure Portal, click on the +New Job icon, and then paste this code into the new job window:

```
//EXPORT data from ADLA Database Table to .CSV files by Business Entity

// Export #1 - WigiTech
@table1 = SELECT * FROM [IOTStreamingDataMLHistoryDB].[dbo].[StreamingDataMLHistory]
WHERE companyname =="WigiTech";

OUTPUT @table1
    TO "/output/StreamingDataMLHistory-WigiTech.Csv"
    USING Outputters.Csv();

// Export #2 - Tall Towers
@table2 = SELECT * FROM [IOTStreamingDataMLHistoryDB].[dbo].[StreamingDataMLHistory]
WHERE companyname =="Tall Towers";
```

```
OUTPUT @table2
    TO "/output/StreamingDataMLHistory-Tall-Towers.Csv"
    USING Outputters.Csv();

// Export #3 - The Complicated Badger
@table3 = SELECT * FROM [IOTStreamingDataMLHistoryDB].[dbo].[StreamingDataMLHistory]
WHERE companyname =="The Complicated Badger";

OUTPUT @table3
    TO "/output/StreamingDataMLHistory-The-Complicated-Badger.Csv"
    USING Outputters.Csv();
```

Click on the Save As icon to save the U-SQL script. Then submit the job and check for the creation of the .CSV output result files.

CREATE AZURE SQL DATABASES AND TABLES (ONE FOR EACH BUSINESS ENTITY) TO HOLD THE DATA EXTRACTED FROM THE ADLA DATABASE TABLE

The next step is to create a new Azure SQL database and SQL table to hold the information that we will extract from the ADLA SQL table that we populated from these three CSV text files:

- Historical IoT Hub Streaming Data

- Historical IoT Hub Machine Learning Web Service Call Results

- Reference Data Team Member Company Affiliation

In this exercise, you'll perform a one-time creation of a new Azure SQL database and a new SQL table for each of the three business entities in the reference implementation.

Each of these databases will contain the merged dataset results (for one of the business entities), where you merged the three files into an ADLA SQL table.

To complete this task, you need the following prerequisites:

- Azure SQL Server Database information, such as server, user, and password credentials.

- Azure SQL Server firewall ports opened-up to allow your client IP address to information.

- SQL Server Management Studio (SSMS) or Visual Studio Server Explorer to run the Transact-SQL scripts to create the three Azure SQL databases and tables.

■ **Note** Download SQL Server Management Studio (SSMS): https://msdn.microsoft.com/en-us/library/mt238290.aspx.

Once you have established connectivity to your Azure SQL Server database using either SQL Server Management Studio or Visual Studio Server Explorer, open a new Query window and enter this SQL script:

```sql
USE [master]
GO

DROP DATABASE IF EXISTS [IOTDataMLHistory-WigiTech]
GO

CREATE DATABASE [IOTDataMLHistory-WigiTech]
GO

USE [IOTDataMLHistory-WigiTech]
GO

DROP TABLE  IF EXISTS [dbo].[IOTDataMLHistory]
GO

CREATE TABLE [dbo].[IOTDataMLHistory](
    [UserId] [char](256) NOT NULL,
    [Age] [float] NOT NULL,
    [Height] [float] NOT NULL,
    [Weight] [float] NOT NULL,
    [HeartRateBPM] [float] NOT NULL,
    [BreathingRate] [float] NOT NULL,
    [Temperature] [float] NOT NULL,
    [Steps] [float] NOT NULL,
    [Velocity] [float] NOT NULL,
    [Altitude] [float] NOT NULL,
    [Ventilization] [float] NOT NULL,
    [Activity] [float] NOT NULL,
    [Cadence] [float] NOT NULL,
    [Speed] [float] NOT NULL,
    [HIB] [float] NOT NULL,
    [HeartRateRedZone] [float] NOT NULL,
    [HeartrateVariability] [float] NOT NULL,
    [Status] [int] NOT NULL,
    [Id] [char](256) NOT NULL,
    [DeviceId] [char](256) NOT NULL,
    [MessageType] [int] NOT NULL,
    [Longitude] [float] NOT NULL,
    [Latitude] [float] NOT NULL,
    [Timestamp] [datetime2](7) NOT NULL,
    [EventProcessedUtcTime] [datetime2](7) NOT NULL,
    [PartitionId] [int] NOT NULL,
    [EventEnqueuedUtcTime] [datetime2](7) NOT NULL,
    [FirstName]  [char](256) NOT NULL,
    [LastName]  [char](256) NOT NULL,
    [UserName]  [char](256) NOT NULL,
    [UType]  [char](256) NOT NULL,
```

```
    [Phone]  [char](256) NOT NULL,
    [Email]  [char](256) NOT NULL,
    [Gender]  [char](256) NOT NULL,
    [MLUserid]  [char](256) NOT NULL,
    [MLTimestamp]  [char](256) NOT NULL,
    [ScoredLabels]  [char](256) NOT NULL,
    [ScoredProb]  [float] NOT NULL,
    [Race]    [int] NOT NULL,
    [CompanyName]  [char](256) NOT NULL,
    [Rid]  [char](256) NOT NULL
)
GO
```

After running this script three times (modifying it to reflect each business entity), you will be ready to populate the Azure SQL database tables by using an Azure Data Factory job.

CREATE AZURE DATA FACTORY JOB TO AUTOMATICALLY POPULATE THE AZURE SQL DATABASES (BY BUSINESS ENTITY) USING THE SQL QUERY EXTRACTIONS FROM THE AZURE DATA LAKE DATABASE

This last step will complete the data analysis and reporting journey by exposing the historical IoT sensor data and associated Machine Learning Web Service call results for consumption by the business entities in the reference implementation scenario.

At this point, all the hard work has already been completed, and all you have to do is create an Azure Data Factory job to select the data out of the ADLA SQL database, filter the results by business entity, and then insert the data into the individual Azure SQL databases you created in the last step.

To get started via the Azure Portal, first navigate to your existing Azure resource group. Search for Data Factory and then add a new Data Factory job, as shown in Figure 7-23.

Figure 7-23. *Adding a new Azure Data Factory job to a resource group*

Next, complete the Azure Data Factory Job configuration parameters, as shown in Figure 7-24.

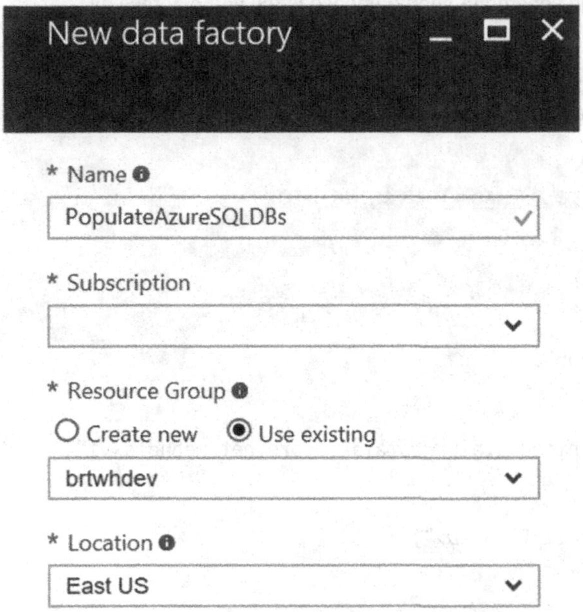

New data factory   _ ☐ ✕

* Name ❶

PopulateAzureSQLDBs   ✓

* Subscription

⌄

* Resource Group ❶

○ Create new   ⊙ Use existing

brtwhdev   ⌄

* Location ❶

East US   ⌄

Figure 7-24. *Azure Data Factory job parameters*

Click on the Create icon, and then the new Data Factory job will be provisioned into your Azure Resource Group after a few minutes.

After the new Data Factory job has been provisioned into your environment, navigate to the new Data Factory job and select the Copy Data (PREVIEW) icon to launch the Copy Wizard.

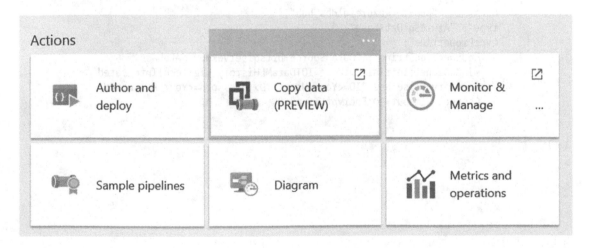

Figure 7-25. *Data Factory Copy Data Wizard*

Next, walk through the Copy Data Wizard to create a Data Factory pipeline job that will copy the data from each individual .CSV file (one for each entity) to the appropriate Azure SQL database (which varies by business entity). The SQL table name and scheme in each database is the same across all databases.

Here are code fragments from a sample Azure Data Factory job to populate an Azure SQL Database for WigiTech, based on a .CSV file exported from the Azure Data Lake Store.

Linked Service: Source Azure Data Lake Store

```
{
    "name": "Source-DataLakeStore-f0g",
    "properties": {
        "hubName": "populateazuresqldbs_hub",
        "type": "AzureDataLakeStore",
        "typeProperties": {
            "dataLakeStoreUri": "https://brtadls.azuredatalakestore.net/webhdfs/v1",
            "authorization": "**********",
            "sessionId": "**********",
            "subscriptionId": "<Your Subscription ID>",
            "resourceGroupName": "brtwhdev"
        }
    }
}
```

Linked Service: Destination: Azure SQL Database

```
{
    "name": "Destination-SQLAzure-f0g",
    "properties": {
        "hubName": "populateazuresqldbs_hub",
        "type": "AzureSqlDatabase",
        "typeProperties": {
            "connectionString": "Data Source=brtsqlserverdev.database.
            windows.net;Initial Catalog=IOTDataMLHistory-WigiTech;Integrated
            Security=False;User ID=<Your User  ID>;Password=<Your Password>;
            Connect Timeout=30;Encrypt=True"
        }
    }
}
```

Input Dataset: .CSV File in Azure Data Lake Store

```
{
    "name": "InputDataset-f0g",
    "properties": {
        "structure": [
            {
                "name": "Column0",
                "type": "String"
            },
            {
                "name": "Column1",
                "type": "Int64"
            },
            {
                "name": "Column2",
                "type": "Int64"
            },
            {
                "name": "Column3",
                "type": "Int64"
            },
            {
                "name": "Column4",
                "type": "Int64"
            },
            {
                "name": "Column5",
                "type": "Double"
            },
            {
                "name": "Column6",
                "type": "Double"
            },
            {
                "name": "Column7",
                "type": "Int64"
            },
            {
                "name": "Column8",
                "type": "Double"
            },
            {
                "name": "Column9",
                "type": "Int64"
            },
            {
                "name": "Column10",
                "type": "Double"
            },
```

```
        {
            "name": "Column11",
            "type": "Double"
        },
        {
            "name": "Column12",
            "type": "Int64"
        },
        {
            "name": "Column13",
            "type": "Int64"
        },
        {
            "name": "Column14",
            "type": "Int64"
        },
        {
            "name": "Column15",
            "type": "Int64"
        },
        {
            "name": "Column16",
            "type": "Int64"
        },
        {
            "name": "Column17",
            "type": "Int64"
        },
        {
            "name": "Column18",
            "type": "String"
        },
        {
            "name": "Column19",
            "type": "String"
        },
        {
            "name": "Column20",
            "type": "Int64"
        },
        {
            "name": "Column21",
            "type": "Double"
        },
        {
            "name": "Column22",
            "type": "Double"
        },
        {
            "name": "Column23",
            "type": "Datetime"
        },
```

```
{
    "name": "Column24",
    "type": "Datetime"
},
{
    "name": "Column25",
    "type": "Int64"
},
{
    "name": "Column26",
    "type": "Datetime"
},
{
    "name": "Column27",
    "type": "String"
},
{
    "name": "Column28",
    "type": "String"
},
{
    "name": "Column29",
    "type": "String"
},
{
    "name": "Column30",
    "type": "Int64"
},
{
    "name": "Column31",
    "type": "Int64"
},
{
    "name": "Column32",
    "type": "String"
},
{
    "name": "Column33",
    "type": "Int64"
},
{
    "name": "Column34",
    "type": "String"
},
{
    "name": "Column35",
    "type": "Datetime"
},
{
    "name": "Column36",
    "type": "String"
},
```

```json
                    {
                        "name": "Column37",
                        "type": "Double"
                    },
                    {
                        "name": "Column38",
                        "type": "Int64"
                    },
                    {
                        "name": "Column39",
                        "type": "String"
                    },
                    {
                        "name": "Column40",
                        "type": "String"
                    }
                ],
                "published": false,
                "type": "AzureDataLakeStore",
                "linkedServiceName": "Source-DataLakeStore-f0g",
                "typeProperties": {
                    "fileName": "StreamingDataMLHistory-WigiTech.Csv",
                    "folderPath": "output/",
                    "format": {
                        "type": "TextFormat",
                        "columnDelimiter": ",",
                        "quoteChar": "\""
                    }
                },
                "availability": {
                    "frequency": "Day",
                    "interval": 1
                },
                "external": true,
                "policy": {}
            }
        }
```

Output Dataset: Azure SQL Database Table

```
{
    "name": "OutputDataset-f0g",
    "properties": {
        "structure": [
            {
                "name": "UserId",
                "type": "String"
            },
            {
                "name": "Age",
                "type": "Double"
            },
            {
                "name": "Height",
                "type": "Double"
            },
            {
                "name": "Weight",
                "type": "Double"
            },
            {
                "name": "HeartRateBPM",
                "type": "Double"
            },
            {
                "name": "BreathingRate",
                "type": "Double"
            },
            {
                "name": "Temperature",
                "type": "Double"
            },
            {
                "name": "Steps",
                "type": "Double"
            },
            {
                "name": "Velocity",
                "type": "Double"
            },
            {
                "name": "Altitude",
                "type": "Double"
            },
            {
                "name": "Ventilization",
                "type": "Double"
            },
```

```
            {
                "name": "Activity",
                "type": "Double"
            },
            {
                "name": "Cadence",
                "type": "Double"
            },
            {
                "name": "Speed",
                "type": "Double"
            },
            {
                "name": "HIB",
                "type": "Double"
            },
            {
                "name": "HeartRateRedZone",
                "type": "Double"
            },
            {
                "name": "HeartrateVariability",
                "type": "Double"
            },
            {
                "name": "Status",
                "type": "Int32"
            },
            {
                "name": "Id",
                "type": "String"
            },
            {
                "name": "DeviceId",
                "type": "String"
        },
            {
                "name": "MessageType",
                "type": "Int32"
            },
            {
                "name": "Longitude",
                "type": "Double"
            },
            {
                "name": "Latitude",
                "type": "Double"
            },
            {
                "name": "Timestamp",
                "type": "Datetime"
            },
```

```
{
    "name": "EventProcessedUtcTime",
    "type": "Datetime"
},
{
    "name": "PartitionId",
    "type": "Int32"
},
{
    "name": "EventEnqueuedUtcTime",
    "type": "Datetime"
},
{
    "name": "FirstName",
    "type": "String"
},
{
    "name": "LastName",
    "type": "String"
},
{
    "name": "UserName",
    "type": "String"
},
{
    "name": "UType",
    "type": "String"
},
{
    "name": "Phone",
    "type": "String"
},
{
    "name": "Email",
    "type": "String"
},
{
    "name": "Gender",
    "type": "String"
},
{
    "name": "MLUserid",
    "type": "String"
},
{
    "name": "MLTimestamp",
    "type": "String"
},
{
    "name": "ScoredLabels",
    "type": "String"
},
```

```
            {
                "name": "ScoredProb",
                "type": "Double"
            },
            {
                "name": "Race",
                "type": "Int32"
            },
            {
                "name": "CompanyName",
                "type": "String"
            },
            {
                "name": "Rid",
                "type": "String"
            }
        ],
        "published": false,
        "type": "AzureSqlTable",
        "linkedServiceName": "Destination-SQLAzure-fOg",
        "typeProperties": {
            "tableName": "[dbo].[IOTDataMLHistory]"
        },
        "availability": {
            "frequency": "Day",
            "interval": 1
        },
        "external": false,
        "policy": {}
    }
}
```

Pipeline: Copy CSV to Azure SQL Database

```
{
    "name": "CopyPipeline-fOg",
    "properties": {
        "activities": [
            {
                "type": "Copy",
                "typeProperties": {
                    "source": {
                        "type": "AzureDataLakeStoreSource",
                        "recursive": true
                    },
                    "sink": {
                        "type": "SqlSink",
                        "writeBatchSize": 0,
                        "writeBatchTimeout": "00:00:00"
                    },
```

```
            "translator": {
                "type": "TabularTranslator",
                "columnMappings": "Column0:UserId,Column1:Age,Column2:Height,
                Column3:Weight,Column4:HeartRateBPM,Column5:BreathingRate,Col
                umn6:Temperature,Column7:Steps,Column8:Velocity,Column9:Altit
                ude,Column10:Ventilization,Column11:Activity,Column12:Cadence,
                Column13:Speed,Column14:HIB,Column15:HeartRateRedZone,Column
                16:HeartrateVariability,Column17:Status,Column18:Id,Column19:
                DeviceId,Column20:MessageType,Column21:Longitude,Column22:Lat
                itude,Column23:Timestamp,Column24:EventProcessedUtcTime,Colum
                n25:PartitionId,Column26:EventEnqueuedUtcTime,Column27:First
                Name,Column28:LastName,Column29:UserName,Column30:UType,Colum
                n31:Phone,Column32:Email,Column33:Gender,Column34:MLUserid,Co
                lumn35:MLTimestamp,Column36:ScoredLabels,Column37:ScoredProb,
                Column38:Race,Column39:CompanyName,Column40:Rid"
            }
        },
        "inputs": [
            {
                "name": "InputDataset-f0g"
            }
        ],
        "outputs": [
            {
                "name": "OutputDataset-f0g"
            }
        ],
        "policy": {
            "timeout": "1.00:00:00",
            "concurrency": 1,
            "executionPriorityOrder": "NewestFirst",
            "style": "StartOfInterval",
            "retry": 3,
            "longRetry": 0,
            "longRetryInterval": "00:00:00"
        },
        "scheduler": {
            "frequency": "Day",
            "interval": 1
        },
        "name": "Activity-0-Data lake path_ output_->[dbo]_[IOTDataMLHistory]"
    }
],
"start": "2016-12-23T03:32:59.874Z",
"end": "2099-12-31T05:00:00Z",
"isPaused": false,
"hubName": "populateazuresqldbs_hub",
"pipelineMode": "Scheduled"
}
}
```

Once you have finished creating the new Azure Data Factory job to copy the CSV file data into the Azure SQL databases, you can easily verify the output. Open SQL Server Management Studio or Visual Studio Server Explorer and run a SQL query over the newly populated SQL table. Figure 7-26 illustrates the results of a SQL query against the `IOTDataMLHistory` SQL table.

Figure 7-26. *Verify import Azure SQL database using a SQL query in SQL Server Management Studio*

At this point, you have completed all the tasks necessary to implement the Azure architecture for the reference implementation, as illustrated in Figure 7-27.

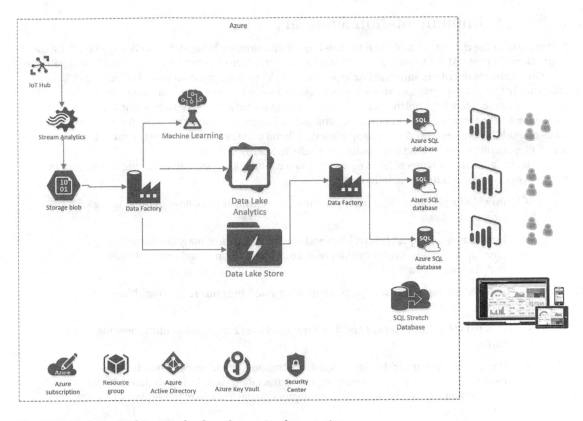

Figure 7-27. *Azure architecture for the reference implementation*

A final step in this process for a full production implementation would be to "lock down" the security aspects of this solution by restricting users and user access to the Azure Data Lake Store and Azure SQL databases via the Azure Portal.

■ **Note** See this link for more information: Security in Azure Data Lake Store: `https://docs.microsoft.com/en-us/azure/data-lake-store/data-lake-store-security-overview`.

Reference Implementation Summary

At this point in the construction of the reference implementation, we have successfully introduced the use of Azure Data Lake and ADLA to provide additional large-scale, batch data processing and analysis capabilities.

One of the more unique and enabling aspects of ADLA applications, built as truly cloud-based solutions, is that you only pay for the resources you consume. It is a pure "consumption-model" approach. In the case of the reference implementation, the incremental Azure billing costs amount to just the costs for the Data Lake Storage (storage consumed) and the ADLA (per job run) costs. This means you can just focus on building and refining the data applications at hand and leave all the infrastructure provisioning, job scheduling, deployment, scaling, and monitoring tasks to Microsoft Azure.

To summarize the progress so far, we provided data capture, analysis, and reporting capabilities by business entity to help achieve the following goals:

- Provided a historical team health monitoring archival and analysis solution using Azure Data Lake.

- Established a comprehensive, historical Machine Learning analysis dataset for creating and refining team health predictions based upon actual or simulated real-time sensor data.

- Enabled full regression analysis scenarios for analyzing and "re-playing" historical events.

- Created the ability to repeat and fine-tune Machine Learning algorithms over the historical data.

- Provided secure, individualized, "self-serve business intelligence" capabilities to each business entity to connect, view, and extract their data. Power BI makes it easy to automatically publish to the web or any mobile device. Chapter 9 explores this topic further.

Summary

This chapter provided a high-level overview of Azure Data Lake Store (ADLS) and Azure Data Lake Analytics (ADLA) and explored the rich set of complementary capabilities offered by both services.

The primary focus of these two cloud services is clearly handling Big Data at scale. One of the more interesting aspects is the flexible and open-ended architecture that enables ingesting *all* types of data via custom or out-of-the-box data extractors and output formatters.

Some of the key value propositions are discussed in the following sections.

Handles Virtually All Types of Data

U-SQL is the language of choice for creating ADLA and it can handle virtually all data ingestion scenarios.

- Unstructured, semi-structured, or structured data.

- Domain-specific user defined types using C#.

- U-SQL queries over Data Lake and Azure blobs.

- Federated Queries over Operational SQL stores and SQL DW, removing the complexity and processing time requirements of traditional Extract-Transform-Load (ETL) operations.

Productive from Day One

The combination of Azure Data Lake Store, ADLA, and U-SQL make it super easy to become instantly productive in the environment.

- Provides effortless scale and performance without the need to manually tune or configure the environment.

- Provides one of best developer experiences throughout the development lifecycle for both novices and experts.

- Allows developers to easily leverage existing skill sets with SQL and .NET.

- ADLA provides easy and powerful data extraction, preparation, and reporting capabilities.

- Easy to use, built-in, text-based connectors for ingesting the most common data formats like tab and comma-delimited text files.

- Simple and rich extensibility model for adding customer–specific data transformations.

No Limits to Scale

Azure Data Lake Store offers virtually limitless storage capacity and the ADLA environment was built from the ground up to handle some of the largest and complex distributed data processing scenarios in the industry today.

- Scales on demand with no code changes required.

- Automatically parallelizes U-SQL and custom code jobs.

- Designed to process literally petabytes of data.

Enterprise Grade

Microsoft Azure leverages other common cloud services such as Azure Active Directory (AAD) to help create a secure, integrated, and easily manageable Big Data cloud environment.

- Azure Data Lake Store offers virtually limitless storage capacity and the Azure Managing, securing, sharing, and discovery of familiar data and code objects (tables, functions, etc.)

- Role-based Authorization capabilities for ADLA SQL catalogs and storage accounts using Azure Active Directory (AAD) integrated security.

- Auditing capabilities are exposed for monitoring of ADLA Catalog objects (databases, tables, etc.).

Reference Implementation

This chapter demonstrates how easy it is to provision, prepare, develop, and publish large datasets that were generated by IoT front-end applications.

You saw how most tasks are accomplished via simple Azure service "configuration activities" vs. the legacy method of doing things, which usually required a dedicated hardware environment, along with all of the additional costs, maintenance, and overhead.

Just Scratching the Surface

It is important to note that we have really only just scratched the surface in terms of the coverage of ADLA features and capabilities. There are many deeper additional topics to explore concerning the functionality and features that are built-in and extensible to the U-SQL programming language and surrounding ADLA services.

Suffice it to say that there are many use case scenarios can easily be implemented via the constructs provided by this set of services for truly handling Big Data in the Azure cloud.

■ ■ ■

## CHAPTER 8

Advanced Analytics Using Machine Learning and R

This chapter explores the exciting new world of Machine Learning and predictive analytics. Machine Learning is currently one of the most exciting technology topics in the IT industry today. With very good reason, as it being used across almost every major industry segment and vertical today.

We are truly living in exciting times as three major trends are converging in the IT industry:

- Big Data and the Internet of Things (IoT)

- Cloud computing and inexpensive cloud-based storage

- Business intelligence capabilities

Some would say that the combination of these forces are helping to usher in the fourth Industrial Revolution. It has been predicted that artificial intelligence and Machine Learning (ML) capabilities will be incorporated into an ever-increasing number of platforms, applications, and software services as we approach the new few years. These new capabilities will enable a new generation of business and IT professionals to take advantage of artificial intelligence and Machine Learning capabilities, all without having to understand exactly how they work.

This creates an enormous opportunity for today's developers and data scientists to help enable these deep integration scenarios and capabilities with current and future software application offerings.

What Is Machine Learning?

Machine Learning can be defined simply as, "Computing systems that improve with experience". There is an old adage which captures the essence quite eloquently and succinctly—"The Past Predicts the Future". As we explore the four major areas of Machine Learning algorithms, you will notice that three of them are based on *historical* data, lending credence to this quote.

Understanding Machine Learning

To understand how Machine Learning works, it helps to compare and contrast it to a traditional approach and highlight the differences. Figure 8-1 illustrates the difference between traditional and Machine Learning approaches.

© Bob Familiar and Jeff Barnes 2017
B. Familiar and J. Barnes, *Business in Real-Time Using Azure IoT and Cortana Intelligence Suite*,
DOI 10.1007/978-1-4842-2650-6_8

Traditional Programming:

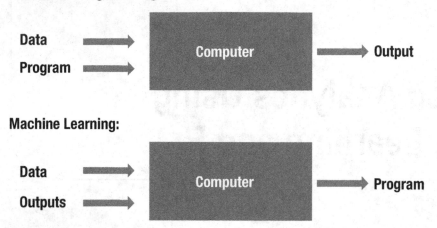

Machine Learning:

Figure 8-1. *Traditional programming versus Machine Learning programming models*

In the world of traditional programming, developers supply data and develop computer programs in order to produce a desired output. In this new world of Machine Learning, the focus is on supplying the data, but also on enriching the data with the known outputs already defined. The computer then calculates a program or Machine Learning "model" that can predict the outcome, within a range of certainty, based on the input data.

One of the key points to emphasize here is the criticality of *data input* requirements for successful Machine Learning algorithm development. The phrase "Data Equals Experience" is the new operating mantra in the world of Machine Learning. More data is always better, and the rise of the cloud, inexpensive storage, Big Data, and ubiquitous computing power, make this period in history truly empowering for Machine Learning technologies at scale.

This leads us to a discussion of the two main types of Machine Learning algorithms:

- *Supervised Learning*: In this case, known outcomes are part of the computer training datasets. When developing the model, the algorithms know exactly what the right predictions should be, since those known outcomes are part of the input provided.

- *Unsupervised Learning*: In this case, the computer is only provided the data to analyze, and the Machine Learning algorithms then attempt to find patterns, associations, logical groupings, and relationships in the data.

These concepts are reinforced by the four major categories of Machine Learning algorithms:

- *Classification*: Relates to predicting whether an input data element fits into a discrete category or type of thing. Typically a string or label is predicted. A common application of this technique is binary classification, where the outcome is one of two values, for instance, hot or cold, on or off, etc.

    - This represents the classic "learn by example" method of teaching.

    - An example is predicting what season a particular date of the year falls into (spring, summer, fall, winter).

- *Binary classification* refers to predicting a result with only two potential outcomes.

    - An example is predicting whether something is Hot/Cold or On/Off.

    - Stay tuned, as we will be using a variation of this algorithm in the reference implementation later in the chapter.

- *Regression*: Refers to predicting a continuous-valued outcome (a "real number") based on various attributes (known as "features") that are provided as inputs.

    - A great example of this algorithm is model that predicts the price of a new car based on the make, model, and features.

- *Recommenders*: This is one of the most common types of Machine Learning algorithms in use today. Such algorithms provide a recommendation based on known history, attributes, or feature similarities.

    - A few common examples of this type of algorithm are:

        - The Amazon.com web site and the personalized recommendations provided as you shop and place items in the cart. The items displayed under the section entitled "People who browsed this item also browsed these items..." is a very powerful sales tool and accounts for 5-15% of their overall web sales.

            - Netflix is another great example of a popular recommender Machine Learning algorithm implementation. By analyzing the prior video viewing history, genre preferences, member recommendations, online video services such as Netflix can provide a personalized movie recommendation list that is highly accurate.

- *Clustering*: These types of algorithms can analyze vast quantities of data and summarily provide logical groupings, segmentation analysis, infer patterns, and mark delineations in the data.

    - This is an example of an *unsupervised* Machine Learning algorithm. This category of algorithms enable users to "see the forest for the trees" if you will, so that patterns and correlations can be established about the data. This is especially valuable for datasets so large that a human could not possibly process them all.

    - One example of this type of algorithm is a sentiment analysis "word cloud," as illustrated in Figure 8-2.

        - In this example, the hash tag #microsoft was sampled from live Twitter feeds and then processed by several R ML packages to extract and analyze the keywords in each tweet.

            - This provides the words that appear. The font-size denotes how often each word was used.

            - Sentiment analysis was also performed on each tweet to determine whether it was positive or negative. The color denotes the predicted emotion.

Figure 8-2. An example of a word cloud clustering algorithm Twitter sentiment analysis of #microsoft"

For those that may be new to the exciting field of data science, we have covered some of the primary concepts such as "supervised" and "un-supervised" learning, and the four major categories of Machine Learning algorithms, as shown in Figure 8-3.

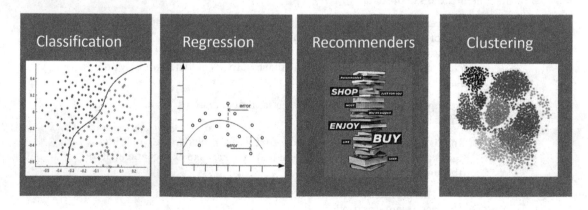

Figure 8-3. The four major types of Machine Learning algorithms

Understanding these basic concepts provides the foundation for a deeper exploration of the fields of data science, Machine Learning, artificial intelligence, and predictive analytics. Understanding how these algorithms work and how they can best be leveraged is a key first step for those embarking on a "digital transformation" and/or a Big Data journey.

Brief History of Machine Learning

Today's modern Machine Learning implementations were more closely aligned with the field of artificial intelligence.

Early research that dates back to the 1940s predominately focused on the ability to mimic human behavior. Back in 1943, Warren McCulloch and Walter Pitts created an early mathematical model for neural network algorithms termed "threshold logic". This early research led to a focus on the application of neural networks to help create "artificial intelligence" capabilities.

In the 1950s, Arthur Samuel from IBM created one of the world's first computer programs that was able to play Checkers against a human. One really exciting part of this early breakthrough was that Samuel found that the computer algorithm was able to actually "learn" from previous game play and thereby improve over time by learning and adapting to the opposing player's strategy.

A great example can be found in the U.S. Postal Service. In the late 1990s, only about 10% of the U.S. postal mail was able to be automatically sorted. This meant the rest had to be processed manually by thousands of postal workers.

Fast-forward to today, where they are now able to automatically process about 98% of the U.S. mail each day using Optical Character Recognition (OCR) technology to understand handwritten and printed addresses of all shapes and sizes. It has been estimated that the U.S. Postal Service now processes 500 million unique pieces of mail every day.

With the rise of the Internet and the World Wide Web, e-commerce companies soon began to leverage and refine Machine Learning and predictive analytics in order to influence web browsing and purchasing behaviors. For example, web log analysis can provide a wealth of information about about customer search patterns, order abandonment rates, advertising effectiveness, and more++. As has been previously noted, Amazon and Netflix are well known and highly successful implementers of these technologies.

Industry Applications of Machine Learning

As can be seen from the examples, very large dividends arise when leveraging Machine Learning and predictive analytics technologies. The potential financial rewards, combined with the rise of the cloud, are a huge motivator for sponsoring continued research and development of these technologies to maximize efficiencies across all kinds of industries.

Here is a list of examples and common use cases of Machine Learning technologies being applied across several key industries today, such as retail, financial services, healthcare, and manufacturing:

- *Retail*
    - Demand forecasting
    - Loyalty programs
    - Cross-sell and upsell
    - Customer acquisition
    - Fraud detection
    - Pricing strategy
    - Personalization
    - Lifetime customer value
    - Product segmentation
    - Store location demographics

- Supply chain management
- Inventory management
- *Financial Services*
  - Customer churn
  - Loyalty programs
  - Cross-sell and upsell
  - Customer acquisition
  - Fraud detection
  - Risk and compliance
  - Loan defaults
  - Personalization
  - Lifetime customer value
  - Call center optimization
  - Pay for performance

- *Healthcare*
  - Marketing mix optimization
  - Patient acquisition
  - Fraud detection
  - Bill collection
  - Population health
  - Patient demographics
  - Operational efficiency
  - Pay for performance

- *Manufacturing*
  - Demand forecasting
  - Marketing mix optimization
  - Pricing strategy
  - Performance risk management
  - Supply chain optimization
  - Personalization
  - Remote monitoring
  - Predictive maintenance
  - Asset management

Horizontal Patterns Across Vertical Industries

In that list, you will note a few common themes, patterns, and use cases that emerge. The following list denotes a few of these common use case scenarios that have many practical applications across most vertical industries:

- Demand forecasting

- Loyalty programs

- Fraud detection

- Personalization

- Lifetime customer value

In today's modern business environment, there are now many open source, academic, and commercial software packages available that leverage various Machine Learning algorithms and models to help enterprises succeed.

To that end, Microsoft has released a set of Azure Machine Learning templates that can be leveraged across many of these vertical and horizontal scenarios:

- *Predictive Maintenance*: Predict physical machine failures based on past history.

- *Customer Churn Prediction*: Predict when a customer churn (loss) may occur.

- *Online Purchase Fraud Detection*: Predict if an online purchase transaction is suspicious or fraudulent.

- *Retail Forecasting*: Provide forecasting for the product sales for an individual retail store.

- *Text Classification*: Classify text records into different categories, such as for sentiment analysis. Machine Learning Templates with Azure ML Studio: `https://gallery.cortanaintelligence.com/Collection/Machine-Learning-Templates-with-Azure-ML-Studio-1`.

We explore more of these templates, packages, libraries, and samples later in the chapter.

Overview of Azure Machine Learning

In July 2014, Microsoft first previewed the Azure Machine Learning service, a fully managed cloud service that enables you to easily build, deploy, and share predictive analytics solutions. At the time, the goal was simple yet visionary:

"Make Machine Learning accessible to every enterprise, data scientist, developer, information worker, consumer, and device anywhere in the world."

Two years later, Microsoft has truly helped democratize the Machine Learning landscape by making the technologies more approachable and accessible to everyone. All you need to get started is a modern web browser and a problem to solve. Microsoft has even made a free version of the Azure Machine Learning Studio available for newcomers to try it out.

■ **Note** See, this link for more information; about the free version. Azure Machine Learning offers free-usage tier: `https://azure.microsoft.com/en-us/updates/azure-machine-learning-now-offers-free-usage-tier/`.

The Traditional Data Science Landscape

To better understand this new world of cloud-based Machine Learning that Microsoft has now enabled, it is helpful to set the context by examining the state of the data science landscape prior to modern cloud offerings like Azure Machine Learning:

- *Expensive*: The huge capital costs for tools, expertise, and compute and storage capacity created unnecessary barriers to entry.

- *Silos of Data*: Cumbersome data management tools, siloed business data, and restricted access to that data limited the amount of sharing of predictive models and datasets.

- *Disconnected tools*: Complex and fragmented tools limited participation for exploring data and building models.

- *Deployment complexity*: Specialized environments supporting data science applications were fairly complex and required highly trained resources to manage them.

Democratizing Machine Learning

In contrast to the traditional data science landscape outlined previously, Microsoft's goal is to make Machine Learning simpler, better, faster, and more collaborative. Microsoft's Machine Learning Studio workspace allows you to invite and share your predictive experiments with virtually anybody in the world.

- *Published Guidance*: Via the online/offline Azure Machine Learning overviews, documentation, tutorials, and walk-thrus.

- *Cortana Analytics Gallery*: An ever-increasing repository of Azure Machine Learning samples and solution templates produced by the Microsoft product group and community members. They can be directly deployed into your Azure Machine Learning workspace to get you started quickly.

- *Machine Learning algorithm cheat sheet*: To help you choose the right algorithm(s) for creating your predictive analytics model, Microsoft provides a great predictive analytics *cheat sheet,* which is like an ML solution flowchart.

■ **Note** See this link for more information. Machine Learning algorithm cheat sheet for Microsoft Azure Machine Learning Studio: `https://docs.microsoft.com/en-us/azure/machine-learning/machine-learning-algorithm-cheat-sheet`.

- *Free Tier*: To get started with zero obligations. Now, you have no excuse to get started.

- *Team Data Science Process (TDSP):* Provides a systematic approach and framework to building intelligent applications that enable teams of data scientists to collaborate effectively over the full lifecycle of a Machine Learning solution.

■ **Note**   Learn more at Team Data Science Process (TDSP): `https://azure.microsoft.com/en-us/documentation/learning-paths/data-science-process/`.

Azure Machine Learning Studio

Microsoft Azure Machine Learning Studio is an online, collaborative, drag-and-drop, environment that you can leverage to build, test, and deploy predictive analytics solutions.

Even though Azure Machine Learning makes it easy for novices and newcomers to easily get started working with predictive analytics, it is also provides a very powerful and updated set of algorithms and integrated tools that even the most seasoned data science professionals will appreciate.

Once you have provisioned a new Azure Machine Learning workspace via the Azure Portal, you can launch Azure Machine Learning Studio in a browser session, as shown in Figure 8-4.

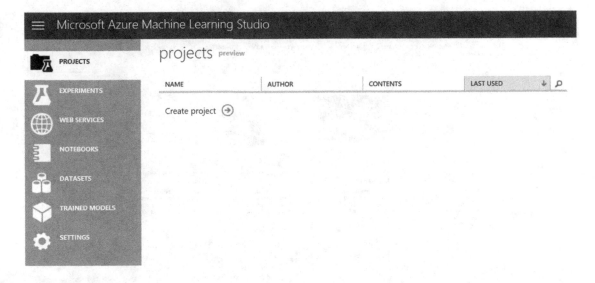

Figure 8-4. *Azure Machine Learning Studio*

After logging in to Azure Machine Learning Studio, you'll see the following tabs on the left:

- *PROJECTS*: This is where you store collections of experiments, datasets, notebooks, and other resources representing a single Machine Learning project.

- *EXPERIMENTS*: This is where experiments that have been created, run, and saved as drafts reside in your workspace. This is the most-often used option.

- *WEB SERVICES*: Azure Machine Learning web services that have been deployed from your experiments can be viewed here.

- *NOTEBOOKS*: This link displays any Jupyter notebooks that you have created. Jupyter Notebook is a web-based interactive computing platform that combines live code, equations, narrative text, visualizations, and interactive dashboards. Microsoft provides cloud-based Jupyter notebook environments at `https://notebooks.azure.com/`.

- *DATASETS*: This link points to any datasets that you uploaded into Azure Machine Learning Studio.

- *TRAINED MODELS*: This link displays a list of Machine Learning models that you trained in experiments and saved in Azure Machine Learning Studio.

- *SETTINGS*: A collection of settings that you can use to configure your Azure Machine Learning account and associated resources.

The Cortana Intelligence Gallery

If you click on the Hamburger menu icon in the top-left of the Azure Machine Learning Studio navigation bar, you will see a link for the Cortana Intelligence Gallery.

The Gallery (see Figure 8-5) is a web site where Microsoft fosters a community of data scientists and developers to share solutions that were created using Azure Machine Learning and components of the Cortana Intelligence Suite.

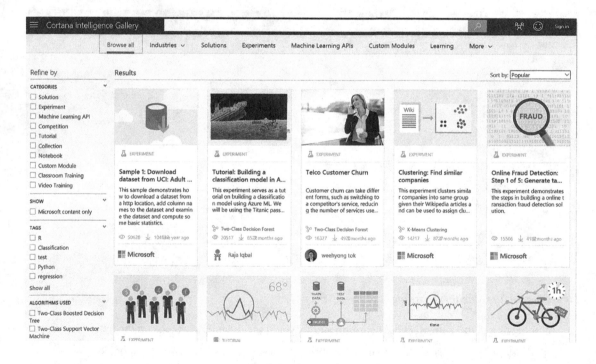

Figure 8-5. *The Cortana Intelligence Gallery*

Notice that there are links on the top navigation bar for other valuable resources such as industry solutions, sample Machine Learning experiments, Machine Learning APIs, custom modules, and a wealth of training resources.

Azure Machine Learning: EXPERIMENTS

The EXPERIMENTS section of Azure Machine Learning Studio is where you will spend most of your time developing and refining Machine Learning experiments. The design surface feels very much like using Microsoft Visio, and the interface is completely drag-and-drop driven. Figure 8-6 depicts a new Machine Learning experiment and the Azure Machine Learning Studio Designer canvas.

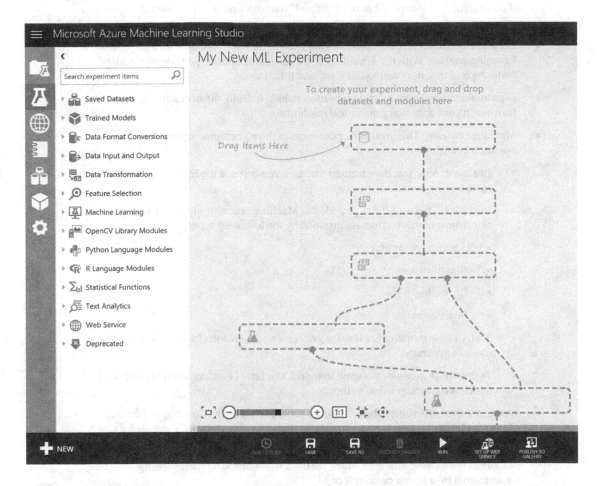

Figure 8-6. *A new, blank, Machine Learning experiment in Azure Machine Learning Studio*

Azure Machine Learning: EXPERIMENT Modules

There are a series of modules and tools that appear on the left side of the Azure ML Studio screen, as shown in Figure 8-6. These modules provide a wealth of functionality and capabilities that can simply be dragged onto the designer surface.

After adding a new module, you can set the individual configuration properties via the Properties section for each module, which appear on the right side of the screen.

The Azure Machine Learning modules are grouped in the following categories:

- *Data Format Conversions*: These modules can help convert data to one of a number of common formats (such as TSV, CSV, and ARFF) used by other Machine Learning tools.

- *Data Input and Output*: Use these modules to read data from other cloud and web data sources. It is also possible read "zipped" datasets and to export data using these modules.

- *Data Transformation*: These modules are used to help prepare data for Machine Learning analysis. With these modules, you can change data types, identify and/or generate features, normalize your data, and much more.

- *Feature Selection*: These modules are used to help identify the best attributes or features in your data, using statistical methods.

- *Machine Learning*: This group contains most of the algorithms supported by Azure Machine Learning.

  - **Evaluate**: After you have trained a model, you can use the Evaluate module to measure the model's accuracy.

  - **Initialize**: These modules provide the Machine Learning algorithms. The algorithms in this section are grouped by the following types:

    - Anomaly detection

    - Classification

    - Clustering

    - Regression

  - *Score*: These modules are used to generate a set of results for evaluating a model's accuracy.

  - *Train*: These modules are used to train a Machine Learning model based on the datasets that you provide as inputs.

- *OpenCV Library Modules*: These modules provide easy access to an open source library for image processing and image classification. The term OCV stands for Open Computer Vision.

- *R Language Modules*: These modules are used to extend Machine Learning experiments by utilizing custom R code.

- *Python Language Machine Learning Modules*: These modules are used to add custom Python code to your Machine Learning experiment.

- *Statistical Functions*: These modules are used to implement various statistical routines to accomplish various numerical analysis tasks.

- *Text Analytics*: These modules can be used to process text and implement text-based functionality such as feature hashing and named entity recognition.

- *Web Service*: These modules can be used to add input or output ports to an existing Azure Machine Learning web service. These are most often utilized to create Machine Learning "re-training" web services implementations.

■ **Tip** See this link for a detailed (A-Z) List of Machine Learning Studio Modules: `https://msdn.microsoft.com/en-us/library/azure/dn906033.aspx`.

An Azure Machine Learning experiment comprises datasets that provide data to analytical modules, which you connect to create a predictive analysis model. A functionally valid Azure Machine Learning experiment has the following characteristics:

- The experiment has at least one dataset and one module.

- Datasets may be connected only to modules.

- Modules may be connected to either datasets or other modules.

- All input ports for modules must have a connection to the data flow.

- All required parameters for each module must be set via the Properties pane on the right side of the designer interface.

We examine the process of building an Azure Machine Learning experiment in detail in the latter portion of this chapter when we cover the specifics of the reference implementation.

The Azure Machine Learning Data Science Flow

Microsoft provides comprehensive guidance and a systematic approach to building Machine Learning applications that follow established data science methodologies and principles. This can be summarized as a five-step process:

1. *Business Understanding:*

    a. Establishing technical needs/requirements

    b. Identifying your scenario for matching to best ML algorithms

2. *Data Acquisition and Exploration:*

    a. Loading data into Azure storage environments

    b. Importing data into Azure Machine Learning Studio

3. *Preparing the Data:*

    a. Exploring the data using built-in tools and utilities

    b. Leveraging sample data

4. *Modeling:*

    a. Engineering features

    b. Selecting features

    c. Learning with counts

    d. Training the model

    e. Evaluating the model

    f. Tuning the model

5. *Deployment:*

    a.   Publishing a model as a web service

    b.   Consuming a model programmatically

    c.   Consuming a model in Excel

■ **Note**   See the following link for more information about Azure Machine Learning's application of the data science process: `https://azure.microsoft.com/en-us/documentation/learning-paths/data-science-process/`.

Microsoft R Server Overview

In April 2015, Microsoft acquired Revolution Analytics and has since released their flagship product as R Server. Revolution Analytics was the leading commercial provider of software and services for R, the world's most widely used programming language for statistical computing and predictive analytics.

Today, the R programming language is one of the most popular statistical and Machine Learning programing languages available to developers and data scientists around the world. The R language is freely available as open source and is popular as a data visualization and reporting tool.

There is a strong and vibrant R community of approximately 2.5 million users. The R language is commonly taught in most universities, and interest in the uses of R is demonstrated by many thriving user groups around the world.

The capabilities of R are extended through user-developed packages, which can add custom statistical or graphical capabilities and extensions. These packages are developed primarily in R but also in other languages such as Java, C, and C++. This has created a very large and healthy ecosystem with over 9,000 R packages contributed to open source repositories to date. Many of these packages and implementations address common business problems and can help solve many use cases related to statistical and predictive analytics.

Processing limitations of Open Source R

Note that there are two flavors of R available today to address specific needs in the data science industry.

- *Open Source R*: A free and widely available distribution from sources such as CRAN (Comprehensive R Archive Network) and `r-project.org`. The software is generally geared for academic use and is supported by the community.

- *Commercial R Packages*: Typically are professionally developed, licensed, and supported for enterprise use for production scenarios.

There are a few significant differences between these R distributions in terms of speed and performance. Open Source R has some limitations such as:

- Operations are limited to in-memory only.

- Data movement/duplication is expensive.

- Lack of parallelism; they are single-threaded only.

- Not enterprise grade:

  - No SLAs or production support models.

  - Lack of guaranteed support timeliness.

  - Community support is inadequate for commercial enterprises.

Enter Microsoft R Server

Microsoft R Server is an enterprise-grade server for hosting and managing parallel and distributed workloads of R processes on servers (Linux and Windows) and clusters (Hadoop and Apache Spark).

It provides an execution engine for solutions built using Microsoft R packages and extends open source R with support for high-performance analytics, statistical analysis, Machine Learning scenarios, and massively large datasets.

To compensate for some of the limitations of open source R outlined previously, Microsoft has filled in the gaps with its Microsoft R Server offerings to provide an enterprise grade, commercially available, R software product offering that offers these features:

- Speed, scalability, flexibility, and efficiency

- Product support and SLA

- Works on data in memory or on disc (ScaleR)

- Wide range of scalable and distributed R functions available

- Works in several computing contexts (including Hadoop, Spark, and SQL Server), and data sources (including disk, HDFS, and SQL)

- R language is portable and includes investment assurance

In addition to extending Azure Machine Learning through the R language module, the Microsoft R Server family allows you to develop and run R models on your platform of choice:

- *Windows*: R Server for Windows ships as R Services in SQL Server 2016.

- *Linux*: Leverage your open source investments to enable advanced predictive and prescriptive analytics use case scenarios.

- *Hadoop/Apache Spark*: Enable your analysis to scale transparently by distributing analytics jobs to run across nodes without complex programming.

- *Teradata Database*: Run advanced analytics in-database for seamless R data analysis.

To summarize, Microsoft has a comprehensive portfolio of R programming offerings (community and commercial) that can run on almost any operating system or platform. Figure 8-7 illustrates the various versions of R that Microsoft now supports.

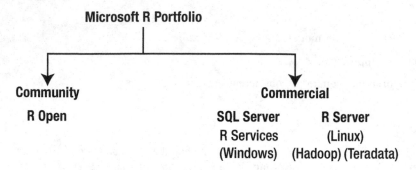

Figure 8-7. *The Microsoft R portfolio of products*

By leveraging the Microsoft supported R environments illustrated in Figure 8-7, you can now easily develop and run R models on your platform of choice in Azure.

Extend Machine Learning Experiments with the R Language Module

By leveraging the R Language module in the Azure Machine Learning Studio Experiment designer, you can instantly extend your Machine Learning model creation and training capabilities by incorporating R code directly into an Azure Machine Learning experiment.

You simply drag and drop the module from the left tool palette in ML Studio onto the design surface. Then you can click on a Properties window on the right, edit your R code in the Designer Editor, and save it when you're done.

Figure 8-8 depicts a screenshot of the Azure Machine Learning Studio Designer with an Execute R Script module. Note that the R code can be edited in the Properties pane on the right.

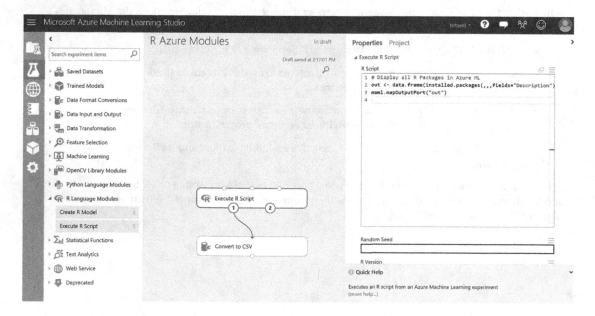

Figure 8-8. *Azure Machine Learning R language modules*

In the Execute R Script sample, the R code will simply list the currently installed R packages via this R statement:

```
out <- data.frame(installed.packages(,,,fields="Description"))
maml.mapOutputPort("out")
```

The next module in the experiment, the Convert to CSV module, provides the ability to download and save a copy of that list of R packages.

Note that for significant R development efforts, we recommend you use other R Developer tools, such as Visual Studio Tools for R or R Studio to create, debug, version, and refine more complex R scripts. Then you can simply paste your R code into the Azure Machine Learning R language module.

The Azure Machine Learning R language module opens up a new world of R code, packages, and additional functionality that can now be accessed via Azure Machine Learning Studio and deployed as a web service for easy consumption. Azure Machine Learning Studio currently includes over 400 of the most popular R packages representing an intersection of the R ecosystem with the agility, collaboration, consumption, and integration aspects of Azure Machine Learning.

■ **Note**   For a complete list of the currently supported packages, see `https://msdn.microsoft.com/en-us/library/azure/mt741980.aspx`.

The use of R is becoming so popular that Microsoft is now including it as a visualization control in Power BI. We explore this new capability and much more in Chapter 9.

R Tools for Visual Studio

If you are a developer and have access to a version of Visual Studio, you can easily turn Visual Studio into a powerful R development environment by installing the R Tools for Visual Studio. There are also free downloads and trial offers for Visual Studio available at this link:

R Tools for Visual Studio: `https://www.visualstudio.com/vs/rtvs/`

Implementing Azure Machine Learning and R in the Reference Implementation

Up to this point, we have explored some of the basic features and capabilities of Azure Machine Learning and provided a brief background on the R programming language and Microsoft's recent R offerings.

Next, we leverage some of our newly acquired knowledge by implementing a few more pieces of our reference implementation.

Business Case for Machine Learning

As a quick refresher, we need to implement a Machine Learning web service that can help predict when a specific team member may have reached the point of physical exhaustion. The inputs will be based on real-time sensor readings that are relayed to the Azure cloud while the team member is working on the job.

The goal is to avoid any kind of accidents, injuries, or incidents that may be caused by team members reaching their individual limits of physical exhaustion. In this way, the business entities can effectively monitor their daily operations and proactively adjust team member workloads and duties to mitigate risk.

Reference Implementation: Assumptions

We make a few practical assumptions to qualify a working prediction model, as follows:

- *Team members may be reluctant to admit signs of physical exhaustion*: This is a fundamental working assumption and could be considered a common reaction based on human nature.

- *Team members may risk financial rewards if they display signs of physical exhaustion*: Since they are financially compensated for the number of hours they work, few will readily admit that they have had enough and want to call it quits.

To overcome these natural human tendencies, we assume that stress tests will be administered to each team member on a monthly basis.

- The stress tests would be able to quickly simulate and accelerate the physical working conditions for a team member, right up to the point of exhaustion.

- Physical exhaustion is signaled when a team member voluntarily pushes an emergency Stop button to cease the stress tests.

- Detailed sensor data will be captured during the entire stress test session. This data will then be used to create training data for our new Machine Learning predictive model.

- The resultant Machine Learning models can also be re-trained on a periodic basis by using updated stress test results.

- The incoming data format for the stress tests will be an Excel spreadsheet with separate tabs containing each team member's individual stress test results.

- In addition to columns holding the sensor data readings, an additional data column will be added to the end to denote when a team member triggered the point of physical exhaustion.

Figure 8-9 depicts a screenshot of a sample team member's stress test spreadsheet results.

	A	B	C	D	E	F	G	H	I	J	K	L	M
1	UserId	BreathingRate	Temperature	Ventiliation	Activity	HeartRateBPM	Cadence	Velocity	Speed	HIB	HeartrateRedZone	HeartrateVarlability	Exhaustion
2	c3ec2fe4-6789-4d3e-8446-852856ce025c	17.44929379	96.29215605	16454.15282	0.133564	90	1	2.898897	0	0	0	0	N
3	c3ec2fe4-6789-4d3e-8446-852856ce025c	17.51138318	96.88186507	16547.12564	0.136821	91	2	5.797794	0	0	0	0	N
4	c3ec2fe4-6789-4d3e-8446-852856ce025c	17.57347257	96.5117878	16640.09846	0.140078	91	3	8.696691	0	0	0	0	N
5	c3ec2fe4-6789-4d3e-8446-852856ce025c	17.63556196	96.31613514	16733.07128	0.143336	92	4	11.59559	0	0	0	0	N
6	c3ec2fe4-6789-4d3e-8446-852856ce025c	17.69765135	96.69531139	16826.0441	0.146593	92	5	14.49448	0	0	0	0	N
7	c3ec2fe4-6789-4d3e-8446-852856ce025c	17.75974074	96.77480951	16919.01692	0.14985	93	6	17.39338	0	0	0	0	N
8	c3ec2fe4-6789-4d3e-8446-852856ce025c	17.82183013	96.71956696	17011.98974	0.153107	93	7	20.29228	0	0	0	0	N
9	c3ec2fe4-6789-4d3e-8446-852856ce025c	17.88391952	96.35834845	17104.96256	0.156365	94	8	23.19118	0	0	0	0	N

Figure 8-9. Sample team member stress test spreadsheet used to train the Azure Machine Learning model

Choosing a Machine Learning Algorithm

One of the first tasks in this endeavor is to determine the appropriate Machine Learning algorithm to use to help solve this problem. Luckily, Microsoft provides a handy cheat sheet (in the form of a free PDF download) to help you determine the best algorithm to use based on the type of problem you are trying to solve.

Figure 8-10 depicts a screenshot of the Azure Machine Learning cheat sheet. Given the actual problem we are trying to solve in our reference implementation, we will attempt to predict a category according to the cheat sheet.

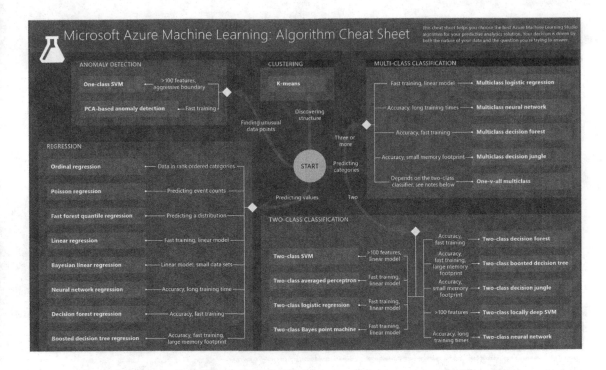

Figure 8-10. *The Azure Machine Learning algorithm cheat sheet*

■ **Note** You can find the Machine Learning algorithm cheat sheet for Microsoft Azure Machine Learning Studio at
https://docs.microsoft.com/en-us/azure/machine-learning/machine-learning-algorithm-cheat-sheet.

In this case, the specific outcome we are trying to predict is exhaustion, and there are exactly two potential states: exhausted and not exhausted. You will recall from earlier in the chapter that *binary classification* algorithms seek to predict one of two possible outcomes such as on/off, red/blue, or hot/cold. Indeed, based on the cheat sheet guidance, we are advised to utilize a binary classification algorithm to provide this Machine Learning model.

Another point to make here is that a binary classification model is an example of supervised learning. This means that we supply the team member training data along with the observed outcome (exhausted or not) for each row of the training data. In this way, once our new Machine Learning model has been trained, it will then be able to predict the outcome (along with a probability percentage) from a set of input attributes (or features).

CREATE AZURE MACHINE LEARNING WORKSPACE

The first step toward realizing our reference implementation is to create the Azure Machine Learning workspace via the Azure Portal. This will be the starting point for creating a Machine Learning experiment and ultimately deploying it as a web service.

To get started, navigate to your previously defined Azure resource group and click on the + Add icon to add another Azure service. Type `Machine Learning Workspace` in the search bar; you will see similar results to what's shown in Figure 8-11.

369

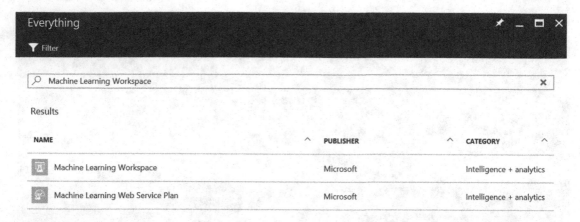

Figure 8-11. *Add a new Machine Learning workspace*

Click on the Machine Learning Workspace. You will then see a confirmation screen similar to the one in Figure 8-12.

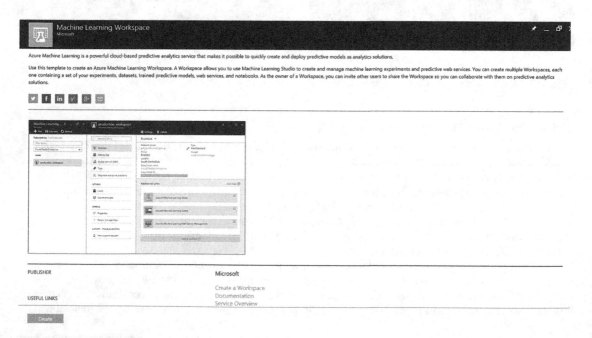

Figure 8-12. *Create an Azure Machine Learning Workspace*

Click on the Create icon at the bottom-left. You will then see a blade appear that will prompt you to enter the parameters required to create your new Azure Machine Learning Workspace, as illustrated in Figure 8-13.

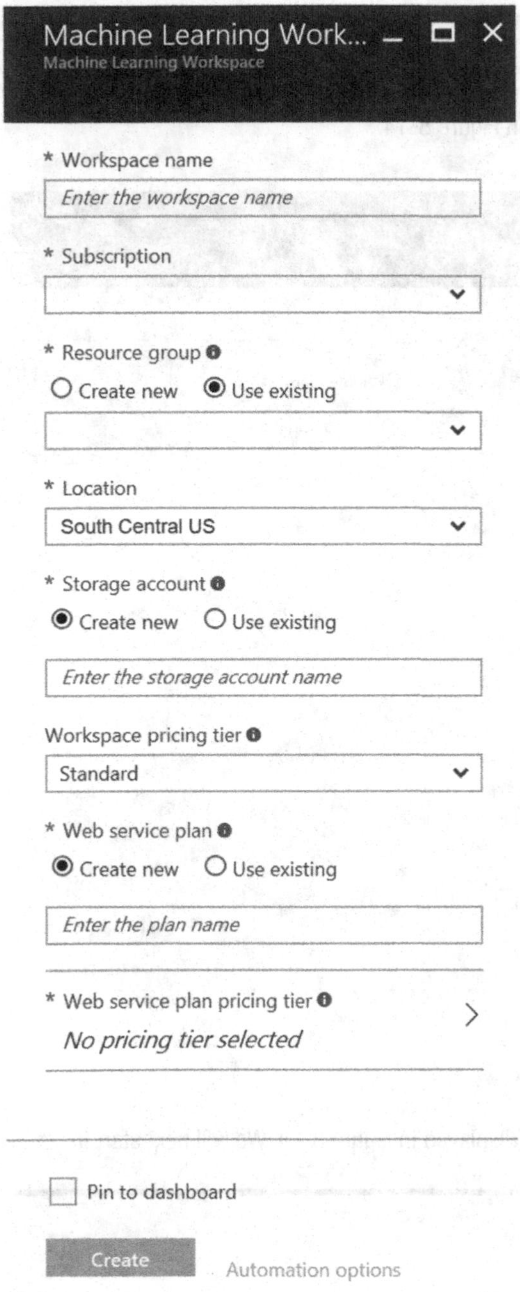

Machine Learning Work... — ☐ ✕
Machine Learning Workspace

* Workspace name

Enter the workspace name

* Subscription

⌄

* Resource group ❶

○ Create new   ⦿ Use existing

⌄

* Location

South Central US   ⌄

* Storage account ❶

⦿ Create new   ○ Use existing

Enter the storage account name

Workspace pricing tier ❶

Standard   ⌄

* Web service plan ❶

⦿ Create new   ○ Use existing

Enter the plan name

* Web service plan pricing tier ❶

No pricing tier selected   ❯

☐ Pin to dashboard

Create   Automation options

Figure 8-13. *Azure Machine Learning: Create New Workspace parameters*

Fill in the required parameters and then click on the Create icon. The new Azure Machine Learning Workspace will be provisioned in a matter of minutes.

After your new workspace has been provisioned, you can navigate to the new Machine Learning workspace blade and view the menu options, as shown in Figure 8-14.

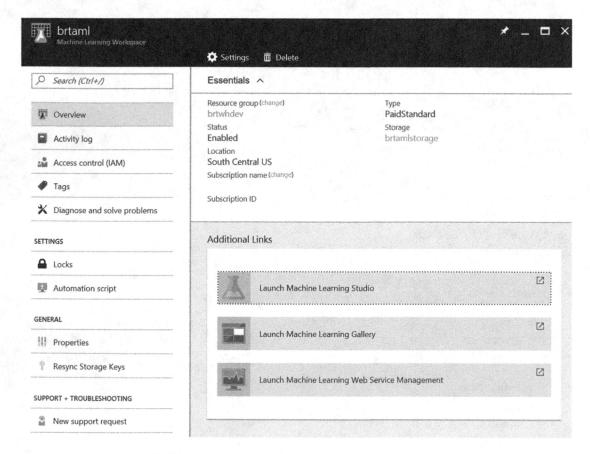

Figure 8-14. *The Azure Machine Learning Workspace blade*

Select the option to Launch Machine Learning Studio, as displayed in Figure 8-14. We will next start to build our new Machine Learning experiment.

CREATE NEW AZURE MACHINE LEARNING EXPERIMENT

After you click on the Launch Machine Learning Studio icon, a new session will open in a new browser tab, as illustrated in Figure 8-15.

Figure 8-15. *Azure Machine Learning Studio landing page*

Click on the My Experiments button and you will be led to the Azure Machine Learning Studio environment.

Now you are ready to create a new Machine Learning experiment. First you need to load training data for this new model. From this book's code base (published on GitHub), download the Excel file named Teammates_AML_Training_Data.xlsx.

After the file has downloaded, open the spreadsheet and click on the Teammates_AML_Training_Data tab. Next, save the spreadsheet as a file in the CSV format by selecting File/Save/Computer and then change the Save As type to CSV (comma delimited) (*.csv).

Upload Training Data File Into Azure Machine Learning Studio

Next, in your Azure Machine Learning Studio browser session, click on the + New icon in the lower-left corner and then click on the Dataset and From Local File options, as shown in Figure 8-16.

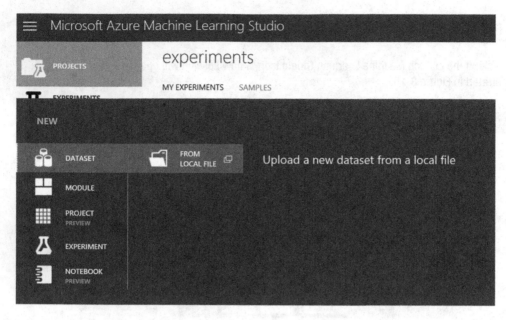

Figure 8-16. *Azure Machine Learning Studio: New dataset from local file options*

Next, you have an opportunity to enter the location of the source data file to upload from your local disk folder. After browsing and selecting your local file that you just saved from the Excel spreadsheet, designate the source file type as a generic CSV file with a header (.csv), as shown in Figure 8-17.

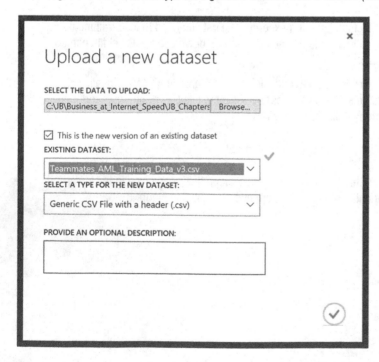

Figure 8-17. *Upload a new Azure Machine Learning dataset from a local CSV file*

Click on the Check Mark icon to start the file upload. A status bar will appear on the bottom of the screen to display progress as your file is uploaded into the Azure ML storage account.

Now that you have uploaded your training data, you can proceed to creating the Machine Learning experiment.

Create New Experiment in Azure Machine Learning Studio

Next, you create and test a new Machine Learning experiment by using Azure Machine Learning Studio to help predict team member exhaustion levels.

Start clicking on the + New icon in the lower-left corner of Azure Machine Learning Studio and then click on the Experiment icon. Then select the Blank Experiment template to create the new Azure Machine Learning experiment from scratch, as shown in Figure 8-18.

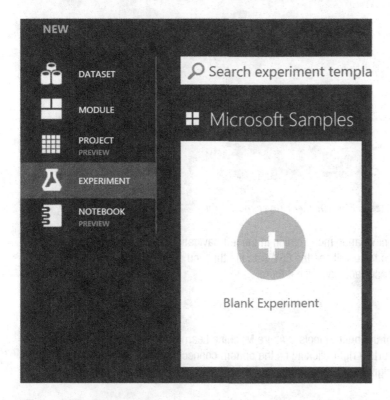

Figure 8-18. *Creating a new, blank Machine Learning experiment in Azure Machine Learning Studio*

This will create a new blank Machine Learning experiment in your workspace. Start simple by clicking on the top name field and renaming the experiment to `Predict Team Health` or something of that nature, as shown in Figure 8-19.

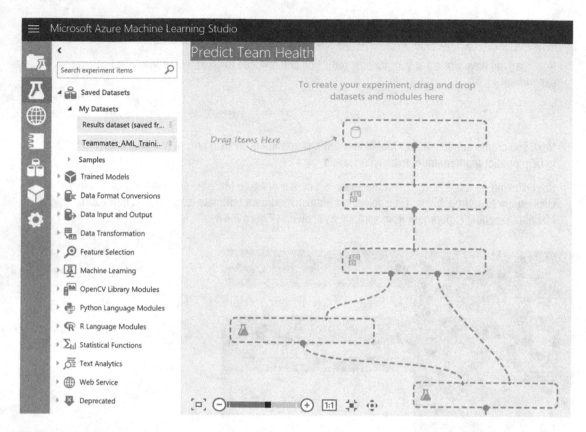

Figure 8-19. *Rename the new blank Azure Machine Learning experiment*

Next, click on the Saved Datasets navigation menu option in the left navigation bar to expand the selections. Click on My Datasets and you will see the CSV data file that you uploaded earlier. Drag this file onto the middle of the designer surface and drop it there.

Visualize the Training Data

You can take advantage of some of the built-in tools in Azure Machine Learning Studio to help visualize and understand the data better. Start by right-clicking on the bottom connector of the input training data that you just dropped onto the designer surface and then on the Visualize icon, as shown in Figure 8-20.

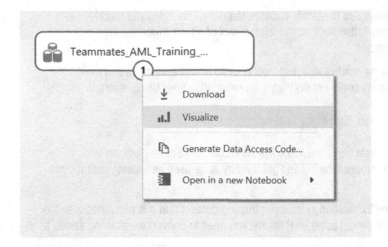

Figure 8-20. Using the built-in tools to help visualize the training data

Next, after clicking on the Visualize icon, you can use the slider bar to select the column named Exhaustion in the last position.

By clicking on the Exhaustion column, you will note that the Visualizations section on the right side of the screen will automatically be filled with a visual display of the distribution of readings.

The credibility of the prediction data would be established based on the recent uploaded stress test training data, as shown in Figure 8-21.

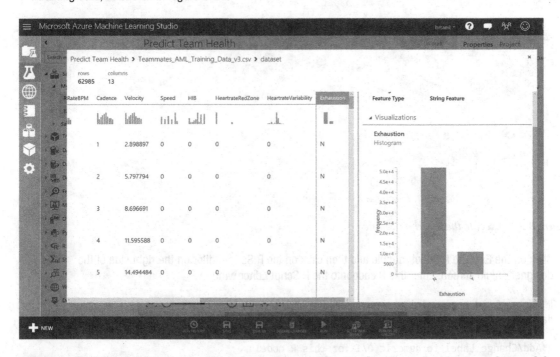

Figure 8-21. Using the built-in Azure Machine Learning studio visualization tools to better understand the distribution of exhaustion levels across team members' training data

Note the histogram (bar chart) format used to quickly visualize the data. This helps you quickly understand key factors in the ML prediction such as the relative mix of stress-triggering data in the Machine Learning input training dataset.

In the bar chart, the bars represent the relative distribution of (Y or N) exhaustion levels and their associated sensor readings that did (Y) or did not (N) trigger an exhaustion level being reached.

Add an Execute R Script Module

Now that you have added the input data file to the Azure Machine Learning Studio Designer and visualized the contents, it is time to process the file and get it ready to be used as training data for this Machine Learning experiment.

Recall that there is a column named Exhaustion in the input training dataset and it is populated with the values of Y or N. In order to train this model using an R library, you need to convert these string values to corresponding numerical values.

To do this, you'll use an R Script module to populate a new column (ExhaustionLabel) with a numerical representation of the value in the Exhaustion column. In short, you will replace Y with a 1 and N with 0.

To do this, expand the R language modules on the left side of the Machine Learning Studio and drag an Execute R Script module to the designer surface. Connect the data input file to the top-left connector of the Execute R Script module, as shown in Figure 8-22.

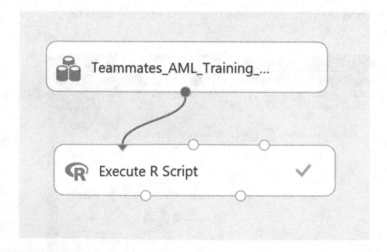

Figure 8-22. *Execute the R Script Module*

Click on the Execute R Script module and then click on the R Script Editor on the right side of the designer studio screen. Enter this R code into the R Script Editor window:

```
# Map 1-based optional input ports to variables
dataset1 <- maml.mapInputPort(1) # class: data.frame

# Add/Change Label to numeric 0/1 for this R model
dataset1$ExhaustionLabel <- ifelse(dataset1$Exhaustion=="N",0,1)
```

```
# Select data.frame to be sent to the output Dataset port
maml.mapOutputPort("dataset1");
```

This R code will to create a new column named ExhaustionLabel and it will be populated it with a 0 or 1 - based on the value of the column named Exhaustion and if it contains an N or Y.

Add a Split Data Module to the Experiment

The next step is to add another module called a Split Data module. The Split Data module will separate the input training data into two distinct streams. The first stream will be for training the new model, and the second stream will be used for evaluating the accuracy of the new model.

You can easily locate the Split Data module by typing Split Data in the Search window on the left side of the Azure Machine Learning Studio Designer screen. You can also find this module by expanding the Data Transformation module under the sub-heading of Sample and Split.

Drag the Split Data module to the designer surface directly under the Execute R Script module. Next, make the connection between the bottom-left connector of the Execute R Script module and the top connector of the Split Data module.

Click on the Split Data module to access the module properties on the right side. Modify the property for Fraction of Rows in the First Output Dataset to the value of 0.80, as shown in Figure 8-23.

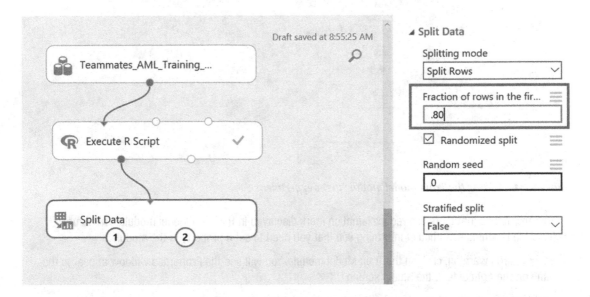

Figure 8-23. *Setting the Azure Machine Learning Split Data module property*

Set the value to 0.80 to denote that you want 80% of the input training dataset to be used to actually train this new model. The remaining 20% of the input training dataset data will be used to check the accuracy of the new Machine Learning model.

Add a Train Model Module to the Experiment

The next step is to add a Train Model module to this experiment. Locate the module by typing **Train Model** in the Search window on the left side of the Azure Machine Learning Studio Designer screen. You can also find this module by expanding the Machine Learning module under the sub-heading of Train.

Drag the Train Model module to the designer surface under the Split Data module and position it at the bottom-left of the Split Data module.

Next, connect the bottom-left of the Split Data module to the top-right connector of the Train Model module, as illustrated in Figure 8-24.

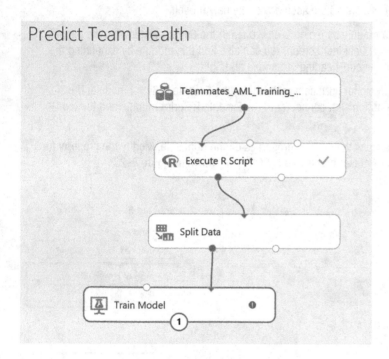

Figure 8-24. *Adding the Train Model module to the experiment*

You may notice that there is a red exclamation mark displayed in the Train Model module. This Azure Machine Learning's method of informing you that you need to set a property in the module.

To fix the red warning, click on the Train Model module. You will see the Properties window appear in the pane on the right side of the Studio screen.

Click on the Launch Column Selector button, as illustrated in Figure 8-25.

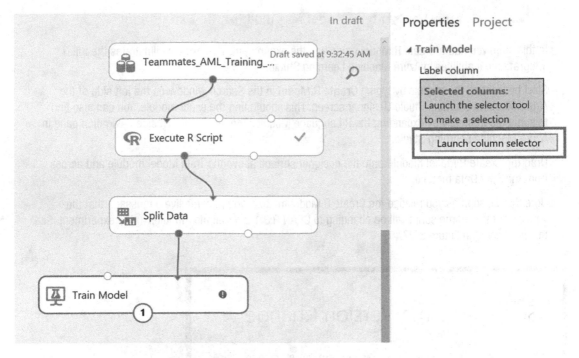

Figure 8-25. *Launch column selector for Train Model module*

The Column Selector is a widely used tool in the Azure Machine Learning Studio that quickly selects all or specific columns to use as the flow of execution passes to each module. For the Train Model module, you need to indicate which column of the incoming data you want the new Machine Learning model to predict. Start by typing in the column named ExhaustionLabel. You will see that AML studio includes a nice feature for IntelliSense/type-ahead in the column name search field. Figure 8-26 depicts the column selector populated with the single column name of ExhaustionLabel.

Select a single column

Figure 8-26. *Set the Train Model module, Column Selector field to denote which column to predict*

Remember to click the check mark icon on the bottom-right of the launch column selector screen to save your changes.

This will set up the experiment nicely for the next step, where you will plug in R code to execute a binary classification algorithm.

Insert a Create R Model Module Into the Experiment

In this step, you add a Create R Model module to the experiment. This exercise illustrates the full R integration capabilities in Azure Machine Learning Studio.

Start by locating the module by typing **Create R Model** in the Search window on the left side of the Azure Machine Learning Studio Designer screen. This should find the exact module. You can also find this module manually by expanding the R Language Modules module in the left side navigation pane in Azure Machine Learning Studio.

Drag the Create R Model module onto the designer surface above the Train Model module and across from the Split Data module.

Note that as soon as you release the Create R Model module, you may receive a message that the version of the runtime script will be changing to CRAN R 3.1.0 for all the modules in the experiment. See the screenshot in Figure 8-27.

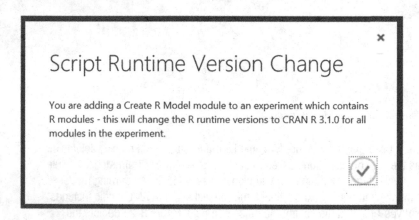

Figure 8-27. *Create R Model: script runtime version change notification*

Next, connect the bottom of the Create R Model module to the top-left connector of the Train Model module.

Now, it is time to modify the Create R Model module and provide the R code.

Click on the Create R Model module and then click on the R Script Editor on the right side of the screen.

You can use the Create R Model module to create an untrained model from R script that you provide. You can base your model on any learner that is included as an R package in the Azure Machine Learning environment.

Note that there are two locations to enter R code in a Create R Model module:

- *Trainer R Script*: An R script that takes a dataset as input and outputs an untrained model.

- *Scorer R Script*: An R script that takes a model and a dataset as input and outputs the scores specified in the script.

You will enter separate blocks of R code into each of these areas. After you create the model, you can use Train Model to train the model on a dataset, like any other learner in the Azure Machine Learning environment.

The trained model can then be passed to the Score Model module to use the model to make predictions. The trained model can then be saved, and the scoring workflow can be published as a web service.

To implement the model, start by entering this R code into the Trainer R Script Editor window:

```
# Trainer R Script
# Input: dataset
# Output: model

# e1071 = pre-installed R package in the Azure Machine Learning environment for
Binary Classification
library(e1071)

# The next three lines get the feature columns and the label column from the dataset
# and combine them into a new R data frame that is named train.data:
features <- get.feature.columns(dataset)
labels   <- as.factor(get.label.column(dataset))
train.data <- data.frame(features, labels)

# The predefined function, get.feature.columns(), selects the columns that were
designated as features in the metadata for dataset.
feature.names <- get.feature.column.names(dataset)

# the predefined function, get.feature.column.names(dataset), is used to get feature
column names from the dataset. Those names are designated
# as the names for columns in train.data.
# a temporary name Class is created for the label column.
names(train.data) <- c(feature.names, "Class")

# Train the "Naïve Bayes" classifier algorithm by using the labels and features in
the train.data data frame.
model <- naiveBayes(Class ~ ., train.data)
```

Next, enter this R code into the Scorer R Script Editor window:

```
# Scorer R Script
# Input: model, dataset
# Output: scores

# Loads the preinstalled R package.
library(e1071)

# Computes the predicted probabilities for the scoring dataset by using the trained
model from the training script.
probabilities <- predict(model, dataset, type="raw")[,2]
```

```
# Apply a default threshold of 0.5 to probabilities when assigning the predicted
class labels.
classes <- as.factor(as.numeric(probabilities >= 0.5))

# Combine the class labels and probabilities into the output data frame, named
"scores".
scores <- data.frame(classes, probabilities)
```

After you have entered the two blocks of R code, you can save your changes by simply clicking anywhere in the Azure Machine Learning Studio Designer that is outside of the Create R Model module.

Insert a Score Model Module into the Experiment

The last step in creating the Azure Machine Learning experiment is to add a Score Model module to it.

You can use Score Model to generate predictions using a trained classification or regression Machine Learning model. The predicted value can be in many different formats, depending on the model and your input data.

In this case, since you are using a classification model (binary) to create the scores, the Score Model module outputs a predicted value for the class, along with the probability of the predicted value.

This is exactly what you need for your reference implementation. You need to make a prediction, based on the current sensor reading data and the historical stress test data, about whether a team member is at risk of physical exhaustion.

Start by locating the module by typing Score Model in the Search window on the left side of the Azure Machine Learning Studio Designer screen. This should find the exact module.

You can also find this module by expanding the Machine Learning category and then the Score sub-category in the left side navigation pane in Azure Machine Learning Studio.

Drag the Score Model module onto the designer surface below and to the right of the Train Model module.

Connect the bottom of the Train Model module to the top-left connector of the Score Model module.

Connect the bottom-right of the Split Data module to the top-right of the Score Model module.

Click on the Save icon on the bottom of the screen and then click on the Run icon to process the new Machine Learning experiment. A green check mark will soon appear next to each module in the Machine Learning experiment as it is processed, as shown in Figure 8-28.

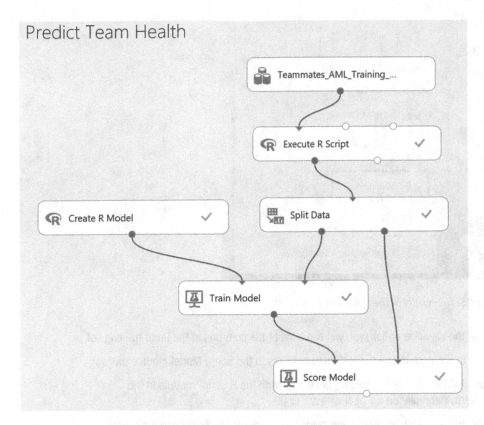

Figure 8-28. *Completed Azure Machine Learning experiment for predicting team members' health*

At this point, you have successfully completed the Azure Machine Learning experiment to predict team members' health based on historical sensor readings from periodic stress tests. This experiment uses a built-in binary classification R package to create the model and score the results. The next step examines how to explore the prediction accuracy of the model.

View Results of Score Model Module to see R Predictions

In this step, you examine the predictions made by this new R Machine Learning model training experiment. To get started, simply right-click on the bottom connector of the Score Model module and then click on the Visualize option in the context menu, as shown in Figure 8-29.

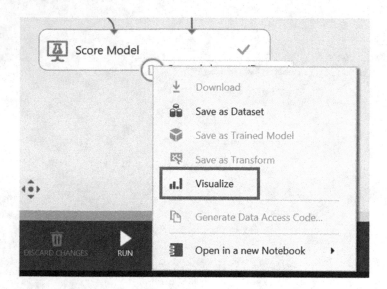

Figure 8-29. *Visualize the results of the Score Model module*

After you click on the Visualize option, you will see a list of the columns in the input training set.

Scroll all the way to the right to see the last three columns in the Score Model module dataset:

- *ExhaustionLabel:* This is the column generated with the R script module in the experiment. You replaced a Y or N with a 1 or 0.

- *Classes:* This is the binary prediction made by the new R Machine Learning model.

- *Probabilities:* This is the calculated probability that the Machine Learning model's prediction will be correct.

Figure 8-30 depicts the visualization of the Score Model result set.

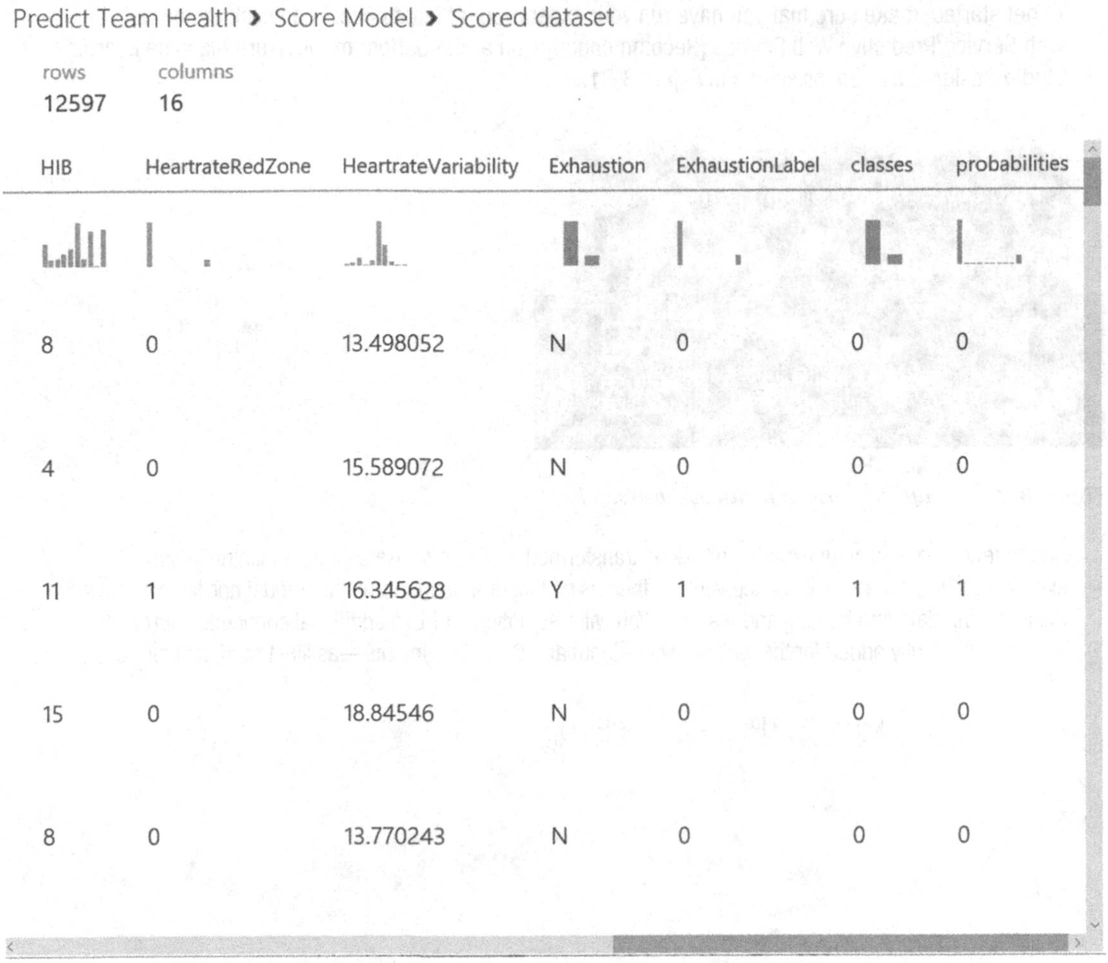

Predict Team Health **>** Score Model **>** Scored dataset

rows	columns
12597	16

HIB	HeartrateRedZone	HeartrateVariability	Exhaustion	ExhaustionLabel	classes	probabilities
8	0	13.498052	N	0	0	0
4	0	15.589072	N	0	0	0
11	1	16.345628	Y	1	1	1
15	0	18.84546	N	0	0	0
8	0	13.770243	N	0	0	0

Figure 8-30. *The visualization of the Score Model module*

You can examine the prediction results and see that the algorithm is reasonably accurate, as Figure 8-30 illustrates nicely where the Exhaustion column = Y on the third row down. Note that prediction is accurate along with the probability being very high, as it is 1.

Create Web Service from R Machine Learning Experiment

Now that you have a working Azure Machine Learning model, it is time to productionalize this experiment by exposing it as an Azure Machine Learning Web Service.

Creating an Azure Machine Learning Web Service allows you to embed your predictive analytics into applications. You can pass new input feature data to the Azure Machine Learning Web Service. The new feature data will be run through the Machine Learning model and the web service will send back the prediction.

387

To get started, make sure that you have run your experiment at least once. Then click on the Set Up Web Service/Predictive Web Service [Recommended] icon at the bottom of the Azure Machine Learning Studio Designer screen, as shown in Figure 8-31.

Figure 8-31. *Set up web service: predictive web service*

After a few moments, your experiment will be transformed into a new, streamlined, Machine Learning experiment. In this new web service version, there is no longer a need to train the model nor, likewise, to split the incoming data into training and test sets. You will also notice that two additional connection ports have been automatically added for the web service—Input and Output endpoints—as illustrated in Figure 8-32.

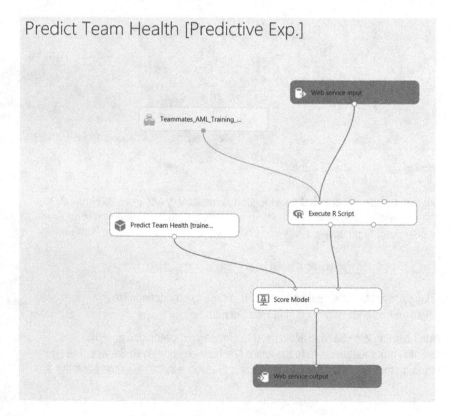

Figure 8-32. *Predictive web service created from the Azure Machine Learning experiment*

Click on the Run icon at the bottom of the designer screen to compile the new web service. You will notice green checkmarks appear next to each module as it has been processed.

Once it's complete, the Deploy Web Service icon will be enabled at the bottom of the Azure Machine Learning Studio Designer screen, as shown in Figure 8-33.

Deploy Web Service [Classic]
Deploy Web Service [New] Preview
RUN
DEPLOY WEB SERVICE
PUBLISH TO GALLERY

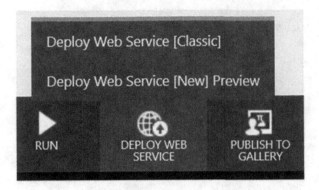

***Figure 8-33.** The deploy web service options*

Select the Deploy Web Service [New] Preview option, and you will be directed to the screen shown in Figure 8-34.

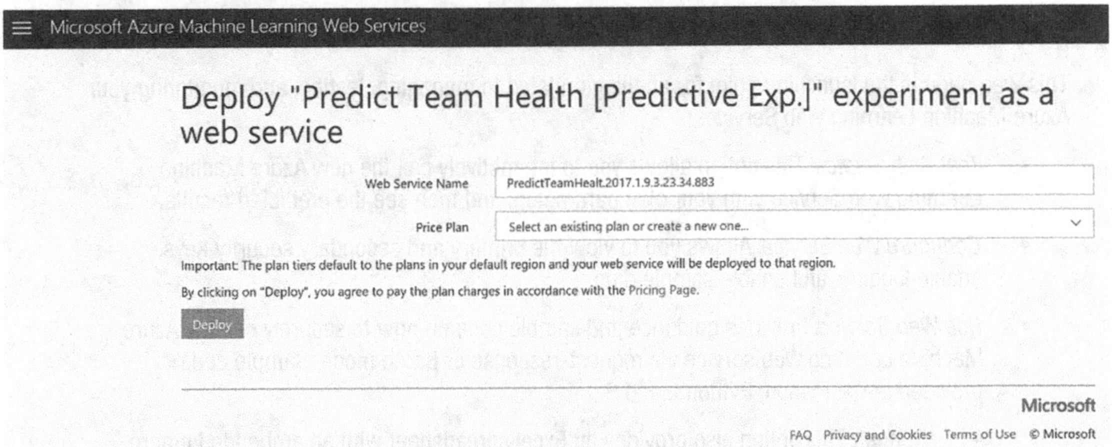

Microsoft Azure Machine Learning Web Services
Deploy "Predict Team Health [Predictive Exp.]" experiment as a web service
Web Service Name
PredictTeamHealt.2017.1.9.3.23.34.883
Price Plan
Select an existing plan or create a new one...
Important: The plan tiers default to the plans in your default region and your web service will be deployed to that region.
By clicking on "Deploy", you agree to pay the plan charges in accordance with the Pricing Page.
Deploy
Microsoft
FAQ Privacy and Cookies Terms of Use © Microsoft

***Figure 8-34.** Deploy web service [new] preview options*

This screen allows you to modify the name of the web service and the Azure price plan under which it will run. Make your selections and click on the Deploy button to deploy the web service.

A new browser tab will open and you will see a screen similar to the one in Figure 8-35.

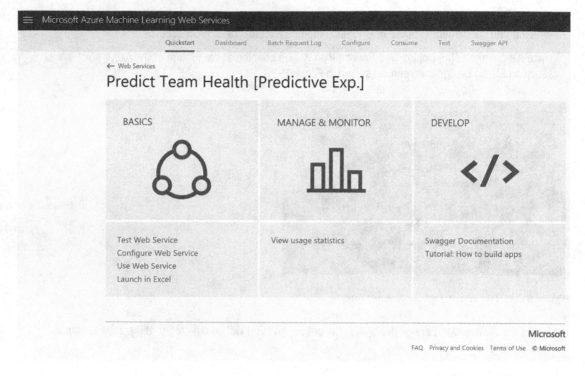

Figure 8-35. *Azure Machine Learning Web Services dashboard*

This web page is the launching point for all things related to managing, testing, and monitoring your Azure Machine Learning Web Services.

- *Test Web Service*: This option allows you to interactively call the new Azure Machine Learning Web Service with your own parameters and then see the predicted results.

- *Configure Web Service*: Allows you to view the primary and secondary security keys, enable logging, and enable sample data.

- *Use Web Service*: Provides guidance and sample code on how to securely call the Azure Machine Learning Web service via request-response or Batch mode. Sample code provided in C#, Python, Python3, and R.

    - **Bonus**: This option also provides an Excel spreadsheet with an embedded macro to interactively call your AML Web Service and test the results.

- *Launch in Excel*: Allows you to launch the test Excel spreadsheet with an embedded macro to interactively call your AML Web Service and test the results.

This is probably one of the best tools and features included with Azure Machine Learning (for free). This feature enables you to populate a spreadsheet with sample data to test your new Azure Machine Learning Web Service without having to create a client application.

Figure 8-36 depicts the Excel spreadsheet with the inputs shown on the top, the Excel Office Add-in panel shown on the right, and the Web Service prediction results displayed on the bottom portion of the spreadsheet.

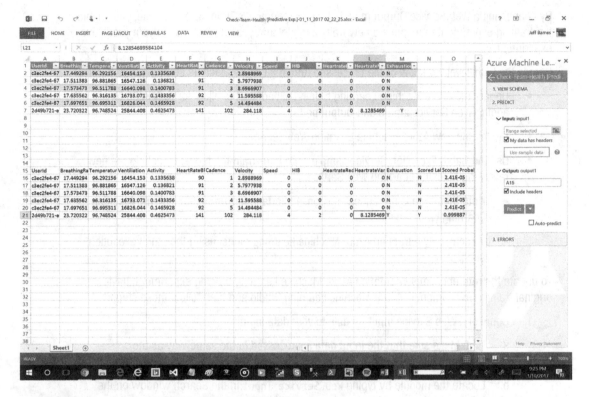

Figure 8-36. Excel 2013 AML web tester spreadsheet

In this exercise, you successfully created a new Web Service from the Azure Machine Learning Experiment. You then deployed it and tested it using an Excel spreadsheet.

There are additional Azure Machine Learning Web Service tools to provide support for diagnostics, logging, and generating Swagger API documentation.

Create Re-Training AML Web Service

One of the most exciting features in Azure Machine Learning is the ability to programmatically re-train a Machine Learning model based on new or updated training data. This one singular feature provides the unique capability for computers to be programmed to automatically adapt and learn from experience.

That's right—the same stuff that science fiction books and the *Terminator* movie series are made of. The good news is that we are still in the early days and there is no immediate concern that computers will become self-aware-for at least a few more years.

Recall that you created an Azure Data Factory job back in Chapter 6 to retrain the Azure Machine Learning model via an exposed Azure Machine Learning Web Service. You will create that service in this exercise.

To deploy the training experiment as a retraining web service, you must add web service inputs and outputs to the existing model.

By connecting a Web Service Output module to the experiment's Train Model module, you enable the training experiment to produce a new trained model that you can then use in your predictive experiment.

Here is the high-level workflow of the process to retrain an Azure Machine Learning Web Service:

- Update the Azure Machine Learning training experiment to allow for retraining by adding Web Service Inputs and Output ports.

- Deploy the new Azure Machine Learning Web Service.

- Use the Batch Execution Service sample code to re-train the model by calling the new retraining Machine Learning Web Service.

    - Note that there is no request-response interface for retraining an Azure Machine Learning Web Service.

    - You can only retrain an Azure Machine Learning model using the batch execution service.

To update the reference implementation Azure Machine Learning training experiment, navigate to the original training experiment in Azure Machine Learning Studio and then follow these steps:

1. Connect a Web Service Input module to your data input:

    a. Hint: Make sure that the input data is processed in the same way as the original training data.

    b. Locate the module by typing `Web Service Input` in the Search window on the left side of the Azure Machine Learning Studio Designer screen. You can also find this module by expanding the Web Service module.

    c. Drag the Web Service Input module to the designer surface right above the Execute R Script module.

    d. Connect the Web Service Input module to the top-left connector of the Execute R Script module.

2. Connect a Web Service Output module to the output of the Train Model module.

    a. Locate the module by typing `Web Service Output` in the Search window on the left side of the Azure Machine Learning Studio Designer screen. You can also find this module by expanding the Web Service module.

    b. Drag the Web Service Output module to the designer surface right below the Train Model module.

    c. Connect the Train Model module to the top of the Web Service Output module.

3. Run the experiment.

Figure 8-37 shows the updated Azure Machine Learning experiment after adding the Web Service Input and Output modules.

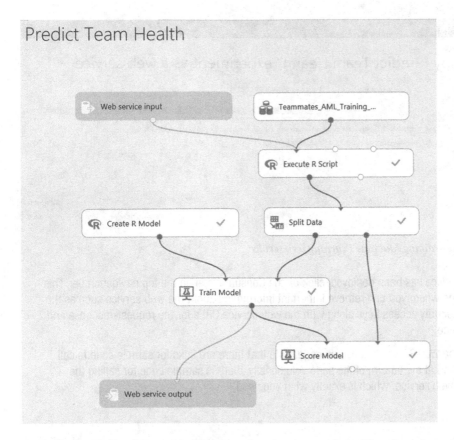

Figure 8-37. Updated Azure Machine Learning experiment after adding the web service input and output modules

Next, you must deploy the updated Azure Machine Learning training experiment as a web service that produces a trained model along with model evaluation results.

To do this, follow these steps:

- At the bottom of the experiment canvas, click Set-Up Web Service, and then select Deploy Web Service [New].

- The Azure Machine Learning Web Services portal will then open a new browser tab to the Deploy Web Service page.

- Type a name for your web service, choose a payment plan, and then click Deploy.

  - You can only use the Batch Execution method when creating trained models.

You will see a screen similar to Figure 8-38.

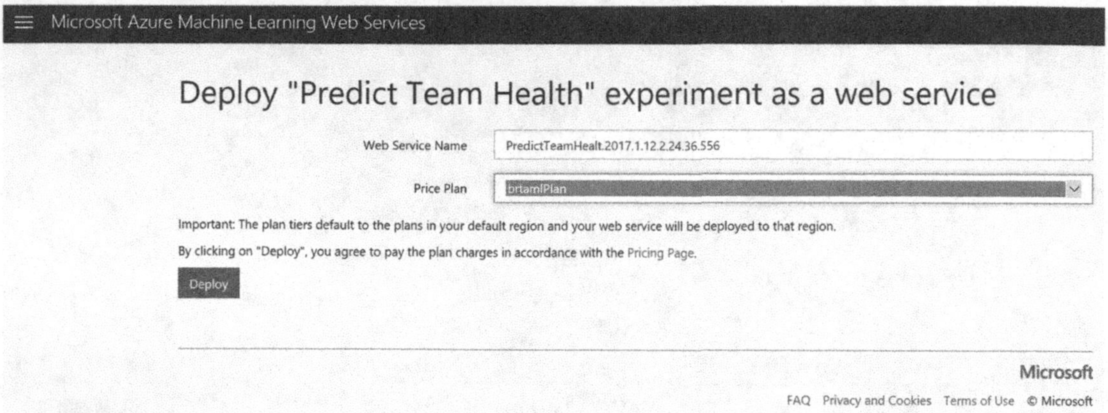

> Microsoft Azure Machine Learning Web Services

Deploy "Predict Team Health" experiment as a web service

Web Service Name   PredictTeamHealt.2017.1.12.2.24.36.556

Price Plan   brtamlPlan

Important: The plan tiers default to the plans in your default region and your web service will be deployed to that region.

By clicking on "Deploy", you agree to pay the plan charges in accordance with the Pricing Page.

Deploy

Microsoft

FAQ   Privacy and Cookies   Terms of Use   © Microsoft

Figure 8-38. *Deploy a re-training Machine Learning web service*

After the new web service has been deployed, click on the Consume icon on the top navigation bar. This will take you to a page where you can retrieve important information about the web service such as the primary/secondary security access keys along with the web service URLs for the request-response and batch execution service.

Figure 8-39 shows the Web Services Consume page. Note that there are links for sample code to call the web service located at the bottom of the page. Additionally, there is sample code for calling the batch version of the web service, which is exactly what you need.

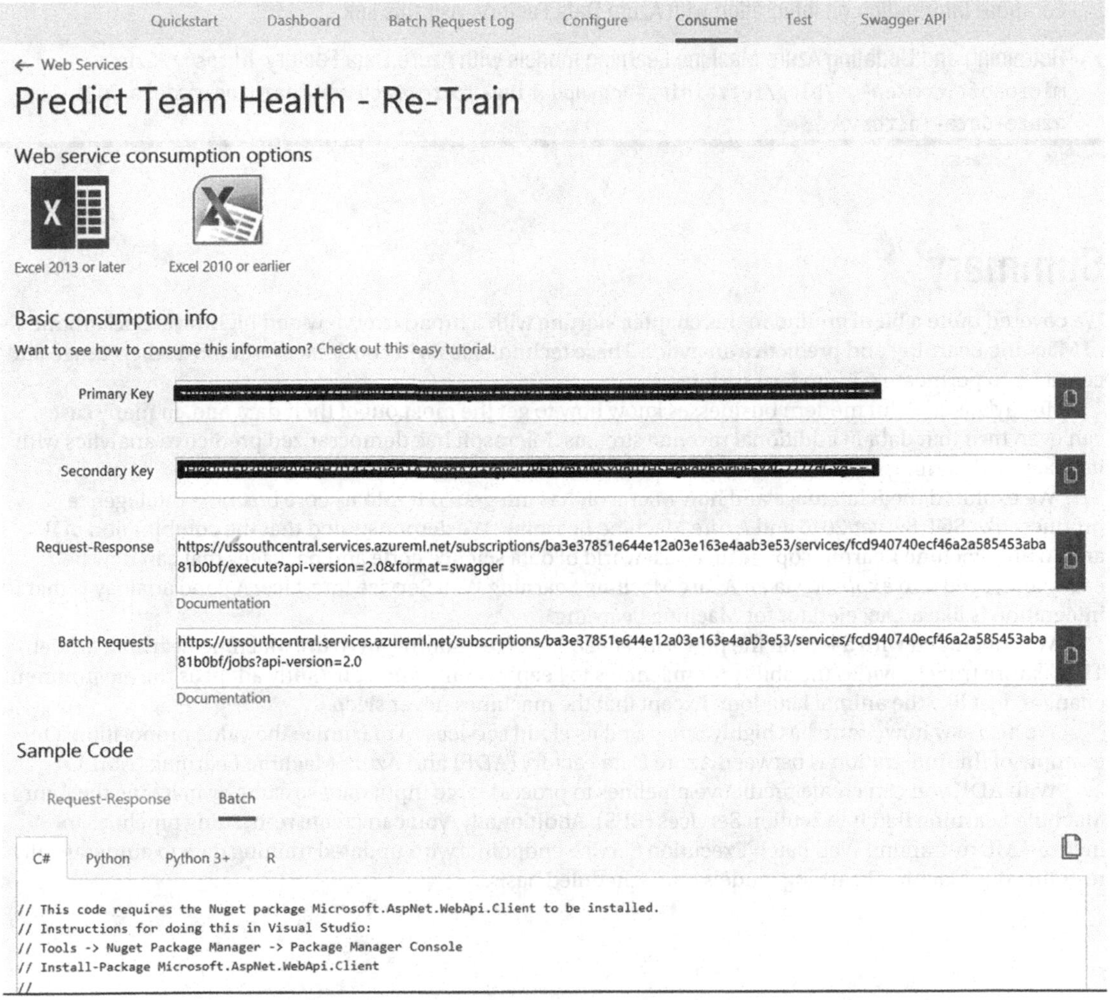

| Quickstart | Dashboard | Batch Request Log | Configure | **Consume** | Test | Swagger API |

← Web Services

Predict Team Health - Re-Train

Web service consumption options

X	X
Excel 2013 or later	Excel 2010 or earlier

Basic consumption info

Want to see how to consume this information? Check out this easy tutorial.

Primary Key	▓▓▓▓▓▓▓▓▓▓▓▓▓▓▓▓▓▓▓▓▓▓▓▓▓▓▓▓▓▓▓▓▓▓▓▓	🗋
Secondary Key	▓▓▓▓▓▓▓▓▓▓▓▓▓▓▓▓▓▓▓▓▓▓▓▓▓▓▓▓▓▓▓▓▓▓▓▓	🗋

Request-Response	https://ussouthcentral.services.azureml.net/subscriptions/ba3e37851e644e12a03e163e4aab3e53/services/fcd940740ecf46a2a585453aba81b0bf/execute?api-version=2.0&format=swagger	🗋
	Documentation	

Batch Requests	https://ussouthcentral.services.azureml.net/subscriptions/ba3e37851e644e12a03e163e4aab3e53/services/fcd940740ecf46a2a585453aba81b0bf/jobs?api-version=2.0	🗋
	Documentation	

Sample Code

Request-Response	**Batch**

| **C#** | Python | Python 3+ | R | 🗋 |

```
// This code requires the Nuget package Microsoft.AspNet.WebApi.Client to be installed.
// Instructions for doing this in Visual Studio:
// Tools -> Nuget Package Manager -> Package Manager Console
// Install-Package Microsoft.AspNet.WebApi.Client
//
```

Figure 8-39. *Web Services Consume tab used to re-train Machine Learning Web Service*

The sample code provided will assist you in creating a C# console application to retrain the Azure Machine Learning model.

■ **Note** For more information about retraining a Machine Learning Model, visit this link: `https://docs.microsoft.com/en-us/azure/machine-learning/machine-learning-retrain-machine-learning-model`.

In addition to creating a custom .NET C# Console application to call the Batch Execution Service for the Machine Learning retraining web service, you can also simply use Azure Data Factory to set up and run an Azure Machine Learning job. All that is required is that you pass in the associated web service URL for retraining and provide the Azure storage location for the retraining data.

For more information on integration with Azure Data Factory, visit this link:

Retraining and Updating Azure Machine Learning models with Azure Data Factory: `https://azure.microsoft.com/en-us/blog/retraining-and-updating-azure-machine-learning-models-with-azure-data-factory/`.

Summary

We covered quite a bit of ground in this chapter, starting with a broad overview and high-level background of Machine Learning and predictive analytics. These technologies will continue to expand in their usage and continue to permeate our modern society.

Today's successful modern businesses know how to get the most out of their data and, in many cases, can even turn that data in additional revenue streams. Microsoft has democratized predictive analytics with its Machine Learning offering.

We explored the R language and how Microsoft has integrated R into its core business intelligence products like SQL Server 2016 and Azure Machine Learning. We demonstrated that the combination of R and Azure Machine Learning opens up a vast world of data science code and packages that can now be easily leveraged and exposed via an Azure Machine Learning Web Service interface. A good analogy is that R integration is like an accelerator for Machine Learning.

We concluded with a look at the powerful capability of re-training an Azure Machine Learning model. This feature truly provides the ability for machines to keep learning and constantly adapt as the environment changes. Just like the animal kingdom. Except that the machines never sleep.

We also saw how Azure has highly integrated its cloud services to maximize the value proposition. One example of this integration is between Azure Data Factory (ADF) and Azure Machine Learning (AML).

With ADF, you can create predictive pipelines to process large input data streams by invoking the Azure Machine Learning Batch Execution Services (BES). Additionally, you can create re-training pipelines to invoke AML re-training Web Batch Execution Service endpoints with updated training data to automatically re-train your Machine Learning models on a scheduled basis.

CHAPTER 9

■ ■ ■

Data Visualizations, Alerts, and Notifications with Power BI

This chapter explores the use of data visualizations, alerts, and notifications to help today's businesses provide useful communications to their employees and customers in order to successfully manage their operations in real time.

We will start the chapter with a brief look at today's reporting landscape, then take a look at how Microsoft technologies like Power BI and Azure functions can help provide quick-and-easy solutions. We will then walk through enabling these technologies as part of our reference implementation scenario.

We will conclude the chapter by walking through the use of the C# .NET "Simulator" application to automatically funnel thousands of sample test data transactions through our Azure cloud implementation. The simulated data will be processed in real time using Azure Stream Analytics, and we will implement a Power BI dashboard to view of our Lambda cloud architecture. Lambda architectures, as you may recall, are designed to handle massive quantities of data by taking advantage of both batch- and stream-processing methods.

Our reference implementation Power BI dashboard will display outputs for all three "temperatures" of the Lambda architecture processing model via visualizations of the cold, warm, and hot data paths.

The Modern Reporting Landscape

Yesterday's green bar print-outs, stale information, and archaic "TPS" reports have been replaced with real-time, ubiquitous communications, modern mobile devices, and instant communications, feedback, and reporting. Instant text alerts, automatic e-mail updates, web portals, and Key Performance Indicator (KPI) dashboards rule the business landscape today. These features and capabilities now represent a large portion of any good consumer, commercial, or enterprise software specifications for a Minimum Viable Product (MVP).

Today, the emphasis is truly on the use of the term "visual communications" to quickly and elegantly convey meaning to users. Success lies in an organization's ability to render key business information to their users in a clear and concise manner.

At times, *management by exception* can be the guiding principle of the day, and reports, visualizations, and tools that help to isolate, identify, and magnify abnormal trends and exceptions are worth their weight in gold today. It has been said that great data visualization is both an art and a science. We would certainly agree and would also propose having an extensive, flexible, and customizable tool chest of visual control "metaphors" to help provide reporting and notifications.

In addition to reporting on what's happening now, with dashboards and visualizations, predicting what will happen next is quickly becoming the current mega-trend in the world of data science. Advances in technologies like Machine Learning, predictive analytics, and artificial intelligence are all helping to pave the way.

© Bob Familiar and Jeff Barnes 2017
B. Familiar and J. Barnes, *Business in Real-Time Using Azure IoT and Cortana Intelligence Suite*,
DOI 10.1007/978-1-4842-2650-6_9

Today's modern business intelligence landscape requires that successful enterprises rely on a proper mixture of hindsight, insight, and foresight to make effective business decisions to drive success. These days, it is not enough to solely rely on the business strategies of the past; today, there is so much value to be derived from the historical data, market trends, and KPI results that can be easily mined to shape predictive strategies in real time.

All this becomes possible with the advent of pay-as-you-go cloud computing, cheap and ubiquitous cloud storage, and democratized predictive analytics engines like Azure Machine Learning.

In order to compete in today's global marketplaces, businesses must learn how to harness their key data assets and transform them into positive-outcome producing streams. Such outcomes could be realized in the forms of increased revenue results, better customer service, and outstanding customer loyalty.

Figure 9-1 illustrates the business intelligence landscape today. Note that there is a 360-degree analysis depicted, with an emphasis on the use of predictive analytics to help drive future outcomes.

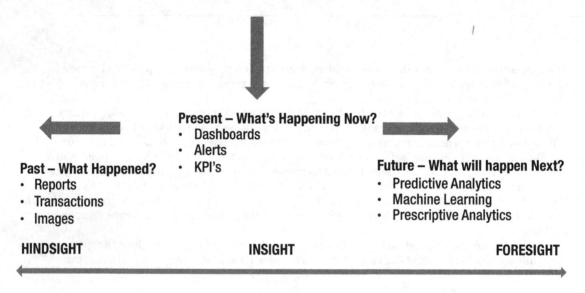

Figure 9-1. *The business intelligence landscape today*

One could argue that in today's modern Internet of Things world, that there is a new meaning for the term AI, or Artificial Intelligence. The reality is that AI is rapidly being replaced with a new meaning; that of "actionable" intelligence. And nowhere is concept of actionable intelligence more important (and necessary) than with the rise of the Internet of Things (IoT) and all the resulting data that these systems can generate.

Due to the sheer volumes of sensor data, humans must increasingly rely on advanced computer systems to track, report, manage, and predict exceptions. Fortunately, as we have seen in the previous chapters, technologies like Azure Stream Analytics (ASA) and Azure Machine Learning (AML) provide valuable features and capabilities to help create and manage these scenarios. These tools can truly enable many "actionable intelligence" use case scenarios, and we will further explore the integration aspects of these technologies when we examine the alerts and notifications topics later in this chapter.

Today, there's data, more data, data overload, and then there's actionable intelligence. Surfacing what is most important—exactly when it is needed—is one of the keys to success when it comes to operationalizing a sensor-based business intelligence platform.

Overview of Power BI

Power BI is a cloud-based analytics service by Microsoft that has the goal of providing "faster time to insight". Power BI has the ability to bring together data from many diverse sources to deliver rich visualizations and comprehensive views of business operations across desktop, web, and mobile devices.

While Power BI certainly appeals to power users, it is also meant for less technical business users and analysts to help them connect with their data and provide self-service business intelligence capabilities. A key feature of Power BI is that it allows you to see all of your data through a "single pane of glass" and then create a complete analytics environment to monitor data and share reports.

The Power BI Service

The Power BI Service, which is located at `www.powerbi.com`, is a Microsoft cloud-based service that allows you to:

- *Create Beautiful Visualizations*: Tell compelling data stories via rich visualization controls.

- *Build Rich, Live Dashboards*: That can help turn business intelligence into business insights by highlighting the exceptions in your data.

- *Create Reports and Datasets*: That can be used to create data visualizations and reporting dashboards.

- *Provide Up-to-Date Data*: Via real-time, automatic, and scheduled data refreshes.

- *Create and Share Power BI Dashboards*: Easily with other people in your organization.

- *Ask Questions of Your Data in Plain English*: Via a natural language query.

- *Allow You to Stay Connected to your Data*: The Power BI Mobile application is available in every major mobile app store.

Power BI Desktop

Power BI Desktop is a visual data exploration and interactive reporting tool that is provided free by Microsoft. It provides a rich, free-form, canvas for deep exploration of your data, along with an extensive library of interactive visualizations. Power BI Desktop offers a highly productive authoring experience for creating reports for the the Power BI service. New features are continually being integrated and the tool is updated on monthly basis. For users who may not have access to Excel 2013, the Power BI Desktop can be used to import data, create data models, and author and share Power BI Reports via the Power BI service.

While Power BI Desktop may not include all the analytical features of Excel, it does provide a simple and elegant solution for creating Power BI reports, visualizations, and dashboards.

Power BI Desktop is a powerful visual data exploration engine that enables you to quickly connect, query, and analyze your data and then quickly create stunning reports and visualizations. With Power BI Desktop, you can:

- *Acquire and Prepare Data*: Using extensive query and filtering capabilities.

- *Manipulate and Consolidate*: Multiple data sources enable users to utilize data from multiple sources in a single report.

- *Establish Data Structures*: Then transform and analyze the data via the built-in tools and visual components.

- *Visualize and Explore Data*: Quickly and easily through a free-form, drag-and-drop, report designer authoring canvas.

- *Author Reports*: With a broad range of modern data visualization tools to fine-tune and polish your dashboards and reports.

- *Publish Beautiful, Interactive Reports*: Directly to `app.powerbi.com`, which makes it easy to share and collaborate on complex reporting projects.

- *Securely Share Reports*: This is done through a unique, curated, enterprise content library approach.

■ **Note**   You can download a copy of Power BI Desktop at: Power BI Desktop: `https://powerbi.microsoft.com/en-us/desktop/`.

Unlocking Data Analysis

Power BI Desktop also enables extensive data analysis capabilities, enabling authors to produce rich data models containing formulas and relationships. For example, you can:

- *Automatically create a data model simply by importing data*:

  - Power BI Desktop can automatically detect relationships in the data and apply default summarizations.

- *Refine data models to enable complex calculations*:

  - Identify key relationships among datasets from a variety of sources.

  - Create relationships between tables manually or by using the Auto-Detect feature.

  - Adjust relationship types (one-to-one, many-to-many, or many-to-one) for deriving specific data insights.

- *Define calculations*: You can define "measures" to generate new fields for use in Power BI reports and dashboards:

  - Measures allow you to create new data from existing data in your data model.

  - One direct benefit of this is that the calculated results of measures are always changing in response to interactions with reports. This allows for fast and dynamic ad hoc data explorations.

  - You can also use the Data Analysis Expression (DAX) library to create calculated tables. For example, instead of querying and loading values into a new table's columns from a data source, you can also create a Data Analysis Expression (DAX) formula that defines the table's values.

■ **Note**   Download the DAX function reference at `https://msdn.microsoft.com/en-us/library/ee634396.`
`aspx`.

- *Define synonyms*: Allow for an improved Q&A experience in the Power BI service for natural language query capabilities.

- *Define row-level security*: Allow you to secure your data at the table and row level by defining security filters. You can define a role and an associated security filter in the Power BI desktop and then assign members to that role in the Power BI service at `app.powerbi.com`.

The Role of Excel and Power BI

Excel 2013 is Microsoft's premier tool for business analytics. It includes additional business intelligence features such as Power Query, Power Pivot, Power View, and Power Map.

With the Excel 2013 edition, business analysts can now publish Excel Workbooks to the web site `app.`
`powerbi.com` to share data, analyses, and reports with other Power BI users.

■ **Note**   Power BI publisher for Excel: `https://powerbi.microsoft.com/en-us/excel-dashboard-`
`publisher`.

Support for R Visualizations

With Power BI Desktop, you can leverage the power of the R programming language to help visualize your data. To use R with Power BI Desktop, you must first install the R engine. To run R Scripts in Power BI Desktop, you must separately install R on your local computer. You can download and install R free from many locations, including the Revolution Open download page and the CRAN Repository.

■ **Note**   Visit this link to get started with R and Power BI Desktop: Running R Scripts in Power BI Desktop:
`https://powerbi.microsoft.com/en-us/documentation/powerbi-desktop-r-scripts/`.

Microsoft R Open

Microsoft R Open, formerly known as Revolution R Open, is the enhanced distribution of R from Microsoft. It is a complete open source R platform for statistical analysis and data science.

Microsoft R Open 3.3.2 (the current version at the time of this writing) is based on (and 100% compatible with) R-3.3.2, and is fully compatible with all packages, scripts, and applications that work with that specific version of R.

Microsoft R Open also includes additional capabilities for improved performance on both Windows and Linux-based platforms.

■ **Note** You can download Microsoft R Open via this link: Microsoft R Open 3.3.2: `https://mran.revolutionanalytics.com/download/`

Power BI Desktop: R Script Visualizations

After you have installed and configured Microsoft R Open to work with Power BI Desktop, you can proceed to create some amazing visuals by leveraging the power of some of the more popular R visualization packages like ggplot2.

"ggplot2" is a powerful data visualization package for use in R programs. It is an implementation of a "grammar of graphics," which is a common playbook for data visualizations. The term comes from a seminal book by Leland Wilkinson and was written in the early 2000s. The graphics grammar scheme seeks to decompose graphs into semantic components such as scales and layers.

■ **Note** You can download a handy ggplot2 cheat sheet at: ggplot2 cheat sheet: `http://www.rstudio.com/wp-content/uploads/2015/12/ggplot2-cheatsheet-2.0.pdf`.

Once you are in the Power BI Desktop environment, you can drag the R Script Visual control to the designer canvas, as illustrated in Figure 9-2.

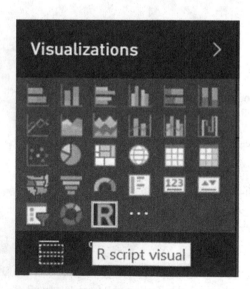

Figure 9-2. The R Script visual control, in the Power BI Visualizations toolbox

After you drag the R visual control to the Power BI designer surface, all you need to do is:

1. Select a column of data to plot. In this example, we are using the Temperature column.

2. Add these lines of R code to the Power BI R Script visual control:

```
# LOAD the ggplot2 package
library(ggplot2)

# RENDER the ggplot2 Visual
ggplot(data=dataset,aes(x=Temperature)) + geom_freqpoly(color="blue")
```

After populating the control with the R code and clicking on the Run arrow in the R Script Editor, you should see a very rich graphic visualization appear. In this case, a geometric frequency polygon is depicted, showing various temperature fluctuations in the sample data. Figure 9-3 illustrates the Power BI R control visualization.

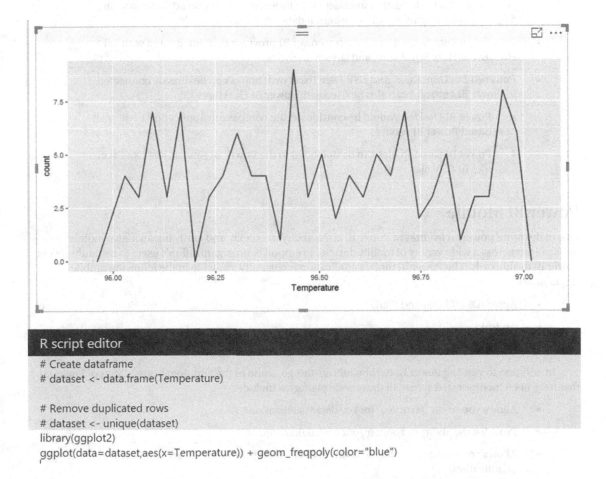

Figure 9-3. *Power BI R module using the ggplot2 R package to render temperature sensor readings visualization*

As you can see from Figure 9-3, Power BI makes it extremely easy to leverage the R language and the extensive library of packages to create very powerful graphic visualizations.

Note that in addition to providing rich visualizations, R can also be used as an input source in Power BI desktop.

Power BI Data Sources

Power BI can connect to a wide variety cloud and on-premises data sources, including:

- *Popular SaaS Solutions*: Such as Salesforce, GitHub, and Dynamics CRM.

- *On-Premise Databases*: Power BI offers live connectivity to SQL Server analysis services. Using a gateway solution, Power BI can also connect to other database solutions.

- *Custom Data Sources*: Power BI also has the ability to connect to almost any data source via powerful ReST APIs. This is a key extensibility point and means that you can now provide custom interfaces into proprietary corporate data sources in addition to leveraging additional external data services.

- *Integration with Other Azure Services*: Power BI provides tight integration with IoT Hub, Event Hub, SQL Azure, and stream analytics.

- *Power BI Desktop, Excel, and CSV Files*: Excel workbooks can be directly connected to Power BI.com and can also be used with Power BI Desktop.

  - Power BI Desktop should be considered the companion application to the web-based Power BI service.

  - Power BI Desktop files can be uploaded to the Power BI service, just like Excel files or CSV files.

Power BI Mobile

One of the more powerful features of Power BI is the ability to quickly and easily install native mobile applications across a wide variety of mobile devices, to empower an organization's users to instantly access Power BI dashboards. The Power BI mobile application is currently available in the following mobile marketplaces:

- Apple iOS (iPhone and iPad)

- Android

- Windows 10

In addition to viewing Power BI dashboards on-the-go, some of the additional capabilities of Power BI that have been incorporated across all the mobile platforms include:

- Allows you to set "favorites" for key data visualizations.

- Provides the ability to zoom in/out of visualizations.

- Allows you to annotate visualizations and share snapshots with others in your organization.

- Allows you to easily configure alerts to receive notifications when critical business metrics reach prescribed thresholds.

Figure 9-4 depicts a Power BI Desktop dashboard automatically rendered into a mobile device view.

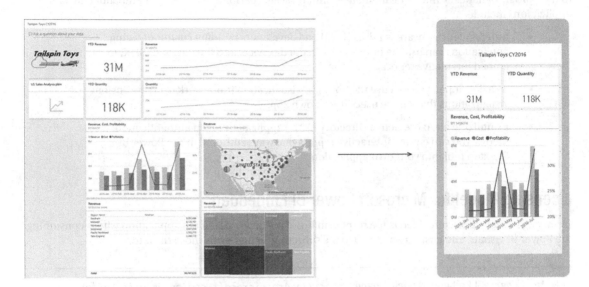

Figure 9-4. *Power BI Dashboard view from a desktop/web browser and on a mobile device*

Power BI mobile application reports support viewing dashboards, reports, SQL Server reporting services reports, and Excel spreadsheets.

The application can also access data that resides both on-premise and in the cloud by connecting to both SQL Server reporting services reports (on-premises) and Power BI dashboards and reports (in the cloud) through a single app experience.

Power BI Embedded

Power BI Embedded is an Azure service that enables developers to leverage Power BI features in their own custom applications. Possible embedded artifacts include charts, visualizations, and reports. One key advantage of Power BI Embedded over the standard Power BI offering is that it can be used anonymously, without requiring any account login information to access it.

With Power BI Embedded you can create and deploy stunning data visualizations and compelling reports directly in your applications using simple ReST APIs and the Power BI Embedded SDK.

Additional features of Power BI Embedded include the following:

- Power BI Embedded provides friction-free authentication and authorization user experiences for embedded reporting scenarios.

- Application developers can easily embed Power BI tiles and reports as an HTML Iframe control in a mobile or web applications.

A Power BI Embedded JavaScript API enables developers to embed reports into applications and to then programmatically interact with them. Common scenarios for using Power BI Embedded in your applications include:

- Independent software vendors (ISVs) and developers building customer facing applications can use the Power BI Embedded service, and the Power BI SDK, to embed interactive reports.

- As a developer, you can use the Power BI visualization framework to create custom visualizations that can be used in your own app.

- By utilizing an Azure Active Directory (AAD) application token authentication model, you can embed interactive reports that were authored in the Power BI Desktop tool into your own application.

Licensing Model for Microsoft Power BI Embedded

Licensing for Power BI embedded is the responsibility of the developer of the application who is consuming the Power BI visuals, and costs are charged to the subscription that owns those resources.

■ **Note** Power BI Embedded pricing page: `https://azure.microsoft.com/en-us/pricing/details/power-bi-embedded/`.

Power BI ReST APIs

Power BI ReST APIs allow developers to programmatically extend their applications to deliver custom, real-time data payloads that drive key dashboard scenarios. Following are some of the key use cases for Power BI ReST APIs.

- Developers can use the Power BI ReST APIs to programmatically push both static and real-time data directly from an application into Power BI.

- Power BI ReST APIs can provide programmatic access to other Power BI resources such as datasets, tables, and schemas.

Power BI Custom Visuals

Power BI is an open and extensible platform. You can download or develop custom visuals as needed to support specific business requirements. To create custom visuals, developers can get started quickly with Microsoft's open source, production-quality, sample Power BI visualization codebase.

In addition to the rich set of (25+) Power BI visual controls, developers also have the following options for obtaining additional Power BI visualizations:

- *Power BI Custom Visuals Gallery*:

  - This is a gallery of (free) visuals created by the Power BI community.

  - You can also install R-powered Power BI visuals. See this link for more information: `https://app.powerbi.com/visuals/`.

- *Create Your Own Power BI Custom Visuals*:

  - Developers also have the option of creating their own custom Power BI visualizations for use in dashboards, reports, and content packs.

  - The Microsoft Power BI visuals project provides high-quality data visualization that you can use to extend Power BI.

  - The project contains over 20 visualization types, the framework to run them, and the testing infrastructure that enables you to build high-quality visualizations. See `https://powerbi.microsoft.com/custom-visuals`.

  - Microsoft has published the source code for all of the Power BI visualizations to GitHub at `https://github.com/Microsoft/PowerBI-Visuals/`.

  - Microsoft enables developers to create their own custom visuals from the published open source visuals along with the provided framework, and then submit them back to the community.

Power BI Natural Language Query

One unique feature of Power BI the ability to ask a question about your data using a natural query language known as Q&A. Power BI Q&A is different from a search engine in that Q&A only provides results about the data hosted in Power BI.

You can use Power BI Q&A to explore your data using statements like "**Show Stores with sales greater than 50,000**" and then receive the answers in the form of charts and graphs. Power BI Q&A also picks the best visualization based on the underlying data types being displayed.

The Power BI Q&A question box is where you type your question using natural language. Power BI Q&A recognizes the words you type and then automatically figures out which dataset to query in order to find the answer. Power BI Q&A also helps you form your question correctly with auto-completion, re-statement, and other textual and visual aids.

The answer to your question is displayed as an interactive visualization and automatically update as you modify the question. Power BI Q&A can intelligently filter, sort, summarize, and display the data based on the question.

Depending on the underlying dataset, the Power BI Q&A service can determine how to best display it. For example, if data is defined as a city or state is more likely to be displayed as a map visualization. Once your Power BI Q&A answers are displayed, you can pin the answers to your dashboard for future reference.

It is possible to even add your own suggested questions for each dataset. As an example, you can create a set of frequently asked questions to help prompt the users of your Power BI datasets. Figure 9-5 depicts a screenshot of the Power BI Q&A screen for the Supplier Quality Analysis sample dashboard, which is available from the `app.powerbi.com` service.

Figure 9-5. *Power BI Q&A showing total quantity of rejected defects*

In this example, we asked for the "plant with total downtime minutes" and quickly received the visual map in Figure 9-5. Note the visual clues offered by the size of the circles on the map, which indicate the relative length of downtime for each individual plant.

Power BI Cortana Integration

Microsoft has recently integrated Cortana (the personal digital assistant) into Power BI to assist humans looking for answers in their data. The Cortana voice integration works seamlessly with Power BI dashboards and allows users to ask questions about their data—similar to the Q&A feature.

Users can ask Cortana questions either verbally or by typing them in such as "what plant had the most defect reports". Cortana can then find answers directly from datasets or from Power BI report pages that are designed specifically for Cortana (these are called Answer Pages).

■ **Tip** Use Power BI to create a custom Answer Page for Cortana: `https://powerbi.microsoft.com/en-us/documentation/powerbi-service-cortana-desktop-entity-cards/`.

Note that there are several prerequisites required before you can begin using Cortana with Power BI:

- The users have Windows 10 version 1511 or later (November 2015 update).

- The users must add their Power BI accounts to Windows 10.

- The dataset supports Q&A and is enabled for Cortana to access. See Figure 9-6.

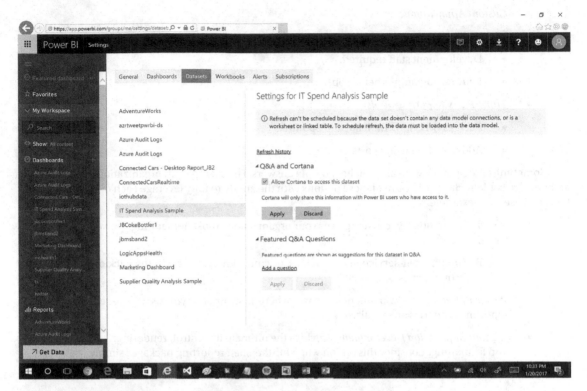

Figure 9-6. *Power BI Settings for Allowing Q&A and Cortana Integration*

Note that you can also easily add Q&A question suggestions. Cortana will return and rank the answers from Power BI, providing one or more best matches for the results. You can continue to interact with the returned visualizations just as you would in Power BI.

Cloud Reporting Cost Architectures

In many cases, the topic of licensing models for reporting, dashboards, and visualizations can have a significant impact on the final implementation details of a modern cloud architecture.

Noting the phrase "your mileage may vary," keep in mind that deeper exploration and analysis is often recommended to determine the best and most cost-effective approach for your organization.

The various strategies for implementing cloud-based dashboards, visualizations, and reporting services for an organization might consist of the following options:

- *Power BI Desktop/Mobile*:

  - Allows you to rapidly configure and enable a self-service BI capabilities in an organization.

  - Per user licensing model.

- *Power BI Embedded*:

  - Provides the ability to embed Power BI visualizations and reporting directly into your custom applications.

  - Limited to static designs and interactivity.

  - Licensed by usage within applications.

- *Custom Applications*:

  - Web/mobile applications.

  - Development staff required.

  - Fully custom implementations.

- *Third-Party Reporting Tools*:

  - Such as QlikView, Tableau, and Spotfire.

  - Additional licensing costs.

Sometimes the right answer can even be multiple answers. For example, an organization's reporting architecture could include a mixture of these options with the ability to fully leverage each option for its own best use cases. For example:

- *Power BI*: Can quickly fully-empower your organizations most demanding "power" users.

  - By enabling self-service BI capabilities, organizations can lighten the backlog of reporting requests for IT staff.

- *Power BI Embedded*: Implement it in cases where static or anonymous web-based reporting scenarios are required.

- *Custom Application Development*: Provides the ultimate in control, rendering, and formatting. Consider this option when off-the-shelf reporting packages simply won't do.

Alerts and Notifications

No discussion about today's modern reporting landscape would be complete without the mention of alerts and notifications. One of the more important aspects of implementing and managing a Big Data cloud application is the ability to provide "management by exception" and thereby focus on the higher value activities such as refining Machine Learning algorithms.

As we have seen, having an awesome, graphically stunning, operations dashboard in Power BI is great, as long as someone is watching it! Alerts and notifications allow you to be automatically informed and contacted when certain thresholds or KPI metrics have been reached. This is where the concept of actionable Intelligence becomes a business differentiator .

In today's fast-paced business environment, communicating with multiple people at the same time is extremely challenging. And to that add the the multitude of communication devices and protocols such as e-mail, SMS, and voice mail.

Another aspect to consider is the associated "escalation schedule" that could be associated with any metric that might trigger an alarm. This refers to a schedule for contacting individuals using different protocols and devices, depending on the severity of the alarm and the amount of elapsed time since the last notification.

In terms of consistency, some employees check their e-mail often, some a few times per day, and some only on an irregular basis. Most employees have smart phones these days with SMS text messaging capabilities. When it comes to communication protocols, the common denominators become those technologies which are the most ubiquitous, widespread, and widely adopted. As a result, e-mail, SMS text messaging, and web alerts quickly rise to the top as the best options for notifications that will reach the largest base of existing users.

The appealing feature of great notification systems is that they streamline communications by alerting all employees about emergencies via their various preferred communication channels. This process should occur within a few seconds from the time the initial alert message is sent. This means that no matter what device your employee has on hand, he or she can receive your important and urgent messages and alerts in a timely manner.

Microsoft Azure has some great managed services capabilities that make handling these types of notifications and alerts easier than ever before. Later in this chapter, we will explore the use of Azure Event Hubs to receive alert messages from our reference implementation and then configure Azure Functions to be automatically "triggered" whenever a new message arrives at the Event Hub.

Establishing a robust alert and notification system allows for the instantaneous broadcasting of important and urgent news regarding (potential) emergencies in the workplace. As a result, a well-tuned alerting system can be an invaluable asset to any business, its customers, and its employees.

In this section, we examine the following Azure technologies to achieve our goals for the reference implementation:

- *Azure Event Hubs*: A large-scale, managed, messaging service that can provide intake for massive data streams from various sources including, applications, devices, and web sites.

- *Azure Stream Analytics*: We will briefly re-visit Azure Stream Analytics and explore adding an additional output option for Event Hubs.

  - In addition to having a "hot path" for real-time Power BI dashboard metrics for our reference implementation, we will also implement a "hot path" to an Azure Event Hub for dropping alert and notification messages that require immediate action.

- *Azure Functions*: This PaaS offering is an extremely lightweight, event-based, serverless, cloud computing platform.

  - Azure Functions can be quickly and easily configured and coded to accelerate development of alerts and notification solutions.

  - They provide programmatic "hooks" into popular Azure-based events for implementing instant integration scenarios.

Azure Event Hub

Azure Event Hub is a highly-scalable, data ingestion service that can scale to millions of events per second, originating from a diverse set of devices and services, with low latency and high reliability.

We will be looking at using the Azure Event Hub service as the primary message queue for staging outbound alerts and notifications for our reference implementation.

The design goal of Event Hubs includes managing what are sometimes referred to as the "three Vs" of Big Data processing:

- *Volume*: Ability to handle massive amounts of data.

- *Velocity*: Ability to handle data ingestion and data egress at scale.

- *Variety*: Ability to handle a wide range of data types and data sources.

Microsoft Azure Event Hubs can support up to 1 million subscribers and support thousands of gigabytes of inbound data. Figure 9-7 illustrates the Azure Event Hub architecture.

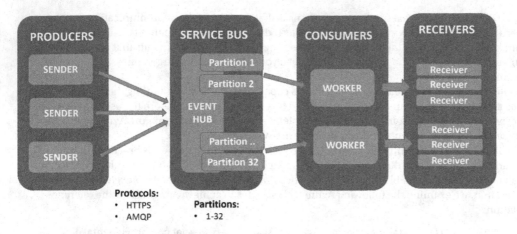

Figure 9-7. Azure Event Hub architecture

Event Publishers

Any application that sends data to an Azure Event Hub is referred to as an event publisher. Event publishers can emit events using the AMQP, AMQP over WebSockets and HTTP protocols. When sending messages, publishers can use a Shared Access Signature (SAS) token to authenticate to an Event Hub.

Event Hub Partitions

Azure Event Hubs provides message streaming functionality via a partitioned consumer pattern. A partition is an ordered sequence of events that is held in an Event Hub. As newer events arrive, they are added to the end of this sequence. This pattern requires that each consumer only reads a specific subset of the message stream. This partitioning pattern also enables horizontal scalability for event processing.

The number of Azure Event Hub partitions is specified at the time of initial provisioning in Azure and can have a value between 2 and 32. The number of partitions specified in an Azure Event Hub directly relates to the number of concurrent "workers" that will be assigned to process the messages in the background.

Event Consumers and Consumer Groups

Any application that reads data from an Event Hub is referred to as an event consumer. All Event Hub consumers connect via the session protocol and events are delivered through the session as they become available. The client does not need to poll for data availability.

The publish/subscribe capabilities in Azure Event Hubs are enabled through the notion of consumer groups. A consumer group is defined as a view (a bookmark, position, or offset) of the message data contents of an Event Hub. Consumer groups enable multiple consuming applications to each have their own separate slice or view of the event hub data stream, and to then be able to read and process the event stream data in a completely isolated and independent manner.

Throughput Units

The processing capacity of Azure Event Hubs is measured in throughput units. Throughput units equate to pre-purchased units of Azure Event Hub message processing capacity and each unit includes the following processing components:

- *Data Ingress*: Up to 1MB per second or 1000 events per second (whichever comes first) for inbound operations.

- *Data Egress*: Up to 2MB per second for outbound operations.

A best practice for optimizing the performance of Event Hubs is to balance the throughput units and partitions to achieve an optimal scaling architecture in Azure. As a general rule, the number of throughput units should be less than or equal to the number of partitions in an Event Hub.

Streaming Analytics: Output to Event Hub

Now that we have a good understanding of Azure Event Hubs, we will re-examine Azure Stream Analytics and how it can integrate with Azure Event Hubs to trigger an alert or notification workflow.

Figure 9-8 illustrates the various output options available to an Azure Stream Analytics job. Note that one of these output options is for Event Hub.

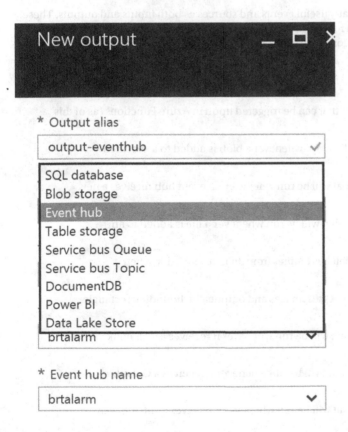

Figure 9-8. Azure Streaming Analytics output option for event hub

You now have the ability to define another hot path for our Streaming Analytics job (in addition to Power BI) for real-time alerting. This additional path allows you to:

- Monitor the incoming stream of sensor data.

- Invoke the Machine Learning Web Service to predict if a team member may be physically exhausted.

- Drop an alert or notification message onto the Azure Event Hub in the case that exhaustion was predicted.

- Perform an activity in response to the alert or notification, such as sending an e-mail or SMS. Azure Functions, the topic of the next section, is a recommended approach for implementing such actions.

Azure Functions

Azure Functions provide an extremely lightweight, server-less, event-driven, computing experience that can help accelerate your development and deployment productivity. Application development is accelerated due to the fact that there is zero server provisioning, configuration, or management involved. Focus is exclusively on refining the workflow and business logic for connecting events to actions in Azure versus how that functionally will be hosted and scaled.

Azure Functions provide hooks into many useful events and sources as both inputs and outputs. These include predefined event triggers such as HTTP requests, storage update, queue dispatches, and event streams, allowing you to quickly build solutions with less code.

Input Bindings

Here is a list of the various INPUT event types that can be triggered upon in Azure Functions (as of this writing):

- *Blob Trigger*: A function that will be run whenever a blob is added to a specified container.

- *Event Hub Trigger*: A function that will be run whenever an event hub receives a new event.

- *External File Trigger*: A function that will be run whenever a file is added to an External File provider.

- *External Table*: A function that fetches entities from an External Table when it receives an HTTP request.

- *Face Locator*: A function that processes images and outputs the bounding rectangle of faces.

- *Generic Web Hook*: A function that will be run whenever it receives a web hook request.

- *GitHub Commenter*: A function that will be run whenever it receives a GitHub Commenter web hook request.

- *GitHub Web Hook*: A function that will be run whenever it receives a GitHub web hook request.

- *Http GET (CRUD)*: A function that fetches entities from a Storage Table when it receives an HTTP request.

- *Http POST (CRUD)*: A function that adds entities to a Storage Table when it receives an HTTP request.

- *Http PUT (CRUD)*: A function that adds entities to a Storage Table when it receives an HTTP request.

- *Http Trigger*: A function that will be run whenever it receives an HTTP request.

- *Image Resizer*: A function that creates resized images whenever a blob is added to a specified container.

- *Manual Trigger*: A function that is triggered manually via the portal Run button.

- *Queue Trigger*: A function that will be run whenever a message is added to a specified Azure Storage Queue.

- *SAS Token*: A function that generates a SAS token for Azure Storage for a given container and blob name.

- *Scheduled Mail*: A function that will periodically send e-mails.

- *Send Grid*: A function that sends a confirmation e-mail when a new item is added to a particular queue.

- *Service Bus Queue Trigger*: A function that will be run whenever a message is added to a specified Service Bus queue.

- *Service Bus Topic Trigger*: A function that will be run whenever a message is added to the specified Service Bus topic.

- *Timer Trigger*: A function that will be run on a specified schedule.

External Bindings

Here is a list of the various OUTPUT event types that can be integrated into an Azure Function (as of this writing):

- Azure Event Hub

- Azure Queue Storage

- Azure Blob Storage

- External File (Preview)

- External Table (Experimental)

- HTTP

- Azure Service Bus

- Azure Table Storage

- Azure DocumentDB Document

- Azure Mobile Table Record

- Azure Notification Hub

- SendGrid (Preview)
- Twilio SMS (Preview)
- Bot Framework

Developer BYOL (Bring Your Own Language)

Azure Functions can be written in a variety of programming languages, such as C#, Node.js, Bash, F#, PHP, PowerShell, and PHP. As a result, application developers can leverage their existing development skillsets when implementing Azure Functions.

You can develop Azure Functions in a variety of tools, including the Azure Portal, Visual Studio, and your favorite text editor. Source control integration enables continuous deployment scenarios, and you can test and debug your function code locally using Visual Studio or the command-line tools.

Cost Effective Scaling

Microsoft offers two hosting options for Azure Functions: the consumption plan and the app service plan. The choice of hosting plan affects the cost and scalability of your particular solution.

- *Consumption Plan Approach*: With this plan, the Azure Function runs in parallel across multiple app instances that automatically scale based on resource utilization. You don't have to reserve resources and you will only be charged for the number of executions and resources actually consumed.

- *App Service plan Approach*: With this plan, an Azure Function runs on a dedicated virtual machine, and an Azure Function may share the server with other apps running in the user's account.

  - Dedicated VMs are allocated to your App Service apps.

  - The VMs are always available whether the code is being actively executed or not.

  - This may be a good option if your scenario requires that functions run near continuously.

■ **Note**　See the following link for more information regarding scaling and pricing for Azure Functions: Scaling Azure Functions: `https://docs.microsoft.com/en-us/azure/azure-functions/functions-scale`.

DevOps Integration with Azure Functions

Organizations can implement deep DevOps integration to enable key functionality like continuous deployment scenarios by leveraging Azure Functions. Multiple Azure Functions can be combined to hook into events associated with many popular source code control applications such as Visual Studio Team Services, GitHub, Bit Bucket, and other popular DevOps tools.

Note that there are a few GitHub specific event hooks with Azure Functions such as `GitHubCommentator` and `GitHubWebHook`. These event hooks provide specific integration points with GitHub repositories, actions, and activities.

Scheduled Functions

One of the more powerful features of Azure Functions is the ability to schedule Azure Functions to be called on set time intervals.

You can use the CRON job syntax to trigger an Azure Function to execute tasks such as data cleaning or synchronizing databases with external systems. A CRON expression usually includes six fields: {minute} {hour} {day} {month} {day of the week} {Year}.

As an example, the CRON setting for a scheduled Azure Function to be triggered once every five minutes would be:

```
"schedule": "0 */5 * * * *"
```

Figure 9-9 depicts an Azure Function that is triggered by a scheduled timer.

```
public static async Task Run(TimerInfo myTimer, TraceWriter log)
{
    var str = ConfigurationManager.ConnectionStrings["sqldb_connection"].ConnectionString;
    using (SqlConnection conn = new SqlConnection(str))
    {
        conn.Open();
        var text = "DELETE from dbo.TodoItems WHERE Complete='True'";
        using (SqlCommand cmd = new SqlCommand(text, conn))
        {
            // Execute the command and log the # rows deleted.
            var rows = await cmd.ExecuteNonQueryAsync();
            log.Info($"{rows} rows were deleted");
        }
    }
}
```

Figure 9-9. *A sample Azure Function to perform database cleanup operations*

Reference Implementation

Up to this point in the chapter, we have provided an overview of the core features and capabilities of Power BI, Azure Event Hubs, and Azure Functions. This will serve as valuable background information when we next revisit the reference implementation and leverage these Azure services for the solution.

Implementation Overview

We continue our technical reference implementation in this chapter with this stage being all about visualizations, alerts, and notifications.

Figure 9-10 provides a high-level overview of the functionality we will implement in the remaining sections of this chapter.

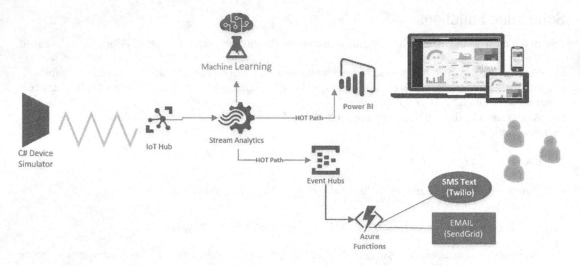

Figure 9-10. *Reference implementation overview for visualizations, alerts, and notifications*

Let's explore the components in this solution as depicted in Figure 9-10:

- *C# Device Simulator*: This is utility program that we can use to generate random sensor readings and send them securely into the Azure IoT Hub.

- *IoT Hub*: This is the primary ingestion point for the sensor readings.

- *Stream Analytics*: Used for processing incoming sensor readings at scale.

  - *Machine Learning Web Services* are invoked from Stream Analytics as each set of team member readings is processed, and a prediction is made as to the physical exhaustion level of the team members.

  - *Hot Paths* for Power BI and Event Hubs output are defined; data is streamed to each of these in real time.

- *Power BI*: Datasets are populated in real time from the Azure Stream Analytics service. Graphical visualizations, reports, and dashboards are then generated and exposed to users.

- *Event Hubs*: Used to send high priority outbound alerts and notifications.

  - *Stream Analytics Query* will filter data output to the Alarm Event Hub: based upon the results of the Machine Learning Web Service Call.

    - Only Positive results for the Machine Learning Web Service calls will dropped into the Alarm Event Hub.

    - This means that a team member is potentially at or near the point of physical exhaustion. Action must be taken immediately!

- *Azure Functions*: Triggered whenever a new item is added to the Alarm Event Hub.

    These events then trigger the associated Azure Functions and send messages as SMS and e-mail via the third-party services as Twilio and SendGrid respectively.

    - *Send SMS Test Message*: Azure Functions can be configured to automatically send SMS text messages via a third-party communications service (Twilio).

    - *E-mail Notifications*: Can be configured in Azure Functions and automatically sent via a third-party e-mail service (SendGrid).

MODIFY THE STREAMING ANALYTICS SQL QUERY

In this section, we revisit the Azure Stream Analytics query we created in Chapter 5 and make a few modifications.

Review the Existing Streaming Analytics SQL Query Output to Power BI

Navigate to your Azure Stream Analytics job in the Azure Portal and click on the Query pane, as shown in Figure 9-11.

Figure 9-11. Azure Streaming Analytics Query pane

You will see the query displayed in the editor window. The first portion of the query is reprinted here for your reference.

```
-- ***********************
-- * HOTPATH - POWER BI
-- * Invoke Machine Learning As Function "ChkTeamHealth()"
-- * Via ASA SQL Subquery
-- * then output to PowerBI (Hot)/SQL (WARM)/BLOB (COLD)
-- ***********************
```

```
WITH [subquery] AS
(
    SELECT UserId,
    [Timestamp],
    EventProcessedUtcTime,
    PartitionId,
    EventEnqueuedUtcTime,
        ChkTeamHealth(
            UserId,
            BreathingRate,
            Temperature,
            Ventilization,
            Activity,
            HeartRateBPM,
            Cadence,
            Velocity,
            Speed,
            HIB,
            HeartrateRedZone,
            HeartrateVariability,
            "N")
    as result from [input-iothub]
    TIMESTAMP BY [Timestamp]
)
SELECT  SQ.UserId,
        SQ.[Timestamp],
        SQ.EventProcessedUtcTime,
        SQ.PartitionId,
        SQ.EventEnqueuedUtcTime,
        CAST(SQ.result.[BreathingRate] as float) as [BreathingRate],
        CAST(SQ.result.[Temperature] as float) as [Temperature],
        CAST(SQ.result.[Ventilization] as float) as [Ventilization],
        CAST(SQ.result.[Activity] as float) as [Activity],
        CAST(SQ.result.[HeartRateBPM] as bigint) as [HeartRateBPM],
        CAST(SQ.result.[Cadence] as float) as [Cadence],
        CAST(SQ.result.[Velocity] as float) as [Velocity],
        CAST(SQ.result.[Speed] as float)as [Speed],
        SQ.result.[HIB],
        SQ.result.[HeartrateRedZone],
        SQ.result.[HeartrateVariability],
        SQ.result.[Scored labels],
        SQ.result.[Scored Probabilities],
        RF.id,
        RF.companyname,
        RF.imageUrl,
        RF.firstname,
        RF.lastname,
        RF.username,
        RF.[type],
        RF.[phone],
```

```
        RF.[email],
        AD.firstname as [adminfname],
        AD.lastname as [adminlname],
        AD.username as [adminuname],
        AD.type as [admintype],
        AD.phone as [adminphone],
        AD.email as [adminemail]

INTO [output-powerbi]

FROM subquery SQ

JOIN [input-refdata-team] RF
    ON SQ.UserId = RF.id

JOIN [input-refdata-team] AD
    ON RF.companyname = AD.companyname
    WHERE    AD.[type] = '2'
```

Here are a few things that are noteworthy in the code sample:

- A WITH clause is used to create a SQL subquery to invoke the Machine Learning Web Service via an ASA inline function call and return the results.

  - The subquery is reused several times in the larger SQL statement. This is actually a best practice to improve performance; avoid re-querying the same data source by holding the temporary results from a WITH clause.

- The Machine Learning Web Service is invoked via an ASA Function called ChkTeamHealth.

- CAST statements have been added to transform certain fields into numeric outputs (instead of "strings") for improved Power BI output visualizations.

  - Example: CAST(SQ.result.[BreathingRate] as float) as [BreathingRate]

- There is a JOIN clause at the end of the statement to the reference data input named [input-refdata-team].

  - This is considered an *enrichment* Query so that supplemental team member information can be appended to the dataset.

  - This enables you to determine additional information for alerts, such as the contact information for a team member's supervisor.

- In the event that a team member is predicted to be at or near physical exhaustion levels, you need to alert the supervisor *immediately*.

  - We now have the supervisor information available in the "hot path" dataset via the JOIN clause addition to the basic query.

Add a New ASA Output Alias for Event Hub for Alarms

The next step is to create a new Azure Event Hub via the portal, so that you can send messages to it via the Azure Stream Analytics query.

Messages that land in this event hub will be used to trigger alerts via an Azure Function.

The Azure Function will, in turn, send SMS text and e-mail messages to the team member's supervisor contact information via third-party communications providers such as Twilio and SendGrid.

Navigate to the Azure resource group for your solution and click on the + Add icon to add another Azure service. Type Event Hub in the search bar and you will see similar results to Figure 9-12.

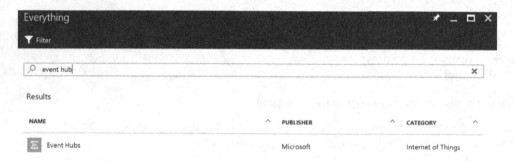

Figure 9-12. *Add a new event hub to the Azure resource group*

Click on Event Hub and you will see a confirmation screen similar to the one in Figure 9-13.

Azure Event Hubs is a highly scalable publish-subscribe service that can ingest millions of events per
connected devices and applications.

Use Event Hubs to:

- Log millions of events per second in near real time.
- Connect devices using flexible authorization and throttling.
- Use time-based event buffering.
- Get a managed service with elastic scale.
- Reach a broad set of platforms using native client libraries.
- Pluggable adapters for other cloud services.

Figure 9-13. *Create a new Azure Event Hub*

Click on the Create icon at the bottom left and then you will see a blade appear that will prompt you to
enter the parameters required to create your new Azure Event Hub, such as illustrated in Figure 9-14.

Figure 9-14. *Create new Azure Event Hub parameters*

Fill in the required parameters and click on the Create icon. The new Azure Event Hub will be provisioned in a matter of minutes.

After your new event hub has been provisioned in your resource group, you can navigate to the new Event Hub blade to retrieve the settings required for defining an output alias in Azure Streaming Analytics.

To retrieve the connection settings:

1. Click on Settings/Shared Access policies.

2. Click `RootManagerSharedAccessKey`.

3. Retrieve these primary or secondary key settings:

    a. Key.(Primary/Secondary)

    b. Connection String

Save these settings for the next step.

Add a New ASA Output Alias for Event Hub for Alerts

Now that we have defined a new Azure Event Hub and retrieved the access keys, the next step is to define a new Stream Analytics Output definition.

To get started, navigate to your Azure Stream Analytics job via the Azure Portal and then click on the Outputs pane shown in Figure 9-15.

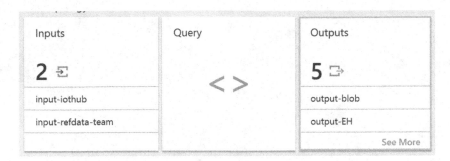

Figure 9-15. *Streaming Analytics Output definitions*

Next, click on the + Add icon on the top navigation bar. You will see a screen similar to Figure 9-16.

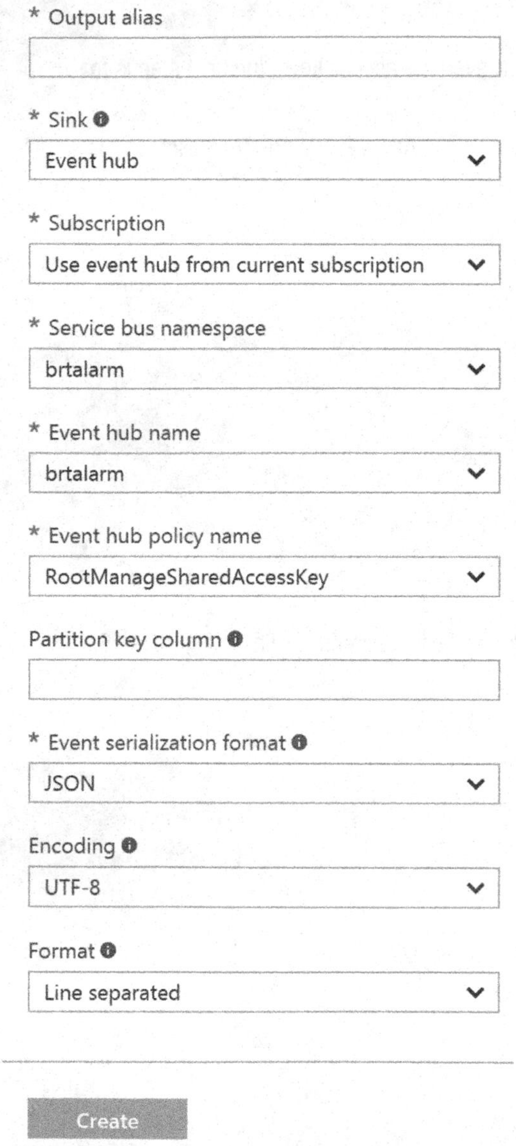

* Output alias

[   ]

* Sink ❶

[Event hub   ⌄]

* Subscription

[Use event hub from current subscription ⌄]

* Service bus namespace

[brtalarm   ⌄]

* Event hub name

[brtalarm   ⌄]

* Event hub policy name

[RootManageSharedAccessKey   ⌄]

Partition key column ❶

[   ]

* Event serialization format ❶

[JSON   ⌄]

Encoding ❶

[UTF-8   ⌄]

Format ❶

[Line separated   ⌄]

[Create]

Figure 9-16. *Add Output Alias parameters for an event hub*

Fill in the required parameters and click on the Create icon. The new Output Alias for the Azure Event Hub will be created.

Modify ASA Query to Add Output to Event Hub for Alerts

Now that you have defined your new Azure Event Hub and Output alias, you will add a new SQL query to output alerts to this event hub, and that, in turn, will trigger an Azure Function for further routing.

Navigate to your Azure Stream Analytics job in the Azure Portal and click on the Query icon.

Here is the code for adding the new Azure Event Hub as an additional output destination. Paste it into the query right after the output to Power BI.

```
-- ***************************
-- * HOTPATH - OUTPUT to Event Hub
-- * If Machine Learning Predicts Stress
-- ***************************
SELECT   SQ.UserId,
         SQ.[Timestamp],
         SQ.EventProcessedUtcTime,
         SQ.PartitionId,
         SQ.EventEnqueuedUtcTime,
         CAST(SQ.result.[BreathingRate] as float)
as [BreathingRate],
         CAST(SQ.result.[Temperature] as float)
as [Temperature],
         CAST(SQ.result.[Ventilization] as float)
as [Ventilization],
         CAST(SQ.result.[Activity] as float)
as [Activity],
         CAST(SQ.result.[HeartRateBPM] as bigint)
as [HeartRateBPM],
         CAST(SQ.result.[Cadence] as float)
as [Cadence],
         CAST(SQ.result.[Velocity] as float)
as [Velocity],
         CAST(SQ.result.[Speed] as float)
as [Speed],
         SQ.result.[HIB],
         SQ.result.[HeartrateRedZone],
         SQ.result.[HeartrateVariability],
         SQ.result.[Scored labels],
         SQ.result.[Scored Probabilities],
         RF.id,
         RF.companyname,
         RF.imageUrl,
         RF.firstname,
         RF.lastname,
         RF.username,
         RF.[type],
         RF.[phone],
         RF.[email],
         AD.firstname as [adminfname],
         AD.lastname as [adminlname],
         AD.username as [adminuname],
         AD.type as [admintype],
         AD.phone as [adminphone],
         AD.email as [adminemail]

INTO [output-EH]
FROM subquery SQ
```

```
JOIN [input-refdata-team] RF
    ON SQ.UserId = RF.id

JOIN [input-refdata-team] AD
    ON RF.companyname = AD.companyname

WHERE   SQ.result.[Scored labels] = 'Y'
        AND AD.type = '2'
```

You will notice that the WHERE clause contains this expression:

```
SQ.result.[Scored labels] = 'Y'
```

This is a key filter for this SQL query because it will only send a message to the Event Hub if the Machine Learning Web Service returned a "Y" as the predicted level of exhaustion. Hopefully very few messages will be passed to this event hub.

BUILD VISUALIZATIONS TO DISPLAY SENSOR READINGS USING R AND POWER BI DESKTOP

The first step is to use Power BI Desktop to connect to the warm path data source in the reference scenario, namely the output directed to the Azure SQL Database by the Stream Analytics query.

■ **Note**   You can download Power BI desktop from this link: Power Bi Desktop: https://www.microsoft.com/en-us/download/details.aspx?id=45331

After you have installed Power BI, you will connect to the Azure SQL database that is the output destination specified in the Stream Analytics job.

Click on Get Data and then SQL Server. After that a new window will appear and ask for the SQL database connection information, as shown in Figure 9-17.

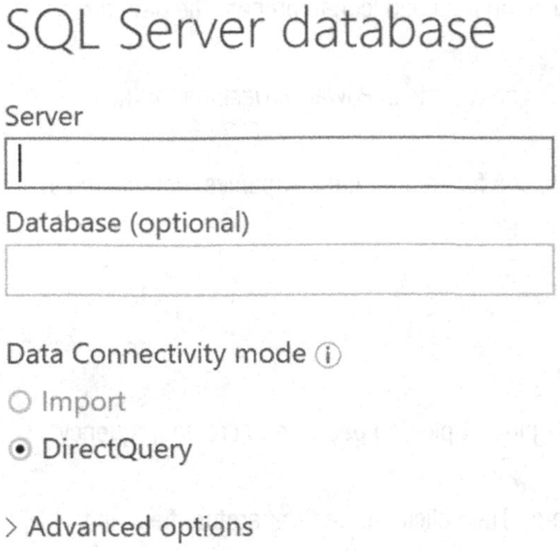

SQL Server database

Server

| |

Database (optional)

| |

Data Connectivity mode ⓘ

○ Import

◉ DirectQuery

› Advanced options

Figure 9-17. *Power BI SQL Server connection information parameters*

Enter the server name for the Azure SQL database in this format: `<YOUR-SERVER-NAME>.database.windows.net`.

It is a good idea to specify `DirectQuery` to get the latest information from the database, rather than `Import`, which creates a snapshot of the data.

Click on the OK icon, and you will see a screen similar to Figure 9-18, where you can select the tables to use with Power BI Desktop.

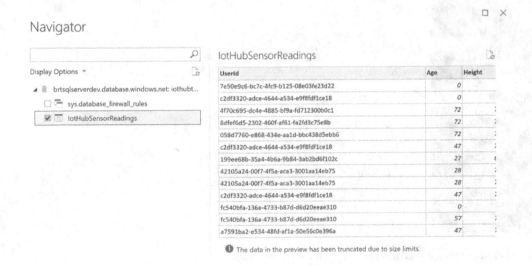

Figure 9-18. *Get Data from Azure SQL database: select table*

Select the [dbo].[IotHubSensorReadings] table and click on the Load icon to prepare the data for use with Power BI Desktop.

At this point, you are ready to start creating visual controls and reports in Power BI Desktop for the reference implementation.

We will create three separate Power BI dashboard reports, one for each of the companies represented in the sample:

- Tall Towers

- The Complicated Badger

- WigiTech

We will use the R Power BI script control along with the ggplot2 R plotting package to create frequency polygon controls.

Click on the R Script control in the Power BI Desktop palette. Then click on the Temperature field and drag it to the Values window for the control.

Right-click on the temperature value and select Average, as shown in Figure 9-19.

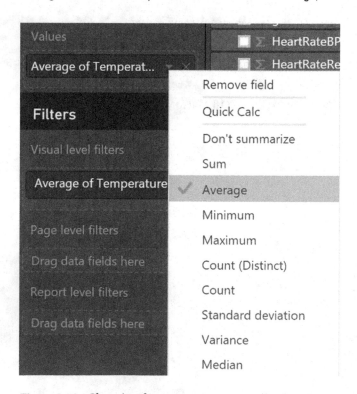

Figure 9-19. *Changing the summarization type for the temperature field*

While the R Script control is still highlighted, right-click on the companyname field and select Add Filter. This will add a new filter control to the report, so that you can filter on each of the three companies in the reference implementation.

After the companyname filter has been added, click on the filter and select Tall Towers, as shown in Figure 9-20.

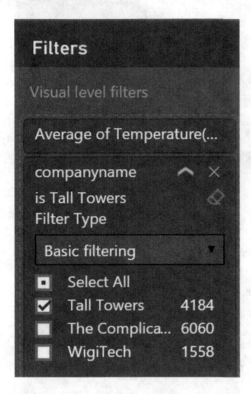

Figure 9-20. *Apply filter criteria to the companyname field*

While you are at it, right-click on the page tab at the bottom of the Power BI designer and select Rename Page. Set the Power BI Report page name to Tall Towers.

Now, you are ready to add the R code to the control. Click on the R Script control and paste the following code into the R editor window:

```
# LOAD the ggplot2 package
library(ggplot2)

# RENDER the ggplot2 Visual
ggplot(data=dataset,aes(x=Temperature)) + geom_freqpoly(color="orange")
```

After you have pasted the R code into the control, click on the arrow ➤ to compile and run the R Script. Your control should render similar to Figure 9-21.

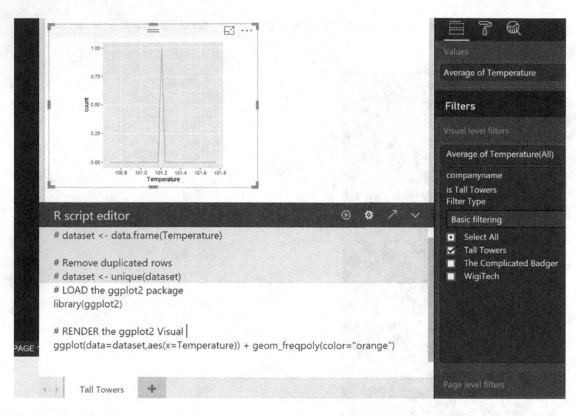

Figure 9-21. *The Power BI R Script control in action, displaying the average temperature for Tall Towers*

Now that you have configured a Power BI R Script control for displaying the average temperature sensor readings for Tall Towers, you can easily repeat the process to create two more R Script controls for HeartRateBPM and BreathingRate. We will use color coding to distinguish the values. Figure 9-22 depicts the completed R Script controls in the Power BI Desktop.

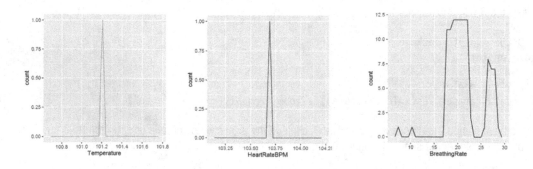

Figure 9-22. *R Script controls rendering frequency plots for various sensor readings*

Before you publish the reports to the Power BI Service, save the Power BI Desktop file as
`TallTower.pbix`.

The reason for providing a descriptive filename is because the next step will be to publish the reports to
the Power BI service and this will be the name that the report is given.

Click on the Publish icon in the top navigation bar, as shown in Figure 9-23.

Figure 9-23. *Publish Power BI Report with custom R controls to the Power BI Service*

After a few moments, you will see a completion window appear, as shown in Figure 9-24.

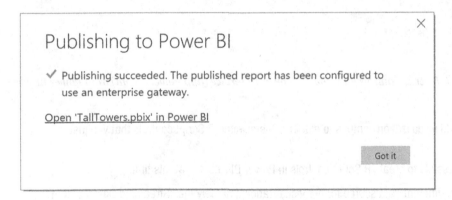

Figure 9-24. *Completion message for publish Power BI report to the Power BI service*

At this point, you can click on the link to Open 'Tall Towers.pbix' in Power BI and it will open a
browser session at the Power BI service located at `http://app.powerbi.com`.

BUILD VISUALIZATIONS USING POWER BI SERVICE FOR REAL-TIME SENSOR READINGS DASHBOARD

After clicking on the link to Open 'Tall Towers.pbix' in Power BI in the last step, you will then be asked for your credentials to gain access to the Power BI app service.

After entering your credentials, you will see that the Power BI Desktop report that we created using R Script controls has been published to the Power BI app service, as shown in Figure 9-25.

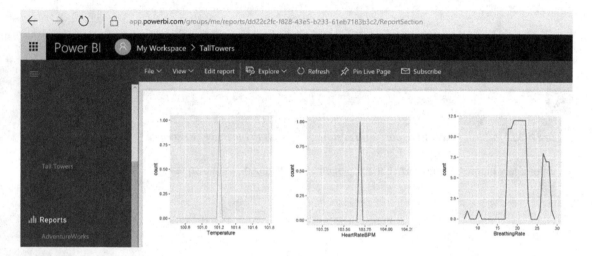

Figure 9-25. *Report with R Script controls published to Power BI service (app.powerbi.com) from Power BI Desktop*

The next step is to add visualization controls to enhance the existing R Script controls that you just uploaded.

Note that it is only possible to create R Script controls in Power BI Desktop at this time.

We will want to use a different data source for our visualizations, namely the "Streaming Dataset" that was populated by the Azure Stream Analytics job you previously modified in this chapter.

Click on the bottom-left navigation bar while in the Power BI app service and click on the Streaming Datasets option, as shown in Figure 9-26.

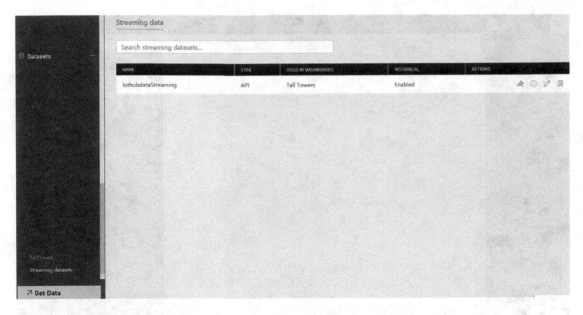

Figure 9-26. *Bottom-left navigation bar to access streaming datasets from the Power BI service*

A list will appear containing the streaming datasets that have already been created. If you have never started your Azure Stream Analytics job nor processed any data (using the simulator, for example), this list may be empty. If that is the case, feel free to skip ahead to the section on running the simulator, and then return to this section to see dataset populated here.

Click on the Create Report icon for the streaming dataset named `iothubdataStreaming`, as shown in Figure 9-27.

Figure 9-27. *Power BI Service streaming datasets, Create Report icon*

Next, the Power BI designer surface load and populate with the dataset that is being output from the Stream Analytics job in real time.

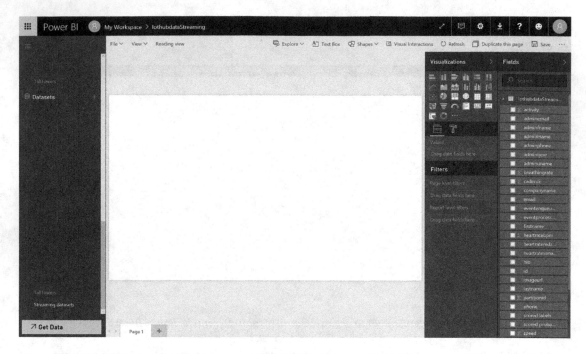

Figure 9-28. *Power BI App Service Designer with iothubdataStreaming dataset*

The first Power BI control we will make will be a real-time sensor gauge showing the average temperature of the team members from the Tall Towers organization.

Click on the gauge control in the Power BI control palette. This populates the designer surface with a new control. Next, click on the temperature field, and it will automatically display in the gauge. Note though, that by default, it shows the sum of the temperature field.

To change this, right-click on the temperature field in the Value area and then select Average. The gauge control will then display the average for the temperature sensor readings processed so far.

The next thing you need to do is add a filter for the correct company. Right-click on the companyname field in the list of dataset fields and select the Add Filter option. This will append a filter control under the properties for the gauge control. Adjust the filter properties to only show data for Tall Towers.

Next, set the color of this gauge control for the temperature sensor to match the previous R Script control, which was rendered in orange.

To do this, simply click on the Paint Roller Brush icon under the properties for the gauge control. Expand the Data Colors property and then choose an orange color for the fill value.

At this point, your Power BI Gauge control should look similar to the one in Figure 9-29.

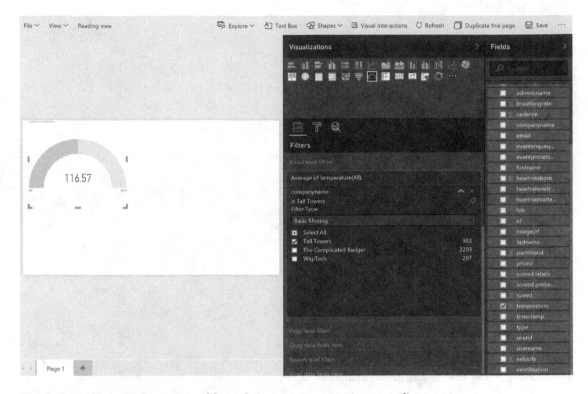

Figure 9-29. *Power BI Gauge control for real-time average temperature reading*

Next, rename the current page by right-clicking on the page tab, selecting the option to Rename Page, and changing it to `Tall Towers Real-Time`.

Click on the Save icon in the top-right navigation bar and you will be prompted to enter a name for your report so it can be saved. Enter `Tall Towers Real-Time`.

Now you will add this gauge control to the Tall Towers dashboard by clicking on the Pin Visual icon in the top-right corner of the gauge control, as illustrated in Figure 9-30.

Figure 9-30. *Power BI app service Pin Visual icon*

After clicking on the Pin Visual icon, you will then be presented with an option to select the dashboard to pin the control to, as shown in Figure 9-31.

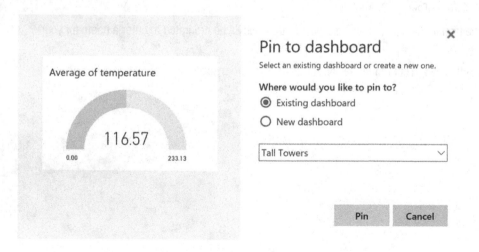

Figure 9-31. *Select Power BI dashboard to pin control to*

The Tall Towers dashboard should already exist since you published the dashboard from Power BI Desktop. Select this option (if available) or you can create a new dashboard.

This will add the gauge control to the existing Tall Towers dashboard with the three R Script controls for the sensor readings.

Repeat the previous steps to create two additional gauge controls for HeartRateBPM and BreathingRate, apply a color theme, and pin the gauge visuals to the Tall Towers dashboard.

At this point, the Tall Towers dashboard should look like Figure 9-32.

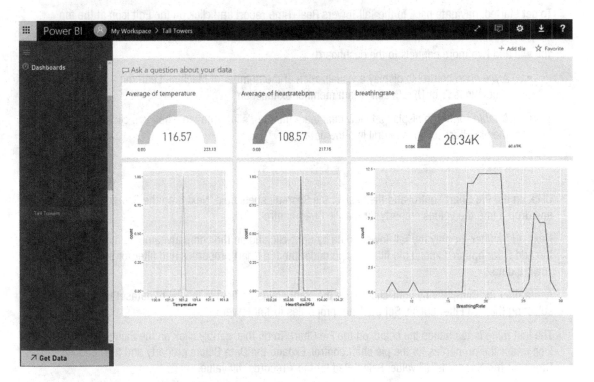

Figure 9-32. Power BI dashboard for Tall Towers

Note that gauge controls on the top row of the Tall Towers dashboard represent real-time data, the hot data path that is being streamed directly into the Power BI service from the Stream Analytics service.

The R Script controls located below the gauge controls in Figure 9-32 are based on data from an Azure SQL database that is also populated from the Stream Analytics service. This data is considered warm due to increased latencies associated with data retrieved from a relational database.

In this way, you have created a dashboard for Tall Towers that displays both real-time and batch KPI metrics.

BUILD POWER BI VISUALIZATIONS FOR MACHINE LEARNING PREDICTIONS

We need to configure one more set of Power BI visualizations to convey the Machine Learning Web Service predictions for exhausted team members.

To get started, navigate back to the Tall Towers Real-Time report and click on the Edit icon at the top navigation bar.

You will add two more controls to the dashboard:

- A *pie chart* control to display a visualization of the number of Machine Learning predictions (Y or N) reflecting team member exhaustion.

- A *table* control to display an individual team member's information when you click on the pie chart sections to drill into the data.

Pie Chart Control

Click on the Pie Chart control and then select the Scored Labels field. Next drag the Scored Labels field and drop it into the Values property for the Pie Chart control.

Next, add a filter for only the Tall Towers data by right-clicking on the companyname field and selecting the Add Filter option. Expand the filter setting under the Pie Chart properties and filter for only the Tall Towers data.

Add a filter for Company by right-clicking on the companyname field in the list of dataset fields and then selecting the Add Filter option. Set the Filter properties to Tall Towers.

The last thing is to change the colors on the Pie Chart. To do this, simply click on the Paint Roller Brush icon under the properties for the pie chart control. Expand the Data Colors property and then choose Green for the N records' fill value. Select Red for the Y records' fill value.

Table Control

Start by clicking on the Table control and then select the following fields to display in the control:

- timestamp
- scored labels
- firstname
- lastname
- breathingrate
- heartrateBPM
- temperature

- velocity

- speed

- phone

- adminemail

- adminphone

Next, add a filter for only the Tall Towers data by right-clicking on the companyname field in the list of dataset fields and then selecting the Add Filter option. Set the Filter properties to Tall Towers.

At this point, the new Pie Chart and Table controls should resemble Figure 9-33.

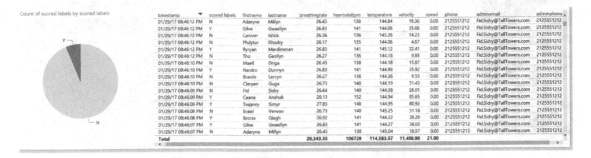

Figure 9-33. *Power BI pie chart and table display for Machine Learning prediction*

A few things are noteworthy about how these controls automatically interact:

- The Pie Chart control and the Table control work together via the filter properties.

  - If you click on the green portion of the pie chart, the data in the Table control is automatically filtered to only records with an N prediction in the Scored Labels field.

  - If you click on the red portion of the pie chart, the data in the Table control is automatically filtered to only records with a Y prediction in the Scored Labels field.

  - If you click anywhere outside of the Pie Chart control, you will see all the data displayed in the Table control.

Next, save the Power BI report and pin the Pie Chart and the Table controls to the Tall Towers dashboard.

You can then rearrange and resize the controls on the Power BI dashboard for Tall Towers to make the display visually appealing. Figure 9-34 depicts the updated dashboard for Tall Towers.

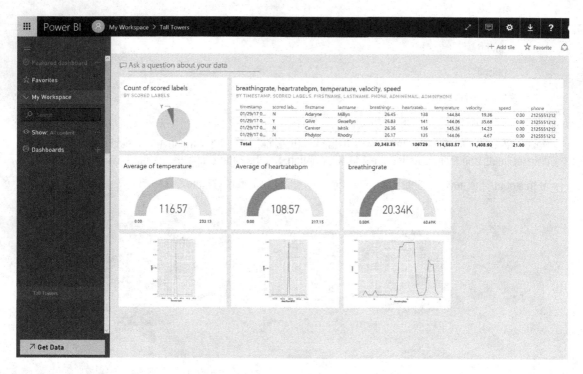

Figure 9-34. *The completed Power BI dashboard view for Tall Towers*

Power BI Q&A

Recall that Power BI has a powerful feature called Q&A that you can use to "ask" questions of your data. To start using Power BI's natural language query feature, simply type in the Q&A window at the top of the Power BI dashboard. You can see the Q&A window at the top of the dashboard depicted in Figure 9-34.

Power BI Q&A recognizes words as you them type and figures out field names and in which datasets to find the answers. Q&A helps you form your natural language questions with auto-completion, re-statement, and other textual aids.

To demonstrate how Q&A works, let's say that you want to see the names of team members who have been predicted to be at risk of physical exhaustion.

You can simply type in the following statement in the Power BI Q&A window at the top of the dashboard:

```
which firstname, lastname, adminemail, adminphone has scored label = Y
```

When you stop typing, Power BI Q&A immediately returns the answers shown in Figure 9-35.

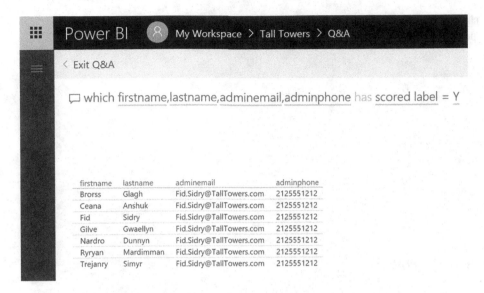

Figure 9-35. *The Power BI Q&A natural language query results*

Note that in addition to having the critical information about the team members, you also have the administrator's e-mail and phone number for each team member with a positive prediction.

You will use this information in the next section to trigger an automatic alert to the admin using Azure Functions.

■ **Note**   You can learn more about Power BI Q&A at: Ask questions of your data using natural language: https://powerbi.microsoft.com/en-us/documentation/powerbi-service-how-to-use-q-and-a/.

Power BI Alerts

Power BI also has the ability to configure alerts to receive notifications when critical business KPIs and key metrics exceed thresholds that you set.

Only you can see the data alerts you set, even if you share a dashboard with someone else. Alerts only work for Power BI controls that display a single number, such as a "card" or "gauge" control.

This will work perfectly for this reference implementation, since you configured three individual gauge controls in your dashboard to monitor the average temperature, heart rate, and breathing rates of team members.

To get started, click on the three dots (or ellipses) at the top-right corner of the gauge control you created for temperature. You will then see an Alert icon, as shown in Figure 9-36.

Figure 9-36. *Configure Power BI alerts*

After you click on the Alert icon, you will see a new window where you can add a new alert rule. Figure 9-37 depicts the properties you can set for a new alert rule.

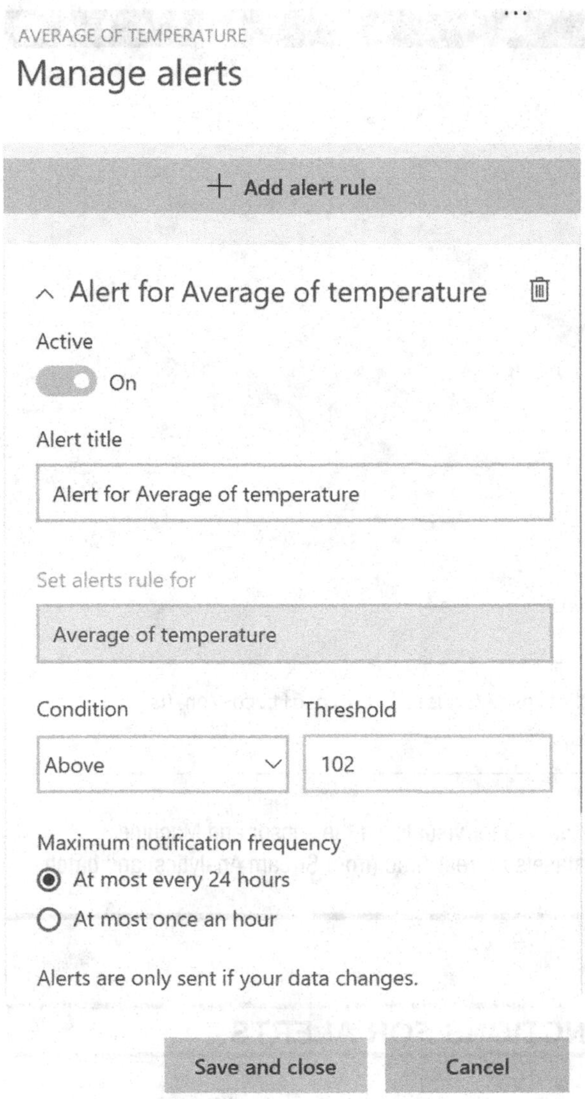

···

AVERAGE OF TEMPERATURE

Manage alerts

+ Add alert rule

∧ Alert for Average of temperature 🗑

Active

⬤ On

Alert title

Alert for Average of temperature

Set alerts rule for

Average of temperature

Condition	Threshold
Above ∨	102

Maximum notification frequency

◉ At most every 24 hours

○ At most once an hour

Alerts are only sent if your data changes.

Save and close   **Cancel**

Figure 9-37. *Power BI alerts: add new alert rule properties*

After you have set alerts for your dashboard controls, you will receive notifications via the Power BI notification center, as shown on the right in Figure 9-38.

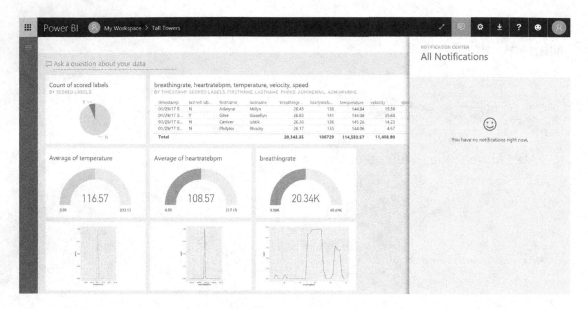

Figure 9-38. *The Power BI notification center window*

■ **Note**   See this link for more about Power BI alerts: `https://powerbi.microsoft.com/en-us/`
`documentation/powerbi-service-set-data-alerts/`.

At this point, you have completed the Power BI dashboard for visualizing the sensor and Machine
Learning data. In this dashboard, you combined datasets for real-time (from Stream Analytics) and batch
(from Azure SQL Database) data sources.

CREATE AZURE FUNCTIONS FOR ALERTS

In this section, we cover the implementation of Azure Functions to send alerts and notifications for the
reference implementation.

Recall that earlier in this chapter, you added a new Azure Event Hub to hold alert notifications that were
generated by the predictions from your Machine Learning Web Service.

You then modified the Stream Analytics query to output notification messages to the event hub if the
prediction was Y.

Reference Implementation Scenario

In the reference implementation, you will be sending alerts to the administrator in charge of each team
member for a specific company.

When you modified the Streaming Analytics query, you inserted SQL-like code that performed a JOIN operation to obtain the team members' administrator information:

```
JOIN [input-refdata-team] AD
    ON RF.companyname = AD.companyname
WHERE   SQ.result.[Scored labels] = 'Y'
    AND AD.type = '2'
```

As as result of the JOIN clause, you had access to the following fields in the query:

```
AD.firstname as [adminfname],
AD.lastname as [adminlname],
AD.username as [adminuname],
    AD.type as [admintype],
    AD.phone as [adminphone],
    AD.email as [adminemail]
```

Figure 9-39 is an updated view of Figure 9-35 that highlights the team members' administrator information that was returned as a result of the Q&A query.

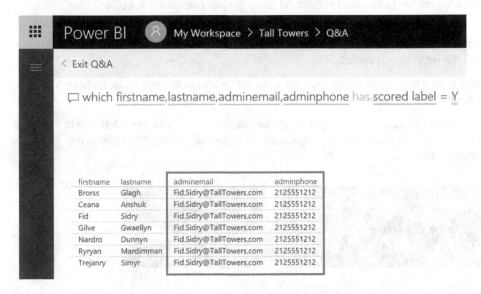

Figure 9-39. *Power BI Q&A displaying administrator information in the returned dataset*

This information is the basis for sending alert messages, and you will send SMS text notifications to administrators for immediate action. As a backup, you'll also send a high-priority e-mail. Each of these notification scenarios will be implemented using Azure Functions.

Create Azure Function to Send Text Alerts via Twilio

The first Azure Function you create is for sending SMS text messages. One of the output bindings available in Azure Functions is via Twilio, a third-party cloud communications platform for building voice and messaging applications via a ReST API. Twilio has a robust API for sending SMS text messages.

■ **Note**   For more information, see this link: Azure Functions Twilio output binding: `https://docs.microsoft.com/en-us/azure/azure-functions/functions-bindings-twilio`.

To register for free developer access, visit `www.twilio.com` to get a free API key.

Note that there are two sets of credentials granted, one for live credentials and one for testing. You need to record your information for the following test credentials:

- Account SID
- Account Token

In addition, be sure to read the Twilio documentation for using the test credentials at `https://www.twilio.com/docs/api/rest/test-credentials`.

One big takeaway from the previous link is that there are special "magic" phone numbers you can use when testing with the Twilio test credentials.

It is also important to note that a real SMS text message will not be sent to any real phone number while using the Twilio test credentials.

To get started, navigate to the Azure resource group for your solution and click on the + Add icon to add another Azure service. Type `Function App` in the search bar. You will see results similar to the screenshot in Figure 9-40.

Figure 9-40. *Adding a new Azure Function app to a resource group*

Click on Function App and you will then see a confirmation screen like the one in Figure 9-41.

Figure 9-41. *Function app confirmation page*

Click on the Create icon at the bottom left and then you will see a blade appear. This blade will prompt you to enter the properties required to create your Azure Function, as illustrated in Figure 9-42.

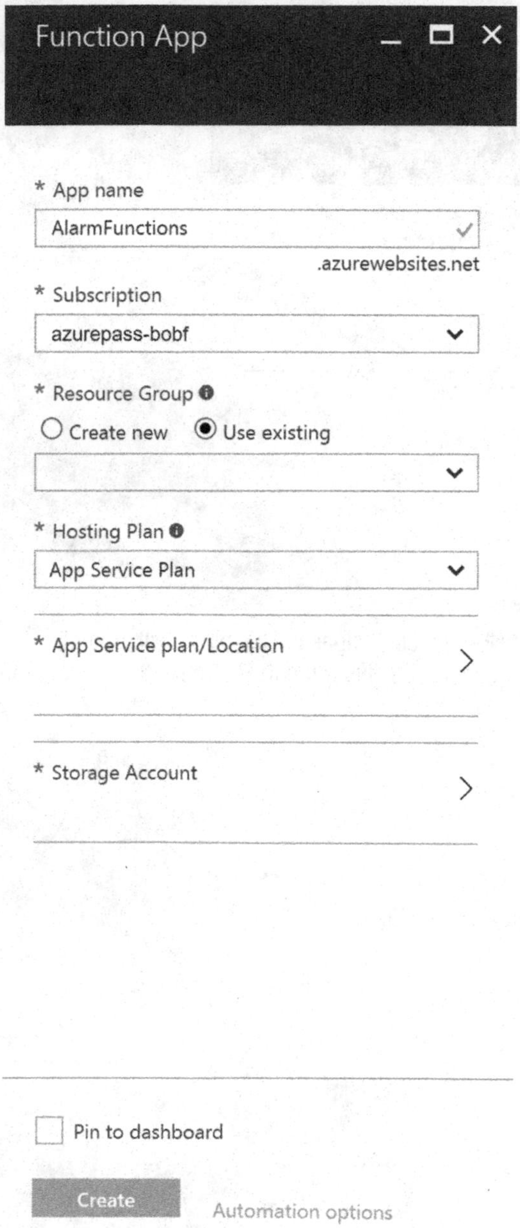

Function App — ▢ ✕

* App name

AlarmFunctions ✓

.azurewebsites.net

* Subscription

azurepass-bobf ⌄

* Resource Group ❶

○ Create new   ◉ Use existing

⌄

* Hosting Plan ❶

App Service Plan ⌄

* App Service plan/Location

⟩

* Storage Account

⟩

☐ Pin to dashboard

Create   Automation options

Figure 9-42. *Create new Azure Function parameters*

After your Azure Function has been provisioned in your resource group, you can navigate to the new Azure Function blade, as depicted in Figure 9-43.

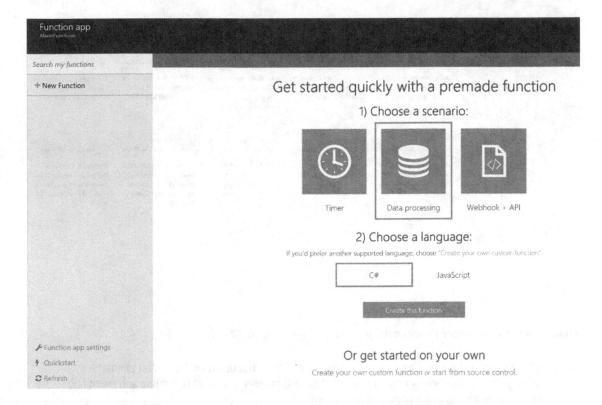

Figure 9-43. *Azure Function blade*

Note that the main screen contains a wizard to help guide you through creating a new function using function templates for common scenarios.

Click on the + New Function icon to add a new Azure Function.

Next, you will see a screen similar to Figure 9-44, where Data Processing has been selected in the drop-down filter for the Scenario template.

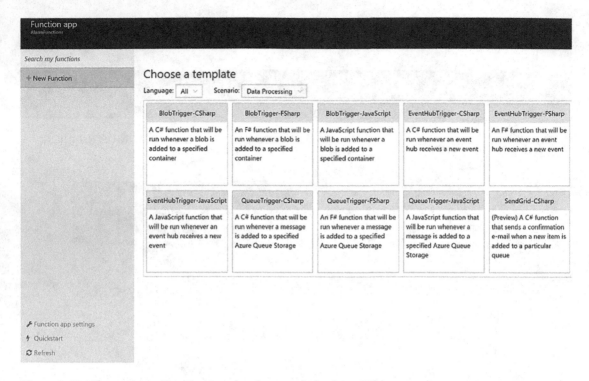

Figure 9-44. *Choose Azure Function template for event hub trigger CSharp*

Select the scenario for EventHubTrigger-CSharp and then scroll down on the screen to enter a name for your new function. Note that you will also need to enter the event hub name and event hub connection information at the bottom of the screen.

After you have entered the required parameters, click on the Create button. You will then see a screen similar to Figure 9-45.

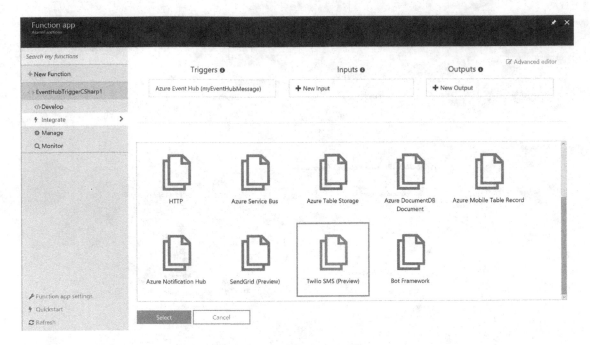

Figure 9-45. *Adding an output binding for Twilio SMS text messaging*

The first thing you need to do is add a new output for the event hub trigger function. To do this, click on the Integrate option on the left navigation bar. Then click on the + New Output icon on the top-left of the screen to add a new output.

Scroll all the way down until you see Twilio SMS (Preview) and select that tile, as shown in Figure 9-45.

Then click on the Select command at the bottom of the screen. You will then be presented with a screen similar to Figure 9-46. Here, you will set specific parameters for the event hub trigger function.

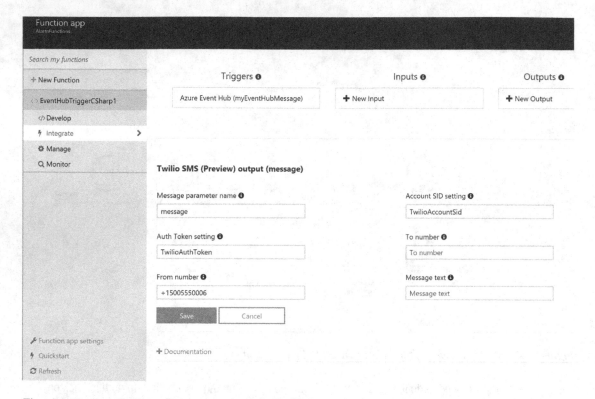

Figure 9-46. *Function integration parameters for Twilio integration*

Enter the following parameter values:

- *Message Parameter Name*: message

  - Note: This value *must* match the value in the function.

- *Auth Token Setting*: TwilioAuthToken

  - Note: This is only a variable name for an app setting variable that will hold the actual value.

- *From Number*: +15005550006

  - Note: This is a magic Twilio number used for sending SMS texts with test credentials.

- *Account SID Setting*: TwilioAccountSid

  - Note: This is only a variable name for an app setting variable that will hold the actual value.

- *To Number*: Leave blank, as you will populate it via code.

- *Message Text*: Leave blank, as you will populate it via code.

Click on the Save command at the bottom after you have entered the required parameters.

The next step is to create app settings for the two new variables you will use to hold the Twilio credentials.

To do this, click on the Function App Settings link on the bottom-left side navigation pane.

Next, you will see a screen similar to Figure 9-47, where you can view and update all the relevant settings for this Azure Function.

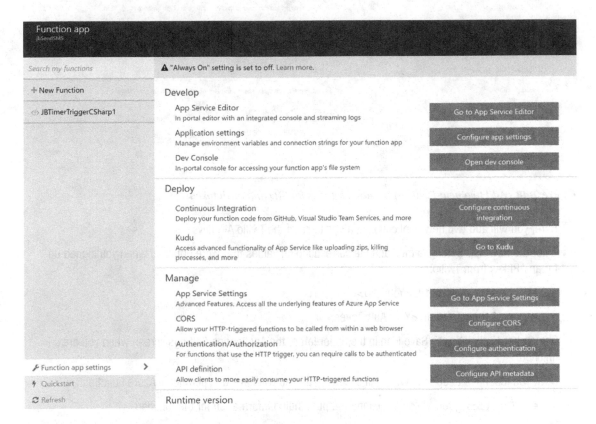

Figure 9-47. Configure application settings

Since you need to add two app setting variables to hold the Twilio SID and authentication token, click on the link for Configure App Settings.

This will take you to the Application Settings pane for your Azure Function. The screen should appear similar to Figure 9-48.

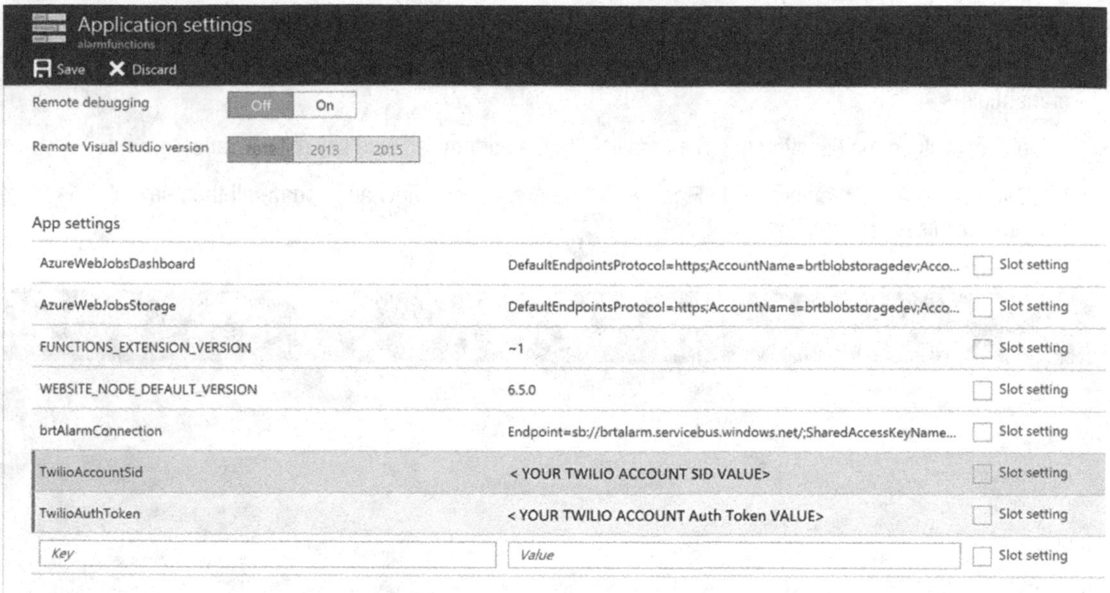

Figure 9-48. *Add two new Twilio application settings for SID and auth token*

Here, you will add two new application settings to store the Twilio API keys.

Enter the new App Setting names and the corresponding values that were obtained when you signed up for an API key from Twilio:

- TwilioAccountSid: <Your SID>

- TwilioAuthToken: <Your Auth Token>

Remember to click on the Save icon in the upper left of the Application Settings screen when you are finished.

Now, you just have to update two small code file and you will have an operational Azure Function:

- Function.json: Holds basic input/output binding information for the function.

- Run.csx: Contains the C# code that will be run when the function is triggered which, in this case, is whenever a new item is added to the event hub to signal an alarm condition.

To update the code for the Function.json file, click on the </>Develop icon on the left navigation bar.

To make the file visible for editing, you must click on the View Files icon on the top right navigation bar. You will then be able to view the files associated with the function.

Click on the Function.json file and it will open in the editor window.

Replace the existing code with the following JSON code and then click on the Save command to save the file.

```json
{
  "bindings": [
    {
      "type": "eventHubTrigger",
      "name": "myEventHubMessage",
      "direction": "in",
      "path": "brtalarm",
      "connection": "brtalarm2nd"
    },
    {
      "type": "twilioSms",
      "name": "message",
      "accountSid": "TwilioAccountSid",
      "authToken": "TwilioAuthToken",
      "from": "+15005550006",
      "direction": "out"
    }
  ],
  "disabled": false
}
```

Code: Function.json

Figure 9-49 depicts the entire Function.json code in the editor window.

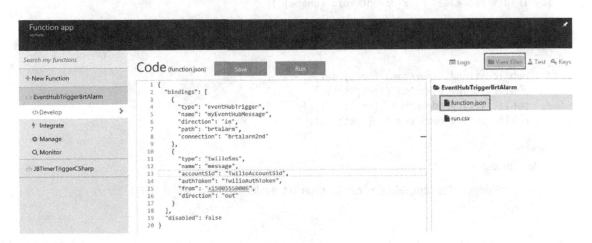

Figure 9-49. *New Azure Function code for Function.json*

Next, click on the run.csx file, and it will open the contents of the existing file into the editor window.

Replace the existing code with the following C# code and then click on the Save command at the top of the screen to save the file.

```csharp
#r "Microsoft.ServiceBus"
#r "Newtonsoft.Json"
#r "Twilio.Api"

using System;
using Microsoft.ServiceBus.Messaging;
using Newtonsoft.Json;
using Twilio;

public static void Run(string myEventHubMessage, out SMSMessage message, TraceWriter
log)
{
string jsonContent = myEventHubMessage.ToString();
var alert = JsonConvert.DeserializeObject<EventHubData>(jsonContent);

string eventtime = alert.timerstamp;
string uname = alert.username;
string adminph = alert.adminphone;

message = new SMSMessage();
message.Body = "Team Member " + uname + " Exhaustion Alert at: " + eventtime;
message.From = "+15005550006";
message.To = adminph;

log.Info($"Processed ALERT Event for: {uname}");

}
public class EventHubData
{
    public string timerstamp { get; set; }
    public string username { get; set; }
    public string adminphone { get; set; }
    public string adminemail  { get; set; }
}
```

Code: run.csx

Figure 9-50 depicts the complete run.csx C# code in the editor window.

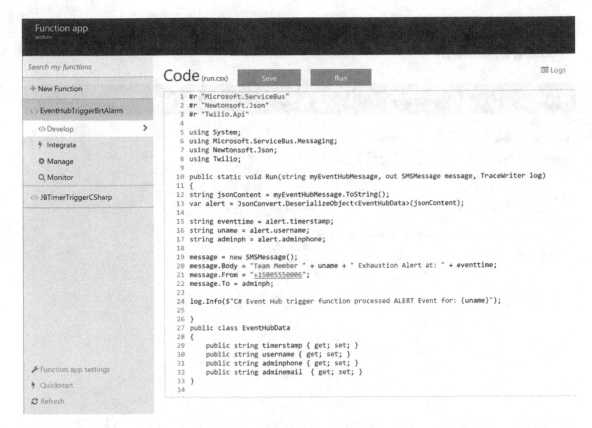

Figure 9-50. *New Azure Function C# code for run.csx in the editor window*

Recall that messages to this event hub are generated from the Azure Stream Analytics Query job that you defined earlier in the chapter. In that job, you defined SQL-like logic to output an alert message to the event hub if the web service predicted a team member is at physical exhaustion levels.

Note that in the function, we defined a class named EventHubData to describe the layout of the incoming event hub message.

We will use this class to deserialize the JSON string that is passed from the event hub. This is so that you can retrieve the specific message fields that are needed to send an SMS text message to the administrator who is responsible for that specific team member.

Create Azure Function to Send E-Mail Alert via SendGrid

The next step is to extend the existing function to send an e-mail to the team member's administrator.

To do this, you will add an output for SendGrid and then modify the code in the two Azure Functions code files (Function.json and run.csx) to handle the additional outbound connection and logic.

To leverage SendGrid to send e-mails, you need to first register for a free developer API key at www.SendGrid.com.

Once you have your SendGrid key, click on the Integrate option on the left navigation bar of the Azure Function Editor blade. Then click on the +New Output icon in the top-right corner of the screen, as depicted in Figure 9-51.

Figure 9-51. *Azure Function Integrate option, add new output*

Scroll all the way down to the bottom and select the option for SendGrid (Preview) and click on Select, as depicted in Figure 9-52.

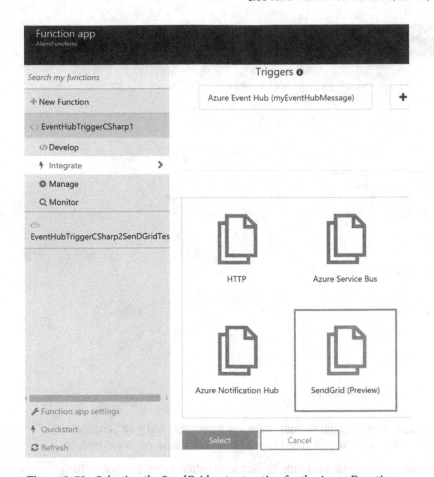

Figure 9-52. *Selecting the SendGrid output option for the Azure Function*

After clicking on the Select button in Figure 9-52, you will next see a screen similar to Figure 9-53, where you can enter specific information to configure the output binding for SendGrid.

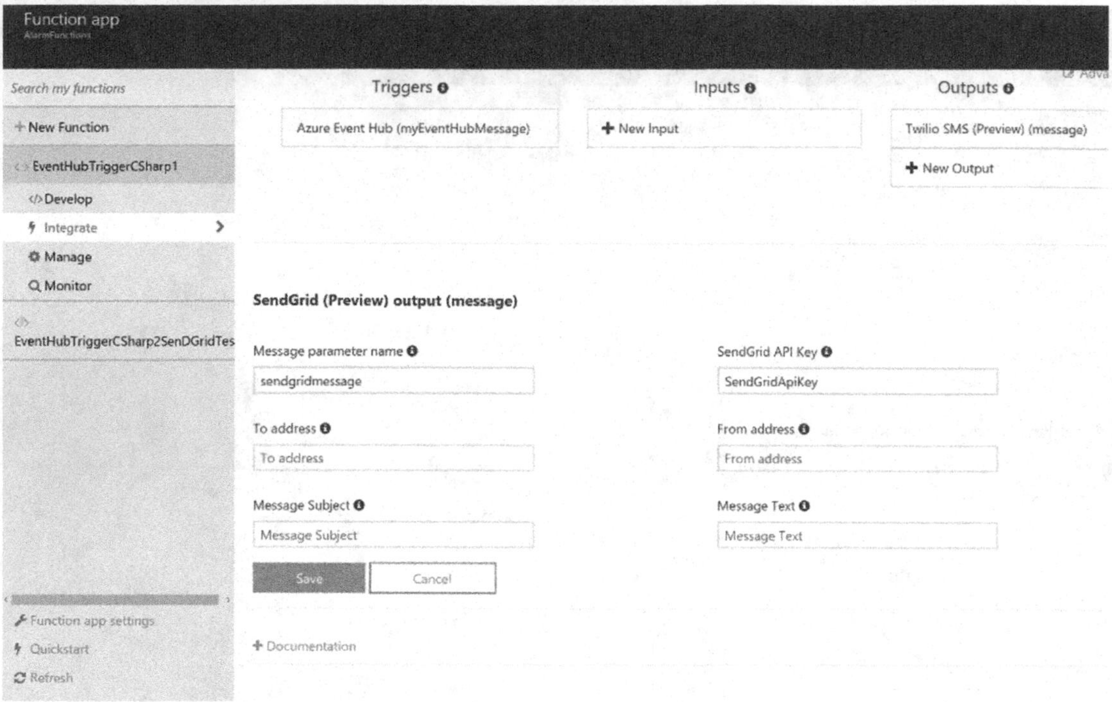

Figure 9-53. *Add new output SendGrid parameters*

All you need to populate here is a different name for your "message parameter" and your SendGrid API key. We will populate the remaining fields from C# code in the function. Click Save when you're done.

To update the code for the `Function.json` file to include the SendGrid output definition, click on the </>Develop icon on the left navigation bar.

Next, click on the View Files icon on the top right navigation bar in order to make the files visible for editing. Click on the `Function.json` file and it will open the contents of the existing file into the editor window.

Replace the existing code with the following JSON code and then click on the Save command to save the file.

```
{
  "bindings": [
    {
      "type": "eventHubTrigger",
      "name": "myEventHubMessage",
      "direction": "in",
      "path": "brtalarm",
      "connection": "brtAlarmConnection"
    },
    {
      "type": "twilioSms",
      "name": "message",
```

```
      "accountSid": "TwilioAccountSid",
      "authToken": "TwilioAuthToken",
      "from": "+15005550006",
      "direction": "out"
    },
    {
      "type": "sendGrid",
      "name": "sendgridmessage",
      "apiKey": "SendGridApiKey",
      "from": "AzureAlerts@TallTowers.com",
      "direction": "out"
    }
  ],
  "disabled": false
}
```

Code: `Function.json`

Next, click on the `run.csx` file and it will open the contents of the existing file into the editor window.

Replace the existing code with the following C# code and then click on the Save command at the top of the screen to save the updated C# file.

```csharp
#r "Microsoft.ServiceBus"
#r "Newtonsoft.Json"
#r "Twilio.Api"
#r "SendGrid"
#r "Microsoft.Azure.WebJobs.Extensions.SendGrid"
using System;
using Microsoft.ServiceBus.Messaging;
using Newtonsoft.Json;
using Twilio;
using SendGrid;
using SendGrid.Helpers.Mail;

public static void Run(string myEventHubMessage, out SMSMessage message, out Mail
sendgridmessage, TraceWriter log)
{
string jsonContent = myEventHubMessage.ToString();
var alert = JsonConvert.DeserializeObject<EventHubData>(jsonContent);
string eventtime = alert.timerstamp;
string uname = alert.username;
string adminph = alert.adminphone;
string admemail = alert.adminemail;

//Send SMS TEXT ALERT via Twilio API
message = new SMSMessage();
message.Body = "Team Member " + uname + " Exhaustion Alert at: " + eventtime;
message.From = "+15005550006";
message.To = adminph;

//Send EMAIL ALERT via SendGrid API
var personalization = new Personalization();
```

```
personalization.AddTo(new Email(admemail));
string subject = "ALERT NOTIFICATION - Team Member " + uname + " Exhaustion Alert
received at: " + eventtime;
var messageContent = new Content("text/html", "ALERT NOTIFICATION - Team Member " +
uname + " Exhaustion Alert received at: " + eventtime);

sendgridmessage = new Mail();
sendgridmessage.Subject = subject;
sendgridmessage.AddContent(messageContent);
sendgridmessage.AddPersonalization(personalization);

log.Info($"Processed ALERT Event for: {uname}");
}
public class EventHubData
{
    public string timerstamp { get; set; }
    public string username   { get; set; }
    public string adminphone { get; set; }
    public string adminemail { get; set; }
}
```

Code: `run.csx`

The next thing you need to do is add a new Application Configuration setting for the SendGridAPI key. It must match the same name as the one used in the `Function.json` file, which was `SendGridApiKey`.

Start by navigating to your Azure Function via the portal and then click on the link for Function App Settings on the bottom left of the screen.

Next, click on the Application Settings command. This will take you to the Application Settings pane for your Azure Function. The screen should appear similar to Figure 9-54.

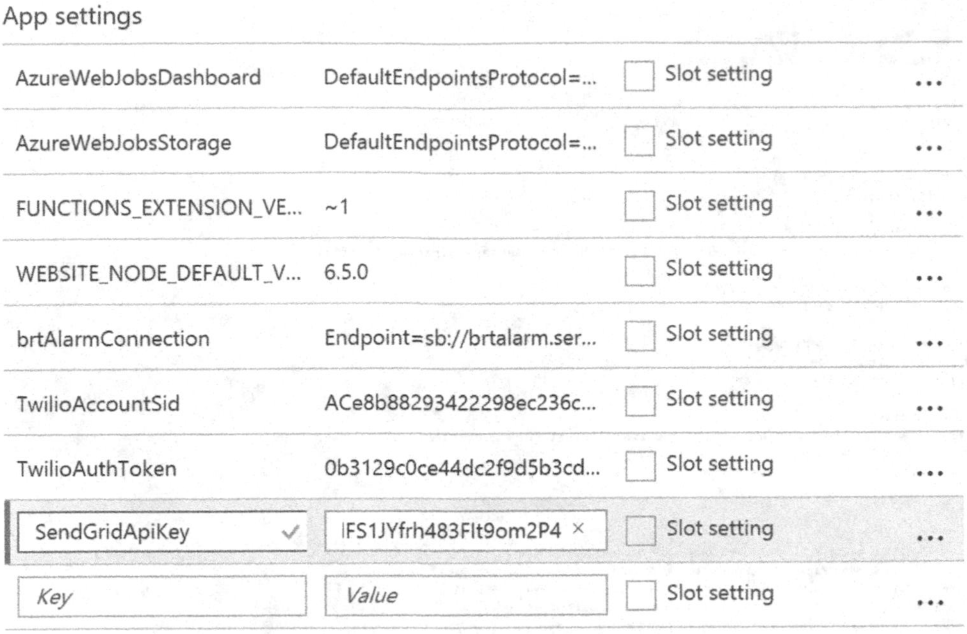

App settings

AzureWebJobsDashboard	DefaultEndpointsProtocol=...	☐ Slot setting	...
AzureWebJobsStorage	DefaultEndpointsProtocol=...	☐ Slot setting	...
FUNCTIONS_EXTENSION_VE...	~1	☐ Slot setting	...
WEBSITE_NODE_DEFAULT_V...	6.5.0	☐ Slot setting	...
brtAlarmConnection	Endpoint=sb://brtalarm.ser...	☐ Slot setting	...
TwilioAccountSid	ACe8b88293422298ec236c...	☐ Slot setting	...
TwilioAuthToken	0b3129c0ce44dc2f9d5b3cd...	☐ Slot setting	...
SendGridApiKey ✓	IFS1JYfrh483Flt9om2P4 ✕	☐ Slot setting	...
Key	Value	☐ Slot setting	...

Figure 9-54. *Adding a new app setting for SendGridAPIKey*

Here, you will add a new application setting to store the SendGrid API key.

Enter the new App Setting ID as `SendGridAPIKey` and your corresponding API key as the value.

Remember to click on the Save icon in the upper left of the Application Settings pane when you are finished.

Monitoring Azure Functions

After you have completed configuring your Azure Function bindings and logic, there are a few ways you can monitor your function.

You can get direct feedback about how your function is running is via the Logs display, which is visible underneath the code editor window in Figure 9-55.

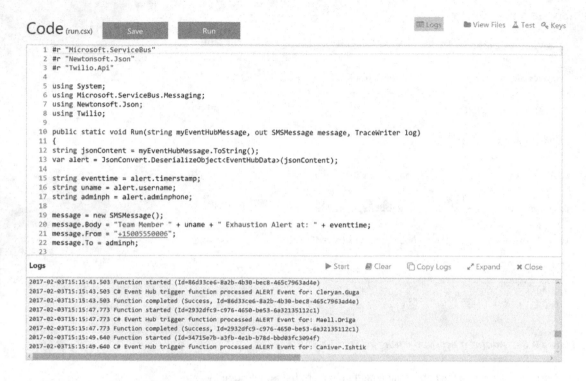

Figure 9-55. *Azure Function Logs window displaying real-time logging output*

Note that you can see the output from the `log.Info()` command such as the one you used in the C# function:

```
log.Info($"Processed ALERT Event for: {uname}");
```

Another method is to use the built-in monitoring tool in the Azure Portal for Azure Functions.

Start by clicking on the Monitor icon on the left navigation bar on the Azure Function blade. Next, you will see a list of all the events and logging output messages that have been generated by this Azure Function call.

Figure 9-56 shows a screenshot of the Azure Function monitoring window.

Figure 9-56. *Azure Functions: monitoring function events*

If you click on an event for a function, you will see a panel that displays the invocation details about the function call.

Figure 9-57 depicts a sample invocation panel for a selected Azure Function event call.

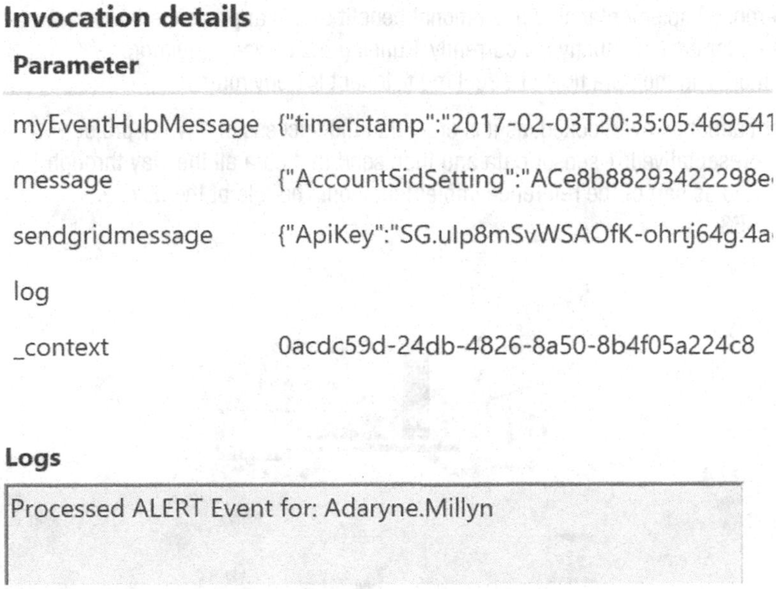

Invocation details

Parameter

myEventHubMessage	{"timerstamp":"2017-02-03T20:35:05.469541
message	{"AccountSidSetting":"ACe8b88293422298e
sendgridmessage	{"ApiKey":"SG.uIp8mSvWSAOfK-ohrtj64g.4a
log	
_context	0acdc59d-24db-4826-8a50-8b4f05a224c8

Logs

Processed ALERT Event for: Adaryne.Millyn

Figure 9-57. *Viewing invocation details for an event*

Note that the Parameter and Logs data displayed in Figure 9-57 can be extremely useful for resolving configuration data or debugging C# programming statements.

RUN SIMULATOR

Hidden within the deep, dark depths of the GitHub repository for this book is a highly useful C# console application that can act as a effective device "simulator" in lieu of real sensor devices, live team members, and actual commercial heavy equipment.

The device simulator is highly useful for generating realistic sensor data for (15) team members for each of the three business entities in the reference implementation.

The business entities are well-known in limited circles and listed here for your reference:

- Complicated Badger

- Tall Towers

- WigiTech

The Github folder path to the device simulator C# code is

```
\devices\device-teamsim
```

After this point in the folder path, you will see three different code paths in the repository—one for each business entity.

This is so that the device simulator for each entity can be then further customized to accommodate each business entity in the reference implementation. An additional benefit of this approach is that you can run the device simulators for each company concurrently. Running the device simulators concurrently helps to facilitate modeling the data flow of a real multi-tenant IoT environment.

The role of the device simulator cannot be over looked, as it is crucial to the success of any IoT project. It is the best way to generate representative IoT sensor data and then send that data all the way through the Azure solution you have created as part of the reference implementation. The role of the device simulator is reflected in Figure 9-58.

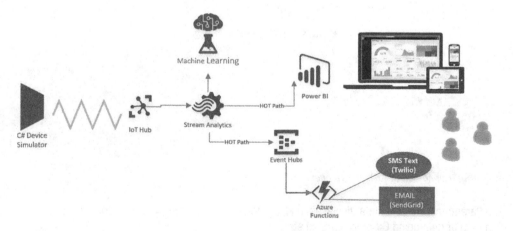

Figure 9-58. *The device simulator role in the reference architecture*

Simulate Sensor Stress Conditions with BRZRKR Mode

One of the primary benefits of the reference implementation solution is the ability to detect issues and automatically send alert notifications.

To that end, the focus of the Power BI dashboard and the alerts and notifications have been on generating visualizations and alerts for these abnormal conditions.

In order to mimic this, there is a feature called BRZRKR mode that can be adjusted to suit your environment. Figure 9-59 illustrates a code fragment in the SendTelemetry function to adjust the BRZRKR mode setting.

```
private static void SendTelemetry(Teammate teammate)
{
    var rowindex = 0;

    const double brzrkr = 1.5; // inflate readings to quickly simulate alarm conditions
```

Figure 9-59. *The Device Simulator BRZKR mode*

To get started, open the C# device simulator project in Visual Studio 2015. Open the Tall Towers solution, which can be found at the following folder location in the GitHub repository: devices\device-teamsim\ talltowers.

Check the Settings in the app.config file to make sure they match your environment. Then you can build and run the simulator. See Figure 9-60.

```
Simulating teammate1
   Profile Id : 8dfef6d5-2302-460f-af61-fa2fd3c75e8b
   Device Id  : 537cfd35-1d39-4aeb-bf45-0ef6faaf300c
Simulating teammate2
   Profile Id : a7591ba2-e534-48fd-af1a-50e56c0e396a
   Device Id  : 2aadb103-fae8-4d84-a07b-15ed48e33a55
Simulating teammate3
   Profile Id : a8569261-b13a-421f-938c-81adef612e25
   Device Id  : bfc37538-9800-4d56-b1da-6ba9a9453f23
Simulating teammate4
   Profile Id : fd36c995-e599-4bc3-8c28-0d5b6fe54624
   Device Id  : bf8e2539-1a0d-4642-94ea-088a44ab0b3f
Simulating teammate5
   Profile Id : 33e37484-31ac-4b34-b928-6520175b5d74
   Device Id  : e4867159-f070-409c-a86e-dcf848088eb3
```

Figure 9-60. *Sample Device simulator output*

After starting the C# device simulator console application, you would typically then start the Azure Stream Analytics job.

After both applications have fully started, you start seeing data appear in your Power BI dashboard.

Depending on your BRZKR mode setting and how you have configured the Azure Functions for alerts, you might also start to see alert messages appear on your cell phone or in your e-mail inbox.

End-to-End: Simulator -> Dashboard and Alerts

In this section, you see how everything comes together in the reference implementation.

We will review some of the dashboard visualizations and alert artifacts that are generated as we run data through the solution using the device simulators.

Figure 9-61 depicts the Power BI dashboard as the device simulator is being run in the background in BRZRKR mode.

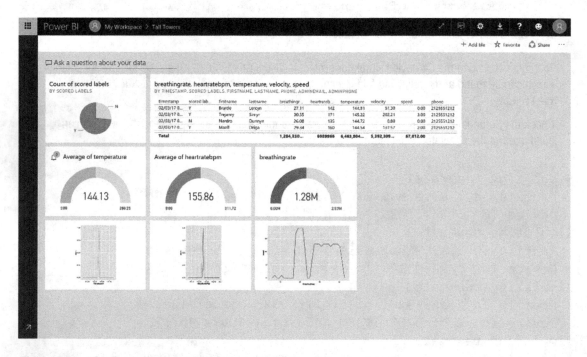

Figure 9-61. *The Power BI real-time dashboard for reference implementation*

Note that in Figure 9-61, there is an alarm icon visible in the top-left corner of the average temperature gauge. This occurred after we manually set the alarm earlier in the chapter.

Figure 9-62 displays the specific Power BI dashboard notification message that was generated for this alarm. You can see that it was triggered by exceeding the threshold you set earlier.

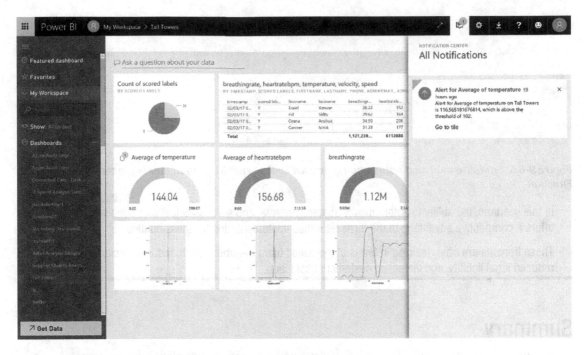

Figure 9-62. *Sample Power BI dashboard alert notification*

In this case, the Power BI notification alert reads as follows (from Figure 9-62):

```
Alert for Average of temperature on
Tall Towers is 116.565181676814, which is above the threshold of 102.
```

Also note that the subject of this Power BI alert is "Alert for Average of temperature a day," which means you will receive this alert once per day.

While this dashboard alerting is certainly useful, we are still in need of a more effective and direct alerting mechanism to contact the appropriate party, on the appropriate device, at the appropriate time.

This capability enables you to deliver vital outbound alert notifications to the most interested parties. And all of this can easily be delivered via the "lowest-common-denominator" methods of modern communication vehicles, namely text and e-mail.

Figure 9-63 represents a sample e-mail that was generated by the C# code and the SendGrid API covered earlier in the chapter.

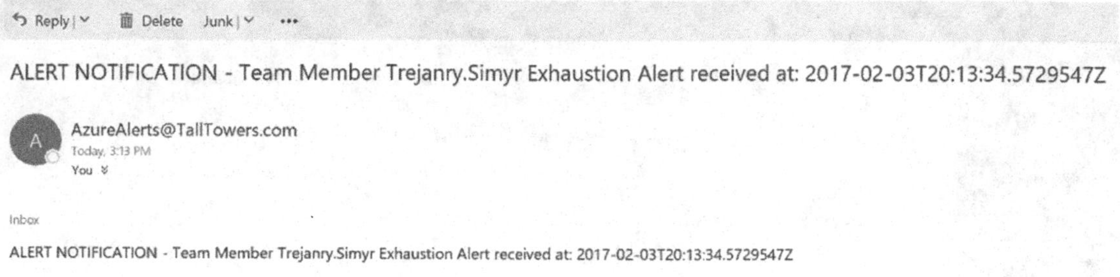

↩ Reply | ⌄   🗑 Delete   Junk | ⌄   •••

ALERT NOTIFICATION - Team Member Trejanry.Simyr Exhaustion Alert received at: 2017-02-03T20:13:34.5729547Z

A   AzureAlerts@TallTowers.com
Today, 3:13 PM
You ⌄

Inbox

ALERT NOTIFICATION - Team Member Trejanry.Simyr Exhaustion Alert received at: 2017-02-03T20:13:34.5729547Z

Figure 9-63. *Sample e-mail alert notification generated by the SendGrid output binding in the Azure Function*

In this scenario, the ability to automatically trigger, generate, and send SMS text and e-mail messages offers a competitive advantage to the three reference implementation business entities.

These benefits are often realized in terms of increased team member health, reduced accidents, reduced legal liability, and increased customer satisfaction.

Summary

This chapter covered the topic of visualizations, alerts, and notifications using Power BI and Azure Functions.

We started with a look at the modern reporting landscape and then provided an overview of the capabilities of the Microsoft Power BI platform, including the following versions and components:

- Power BI Service
- Power BI Desktop
- Power BI Embedded
- Power BI Mobile
- ReST APIs
- Custom Visuals
- Natural Language Query
- Cortana Integration
- Power BI Desktop
- R Script Visualizations

We then explored the use of several Azure services—including event hubs, Stream Analytics, and Functions—to enable an automatic alerts and notifications solution with minimal coding. We examined the following Azure technologies:

- *Azure Event Hubs*: Use as a trigger mechanism for Azure Functions
- *Streaming Analytics*: Output to Event Hub capability
- *Azure Functions*: Send SMS text (via Twilio) and send alert e-mail (via SendGrid)

We then "made it real" by incorporating all of these Azure capabilities into the reference implementation. The final piece was the device simulator and the capability to generate both normal and alarm conditions to test the end-to-end system.

With the device simulators in place, we were then able to quickly create simulated data and generate rich, interactive, dashboard visualizations using Power BI. With minimal additional effort, those same dashboard views are instantly available on all versions of Power BI, including the desktop, web, and mobile versions.

In addition to rich visualizations and dashboards, we were also able to quickly and easily implement alerts and notifications by leveraging several Azure services such as event hubs and Azure Functions.

In today's fast-paced business world, constantly operating at "Internet speed," there are many critical requirements for highly streamlined, adaptive, operational dashboards and visualizations to help improve business outcomes by avoiding unfavorable scenarios.

When you add cloud-enabled capabilities like Machine Learning and predictive analytics, you can start to manage outcomes even before they happen.

Combine this predictive capability with timely, actionable, and effective alerts and notifications and you have all the underpinnings of a great, modern cloud business architecture.

CHAPTER 10

■ ■ ■

Security and Identity

This chapter reviews several key security topics including threat modeling, security protocols, encryption, and key management as well as managing user identities and supporting multi-tenancy in your solution.

Threat Modeling

Cybercrime and IoT security have been front and center in the news this past year. Defining the security strategy for an IoT solution that uses public cloud platforms requires understanding the surface areas of vulnerability and the attack vectors that cyber criminals might leverage. Security is a not a solution; it is an ongoing process that requires discipline and constant analysis, review, and action.

Threat vectors in the context of an IoT solution are defined by zones, where each zone outlines a surface area of attack. The design team uses these zone definitions to articulate a security strategy, technology stack, monitoring, review, and response process. The zones in an IoT solution span the on-premises environment made up of wired, wireless, and cellular networks, the devices you deploy into that environment, the applications that you provide your end users, and everything in between.

Threat modeling helps you understand how an attacker might seek to compromise and gain access to a system. It also defines the process and tools that you would leverage to mitigate the attack. Threat modeling should be an activity that is undertaken at design time and continues throughout the lifetime of the application. It is critical that security mitigation strategies are defined and continually updated as the solution evolves.

The threat modeling activity consists of four steps:

- Modeling the application
- Enumerating threats
- Mitigating threats
- Validating mitigations

© Bob Familiar and Jeff Barnes 2017

B. Familiar and J. Barnes, *Business in Real-Time Using Azure IoT and Cortana Intelligence Suite*,
DOI 10.1007/978-1-4842-2650-6_10

This modeling process starts with creating a solution architecture diagram. All elements in the diagram are potential surface areas of attack. *STRIDE* is a threat classification model that can be used to organize potential threats and well known mitigation strategies as you perform the analysis on your architecture. STRIDE stands for:

- *Spoofing*: The attacker pretends to be someone or some service they are not

- *Tampering*: The attacker modifies data in transit

- *Repudiation*: A user performs an action and then claims they did not actually do it, such as a credit card transaction

- *Information Disclosure*: Can the attacker or user access data they are not allowed to see

- *Denial of Service*: The attacker degrades a service through overloading or redirection

- *Elevation of Privilege*: The attacker can gain privileges that they would not normally have

The *services* within your solution would be subject to different STRIDE classifications. For example:

- Processes can be classified using STRIDE

- Data flows are classified using TID components of STRIDE

- Data stores are classified using TID, and sometimes R, if the data stores are log files

- External entities are classified using SRD

■ **Note**   An excellent reference on STRIDE written by Larry Osterman at Microsoft can be found at https://blogs.msdn.microsoft.com/larryosterman/2007/09/04/threat-modeling-again-stride/.

Threat Modeling Zones and IoT

The zones in an IoT solution can be defined as follows:

- Local

- Device

- Cloud Gateway

- Cloud Service

Local Zone

One of the more critical parts of an IoT solution with respect to security are the devices that are deployed into the world—into physical environments over which we may not have control. This *local zone* is subject to physical and digital attack vectors.

The relationship between end users or sensors and the device defines a data transition boundary. It is at this boundary where attackers will focus their attention. The physical space into which it is deployed, the network segment it belongs to, and how it receives and sends data must all be considered. A short but certainly not exhaustive list of questions the design team should pose during their analysis of the local zone:

- Will the device be into a locked room with limited access?
- Will end users interact directly with the device, such as a lock or a thermostat?
- Is the device attached to an open wireless network, connected to a cellular carrier, or using to a hard-wired LAN?
- Does the device reside on its own network segment?
- How is the device deprovisioned if it fails or is replaced?

Device Zone

The *device zone* focuses on the inner workings of the device. The operating system and firmware that are executing your application logic, connecting to networks, receiving and sending data, storing data locally, and so on are analyzed. One important consideration is how user and admin accounts are created and their passwords maintained. Consumer IoT devices are known to be vulnerable in this area as manufacturers have been lax in their design and end users are may not be technically savvy enough to consider the implications of the password 12345. Here's a short but certainly not exhaustive list of questions the design team should ask during their analysis of the device zone:

- What operating system is embedded on the device?
- What language is the firmware/application implemented in?
- Has the firmware team left ports open for remote connection and debugging?
- How is the firmware upgraded?
- What user/admin accounts are created and how are their credentials maintained?
- How is the device installed on the local network?
- How does the device authenticate to the cloud gateway?
- Is the data encrypted in flight and at rest?
- What data transmission protocols (MQTT, AMQP, HTTPs, or other) are used to communicate locally and with the cloud?

As we covered in previous chapters, we use a two-phase authentication mechanism that combines a secure HTTPs call to the Device API to retrieve the device manifest followed by a secure call over either MQTT or AMQP to IoT Hub to connect and set up the two-way communication between the device and the cloud. We also demonstrated the use of the device twin and direct methods to perform secure device management operations (see Figure 10-1).

Cloud Gateway Zone

The cloud gateway is a cloud-hosted service or services that provide public cloud secure endpoints for devices to register, authenticate, and send and receive messages. A cloud gateway needs to be able to provide these services across multiple device zones. In our solution architecture, IoT Hub and the Device API represent the players in the cloud gateway zone. They expose secure endpoints that allow devices to connect and communicate. A protocol gateway and/or SMS gateway may also reside in this zone if you are connecting to legacy devices in your solution (see Figure 10-1).

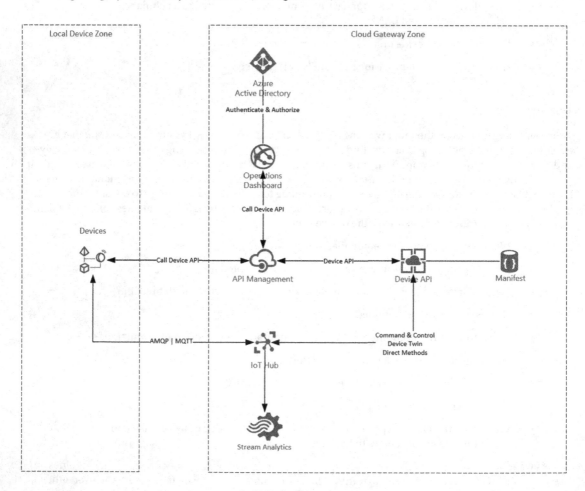

Figure 10-1. *Local, device, and cloud gateway zones*

Cloud Services Zone

The cloud gateway provides access to the incoming messages by internal cloud-hosted services—in the Cloud Services Zone—that provide data ingestion, stream processing, storage, advanced analytics, and application integration through APIs, queues, and batch processing (see Figures 10-2 and 10-3).

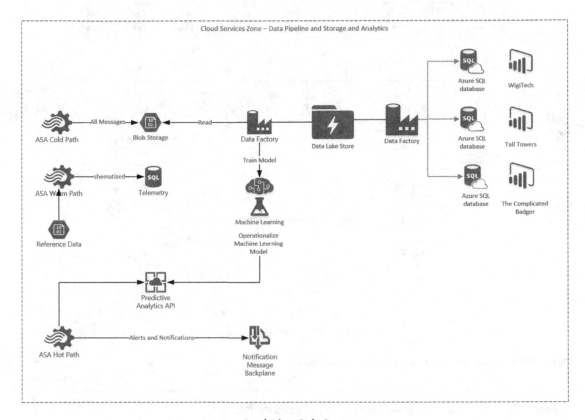

Figure 10-2. *Cloud services zone, data pipeline, storage, and analytics*

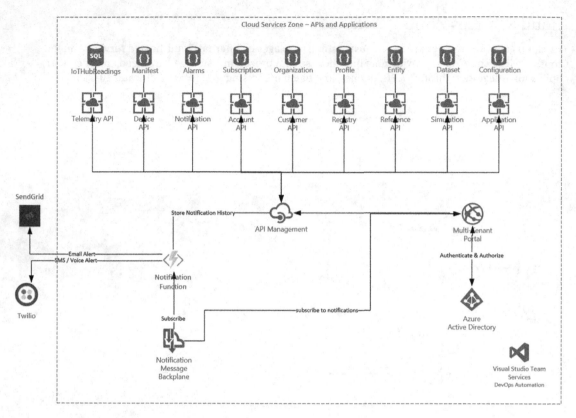

Application Sub-System

Figure 10-3. *Cloud services zone, APIs, and applications*

■ **Note**   Recommended reading on Azure security includes the following:

Protecting Data and Privacy in the Cloud whitepaper

```
http://download.microsoft.com/download/2/0/A/20A1529E-65CB-4266-8651-1B57B0E42DAA/
Protecting-Data-and-Privacy-in-the-Cloud.pdf
```

Windows Azure Privacy Overview whitepaper

```
http://download.microsoft.com/download/7/5/9/759E2283-F517-430E-84AF-0151988C117A/
WindowsAzurePrivacyOverview.pdf
```

Microsoft Azure Security, Privacy, and Compliance whitepaper

```
http://download.microsoft.com/download/1/6/0/160216AA-8445-480B-B60F-5C8EC8067FCA/
WindowsAzure-SecurityPrivacyCompliance.pdf
```

Security Protocols

Interactions between infrastructure and the Azure components that comprise an IoT solution can be secured using industry standard protocols including X.509 certificates, role-based access control, firewall rules, and virtual networking.

Data emanating from on-premises IoT devices is unconditionally secured in-flight via TLS over protocols such as HTTP/S on port 443 and secure AMQP on port 5671. Data-at-rest can also be secured through service-based encryption (such as Transparent Data Encryption on Azure SQL Database and Azure Storage Service Encryption) or application-level encryption with Azure Key Vault providing secure storage of access keys. Specific requirements for at-rest security will vary with the nature of the data and the storage mechanisms, which are addressed at the higher layers of the architecture.

■ **Note** For more detail on IoT and Security, see this article by Yuri Diogenes and Dominic Betts from Microsoft: https://docs.microsoft.com/en-us/azure/iot-suite/iot-security-architecture.

Azure Security Center

The Azure Security Center provides you with an overview of your current services with respect to potential threats and verifies that the appropriate security controls are in place and configured correctly. You can set up alerts and notifications for each of your services so that administrators and key members of the team are alerted to potential threats (see Figure 10-4).

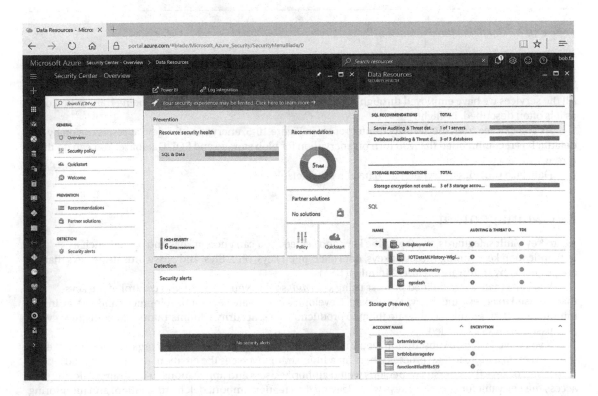

***Figure 10-4.** Security Center reporting on vulnerable services*

The Security Center provides remediation guidance and the ability to turn on encryption, enable auditing, and configure alerts as well as set up threat modeling if appropriate. In Figure 10-5, you can see that threat modeling on the SQL Database is engaged to detect SQL injection and anomalous client logins.

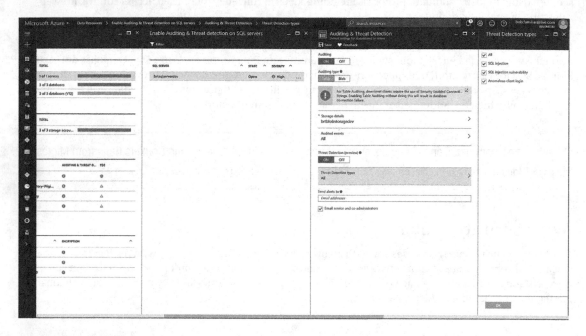

Figure 10-5. *Configure threat modeling*

Data Encryption

All the services we have employed through the solution provide encryption as data is being transmitted or, as it is often described, in-flight.

As you can see from the Security Center report in Figure 10-5, encryption for data at rest is not on by default. It is recommended that you turn on encryption for blob storage and SQL Database. You can do this through the Security Center.

Data lake provides encryption for data at rest by default.

Key Management

Azure Key Vault safeguards cryptographic keys and secrets. You can encrypt keys and secrets such as authentication keys, storage account keys, data encryption keys, .PFX files, and passwords using keys that are protected by Hardware Security Modules (HSMs).

You can create a streamlined process using *key vault* so that you can maintain control of the keys that are used to access and encrypt your data. Developers can create keys for development and testing in minutes and then seamlessly migrate them to production keys. Security administrators can grant and revoke permission to keys as needed.

If you have an Azure subscription, you can create and use Key Vault. Within an organization, it makes sense to set up a more formal process where an administrator oversees the creation, distribution, and revocation of keys. This person or persons would authorize users and applications to programmatically access the key vault for subsets of keys while leaving the creation, import, delete, revocation, and monitoring a private concern.

> ■ **Note** For more information on Key Vault, visit `https://docs.microsoft.com/en-us/azure/key-vault/key-vault-whatis`.

Identity

Identity is all about who can access your applications, APIs, and the underlying data that are at the heart of your IoT solution. You will want the ability to provide users some level of self-service for registration, password management, and profile updates while maintaining stringent protocols for accessing application capabilities and data.

Authentication and Authorization

Authentication and authorization for customers, employees, and partners is provided through a cloud-hosted identity-as-a-service (IaaS) provider. Azure Active Directory has quickly become a popular choice in the Azure ecosystem to manage multi-tenant identities.

Azure Active Directory (Azure AD) simplifies authentication for developers with support for industry-standard protocols such as OAuth 2.0 and OpenID Connect as well as open source libraries for different platforms to access its application and operations APIs.

Azure AD B2C is a full-featured cloud identity management service for consumer and partner facing web and mobile applications. It is a highly available global service that scales to hundreds of millions of identities. Your users can register, authenticate, and manage their profile using company e-mail or one of their social accounts such as Google+, Facebook, or LinkedIn. The self-service forms are provided by Azure AD B2C, and applications that want to integrate with this service are registered with the directory through the Azure Portal or through the Azure AD automation API called the GraphAPI.

Multi-Tenancy

Multi-tenancy refers to the capability of a single code deployment, often a web application or API, to service a user base from multiple companies and partners (tenants) while providing a potentially distinct experience for each tenant. Upon entry, users will only be able to see the functional areas of the app they are authorized to see and access the data they are authorized to view.

With respect to data access, there are two design patterns that can be applied:

- The data pipeline services create individual, isolated databases for each organization and role-based authorization is overlaid for employees of that company.

- The data pipeline services place all the data into a single, elastic store whose schema provides a security overlay that uses authentication claims to restrict access by company and role.

There is no right or wrong way to go about this; it is a business decision as to which one is appropriate for you. You may have customers who want to be reassured their data is isolated from other organization who are using the same SaaS application. In that case, the tradeoff is that your team will need to design a process by which the databases for each organization are created and managed. If all organizations are accessing the same scalable, elastic store then it is your duty to not only manage this store but also to provide guarantees that data access is properly restricted across organizations and users in organizations.

The reference solution demonstrates both of these patterns. Chapters 7 and 9 introduced the first pattern: how you can design a data pipeline process using Data Factory to generate individual databases for each organization (see Figure 10-6).

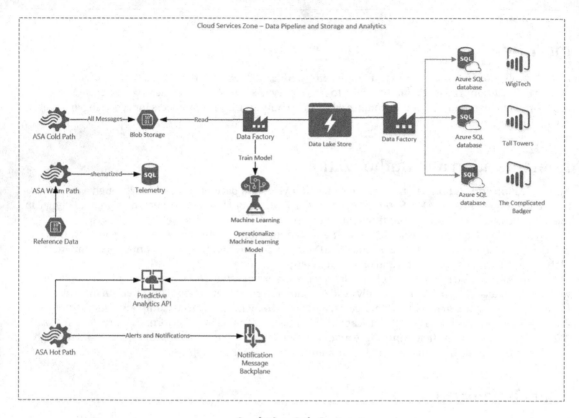

Figure 10-6. *Separate data stores for each organization*

Here we will examine the second pattern: a single, scalable store that defines a schema to provide both company and role-based access.

In addition to the Blob Storage and Data Lake Store depicted in Figure 10-6, the Stream Analytics job sends telemetry to a SQL Database table referred to as the warm path. As the Stream Analytics job processes each of the incoming messages, it transforms the message by joining the biometric data with details about the employee who is wearing the vest such as his name, e-mail, age, weight, and height along with the company name and the type of user. In our scenario, there are two types of users: administrators and employees. An employee can only view his or her own personal data. Administrators can only view data for employees at their companies. Using the company and user type columns in the SQL Database table, we will demonstrate the second pattern: providing a security overlay based on user type and organization to restrict data access (see Figure 10-7).

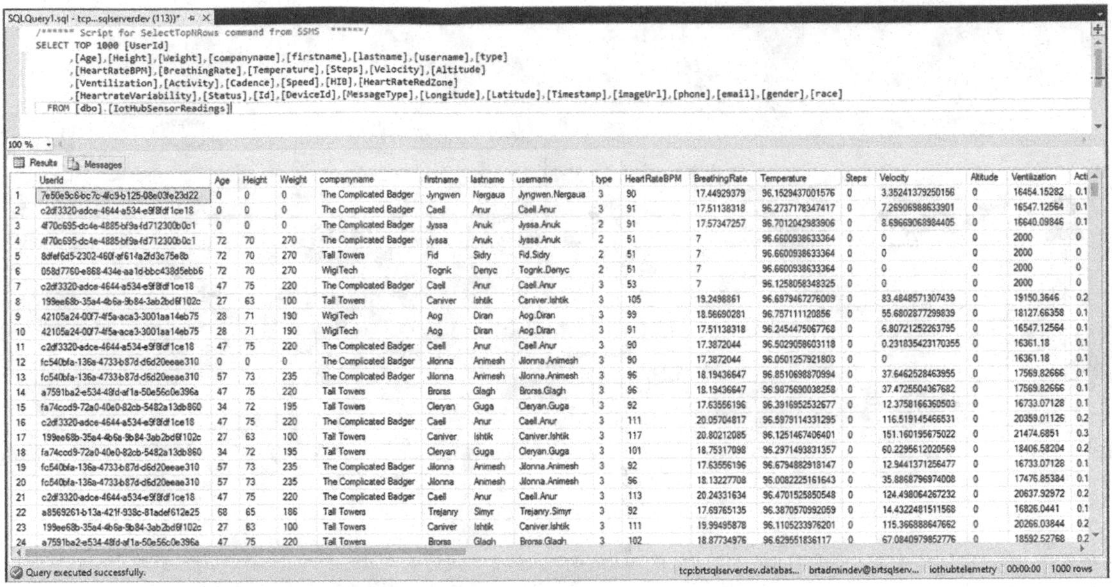

Figure 10-7. *SQL table containing user telemetry*

For this plan to work, we need a secure API that sits on top of the SQL Database table and enforces the requirements of our security model. The Telemetry API will provide a secure endpoint for applications that want to access the underlying data. Any application that wants to call the Telemetry API will need to provide the details of the authenticated user, the company name, and user type as parameters to the call.

This application needs to be registered with Active Directory to establish the trust relationship between the identity provider (Active Directory) and the application itself. Once the user is authenticated, the application has access to "claims" for that user and can use that information to call the platform APIs. Claims are name-value pairs that provide details about the user such as their given name and surname. In addition, you can extend the default claims collection by adding additional properties needed at the application level.

Using the user ID claim, for instance, the application can look up the user's profile via the Registry API, retrieve the user's subscription level from the Account API, organization details from the Customer API, and application configuration details from the Application API (see Figure 10-8).

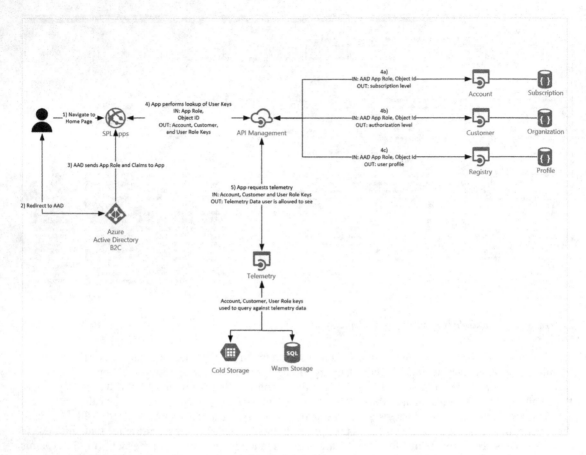

Figure 10-8. *Multi-tenant authentication and authorization*

Figure 10-8 depicts a user authentication, authorization, and telemetry request workflow:

1. The user navigates to the home page of the web application or launches the mobile app.

2. The user is redirected to the Azure AD login page and provides his or her username and password. In the case of a mobile application, the Azure AD login page is presented in a modal popup.

3. Azure AD authenticates the user and, if successful, redirects back to the application with a token that contains a set of standard claims like name, unique ID, etc.

4. The application uses these claims to invoke a set of managed APIs that are secured from the application to the API Management proxy using OAuth bearer tokens and from the proxy to the service using managed certificates, basic authentication, or shared secrets.

    a. The Account API returns a subscription model. The subscription model might define levels of feature capability such as gold, silver, and bronze, which map to a monetization model.

    b.   The Customer API returns an organization model consisting of roles that the user has within the customer's organization, for example, Super Admin, Admin, Technical Services, Read Only, District Manager, Branch Manager, and so on.

    c.   The Registry API returns a user profile model that contains all the details about the user including location, contact information, and preferences.

5.   The user requests to view telemetry.

    a.   The application calls the secure managed Telemetry API passing in the relevant keys for user profile, user role, account, and customer. These keys are used in the WHERE clause along with other parameters in the underlying query to limit the data returned for that user.

The remainder of this chapter takes you through a series of exercises that configure an Azure AD B2C tenant in your subscription, import users from the three organizations, register applications, and leverage the user claims returned from Azure AD B2C to make calls to the Telemetry API, which restricts access to data based on user roles.

CREATE AN AZURE B2C TENANT

To implement an application that leverages Azure AD B2C for identity, you first need to have an instance of Azure AD B2C and then register your application with that instance.

The application registration process creates a unique ID for your app, known as the Application ID. The registration process will also request a Redirect URL that is used to redirect back to your application after authentication has completed.

Azure AD supports several authentication protocols. This scenario leverages OpenID Connect (which in turn relies on OAuth 2.0), so the application communicates with Azure AD using these two endpoints:

- `https://login.microsoftonline.com/{tenant}/oauth2/v2.0/authorize`

- `https://login.microsoftonline.com/{tenant}/oauth2/v2.0/token`

where `{tenant}` is the name of your Azure AD B2C tenant; for example, `mytenant.onmicrosoft.com` (or the GUID associated with that tenant).

To complete the application registration process, you configure a set of policies, one each for the operations that you want Azure AD B2C to perform on your behalf. Policies include:

- Sign Up

- Sign In

- Update Profile

- Password Reset

Follow these steps to create and configure your instance of Azure AD.

1.   Navigate to the Classic Azure Management portal and log in.

    `http://manage.windowsazure.com`

2.   Select New ➤ Directory ➤ Custom Create (see Figure 10-9).

Figure 10-9. *Create an instance of Azure Active Directory B2C*

3. Fill out the form providing the name of your organization, a unique name for your tenant, and the region. Lastly be sure to check the box that is labeled "This is a B2C directory" (see Figure 10-10).

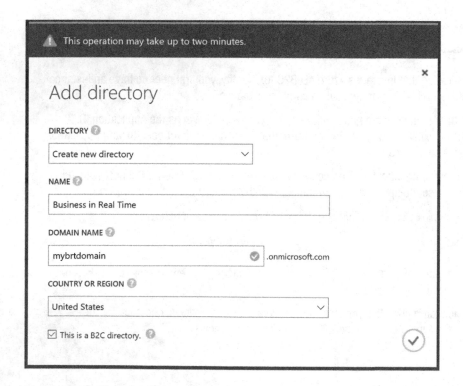

Figure 10-10. *Name and create your B2C tenant*

■ **Note** The default domain will be {your-tenant}.onmicrosoft.com. You can change the domain later in the process if necessary.

---

4. Once the creation process is complete, you will be able to configure the directory (see Figure 10-11).

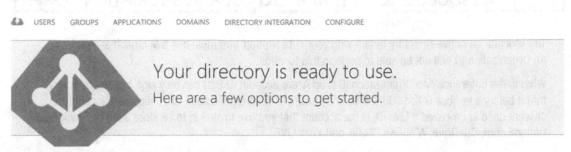

brtb2c

USERS   GROUPS   APPLICATIONS   DOMAINS   DIRECTORY INTEGRATION   CONFIGURE

Your directory is ready to use.
Here are a few options to get started.

LEARN
Read: Azure Active Directory B2C

ADMINISTER
Manage B2C settings

Figure 10-11. Ready to administer B2C Settings

5.   Click Manage B2C Settings. This will take you to the new Azure portal (see Figure 10-12).

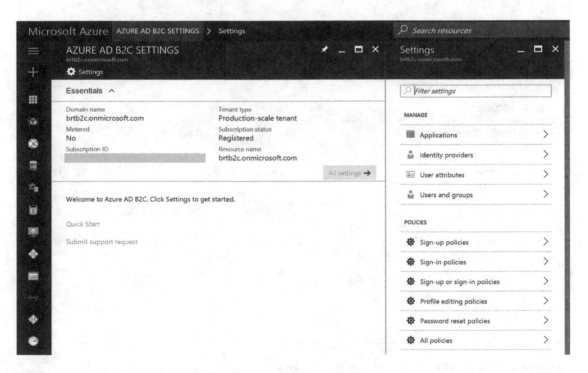

Figure 10-12. Azure AD B2C Settings blade

Next, you will associate your tenant to your subscription.

ASSOCIATE YOUR TENANT TO YOUR SUBSCRIPTION

To associate an Active Directory tenant with your subscription, you must use a Microsoft account. An Organization ID will not be able to perform this function.

What is the difference? An Organization ID is an Azure account ID that can only sign into the directory that it belongs to. Your Office 365 e-mail is an example of an organization ID. A Microsoft account, or what used to be called a Live ID, is the account that you use to sign in to services such as Skype, Outlook.com, OneDrive, Windows Phone, and Xbox LIVE.

1. If necessary, create a Microsoft ID and make that user a co-administrator of your Azure subscription.

   You can do this from the classic portal at `https://manage.windowsazure.com`. Click settings in the left-side navigation bar, click the name of your subscription, and then choose Administrators from the top menu. Then click the Add button in the bottom toolbar (see Figure 10-13).

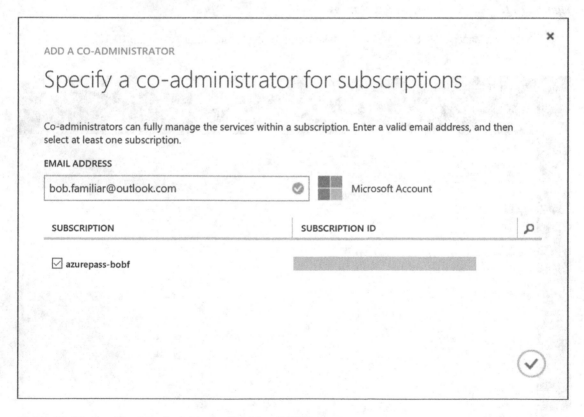

Figure 10-13. Specify a co-administrator for subscriptions

2. Add the Microsoft account to the Azure AD B2C Directory as a Global Administrator (see Figure 10-14).

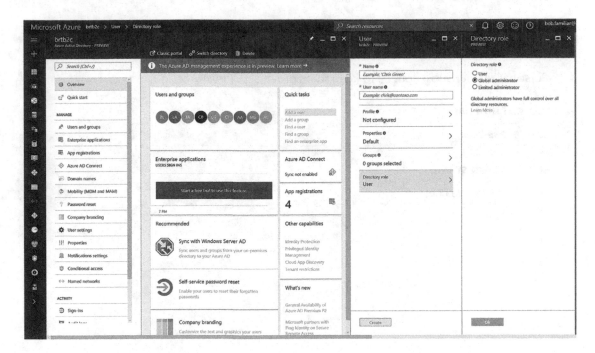

Figure 10-14. *Add a global administrator*

3. Make this user a service administrator of the subscription (see Figure 10-15).

Log in to `https://account.windowsazure.com` using the ID you used to create your Azure subscription and then select your subscription to drill into the details page. Click Edit Subscription Details and set the Microsoft ID as the service administrator.

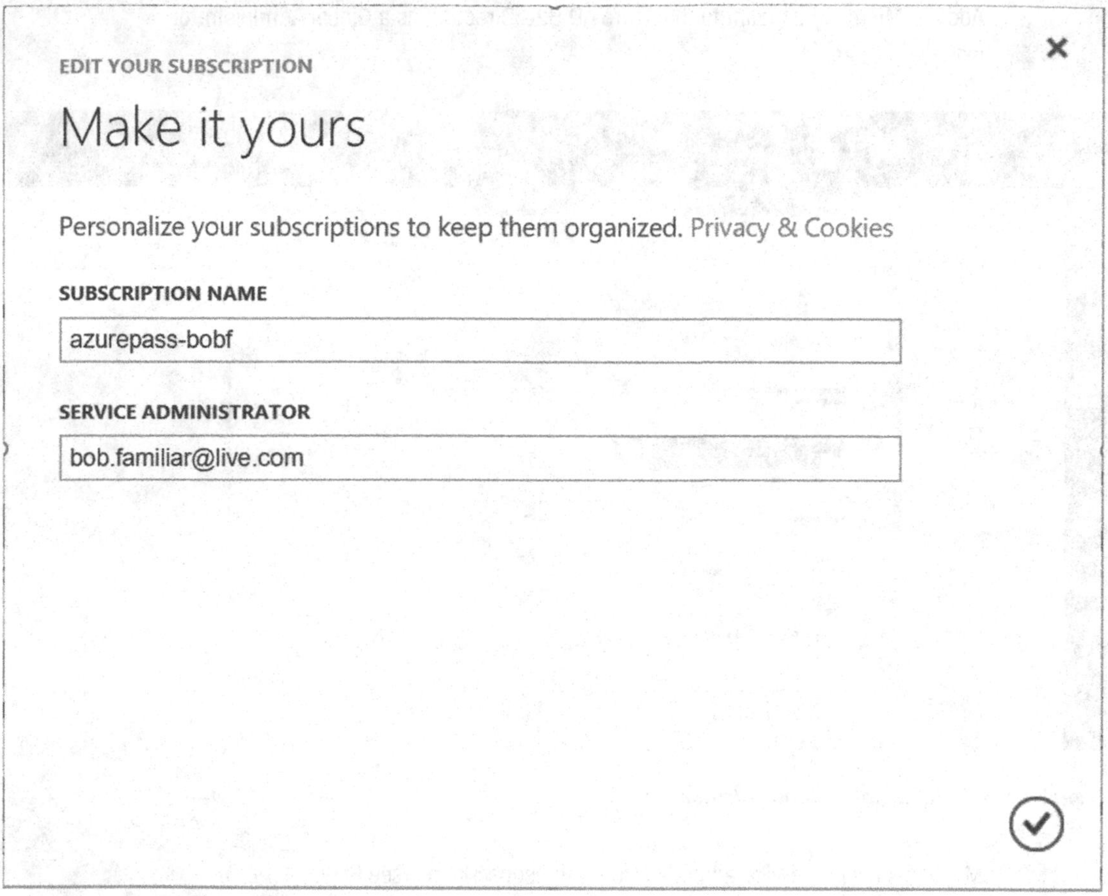

EDIT YOUR SUBSCRIPTION

Make it yours

Personalize your subscriptions to keep them organized. Privacy & Cookies

SUBSCRIPTION NAME

azurepass-bobf

SERVICE ADMINISTRATOR

bob.familiar@live.com

Figure 10-15. *Changing the service administrator*

4. Log out and navigate to the classic portal. Log in using the Microsoft account. Click Settings in the left navigation bar, select the subscription in the list, and then click the Edit button in the bottom toolbar. Select the directory in the drop-down list, click through to Step 2 and save your changes (see Figure 10-16).

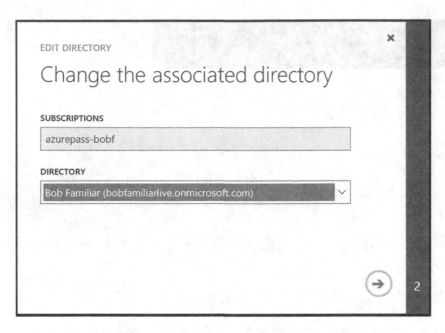

Figure 10-16. *Change the associated directory*

■ **Note** For more details, see this article on how to enable billing:
https://docs.microsoft.com/en-us/azure/active-directory-b2c/active-directory-b2c-how-to-enable-billing

---

REGISTER AN APPLICATION

Only registered applications can integrate with Azure AD B2C.

In this exercise, you will register a web application that provides access to the Telemetry and defines the policies for sign-up, sign-in, and profile management. Note that we will update this app in a later exercise. For now, we are just going to register it with Azure AD.

1. From the Azure AD B2C Management Blade, click Applications, then Add (see Figure 10-17).

2. Enter brtportal for the name

3. Click Yes for Include Web App/Web API.

4. Enter https://localhost:44316/ as the redirect URL.

5. Click the Create button.

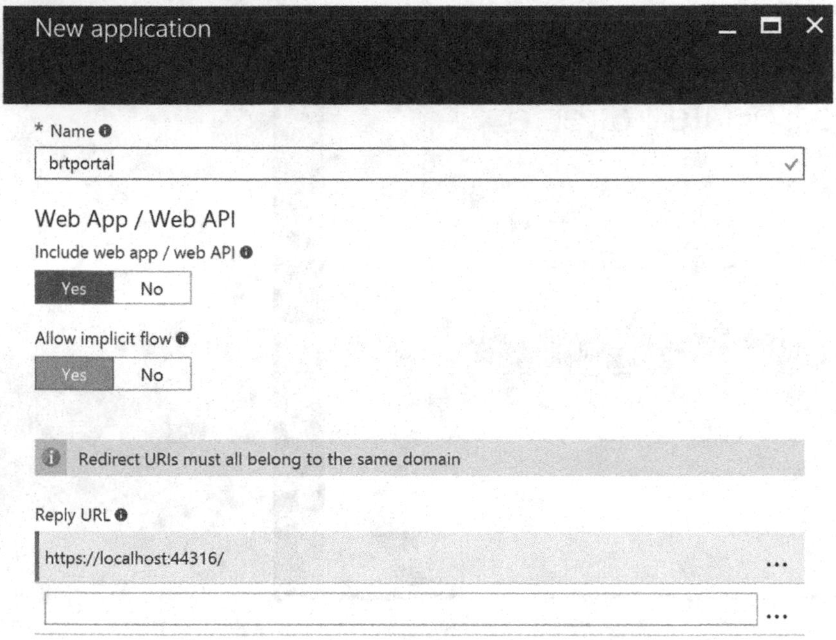

Figure 10-17. Registering an application

6. Once the create process is finished, click on the application name to reveal the generated application ID.

7. Copy the application ID for later use.

   In this next step, we define a set of policies for our registered application. As part of these definitions, we can specify the user attributes that we want to prompt for at sign-up as well as which attributes to return as part of the claims upon authentication. You can access the user attributes from the Azure AD B2C Management Blade (see Figure 10-18). It is also possible to define custom user attributes.

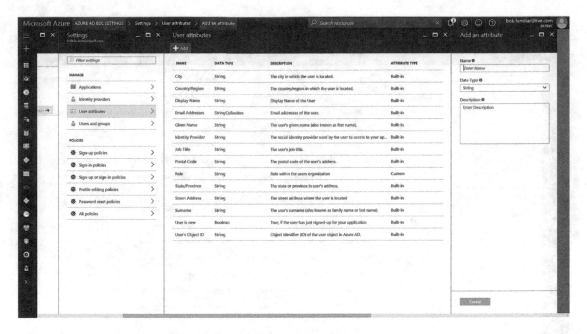

Figure 10-18. *User attributes*

8. Click Add on the User Attributes screen and create a custom attribute called `Role` with a data type of string.

   Now that the application is registered, we can define the policies for this application. Policies define the integration points between Azure AD B2C and the application. Azure AD B2C will provide screens for sign-up, sign-in, profile management, and password reset.

9. In the Azure B2C Management blade, click Sign-Up Policy.

   For Identity providers, choose Email. The sign-up attributes are the fields you want the user to provide on the sign-up form. Choose Email and Display Name. For claims, at a minimum select Display Name but you can choose as many attributes as you want to send back upon a successful sign up. Save your edits and click Create (see Figure 10-19).

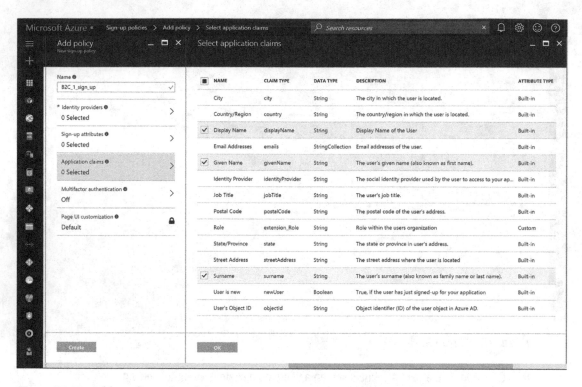

Figure 10-19. *Add a policy, select claims*

10. Once the policy is created, click the name and select the application that this policy applies to. Enter the Reply URL for that application. For this example, that value is `https://localhost:4435644316/` (see Figure 10-20).

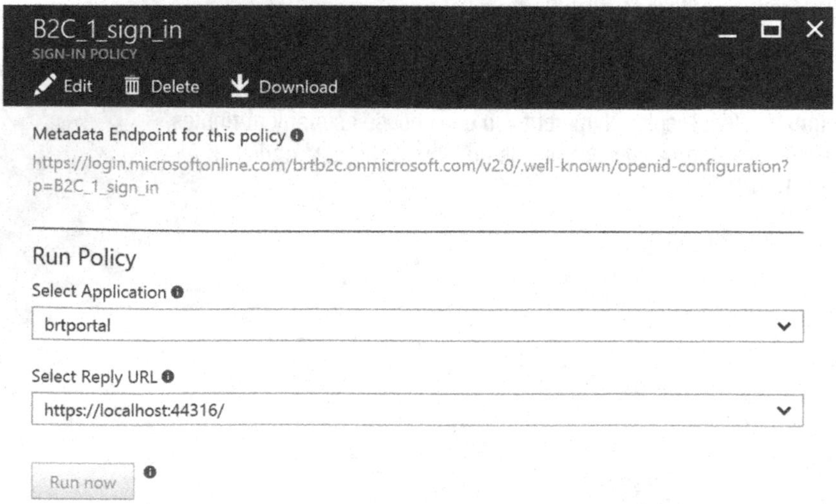

Figure 10-20. *B2C_1_sign_in Policy*

11. Follow the same procedure to create a sign-in policy.

12. Create a Profile Edit policy. This policy will allow the user to update his or her profile to provide a value for the custom attribute we defined. Make sure to select Role as one of the attributes users can edit as part of their profiles (see Figure 10-21).

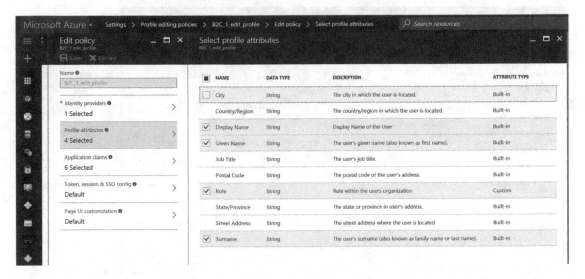

Figure 10-21. *Create Edit Profile policy*

IMPORT USERS TO THE NEW TENANT

In this exercise, you import user accounts into the Azure AD B2C tenant so that you can test the multi-tenant features. Microsoft provides an easy-to-use command-line utility to perform operations against the tenant. The API for Active Directory is called the Graph API, and this exercise will provide insight into how you can automate operations against the AD tenant using this API.

To provide secure access to the Graph API, there is some setup before you can perform these directory operations:

- Create a local global administrator in your tenant.

- Install both the Online Sign-In Assistant and the Active Directory Module for PowerShell.

- Register the command-line utility with Azure AD B2C so that it has the proper credentials to invoke the GraphAPI.

1. In the management blade, click on Users and Groups, All Users, and then click Add.

2. Create a user account for the local admin with the username.

   admin@[your-tenant].onmicrosoft.com

3. Set the password.

4. Set the Directory Role to be Global Administrator.

5. Click Create.

This account will have rights to invoke the GraphAPI against your tenant (see Figure 10-22).

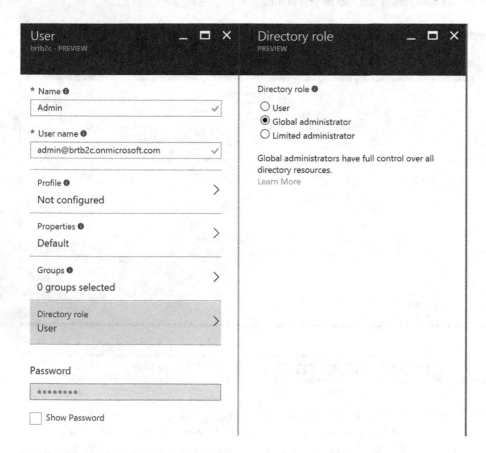

Figure 10-22. *Add a local global administrator account manually*

6. Follow these links to download and install the Online Sign-In Assistant and the Active Directory Module for PowerShell:

   ```
   http://go.microsoft.com/fwlink/?LinkID=286152
   http://go.microsoft.com/fwlink/p/?linkid=236297
   ```

7. When complete, open a command window or PowerShell console window, navigate to the identity folder of your local repo, and clone the command-line utility using Git.

   ```
   git clone https://github.com/AzureADQuickStarts/B2C-GraphAPI-
   DotNet.git
   ```

There are three PowerShell scripts in the identity folder that will assist you through this process.

- 01-RegisterAppInADTenant.ps1: Registers the command-line utility with Azure AD and generates an Object ID, Application Principal ID, and a Client Secret.

- 02-AssignAppPermissions.ps1: Extends the permission of the command-line utility.

- 03-ImportUsers.ps1: Uses the command-line utility to import users. The users have been predefined in a set of JSON files in the identity\UserJson folder.

The command-line utility will use the client secret to authenticate to Azure AD and to acquire access tokens. The Object ID and Application Principal ID are used to assign the extended permissions that the utility needs to perform, namely these CRUD operations: directory readers to read users, directory writers to create and update users, and user account administrator to delete users.

8. Open a PowerShell console window and navigate to the identity folder of the repo. Run the 01-RegisterAppInADTenant.ps1 script. The script will prompt for the name of your Azure subscription and the name of the app you want to register. Note the name of the application is B2CGraphClient (see Figure 10-23).

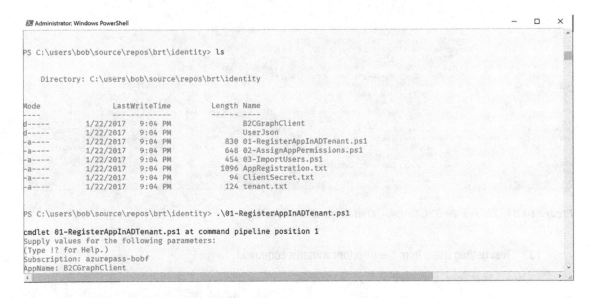

Figure 10-23. *Register the B2CGraphClient command-line utility*

The registration script generates two files—AppRegistration.txt and ClientSecret.txt. The App Registration file contains the App Principal ID and the Object ID. The Object ID is used to extend the permissions of the app registration. The App Principal ID and Client Secret are added to the B2CGraphClient source code so it can authenticate and retrieve tokens from Azure AD B2C.

9. Run the 02-AssignAppPermission.ps1 script, passing in the name of the subscription and the Object ID.

10. Open the B2CGraphClient solution in Visual Studio and then open the app.config file. Update the following app settings:

    key="b2c:Tenant" value="[your-tenant].onmicrosoft.com"
    key="b2c:ClientId" value="[your-app-principal-id]"
    key="b2c:ClientSecret" value="[your-client-secret]"

11. Build the solution.

12. To test the app, navigate to the B2C-GraphClient-DotNet\B2CGraphClient\Bin\ Debug folder and type the following command to get the help for the utility (see Figure 10-24).

    > .\b2c.exe help

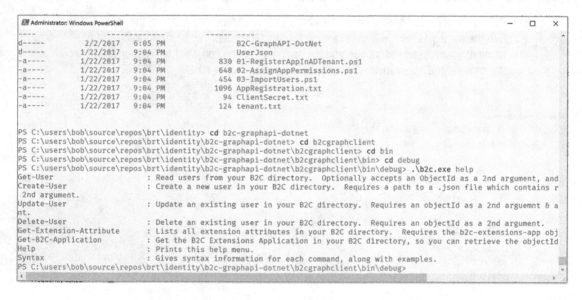

Figure 10-24. *Testing the B2C Graph Client command-line utility*

13. Test getting users from the directory with this command:

    > .\b2c.exe get-user

    You should see the administrator account returned as a JSON stream.

14. Navigate back to the identity folder and execute the third script, 03-ImportUsers.ps1.

    This script will use the contents of the identity\UserJson folder to import users for each of the three pseudo-companies we defined.

15. When the script completes, navigate back to the application bin folder and re-run the get-user command:

    > .\b2c.exe get-user

    You should see 50+ users returned from the directory (see Figure 10-25).

```
Administrator: Windows PowerShell                                          —    □    ×
      "mailNickname": "Brorss.Glagh",
      "mobile": "2125551212",
      "onPremisesSecurityIdentifier": null,
      "otherMails": [],
      "passwordPolicies": "DisablePasswordExpiration",
      "passwordProfile": null,
      "physicalDeliveryOfficeName": null,
      "postalCode": "10018",
      "preferredLanguage": null,
      "provisionedPlans": [],
      "provisioningErrors": [],
      "proxyAddresses": [],
      "refreshTokensValidFromDateTime": "2017-01-23T00:31:30Z",
      "showInAddressList": null,
      "sipProxyAddress": null,
      "state": "NY",
      "streetAddress": "53 WEST 36TH STREET",
      "surname": "Glagh",
      "telephoneNumber": "2125551212",
      "thumbnailPhoto@odata.mediaEditLink": "directoryObjects/feffacce-f87c-44ec-97e9-4ed6ec5c5fdf/Microsoft.DirectorySer
      "usageLocation": null,
      "userPrincipalName": "07a4e71f-09ab-4828-8988-0e113118c96b@brtb2c.onmicrosoft.com",
      "userType": "Member"
    }
  ]
}
PS C:\users\bob\source\repos\brt\identity\b2c-graphapi-dotnet\b2cgraphclient\bin\debug>
```

Figure 10-25. *Use the utility to list all users in the directory*

16. Return to the Azure AD B2C management blade and click on Users and Groups and then All Users. You will see that the directory has been populated and that you can view the users and their properties (see Figure 10-26).

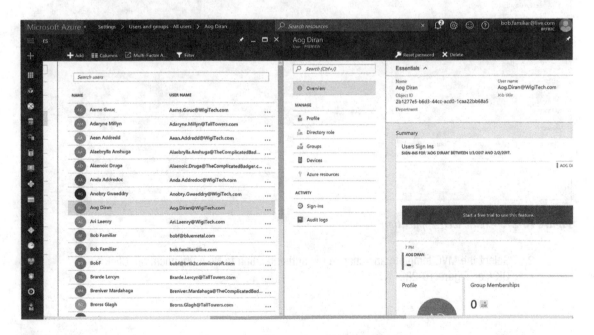

Figure 10-26. *Users successfully imported into the tenant*

CREATE A MULTI-TENANT APPLICATION

In this exercise, you will create a web application that will use Azure AD B2C to authenticate users, and you will define the Azure AD B2C Policies for sign-in, sign-up, and profile management.

1. Open Visual Studio and create a new project using the ASP.NET MVC template. Select the dashboard folder in the repo and set the framework version to 4.6.1. Call the mtauth solution. Click the OK button to advance to the next step in the wizard (see Figure 10-27).

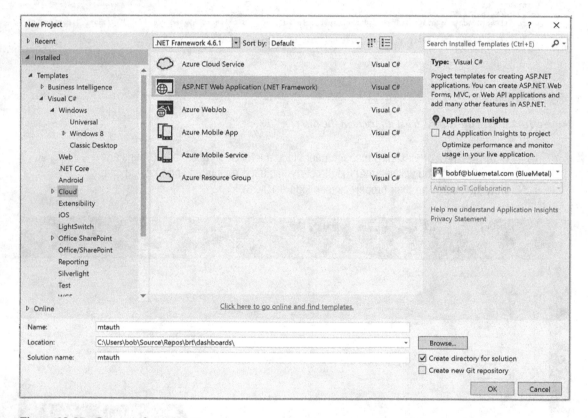

Figure 10-27. Create web application

2. Select the MVC template and change the authentication to No Authentication. Click OK (see Figure 10-28).

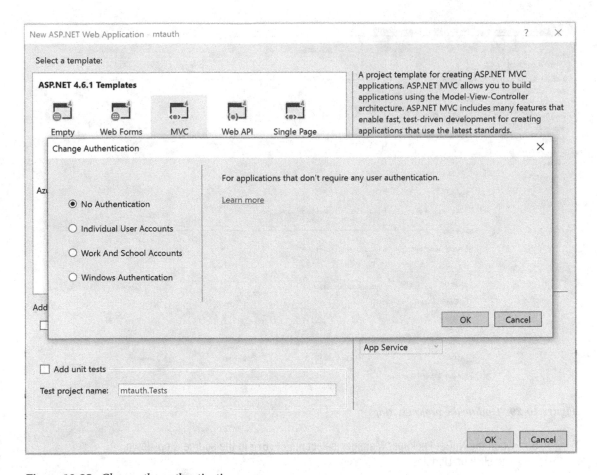

Figure 10-28. *Change the authentication*

3. From the menu, select Tools ➤ NuGet Package Manager ➤ Package Manager Console. Install these NuGet packages, which provide the scaffolding for authenticating to Azure AD using Open ID Connect:

```
Install-Package Microsoft.Owin.Security.OpenIdConnect
Install-Package Microsoft.Owin.Security.Cookies
Install-Package Microsoft.Owin.Host.SystemWeb
```

4. Open the project settings, select the Web tab and update the project URL to be https://localhost:44316/. When prompted to create the virtual directory, click OK (see Figure 10-29).

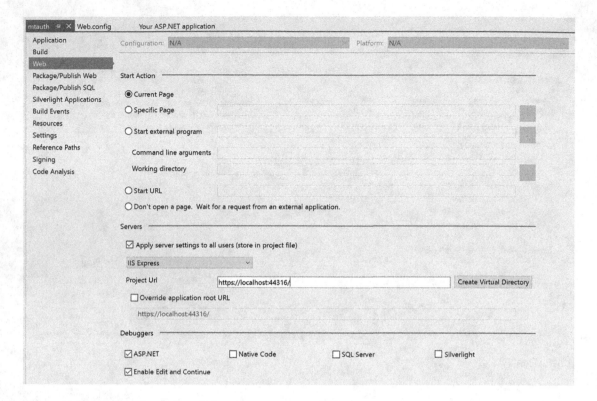

Figure 10-29. *Update the project settings*

5. Open the NuGet Packager Manager, select `nuget.org` in the source drop-down, and click on Updates.

    Select all the packages to be updated except for the `System.IdentityModel.Tokens.JWT` package.

    That package should remain at version 4.0 (see Figure 10-30). Note that you may have to restart Visual Studio after these package updates.

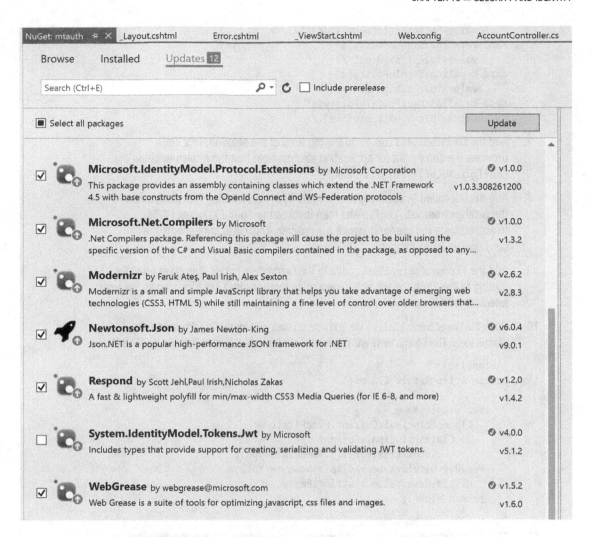

Figure 10-30. Update the NuGet packages for the solution

There are several files that you need to add to this project. They have been supplied in the repo in the `dashboards\mtauth-files` folder.

6. Add the `web.config` file from the `mtauth-files` folder and update the following app settings. Note that this Application ID is the one that was generated when you registered this app with Azure AD in Exercise 2.

```
<add key="ida:Tenant"
     value="[your-tenant].onmicrosoft.com" />
<add key="ida:ClientId"
     value="[your-app-id]" />
<add key="ida:AadInstance"
     value="https://login.microsoftonline.com/{0}/v2.0/.well-known/
     openid-configuration?p={1}" />
<add key="ida:RedirectUri"
```

```
        value="https://localhost:44316/" />
<add key="ida:SignUpPolicyId"
        value="b2c_1_sign_up" />
<add key="ida:SignInPolicyId"
        value="b2c_1_sign_in" />
<add key="ida:UserProfilePolicyId"
        value="b2c_1_edit_profile" />
```

7. Add the file called `Startup.cs` to the top level of the solution. This class provides the entry point for application startup. Note that the implementation of `ConfigureAuth()` is not yet defined.

8. Add the file called `Startup.Auth.cs` in the `App_Start` folder. This class loads the settings from `Web.config` and then invokes the Open ID Connect APIs to authenticate the user and invoke the policies. This class implements the `ConfigureAuth()` routine.

9. Add the `AccountController.cs` file to the Controllers folder. This class provides routing to the Startup class policy invocation methods that are triggered as the user interacts with the user interface.

10. Open the `HomeController.cs` file and add an endpoint for routing the user to the Claims view. The Claims view will display the claims data returned from Azure AD B2C.

```
[Authorize]
public ActionResult Claims()
{
    var displayName =
      ClaimsPrincipal.Current.FindFirst(
         ClaimsPrincipal.Current
            .Identities.First().NameClaimType);
    ViewBag.DisplayName = displayName != null ?
      displayName.Value : string.Empty;
    return View();
}
```

11. There are updated View files in the `mtauth-files` folder. Copy those over the existing files in your solution and then add the `Claims.cshtml` file using the Add Existing Item menu command in Visual Studio.

12. Add the `profile-dropdown.js` file to the `Scripts` folder in your solution using the Add Existing Item menu command in Visual Studio.

13. Build and run the solution. The home page will appear showing the Sign Up, Sign In, and Claims menu options (see Figure 10-31).

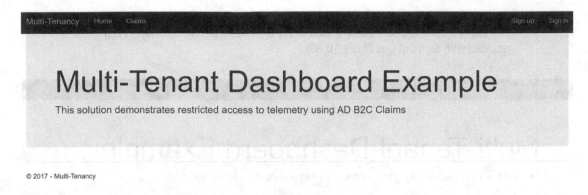

Figure 10-31. Multi-tenant dashboard home page

14. Click on Sign In. You will be routed to the Azure AD B2C Sign-In Policy Page. Note that this is the default look and feel. It is possible to apply your own style to these pages.

15. Tognk is an employee at WigiTech. He is an administrator there so he has raised privileges in the solution, as you will see in a later exercise (see Figure 10-32). Log in using his credentials:

    Username: Tognk.Denyc@WigiTech.com
    Password: P@ssword!

Figure 10-32. Log in to the dashboard

16. Once authenticated, you will be redirected back to the home page, and you will see that Tognk's name appears where it used to say Sign Up, and that Sign In has been replaced with Sign Out (see Figure 10-33).

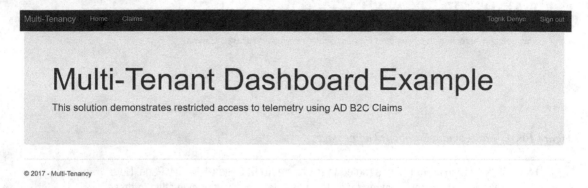

Figure 10-33. User authenticated

17. Click on the Claims menu option. You will be redirected to the Claims view, which will display the claims that have come back from Azure AD B2C for this user (see Figure 10-34).

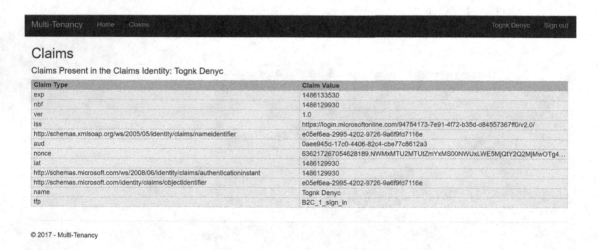

Figure 10-34. User claims

18. Test the application with other users from the same company and from the other companies. Note that the password for all user accounts is P@ssword!. Here are some accounts that you can use to test:

WigiTech
Admin - Tognk.Denyc@WigiTech.com
Employee - Aog.Diran@WigiTech.com

Tall Towers
Admin - Fid.Sidry@TallTowers.com
Employee - Maell.Driga@TallTowers.com

The Complicated Badger
Admin - Jyssa.Anuk@TheComplicatedBadger.com
Employee - Jill.Aniua@TheComplicatedBadger.com

UPDATE THE APP TO CALL THE PLATFORM APIS

The application is now multi-tenant. You can log into the application using accounts from any of the three supported organizations. The next step is to use the information in the claims to call the platform APIs and retrieve details about the user.

■ **Note** If you have not done so already, you will need to build and deploy the Telemetry Model NuGet package and Telemetry API and then import the Swagger definition into API Management following the build and deploy process outlined in Chapter 2.

---

1. Add references to the Wire, Registry Model, and Telemetry Model NuGet packages in the mtauth solution (see Figure 10-35).

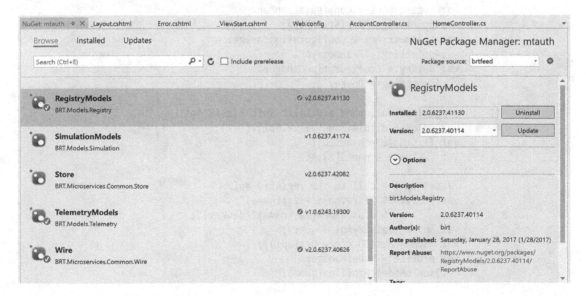

Figure 10-35. Add NuGet packages

509

2. Add the following settings in the Web.config file:

```
<add key="RegistryAPI" value="https://[your-apim-host].azure-api.net/
dev/v1/registry/profiles" />

<add key="TelemetryAPI" value="https:// ://[your-apim-host].azure-api.net/
dev/v1/telemetry/events" />

<add key="DevKey" value="subscription-key=[your-key]" />
```

3. Open the HomeController.cs file and replace the Claims method with the following code.

This code looks up the user's profile and, using the type property from the profile, sets up a call to the Telemetry API.

The Telemetry API takes as parameters the name of the company, the type of user, the user's e-mail, the number of data records to retrieve, and the APIM subscription key. The collection returned is loaded into the ViewBag object for processing by the Claims view.

```
[Authorize]
public ActionResult Claims()
{
    var displayName = ClaimsPrincipal.Current.FindFirst(
        ClaimsPrincipal
            .Current
            .Identities
            .First().NameClaimType);

    if (displayName != null)
    {
        ViewBag.DisplayName = displayName.Value;

        var registryApi = ConfigurationManager
            .AppSettings["RegistryAPI"];
        var telemetryApi = ConfigurationManager
            .AppSettings["TelemetryAPI"];
        var devKey = ConfigurationManager
            .AppSettings["DevKey"];

        // get the full name and split into first, last
        var names = displayName.Value.Split(' ');
        var firstname = names[0];
        var lastname = names[1];

        // set up the call to the registry api
        var query = $"/firstname/{firstname}" +
$                   $"/lastname/{lastname}?{devKey}";
        var api = registryApi + query;
        var json = Rest.Get(new Uri(api));
        var profile = ModelManager
            .JsonToModel<Profile>(json);
```

```
// NOTE: only type 2 (admin) and type 3
// (employee) are able to access telemetry.
// All other user types will return an empy
// telemetry collection
var type = 0;

if (profile != null)
{
    switch (profile.type)
    {
        case ProfileTypeEnum.NotSet:
            type = 0;
            break;
        case ProfileTypeEnum.Organization:
            type = 1;
            break;
        case ProfileTypeEnum.Administrator:
            type = 2;
            break;
        case ProfileTypeEnum.Employee:
            type = 3;
            break;
        case ProfileTypeEnum.Contractor:
            type = 4;
            break;
        case ProfileTypeEnum.Temporary:
            type = 5;
            break;
        case ProfileTypeEnum.Partner:
            type = 6;
            break;
        default:
            throw new
                ArgumentOutOfRangeException();
    }

    query = "/companyname/" +
            $"{profile.companyname}" +
                $"?usertype={type}" +
            $"&username={profile.username}" +
            $"&count=15&{devKey}";

    api = telemetryApi + query;

    json = Rest.Get(new Uri(api));
    var telemetryList = ModelManager
      .JsonToModel<TelemetryList>(json);

    ViewBag.UserProfile = profile;
    ViewBag.Telemetry = telemetryList.list;
}
}

return View();
}
```

4. Open the `Views\Home\Claims.cshtml` file and update the contents of the file with the following code.

This code will output a table of the user's claims as well as display a list of the 15 most recent telemetry readings that this user can see. If logged in as an employee, the user will see only his or her own telemetry readings. If logged in as an administrator, they will see readings from their employees.

```
@using System.Security.Claims
@using BRT.Models.Telemetry
@{
    ViewBag.Title = "Claims";
}
<h2>@ViewBag.Title</h2>

<h4>Claims Present for @ViewBag.DisplayName</h4>

<table class="table-hover claim-table">
    <tr>
        <th class="claim-type claim-data claim-head">Claim Type</th>
        <th class="claim-data claim-head">Claim Value</th>
    </tr>

    @foreach (Claim claim in
        ClaimsPrincipal.Current.Claims)
    {
        <tr>
            <td class="claim-type claim-data">
                @claim.Type
            </td>
            <td class="claim-data">
                @claim.Value
            </td>
        </tr>
    }
</table>
<br/>
<table>
    <tr>
        <td class="claim-data">Lastname</td>
        <td class="claim-data">Age</td>
        <td class="claim-data">Weight</td>
        <td class="claim-data">Height</td>
        <td class="claim-data">Activity</td>
        <td class="claim-data">Altitude</td>
        <td class="claim-data">Breathing Rate</td>
        <td class="claim-data">Cadence</td>
        <td class="claim-data">Heart Rate</td>
        <td class="claim-data">Red Zone</td>
        <td class="claim-data">Variability</td>
        <td class="claim-data">Speed</td>
        <td class="claim-data">Steps</td>
```

```
            <td class="claim-data">Temperature</td>
            <td class="claim-data">Velocity</td>
            <td class="claim-data">Ventilization</td>
    </tr>

    @foreach (UserTelemetry telemetry in
        ViewBag.Telemetry)
    {
        <tr>
            <td class="claim-data">
                @telemetry.User.lastname
            </td>
            <td class="claim-data">
                @telemetry.Readings.age
            </td>
            <td class="claim-data">
                @telemetry.Readings.weight
            </td>
            <td class="claim-data">
                @telemetry.Readings.height
            </td>
            <td class="claim-data">
                @telemetry.Readings.activity
            </td>
            <td class="claim-data">
                @telemetry.Readings.altitude
            </td>
            <td class="claim-data">
                @telemetry.Readings.breathingRate
            </td>
            <td class="claim-data">
                @telemetry.Readings.cadence
            </td>
            <td class="claim-data">
                @telemetry.Readings.heartRateBPM
            </td>
            <td class="claim-data">
                @telemetry.Readings.heartRateRedZone
            </td>
            <td class="claim-data">
                @telemetry.Readings.heartrateVariability
            </td>
            <td class="claim-data">
                @telemetry.Readings.speed
            </td>
            <td class="claim-data">
                @telemetry.Readings.steps
            </td>
            <td class="claim-data">
                @telemetry.Readings.temperature
            </td>
            <td class="claim-data">
```

```
                        @telemetry.Readings.velocity
                </td>
                <td class="claim-data">
                        @telemetry.Readings.ventilization
                </td>
            </tr>
        }
    </table>
```

5. Run the telemetry simulators (see Chapter 4). Note that the Stream Analytics job must be running for the data to be routed to the SQL Database table.

6. Test the portal application by logging in as both administrators and employees of the different companies. See Figures 10-36 and 10-37.

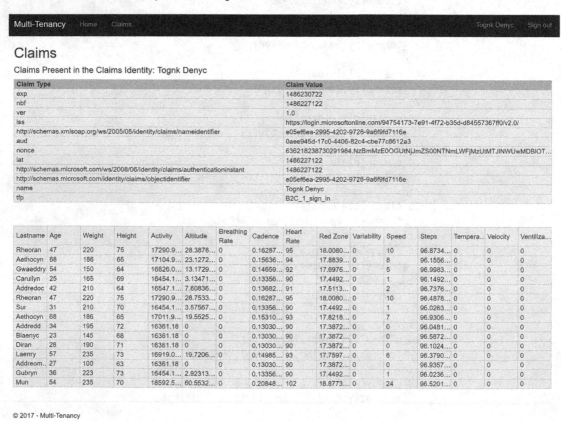

Figure 10-36. *Logged in as Tognk Denyc, an administrator at WigiTech*

We will use the claims returned from AD to look up the user in the system and pass the users profile information to the Telemetry API to demonstrate restricting access to the telemetry.

The users we will use for testing are from the WigiTech organization. Tognk Denyc is an administrator, so he can see all employee information from WigiTech. Aog Diran is an employee, so Aog can only see his own information.

| Multi-Tenancy | Home | Claims | | Aog Diran | Sign out |

Claims

Claims Present in the Claims Identity: Aog Diran

Claim Type	Claim Value
exp	1486230940
nbf	1486227340
ver	1.0
iss	https://login.microsoftonline.com/94754173-7e91-4f72-b35d-d84557367ff0/v2.0/
http://schemas.xmlsoap.org/ws/2005/05/identity/claims/nameidentifier	2b1277e5-b6d3-44cc-acd0-1caa22bb68a5
aud	0aee945d-17c0-4406-82c4-cbe77c8612a3
nonce	636218241016037504.OWVhOGVkNWYtZDVhYS00MzA2LWFiOGYtOWJINDg3NzIwZm..
iat	1486227340
http://schemas.microsoft.com/ws/2008/06/identity/claims/authenticationinstant	1486227340
http://schemas.microsoft.com/identity/claims/objectidentifier	2b1277e5-b6d3-44cc-acd0-1caa22bb68a5
name	Aog Diran
tfp	B2C_1_sign_in

Lastname	Age	Weight	Height	Activity	Altitude	Breathing Rate	Cadence	Heart Rate	Red Zone	Variability	Speed	Steps	Tempera..	Velocity	Ventiliza...
Diran	28	190	71	16361.18	0	0	0.13030...	90	17.3872...	0	0	96.1024...	0	0	0
Diran	28	190	71	16361.18	0	0	0.13030...	90	17.3872...	0	0	96.6383...	0	0	0
Diran	28	190	71	16361.18	0	0	0.13030...	90	17.3872...	0	0	96.1907...	0	0	0
Diran	28	190	71	16361.18	0	0	0.13030...	90	17.3872...	0	0	96.1996...	0	0	0
Diran	28	190	71	16361.18	0	0	0.13030...	90	17.3872...	0	0	96.6571...	0	0	0
Diran	28	190	71	16361.18	0	0	0.13030...	90	17.3872...	0	0	96.4389...	0	0	0
Diran	28	190	71	16361.18	0	0	0.13030...	90	17.3872...	0	0	96.0501...	0	0	0
Diran	28	190	71	16361.18	0	0	0.13030...	90	17.3872...	0	0	96.8051...	0	0	0
Diran	28	190	71	16361.18	0	0	0.13030...	90	17.3872...	0	0	96.4103...	0	0	0
Diran	28	190	71	16361.18	0	0	0.13030...	90	17.3872...	0	0	96.0208...	0	0	0
Diran	28	190	71	16361.18	0	0	0.13030...	90	17.3872...	0	0	96.0073...	0	0	0
Diran	28	190	71	16361.18	0	0	0.13030...	90	17.3872...	0	0	96.1677...	0	0	0
Diran	28	190	71	16361.18	0	0	0.13030...	90	17.3872...	0	0	96.0812...	0	0	0
Diran	28	190	71	16361.18	0	0	0.13030...	90	17.3872...	0	0	96.1042...	0	0	0
Diran	28	190	71	16361.18	0	0	0.13030...	90	17.3872...	0	0	96.1397...	0	0	0

© 2017 - Multi-Tenancy

Figure 10-37. Logged in as Aog Diran, a WigiTech employee

The last thing that we want to validate in our application is that users can update their profiles. In an earlier exercise, we defined a profile edit policy that allowed a user to update a few of attributes, including a custom attribute called Role.

Follow these steps to validate that this feature is working.

7. Click the username in the upper-right corner of the application. An Edit Profile link is displayed (see Figure 10-38).

Figure 10-38. *Edit Profile menu option*

8. Click the link. You will be redirected to a page provided by Azure AD B2C that allows the user to update the profile based on the policy definition. Note that the Role field is available for edit (see Figure 10-39).

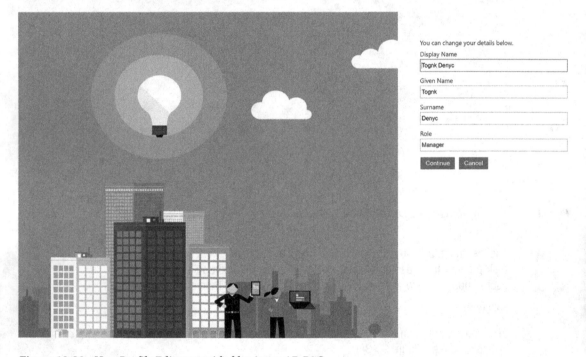

Figure 10-39. *User Profile Editor provided by Azure AD B2C*

Summary

This chapter looked at using threat modeling to define an analysis process and outlined mitigation strategies for ongoing security audits. It also examined Azure AD B2C as a foundation for managing identities and providing multi-tenant access to your application and underlying data.

CHAPTER 11

■ ■ ■

Epilogue

Every business is engaged in or will soon face a digital transformation. To accelerate this transformation and provide customers, partners, and employees the most impactful solutions, these businesses need to incorporate real-time data. While there may be SaaS services that comport to provide a complete end-to-end solution, our experience shows that today there really is no option to buy a product that will truly deliver what organizations need. To drive their digital transformations, organizations have two choices:

- Wait for the ISV market to catch up and risk missing the current window of opportunity.

- Build a solution today that can expand and adapt tomorrow.

Our work with clients over the past several years has engendered an engineering approach highlighted by best practices with respect to the software product lifecycle, a microservices-based architecture, and the power and cohesion of cloud services that are provided by Microsoft Azure. Leveraging Azure's PaaS services eliminates the need to manage resources on virtual machine-based environments, configure and patch operating systems, and develop your own elastic scale infrastructure. Instead, you focus on automation, configuration, and just the code necessary to define and implement your business requirements.

The journey to delivering business-transformative solutions starts with cultivating and integrating a DevOps culture inside your organization. DevOps is all about people, process, and tools working collaboratively to support the high-velocity software development processes that are essential to success. Sure, the technology is awesome, but it does not provision, build, and deploy itself.

Device management is often overlooked when organizations make their first foray into IoT. It's easy to create the initial small-scale solutions with single-board computers and then manually support their deployments. The ability to automate the monitoring and communication with your devices when you have potentially tens of thousands of them out in the wild must be carefully considered.

As important as the devices are, you must never lose sight that IoT is still all about the data. The data is the raw ore that the business hopes to mine for the gold, namely, the keen insight that truly drives transformation. Success here requires designing and implementing a powerful data pipeline that incorporates real-time processing, integrates reference data, and invokes operationalized Machine Learning APIs. Such a pipeline addresses the three paths for data:

- Hot (such as alerts that require immediate action)

- Warm (such as telemetry)

- Cold (for archival and analysis)

This spectrum of data and associated analytics is central to providing the rich visualizations, alerts, and notifications that ultimately drive the transformation.

© Bob Familiar and Jeff Barnes 2017
B. Familiar and J. Barnes, *Business in Real-Time Using Azure IoT and Cortana Intelligence Suite*,
DOI 10.1007/978-1-4842-2650-6_11

Focusing on security from the very start of your product development is paramount. Adopting a threat modeling and mitigation process and leveraging tools such as Azure Security Center can help you identify threats and mitigate risks.

We really hope you have enjoyed reading this book and working through the exercises as much as we have enjoyed researching and crafting it. May all your business endeavors run at Internet speed!

Bob & Jeff

Index

© Bob Familiar and Jeff Barnes 2017

B. Familiar and J. Barnes, *Business in Real-Time Using Azure IoT and Cortana Intelligence Suite*,
DOI 10.1007/978-1-4842-2650-6

519

Get the eBook for only $5!

Why limit yourself?

With most of our titles available in both PDF and ePUB format, you can access your content wherever and however you wish—on your PC, phone, tablet, or reader.

Since you've purchased this print book, we are happy to offer you the eBook for just $5.

To learn more, go to http://www.apress.com/companion or contact support@apress.com.

Apress®

Printed in the United States
By Bookmasters